The Complete Poetry of Robert Herrick

The Anchor Seventeenth-Century Series presents the major—and significant minor—texts in English of the Seventeenth Century in authoritative and inexpensive editions. Prepared especially for Anchor Books by a distinguished group of American and Canadian scholars, these newly edited texts meet the highest standards of scholarship and readability. Each volume incorporates the latest textual and critical discoveries, and the series as a whole is designed to provide a reliable access to the literature of the Seventeenth Century.

The Anchor Seventeenth-Century Series
is published by Doubleday Anchor Books
under the general editorship of
PROFESSOR J. MAX PATRICK, *New York University*

J. Max Patrick is Professor of English in the Graduate School of Arts and Science, New York University. He is the author of numerous articles on seventeenth-century literature, the editor of *Seventeenth-Century News*, and associate editor and founder of *Neo-Latin News*.

He received the B.A. degree from the University of Toronto and the B.Litt. and D.Phil. degrees from Oxford University (Balliol College), and has taught in Queens College, New York, and in the universities of Manitoba, Buffalo, Princeton, Emory, Florida, and Poitiers. His publications include *Hugh Peters: A Study in Puritanism; Francis Bacon* (British Council, Writers and Their Work Series); and, with R. W. Gibson, a comprehensive bibliography of all known works of utopian literature in all languages 1500–1750 (in Gibson's *St. Thomas More: A Preliminary Bibliography*). He is the editor of the *State Papers* and of *Of Prelatical Episcopacy* in the Yale Milton, and, with Glenn Negley, the author of *The Quest for Utopia* (Anchor A326).

Professor Patrick is the general editor of the Anchor Seventeenth-Century Series.

THE COMPLETE POETRY OF ROBERT HERRICK

Edited with an Introduction and Notes

by

J. MAX PATRICK

ANCHOR BOOKS
Doubleday & Company, Inc.
Garden City, New York, 1963

This edition has been specially prepared for Anchor Books and has not been published before in book form.

LIBRARY OF CONGRESS CATALOG CARD NUMBER 63-8753

PRINTED IN THE UNITED STATES OF AMERICA
FIRST EDITION

INTRODUCTION

Herrick is the delight of true lovers of poetry and the despair of some critics. To his contemporaries, his lyrics aptly expressed and successfully communicated the meanings and emotions which he intended to convey. He thus accomplished the prime task of an artist, providing works of art which were so self-communicative that their appreciation and understanding required no explanation or commentary. His lyrics have been justly admired by later generations for their exquisite and unerring artistry and their perfect decorum. Such appreciation is like the appreciation due natural perfection; analysis is possible but extraneous.

But Herrick wrote for a coterie of seventeenth-century English gentlemen educated in the classics. What was easily recognized by them is no longer familiar: meanings, allusions, and modes of expression have changed. Accordingly, to restore to Herrick's poems their original clarity and meaningfulness, some explanatory footnoting and occasional interpretation and commentary are now necessary, especially for the majority of the English-speaking peoples whose background is radically different from those of Herrick's contemporaries. A twentieth-century edition of a seventeenth-century poet is inadequate if, as in Martin's otherwise admirable edition of Herrick, it is formulated primarily for that relatively small and ever diminishing group of educated men who have enjoyed training in the Greek and Latin classics.

The notes in the present text are fuller than most readers will require, and should be consulted only when needed. For Herrick's poems were written primarily to be enjoyed; and once the barriers of period and cultural differences are overcome, his lyrics are exceptionally self-sufficient. In some measure they contain the ironies, ambiguities, paradoxes, and complex allusions so prized by modern critics; and they also reveal metaphysical strains and meditative techniques; but Herrick communicates so directly that a sensitive and intelligent reader can discover these qualities for himself.

Herrick has been cherished chiefly for his graceful fancy, sweet innocence, fairy lore, and love of the countryside. But such works constitute only about half of his poetic output. His epigrams and coarse, even vulgar, poems have received less intelligent attention than is their due. Indeed, their earthy gusto is the complement of Herrick's "prettiness," and both are best enjoyed if used as foils to each other. The seeming jumble in the arrangement of his poems is no accident: the mixture serves to save the sweet and the trivial from cloying. And further relief is provided by Herrick's heroic strain, especially in his tributes to royalty and high patrons. Uniting all the poems is a versatile wit, from the baldly, even insipidly, obvious to the subtle and the complex.

Herrick's range is extraordinarily wide, extending from the pastoral to the cynical, from the gross to an almost rococo elegance, and from the prosaic and didactic to the dramatic. Narrative and profoundly philosophic content is largely lacking, and the religious poems are not imbued with passion or emotional depth. On the other hand, even when they descend to bathos, they are characterized by a sweet reasonableness which anticipates eighteenth-century rationalism and common sense. Herrick has been called *pagan*, but the label is misleading; for his poems constantly echo Scripture, and what at first seems heathenish proves to be not so much Roman and classical as a universalized religious sentiment expressive of Latitudinarian Anglicanism.

He demands from the reader a multiple sensibility; not only a capacity to respond to exquisite miniatures, to delight in disorder, to relish phrases like "the liquefaction of her clothes"; but also a capacity for brutal realism, for a sense of the mutability of things, and for an awareness of man's mortality. Indeed, the fluctuations in his reputation have occurred mainly because readers attracted by his charm have been repulsed by his earthiness, while those who savored this quality were repelled by what they considered insipid daintiness. But twentieth-century readers are peculiarly fortunate. For the expansion of sensitivity to extremely diverse kinds of poetry in recent years makes possible, perhaps for the first time since Herrick's own period, healthy, free appreciation of all aspects of his many-faceted genius.

CONTENTS

PUBLICATION AND REPUTATION

In the first half of the seventeenth century, genteel and noble authors hesitated to have their works appear in print but often allowed them to circulate in manuscript. Donne and Herbert saw only a few of their poems printed, and when Milton's *Comus* appeared in 1637, it was "not openly acknowledg'd by the Author." Before the publication of *Hesperides* in 1648, when Herrick was fifty-seven, only ten of his known poems were printed,[1] and his name was associated with only one of them. Accordingly, his reputation before 1648 rested almost entirely on manuscripts.

The period was singularly deficient in literary criticism and comment, apart from Jonson's *Timber* and Drummond's *Conversations*. Any attempt to gauge an author's reputation from incidental comments which have survived is likely to be misleading. However, Richard James's ranking of Herrick with Jonson and Drayton in 1625 as a poet of acknowledged eminence is significant. Otherwise the best means of measuring a writer's fame in the period before 1675 is probably the frequency with which his poems in manuscript have survived. L. C. Martin, in his edition of Herrick, records that 40 of the poems published in 1648 occur in the manuscripts known to him (138 appearances if repetitions are counted). This tally

[1] H-376 in Stow's *Survey of London*, 1633; H-293B in a collection of fairy poems, 1634–35; H-263 and H-580 in Carew's *Poems*, 1640; H-164, H-575, H-580 among verse "By other Gentlemen" included in *Poems written by Wil. Shake-speare. Gent.*, 1640 (Herrick was identified as a contributor in the Stationers' Register entry, Nov., 1639); H-128 and S-6 in *Recreation for Ingenious Head-peeces*, 1645; H-208 and H-263 in *The Academy of Complements*, 1646; and S-1 credited to Herrick, in the 1647 folio of Beaumont and Fletcher's plays.

is incomplete (for example, H-445 occurs in B.M. Add MS 18,044; and H-164, H-138B, H-336 occur in Rosenbach MS 188). Judged by this criterion of frequency of manuscripts, Herrick was outshone by Donne, was at least as popular as Milton, was better known than Carew, and had far more reputation than Marvell in the seventeenth century.

Scholars have been somewhat too ready to assume from slight evidence that *Hesperides* was poorly received on publication and had few purchasers. Admittedly copies were still available for sale some twenty years later, but Anthony Wood states that the book was "much admired" especially by Royalists when it appeared. The fact that numerous copies survived the Great Fire of 1666 and times transhifting since then and are today available in libraries throughout the world suggests that the original printing was exceptionally large.

The very nature of the 1648 volume suggests that its publishers expected a large sale because of its multiple appeals. It is reasonable to assume that at least 100 copies came into the hands of the patrons, friends, and relatives mentioned in the poems, and their associates. The times were turbulent, but, as Marchette Chute observes, a great deal of poetry was being published in London and most of it sold well, including Thomas Randolph's verse which was similar in genre to Herrick's: the notion that there was a demand only for metaphysical poetry has no sound basis. Royalists were doubtless expected to buy *Hesperides*, and their number was not small. Moreover the volume's contents provided appeals to scholars, men of piety, lovers of fairy lore and country life, wits, sentimentalists, and readers who delighted in cleanly wantonness and none-too-dainty epigrams. In the lack of substantial evidence to the contrary, it seems wisest to conclude that the reception of *Hesperides* was not ungratifying. It is true that Herrick's name does not seem to have become well known; but his poems do seem to have gained in popularity: between 1649 and 1674, almost a hundred of them were reprinted, usually without credit to him, in 28 different collections.

Herrick's confidence in his own ultimate reputation found little further justification before the nineteenth century. He was briefly but not very favorably mentioned in *Musarum Deliciae* (1655) and *Naps upon Parnassus* (1658). In 1675 Edward Phillips deplored his triviality but approved of his occasional "pretty Floury and Pastoral gale of Fancy." In the eighteenth century he received a short biographical notice and in 1790 three of his poems were reprinted. Seven years later enquiries about him in the *Gentleman's Magazine* led to replies; and in 1804 Nathan Drake's *Literary Hours* devoted three appreciative articles to him.

These articles initiated Herrick's real rise to fame. In 1810 J. Nott printed 284 of the poems in the first edition since 1648; Campbell included some representation in his *Specimens*, 1819. In 1823, Thomas Maitland published a complete edition of *The Works*, which inspired an attack by Southey on the alleged unwisdom of making the "naughty" material available. But his was a small voice, and Herrick met with growing acclaim and numerous reprints thereafter. Among the noteworthy editions are those by W. C. Hazlitt, 1869; Alexander B. Grosart, 1876; Alfred Pollard, 1891; George Saintsbury, 1893; F. W. Moorman, 1915; and L. C. Martin, 1956. These editors take advantage of each other's discoveries and notes, and, in various ways, the present edition, following in their tradition, is likewise indebted to them. Except in a few instances, where acknowledgments are made, their findings have been checked against original sources, however.

Herrick's place as one of the greatest English lyric poets is now secure. His epigrams are admired by the few but fit who cherish that genre. Following the lead of S. Musgrove in *The Universe of Robert Herrick*, critics are now beginning to perceive that the poems contain hitherto neglected depths, subtleties, and complexities.

enquiries about him in the Gentleman's Magazine led to replies, and in 1809 Nathan Drake's Literary Hours devoted three appreciative articles to him.

These articles launched Herrick's real rise to fame. In 1810 J. Nott printed 284 of the poems in the first edition since 1648; Campbell [illegible] some representation in his Specimens (1819). In 1823, Thomas Maitland published a complete edition of The Works, which inspired an attack by Southey on the alleged unwisdom of making the [illegible] material available. Full editions, small volumes, and selections with growing acclaim and numerous reprints [illegible]. Among the more scholarly editions are those by W. C. Hazlitt (1869), Alexander B. Grosart (1876), Alfred Pollard (1891), George Saintsbury (1893), F. W. Moorman (1915), and L. C. Martin (1956). These editors took advantage of each other's discoveries and notes and in various ways the present edition, following the usual tradition, is likewise indebted to them. Except in a few instances, where acknowledgments are made, their findings have been checked against original sources, however.

Herrick's place as one of the greatest English lyric poets now seems [illegible]. His epigrams are admired by the few, but it [illegible] who cherish [illegible]. Following the lead of S. Musgrove in 1950 [illegible], [illegible] are beginning to perceive that the poems contain hitherto neglected [illegible] subtleties and complexities.

SELECTED BIBLIOGRAPHY

MALCOLM L. MACLEOD. *A Concordance to the Poems of Robert Herrick.* New York, 1936.

S. A. AND D. R. TANNENBAUM. *A Concise Bibliography.* New York, 1949.

JOHN THOMSON. *Indexes to the First Lines and to the Subjects of the Poems.* Philadelphia, 1901.

P. AIKEN. *The Influence of the Latin Elegists . . . 1600–50, with Particular Reference to Robert Herrick.* Orono, Maine, 1932.

CLEANTH BROOKS. *The Well Wrought Urn.* New York, 1947.

MARCHETTE CHUTE. *Two Gentle Men: The Lives of George Herbert and Robert Herrick.* New York, 1959. –Sound and readable.

FLORIS DELATTRE. *Robert Herrick.* Paris, 1912. –In French; the best scholarly treatment.

EMILY EASTON. *Youth Immortal: A Life of Robert Herrick.* New York, 1934. –Imaginative.

A. H. GILBERT. "Robert Herrick on Death." *MLQ,* V (1944), 61–8.

A. C. JUDSON. "Robert Herrick's Pillar of Fame." *Texas Review,* V (1920), 262–74.

F. R. LEAVIS. *Revaluation.* London, 1936. Pp. 39–41.

ROSE MACAULAY. *The Shadow Flies.* New York, 1932. –Fiction.

KATHRYN ANDERSON MCEUEN. *Classical Influence upon the Tribe of Ben.* Cedar Rapids, 1939.

LEON MANDEL. *Robert Herrick: The Last Elizabethan.* Chicago, 1927.

J. A. MAZZEO, ed. *Reason and Imagination.* New York, 1962. Contains an article by M. K. Starkman on *Noble Numbers.*

F. W. MOORMAN. *Robert Herrick.* London, 1910. –Readable but not always reliable.

S. MUSGROVE. *The Universe of Robert Herrick.* Auckland, 1950. –A profoundly perceptive short study; highly recommended.

JOHN PRESS. *Herrick.* The British Council Writers and their Work series, No. 132. London, 1961. –A capable survey.

G. W. REGENOS. "The Influence of Horace on Herrick." *PQ,* XXVI (1947), 268–84.

N. ROECKERATH. *Der Nachruhm Herricks und Wallers.* Leipzig, 1931.

M. J. RUGGLES. "Horace and Herrick." *Classical Journal,* XXXI (1936).

A. C. SWINBURNE. *Studies in Prose and Poetry.* London, 1894.

BIOGRAPHICAL OUTLINE

1556: Nicholas, 2nd son of John Eyrick, left Leicestershire to become a goldsmith's apprentice in London.

1582: Nicholas Herrick, goldsmith and banker, married Julian (or Juliana), daughter of William Stone, a London mercer.

Aug. 24, 1591: their 7th child and 4th son, Robert, baptized.

Nov. 9, 1592: Nicholas fell from his house in Goldsmith's row and died; suicide suspected.

1592–1607: Herrick's schooling and residence unknown.

1607: apprenticed to his uncle, Sir William Herrick, a prosperous goldsmith, supposedly for 10 years.

1613: entered St. John's College, Cambridge, as a wealthy student, but some years later, to save expense, transferred to Trinity Hall; B.A., 1617; M.A., 1620.

April 24–25, 1623: ordained deacon and priest by the Bishop of Peterborough, possibly to become some nobleman's chaplain.

1627: participated in the disastrous military expedition to the Isle of Rhé as a chaplain to the Duke of Buckingham.

1629: mother died; appointed Vicar of Dean Prior in Devon.

Oct. 29, 1630: installed as Vicar.

April 29, 1640: Stationers' Register entry that Andrew Crooke would publish "Poems written by Master Robert Herrick."

1640: probably in London; see notes to H-979.

1647: expelled from his vicarage because of his royalism; presumably returned to Westminster.

1648: publication of *Hesperides*.

1648–60: probably supported by relatives; no definite information.

1660: returned to his vicarage from Westminster.

Oct. 15, 1674: buried at Dean Prior.

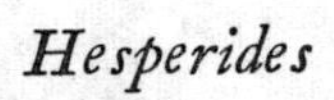
Hesperides

HESPERIDES:

OR,

THE WORKS

BOTH

HUMANE & DIVINE

OF

ROBERT HERRICK *Esq.*

OVID.

Effugient avidos Carmina nostra Rogos.

LONDON,

Printed for *John Williams*, and *Francis Eglesfield*, and are to be sold at the Crown and Marygold in Saint *Pauls* Church-yard. 1648.

A Note on the Title Page and the Text

The Hesperides or Western Maidens were three (or, in some legends four) nymphs. Hesiod made them the fatherless daughters of Night. Diodorus Siculus, followed by Milton (*Comus*, 981), described them as the children of Atlas and his niece, Hesperis, daughter of Hesperus. According to myth, the goddess of Earth presented Juno with a wedding present of branches bearing golden apples. Juno had them planted in a garden, also known as Hesperides, which was guarded by the nymphs. Different authors give different sites for these gardens, but all agree in locating them in the west. Herrick's title suggests that his poems are golden apples, fruits, at least in part, of Devonshire; collectively they constitute a garden of poetry. In another sense, his poems are the daughters of Hesperus, the evening star; as such they are little stars. See the note by G. C. Moore, *MLR*, IX (July, 1914), 373–4.

The Latin inscription is the same as Ovid, *Amores*, III, IX, 28 except for its first word, *defugient* (*diffugiunt; effugiunt*): "Song alone escapes the greedy funeral pyre." Cf. Ovid, *Tristia*, III, VII, 54 and *Ex Ponto*, III, II, 32.

Some copies read, "by Tho. Hunt, Bookseller in Exon. 1648" after the phrase: "and are to be sold."

This edition is based primarily on the two copies in the New York Public Library Berg Collection, the copy in the Rosenbach Foundation Library in Philadelphia, and the Harvard Library copy (14454.27.2.25*) of the first issue of the first edition; but superior readings from other copies, most of them already noted by previous editors, have been silently incorporated in the text printed here. The errata listed in the original edition have been corrected in their proper places, and some obvious misprints have been silently rectified; but, for the most part, the text as it occurs in one or other copy of the 1648 edition has been conservatively retained, even in some instances when Martin or other editors make a plausible case for emendations. Throughout the text abbreviations have been expanded and i and j, u and v have been changed when necessary to conform with modern practice. Except in rare instances no attempt is made to record variants which occur in the thirty-five works which contained poems by Herrick and appeared in his lifetime. These are recorded in Martin's edition. He also records, for forty poems published in *Hesperides* and *Noble Numbers,* variants which occur in about fifty-three manuscript collections or single manuscripts. Most of these variants are of doubtful value, for scribes who copied poems in the 17th century were, for the most part, highly inaccurate and were prone to edit and revise texts intentionally as well as accidentally. Moreover, Martin's examination of manuscripts was by no means complete, as he in part acknowledges (p. xxvi, n.1). To supplement his work, collations of versions in the Rosenbach manuscripts are included here and our thanks are due to the Philip H. and A. S. W. Rosenbach Foundation of Philadelphia for access to them. We are also grateful to the Folger, Huntington, British Museum, Bodleian, Harvard University and other libraries mentioned in special connections for allowing use of their manuscript resources. However, we have made no attempt to include all known variants: the scholar who seeks them should consult the critical notes in *The Poetical Works of Robert Herrick*, ed. L. C. Martin, published at Oxford at the Clarendon Press, 1956, and use them in connection with our own supplementary collations from manuscripts not explored by him. The evaluation and full utilization of both printed and manuscript variants remains a formidable task which awaits future editors.

In the meantime it is wisest to rely on the 1648 edition. Herrick was almost certainly in London during the course of its publication; it is reasonable to assume that it was based on copy as he provided it and that, although not perfect, it approximates in general to what he intended.

It is equally obvious that he would not have wished his poems which were not included in the 1648 text to be printed as they occur in the manuscripts, if only because their sparse punctuation renders them very difficult to follow. Accordingly, we have in some instances modernized the spelling and punctuation of these poems, thus providing texts which, though inevitably interpretative in punctuation, will at least enable most readers to enjoy and understand them. However, in a few cases, we retain MSS readings unchanged, so that readers may have both a sense of the interpretative and editorial problems involved and also an opportunity to exercise their own editorial talents.

The arrangement of the lines of poetry in the 1648 edition is obviously significant in shaped poems like N-268; but it is also often functional elsewhere; for example, a short line about dropping blood or tears is likely to be placed far to the right of the main text of a poem in order to heighten the sense of suspense and isolation. In H-316, for similar reasons, "Stay, stay," "Has run," "We die," and "Away" are set off; and in H-283, the fifth line, "Reaching at heaven" is put out of a balanced position to achieve an effect of aspiration. In the present edition such devices are retained as far as possible. The inconsistencies of the original edition in numbering stanzas sometimes with roman, sometimes with arabic, and sometimes with mixed numerals, with or without punctuation have likewise been preserved when possible; for they presumably reflect what appeared on the original manuscripts and may be significant for dating composition. And in an effort to keep something of the quaint flavor of the original printing, its somewhat erratic capitalization of the first two, three, or even more letters of the opening word of poems has been retained, but not the large initial letter. Variety, not consistency, is characteristic of the 1648 edition and probably results from Herrick's own intentions.

A Note on the Original Frontispiece

The frontispiece (to be found in the middle of this edition) shows the bust of a somewhat hook-nosed, curly-headed man, in profile, with a moustache. It is usually assumed that the engraver, William Marshall, intended this to portray Herrick, but the picture may well be merely a generalized representation of a poet. The landscape surrounding the bust includes the Hill of Parnassus, the Spring of Helicon, Pegasus about to soar from the hill, several trees, and nine naked figures—presumably the Muses. Two of these winged figures are flying with wreathes of flowers—flowers from the Garden of the

Hesperides—preparing to crown him. Five others circle in a dance below the largest tree in the garden itself. And two, holding branches of bay or olive leaves, sit in the foreground pointing to a Latin poem on the base of the bust. The initials "I.H.C.W.M." below the poem almost certainly indicate that their author was John Harmar of the College of Westminster (See H-966). The Latin and Grosart's translation are as follows:

> Tempora cinxisset Foliorum densior umbra:
> Debetur Genio Laurea Sylva tuo.
> Tempora et Illa Tibi mollis redimîsset Oliva;
> Scilicet excludis Versibus Arma tuis.
> Admisces Antiqua Novis, Jocunda Severis: 5
> Hinc Juvenis discat, Fœmina, Virgo, Senex
> Ut solo minores Phœbo, sic majores Unus
> Omnibus Ingenio, Mente Lepore, Stylo.

> A denser shade of leaves thy brows should bind;
> A laurel grove is due to such a mind.
> The peaceful olive should those brows entwine,
> For arms are banished from such verse as thine.
> Old things with new thou blendest, grave with gay: 5
> Hence young and old, mother and maid may say,
> Phœbus except, all else thou dost outvie
> In style, and beauty, and capacity.

The Poem Preceding the List of Errata.[1]

> *For these Transgressions which thou here dost see,*
> *Condemne the Printer, Reader, and not me;*
> *Who gave him forth good Grain, though he mistook*
> *The Seed; so sow'd these Tares throughout my Book.*

[1] Since the errata have been corrected in this edition, they are not listed here.

[*The Prefatory Poem*]

TO THE MOST ILLUSTRIOUS, AND Most Hopefull PRINCE, CHARLES, Prince of *Wales*.[1]

WEll may my Book come forth like Publique Day,
When such a *Light* as *You* are leads the way:[2]
Who are my Works *Creator,* and alone
The *Flame* of it, and the *Expansion.*[3]
And look how all those heavenly Lamps acquire 5
Light from the Sun, that *inexhausted Fire:*
So all my *Morne,* and *Evening Stars* from You
Have their *Existence,* and their *Influence* too.[4]
Full is my Book of Glories;[5] but all These
By You become *Immortall Substances.* 10

[1] Charles's birth on May 29, 1630, was followed, within an hour, by the appearance of Hesperus, the evening star, in the mid-day sky. The poets seized on this phenomenon as an auspicious omen, compared it with the Star of Bethlehem, and continued to exploit stellar imagery whenever they wrote about him.

[2] Herrick almost certainly wrote this address for a volume of poems intended for publication about 1640. On April 29, 1640 (Prince Charles's tenth birthday), Andrew Crooke's application to the Stationers' Company led to the following record in their Register: "Entred for his Copie under the hands of Master Hansley and Master Bourne warden, *The severall Poems* written by Master Robert Herrick." The intention was, clearly, to have this volume appear in celebration of the formal presentation of Charles to the British nations as Prince of Wales and also his initiation into the Order of the Garter. Thus Herrick's opening lines signify that Charles's light or star, being made public, led the way for the publication of the poet's little stars or hesperides.

[3] i.e. god-like Charles led to the creation of Herrick's little stars

or poems and inspired them. The Prince's presentation to the public led to their being given expansion both in the sense of publication and in the sense of being given substance. Cf. Gen. i.6, where the margin gives "expansion" as the equivalent of "firmament."

[4] Just as the stars (planets and moon) derive their light from the sun, so Herrick's star-poems not only owe their existence to the sun-prince Charles but also their light and its *influence* or flow to the public.

[5] circles of radiance; laudatory displays.

HESPERIDES.

H-1 *The Argument*[1] *of his Book.*

I Sing of *Brooks*, of *Blossomes*, *Birds*, and *Bowers:*
Of *April*, *May*, of *June*, and *July*-Flowers.
I sing of *May-poles*, *Hock-carts*,[2] *Wassails*,[3] *Wakes*,[4]
Of *Bride-grooms*, *Brides*, and of their *Bridall-cakes*.
I write of *Youth*, of *Love*, and have Accesse 5
By these, to sing of cleanly-*Wantonnesse*.
I sing of *Dewes*, of *Raines*, and piece by piece
Of *Balme*, of *Oyle*, of *Spice*, and *Amber-Greece*.[5]
I sing of *Times trans-shifting;*[6] and I write
How *Roses* first came *Red*, and *Lillies White*. 10
I write of *Groves*, of *Twilights*, and I sing
The Court of *Mab*, and of the *Fairie-King*.
I write of *Hell;* I sing (and ever shall)
Of *Heaven*, and hope to have it after all.[7]

[1] theme. [2] wagons loaded with the last of the harvest. See H-250. [3] drinking to the health of others, especially on Twelfth Night and Christmas Eve. [4] parish festivals; night watches for the dead. [5] ambergris: waxy substance used for perfumes. [6] transience; also parallels and correspondences between men's lives, daily and annual events, and the church calendar, on the one hand, and universal history and the divine story, on the other. [7] Catalogues of this sort are frequent in literature, but this one is like a microcosm and involves in progression natural objects; the seasons; human activities which accompany them; human emotions; the dews and rains of the physical heaven; balms, oils and spices, which symbolize the spiritual; the causes of things; the twilight realm of fairies; hell; and heaven.

H–2

To his Muse.

WHither *Mad maiden* wilt thou roame?
Farre safer 'twere to stay at home:
Where thou mayst sit, and piping please
The poore and private *Cottages.*
Since *Coats,*[1] and *Hamlets,* best agree 5
With this thy meaner Minstralsie.[2]
There with the Reed,[3] thou mayst expresse
The Shepherds Fleecie happinesse:
And with thy *Eclogues* intermixe
Some smooth, and harmlesse *Beucolicks.* 10
There on a Hillock thou mayst sing
Unto a handsome Shephardling;
Or to a Girle (that keeps the Neat)[4]
With breath more sweet then Violet.
There, there, (perhaps) such Lines as These 15
May take[5] the simple *Villages.*
But for the Court, the Country wit
Is despicable unto it.
Stay then at home, and doe not goe
Or flie abroad to seeke for woe. 20
Contempts in Courts and Cities dwell;
No *Critick* haunts the Poore mans Cell:
Where thou mayst hear thine own Lines read
By no one tongue, there, censured.
That man's unwise will search for Ill, 25
And may prevent it, sitting still.

[1] cotes: cottages, and shelters for animals. [2] poetry less lofty than epic and tragedy and closer to common life; i.e. bucolic poetry about shepherds and aspects of country and village life. [3] a rustic musical pipe. [4] oxen or similar cattle. [5] take the fancy of, become popular with.

H–3

To his Booke.

WHile thou didst keep thy *Candor*[1] undefil'd,
Deerely I lov'd thee; as my first-borne child:
But when I saw thee wantonly to roame
From house to house, and never stay at home;

I brake my bonds of Love, and bad thee goe, 5
Regardlesse whether well thou sped'st, or no.
On with thy fortunes then, what e're they be;
If good I'le smile, if bad I'le sigh for Thee.

[1] whiteness, i.e. purity. Throughout the poem there is an undertone of Biblical allusion: cf. Psalm cxix.1; Deut. xxi.15; Luke x.7; Hosea xi.1–4.

H–4 *Another.*

TO read my Booke the Virgin shie
May blush, (while *Brutus* standeth by:)
But when He's gone, read through what's writ,
And never staine a cheeke for it.

H–5 *Another.*

WHo with thy leaves shall wipe (at need)
The place, where swelling *Piles* do breed:
May every Ill, that bites, or smarts,
Perplexe him in his hinder-parts.

H–6 *To the soure Reader.*

IF thou dislik'st the Piece thou light'st on first;
Thinke that of All, that I have writ, the worst:
But if thou read'st my Booke unto the end,
And still do'st this, and that verse, reprehend:
O Perverse man! If All disgustfull be, 5
The Extreame Scabbe take thee, and thine, for me.

H–7 *To his Booke.*

COme thou not neere those men, who are like *Bread*
O're-leven'd; or like *Cheese* o're-renetted.

H–8

When he would have his verses read.

IN sober mornings, doe not thou reherse[1]
The holy incantation of a verse;
But when that men have both well drunke, and fed,
Let my Enchantments then be sung, or read.
When Laurell spirts 'ith fire, and when the Hearth 5
Smiles to it selfe, and guilds the roofe with mirth;
When up the **Thyrse*[2] is rais'd, and when the sound
Of sacred **Orgies*[3] flyes, A round, A round.
When the *Rose*[4] raignes, and locks with ointments shine,
Let rigid *Cato*[5] read these Lines of mine. 10

[1] recite. [2]* A *Javelin* twind with *Ivy* (Herrick's note). [3]* Songs to *Bacchus* (Herrick). [4] symbol of gaiety. [5] Roman who discharged the office of Censor with severity.

H–9

Upon Julias *Recovery.*

DRoop, droop no more, or hang the head
Ye *Roses* almost withered;
Now strength, and newer Purple get,
Each here declining *Violet.*
O *Primroses* ! let this day be 5
A Resurrection unto ye;
And to all flowers ally'd in blood,
Or sworn to that sweet Sister-hood:
For Health on *Julia's* cheek hath shed
Clarret, and Creame commingled. 10
And those her lips doe now appeare
As beames[1] of *Corrall,* but more cleare.

[1] branches.

H–10

To Silvia *to wed.*

LEt us (though late) at last (my *Silvia*) wed;
And loving lie in one devoted bed.
Thy Watch may stand, my minutes fly poste haste;

No sound calls back the yeere that once is past.
Then sweetest *Silvia*, let's no longer stay; 5
True love, we know, precipitates delay.
Away with doubts, all scruples hence remove;
No man at one time, can be wise, and love.

H–11 *The Parliament of Roses to* Julia.

I Dreamt the Roses one time went
To meet and sit in Parliament:
The place for these, and for the rest
Of flowers, was thy spotlesse breast:
Over the which a State[1] was drawne 5
Of Tiffanie,[2] or Cob-web Lawne;
Then in that *Parly*, all those powers
Voted the Rose; the Queen of flowers.
But so, as that her self should be
The maide of Honour unto thee. 10

[1] canopy. [2] transparent silk or muslin.

H–12 *No bashfulnesse in begging.*

TO get thine ends, lay bashfulnesse aside;
Who feares to aske, doth teach to be deny'd.

H–13 *The Frozen Heart.*

I Freeze, I freeze, and nothing dwels
In me but Snow, and *ysicles.*
For pitties sake give your advice,
To melt this snow, and thaw this ice;
I'le drink down Flames, but if so be 5
Nothing but love can supple me;
I'le rather keepe this frost, and snow,
Then to be thaw'd, or heated so.

H–14 To Perilla.

AH my Perilla! do'st thou grieve to see
Me, day by day, to steale away from thee?
Age cals me hence, and my gray haires bid come,
And haste away to mine eternal home;
'Twill not be long (*Perilla*) after this, 5
That I must give thee the *supremest*[1] kisse:
Dead when I am, first cast in salt, and bring
Part of the creame from that *Religious Spring*;[2]
With which (*Perilla*) wash my hands and feet;
That done, then wind me in that very sheet
Which wrapt thy smooth limbs (when thou didst implore
The Gods protection, but the night before)
Follow me weeping to my Turfe, and there
Let fall a *Primrose*, and with it a teare:
Then lastly, let some weekly-strewings[3] be 15
Devoted to the memory of me:
Then shall my *Ghost* not walk about, but keep
Still in the coole, and silent shades of sleep.

[1] ultimate. [2] a fountain sacred to some deity; i.e. her eyes from which spring tears of pious mourning. Cf. Crashaw, *Steps to the Temple* (1646), "The Weeper," lines 1–2, 5–6: "Haile *Sister Springs*, / Parents of Silver-forded rills! / . . . I meane / Thy faire Eyes . . . ." [3] of flowers on the grave.

H–15 *A Song to the Maskers.*[1]

1. COme down, and dance ye in the toyle[2]
   Of pleasures, to a Heate;
   But if to moisture, Let the oyle
   Of Roses be your sweat.

2. Not only to your selves assume[3]
   These sweets, but let them fly;
   From this, to that, and so Perfume
   E'ne all the standers by.

3. As Goddesse *Isis* (when she went,
Or glided through the street)
Made all that touch't her with her scent,
And whom she touch't, turne sweet.[4]

[1] numbers are attached to stanzas in *Hesperides* infrequently and occur more often in songs than in other genres. [2] turmoil. [3] receive. [4] According to Plutarch's *Morals*, trans. Philemon Holland (1657 ed.), p. 1053, the Egyptian goddess Isis, in order to ingratiate herself with the servants of the Queen of Byblus, cast "from her into them a marvellous sweet and pleasing scent issuing from her body."

H–16 To *Perenna.*

WHen I thy Parts runne o're, I can't espie
In any one, the least indecencie:[1]
But every Line, and Limb diffused[2] thence,
A faire, and unfamiliar excellence:
So, that the more I look, the more I prove, 5
Ther's still more cause, why I the more should love.

[1] uncomeliness of form, inelegance. Cf. Milton, "Il Penseroso," line 36, "Over thy decent shoulders drawn." [2] regarded individually.

H–17 *Treason.*

THe seeds of *Treason* choake up as they spring,
He Acts the Crime, that gives it Cherishing.[1]

[1] Cf. Juvenal, XIII, 209–10; trans. Barten Holyday (1673), line 209, "Who thinks a Crime is guilty of the Fact."

H–18 *Two Things Odious.*

TWo of a thousand things, are disallow'd,
A lying *Rich* man, and a *Poore* man proud.[1]

[1] Ecclus. xxv.2, "Three sorts of men my soul hateth . . . a poor man that is proud, a rich man that is a liar, and an old adulterer that doteth."

H–19 *To his Mistresses.*

HElpe me! helpe me! now I call
To my pretty *Witchcrafts* all:
Old I am, and cannot do
That, I was accustom'd to.
Bring your *Magicks, Spels, and Charmes,* 5
To enflesh my thighs, and armes:
Is there no way to beget
In my limbs their former heat?
Æson had (as *Poets* faine)
Baths that made him young againe:[1] 10
Find that *Medicine* (if you can)
For your drie-decrepid man:
Who would faine his strength renew,
Were it but to pleasure you.

[1] In Ovid's *Metamorphoses,* VII, 297 ff., trans. George Sandys (1632), pp. 237–38, an enchantress takes the "age-diseas'd" body of King Æson, "Thrice purges him with waters, thrice with flames," and then replaces his blood with a witches' brew, thus restoring him to manly vigor.

H–20 *The Wounded Heart.*

COme bring your *sampler,*[1] and with Art,
Draw in't a wounded Heart:
And dropping[2] here, and there:
Not that I thinke, that any Dart,
Can make your's bleed a teare: 5
Or peirce it any where;
Yet doe it to this end: that I,
May by
This secret see,
Though you can make 10
That *Heart* to bleed, your's ne'r will ake
For me.

[1] piece of canvas used for embroidery. [2] dropping blood. Herrick probably intended the poem's shape to suggest a torn heart.

H–21 *No Loathsomnesse in love.*[1]

WHat I fancy, I approve,
No Dislike there is in love:
Be my Mistresse short or tall,
And distorted there-withall:
Be she likewise one of those, 5
That an *Acre* hath of Nose:
Be her forehead, and her eyes
Full of incongruities:
Be her cheeks so shallow too,
As to shew her *Tongue* wag through: 10
Be her lips ill hung, or set,
And her grinders black as jet;
Ha's she thinne haire, hath she none,
She's to me a *Paragon.*

1 An example of what Conrad Hilberry calls "a baroque genre that enjoyed an obscure popularity during the first half of the seventeenth century: the praise of an ugly or deformed mistress," in his ed. of *The Poems of John Collop* (Madison, 1962), pp. 19–26.

H–22 *To* Anthea.

IF, deare *Anthea,* my hard fate it be
To live some few-sad-howers after thee:
Thy *sacred Corse*[1] with *Odours* I will burne;
And with my *Lawrell*[2] crown thy *Golden Urne.*
Then holding up (there) such religious Things, 5
As were (time past) thy holy *Filitings:*[3]
Nere to thy *Reverend Pitcher*[4] I will fall
Down dead for grief, and end my woes withall:
So three in one small plat of ground shall ly,
Anthea, Herrick, and his *Poetry.* 10

1 corpse. 2 laurel or bay leaves symbolize poetry. 3 filletings: headbands to ornament hair or hold it in place. 4 funeral urn.

H–23 ## *The Weeping Cherry.*

I Saw a *Cherry* weep, and why?
Why wept it? but for shame,
Because my *Julia's* lip was by,
And did out-red the same.
But pretty Fondling,[1] let not fall 5
A teare at all for that:
Which *Rubies, Corralls, Scarlets,* all
For tincture, wonder at.

[1] foolish little thing.

H–24 ## *Soft Musick.*

THe mellow touch of musick most doth wound
The soule, when it doth rather sigh, then sound.

H–25 ## *The Difference Betwixt Kings and Subjects.*

TWixt Kings and Subjects ther's this mighty odds,
Subjects are taught by *Men;* Kings by the *Gods.*

H–26 ## *His Answer to a Question.*

SOme would know
Why I so
Long still doe tarry,
And ask why
Here that I 5
Live, and not marry?
Thus I those
Doe oppose;
What man would be here,
Slave to Thrall, 10
If at all
He could live free here?

H–27 *Upon* Julia's *Fall.*

JUlia was carelesse, and withall,
She rather took, then got a fall:
The wanton *Ambler*[1] chanc'd to see
Part of her leggs sinceritie:[2]
And ravish'd thus, It came to passe, 5
The Nagge (like to the *Prophets Asse*)
Began to speak,[3] and would have been
A telling what rare sights h'ad seen:
And had told all; but did refraine,[4]
Because his Tongue was ty'd againe. 10

[1] a smooth-moving horse. [2] soundness without deception. [3] When an angel, invisible to Balaam but seen by his ass, barred the way and the animal would not proceed, the prophet struck it. "And the Lord opened the mouth of the ass, and she said unto Balaam, What have I done unto thee . . . ?" Numb. xxii.28. [4] from Latin *refrenare,* to bridle back.

H–28 *Expences Exhaust.*

LIve with a thrifty, not a needy Fate;[1]
Small shots[2] *paid often, waste a vast estate.*

[1] governing principle. [2] debts (especially in taverns).

H–29 *Love what it is.*

LOve is a circle that doth restlesse move
In the same sweet eternity of love.[1]

[1] Burton, in his *Anatomy,* 3,1,1,2 (6 ed., p. 416), describes love as "*Circulus à bono in bonum,* a round circle still from good to good; for love is the beginner and end of all our actions." Cf. H-839.

H–30 *Presence and Absence.*

WHen what is lov'd, is Present, love doth spring;
But being absent, Love lies languishing.

H–31 *No Spouse but a Sister.*[1]

A Bachelour I will
Live as I have liv'd still,
And never take a wife
To crucifie my life:
But this I'le tell ye too, 5
What now I meane to doe;
A Sister (in the stead
Of Wife) about I'le lead;[2]
Which I will keep embrac'd,
And kisse, but yet be chaste. 10

[1] Herrick's sister-in-law Elizabeth kept house for him at Dean Prior. Cf. H-72. [2] I Cor. ix.5, "Have we not power to lead about a sister . . . ?"

H–32 *The Pomander[1] Bracelet.*

TO me my *Julia* lately sent
A Bracelet richly Redolent:
The Beads I kist, but most lov'd her
That did perfume the Pomander.

[1] an aromatic mixture. It was placed in little balls pierced with holes to let the perfume escape. Bracelets were made of these balls.

H–33 *The shooe tying.*

ANthea bade me tye her shooe;
I did; and kist the Instep too:
And would have kist unto her knee,
Had not her Blush rebuked me.

H–34 *The Carkanet.*[1]

INstead of Orient Pearls of Jet,
I sent my Love a Karkanet:
About her spotlesse neck she knit

The lace, to honour me, or it:
Then think how wrapt[2] was I to see 5
My Jet t'enthrall[3] such Ivorie.

[1] carcanet: necklace or collar. [2] wordplay on *wrapped* and *rapt.* [3] like a slave's collar.

H–35 *His sailing from* Julia.

WHen that day comes, whose evening sayes I'm gone
Unto that watrie Desolation:
Devoutly to thy *Closet-gods* then pray,
That my wing'd Ship may meet no *Remora.*[1]
Those Deities which circum-walk the Seas, 5
And look upon our dreadfull passages,
Will from all dangers, re-deliver me,
For one *drink-offering,* poured out by thee.
Mercie and *Truth* live with thee![2] and forbeare
(In my short absence) to unsluce a teare: 10
But yet for Loves-sake, let thy lips doe this,
Give my dead picture one engendring kisse:
Work that to life, and let me ever dwell
In thy remembrance (*Julia.*) So farewell.

[1] a fish which attached itself to a ship by suction and was believed able to stop it. [2] II Sam. xv.20.

H–36

How the Wall-flower came first, and why so called.

WHy this Flower is now call'd so,
List' sweet maids, and you shal know.
Understand, this First-ling[1] was
Once a brisk and bonny Lasse,
Kept as close as *Danae*[2] was: 5
Who a sprightly *Springall*[3] lov'd,
And to have it fully prov'd,
Up she got upon a wall,
Tempting[4] down to slide withall:
But the silken twist unty'd, 10

So she fell, and bruis'd, she dy'd.
Love, in pitty of the deed,
And her loving-lucklesse speed,
Turn'd her to this Plant, we call
Now, *The Flower of the Wall.* 15

[1] first example of this kind of flower. [2] Her father shut her away from men in a brazen chamber because an oracle said that she would bear a son who would kill him. [3] youth, stripling. [4] attempting.

H–37 *Why Flowers change colour.*

THese fresh beauties (we can prove)
Once were Virgins sick of[1] love,
Turn'd to Flowers. Still in some
Colours goe, and colours come.

[1] because of.

H–38 *To his Mistresse objecting to him neither Toying or Talking.*

YOu say I love not, 'cause I doe not play
Still with your curles, and kisse the time away.
You blame me too, because I cann't devise
Some sport, to please those Babies[1] in your eyes:
By *Loves Religion,* I must here confesse it, 5
The most I love, when I the least expresse it.
Small griefs find tongues: Full Casques[2] are ever found
To give (if any, yet) but little sound.
Deep waters noyse-lesse are; And this we know,
That chiding[3] *streams betray small depth below.* 10
So when Love speechlesse is, she doth expresse
A depth in love, and that depth, bottomlesse.
Now since my love is tongue-lesse, know me such,
Who speak but little, 'cause I love so much.

[1] the pupils or their reflected tiny images of him (with further implications). [2] casks, barrels. [3] babbling.

H–39 *Upon the losse of his Mistresses.*

I Have lost, and lately, these
Many dainty Mistresses:
Stately *Julia*, prime of all;
Sapho next, a principall:
Smooth *Anthea*, for a skin 5
White, and Heaven-like Chrystalline:
Sweet *Electra*, and the choice
Myrha, for the Lute, and Voice.
Next, *Corinna*, for her wit,
And the graceful use of it: 10
With *Perilla:* All are gone;
Onely *Herrick's* left alone,
For to number sorrow by
Their departures hence, and die.

H–40 *The Dream.*

ME thought, (last night) love in an anger came,
And brought a rod, so whipt me with the same:
Mirtle[1] the twigs were, meerly to imply;
Love strikes, but 'tis with gentle crueltie.
Patient I was: Love pitifull grew then, 5
And stroak'd the stripes, and I was whole agen.
Thus like a Bee, *Love-gentle* stil doth bring
Hony to salve, where he before did sting.[2]

[1] an emblem of love, sacred to Venus. [2] Cf. Thomas Stanley, "The Chace VII" in his renderings of Anacreon in *Poems* (1651): "With a whip of Lillies, Love / Swiftly me before him drove: / . . . / Till a Snake that lurking lay / Chanc'd to sting me by the way: / Now my soul was nigh to death, / Ebbing, flowing with my breath; / When Love, fanning with his wings, / Back my fleeting spirit brings; / Learn (saith he) another day / Love without constraint t'obey."

H–41 *The Vine.*

I Dream'd this mortal part of mine
Was Metamorphoz'd to a Vine;
Which crawling one and every way,
Enthrall'd[1] my dainty *Lucia.*
Me thought, her long small legs and thighs 5
I with my *Tendrils* did surprize;
Her Belly, Buttocks, and her Waste
By my soft *Nerv'lits* were embrac'd:
About her head I writhing hung,
And with rich clusters (hid among 10
The leaves) her temples I behung:
So that my *Lucia* seem'd to me
Young *Bacchus* ravisht by his tree.[2]
My curles about her neck did craule,
And armes and hands they did enthrall: 15
So that she could not freely stir,
(All parts there made one prisoner.)
But when I crept with leaves to hide
Those parts, which maids keep unespy'd,
Such fleeting pleasures there I took, 20
That with the fancie I awook;
And found (Ah me!) this flesh of mine
More like a *Stock,* then like a *Vine.*

[1] fettered. [2] the grape vine.

H–42 *To Love.*

I'M free from thee; and thou no more shalt heare
My puling Pipe to beat against thine eare:
Farewell my shackles, (though of pearle they be)
Such precious thraldome ne'r shall fetter me.
He loves his bonds, who when the first are broke, 5
Submits his neck unto a second yoke.

H–43 *On himselfe.*

YOung I was, but now am old,
But I am not yet grown cold;
I can play, and I can twine

'Bout a Virgin like a Vine:[1]
In her lap too I can lye 5
Melting, and in fancie die:[2]
And return to life, if she
Claps my cheek, or kisseth me;
Thus, and thus it now appears
That our love out-lasts our yeeres. 10

[1] Cf. Stanley's trans. of Anacreon, "XXXIV," *Poems* (1651): "Though my aged head be gray / And thy youth more fresh than May, / Fly me not; oh rather see / In this wreath how gracefullie / Roses with pale Lillies joyne: / Learn of them, so let us twine" (*Anacreontea,* XXXIX). See H-527 and note. [2] Herrick puns on infancy and on the sexual meaning of *lie* and *die:* each sexual act was supposed to shorten one's life by a day.

H-44 Love's play at Push-pin.[1]

LOve and my selfe (beleeve me) on a day
At childish Push-pin (for our sport) did play:
I put, he pusht, and heedless of my skin,
Love prickt my finger with a golden pin:
Since which, it festers so, that I can prove 5
'Twas but a trick to poyson me with love:
Little the wound was; greater was the smart;
The finger bled, but burnt was all my heart.

[1] Children's game played with pins alternately "put" or placed and pushed.

H-45 The Rosarie.[1]

ONe ask'd me where the Roses grew?
  I bade him not goe seek;
But forthwith bade my *Julia* shew
  A bud in either cheek.

[1] rosegarden.

H–46 *Upon* Cupid.[1]

OLd wives have often told, how they
Saw *Cupid* bitten by a flea:
And thereupon, in tears half drown'd,
He cry'd aloud, Help, help the wound:
He wept, he sobb'd, he call'd to some 5
To bring him *Lint*, and *Balsamum*,
To make a *Tent*,[2] and put it in,
Where the *Steletto*[3] pierc'd the skin:
Which being done, the fretfull paine
Asswag'd, and he was well again. 10

[1] Inspired in part by *Anacreontea*, XXXV, in the Latin version by Henri Estienne (Stephanus), *Anacreontis Teji odae* (Paris, 1554), pp. 104–5: "Inter rosas Cupido / Aspiculam jacentem / Non vidit, éstque punctus. / Manúmque sauciatus, / Mox ejulare coepit. / Et cursitans volánsque / Ad candidam Cytherem, / Heu óccidi, óccidi, inquit, / Vitamque, mater, efflo. / En me minuta serpens / Pennata vulneravit: / Apem vocant coloni. / Tunc illa, Apis si acumen / Tantum facit dolorem, / Quantum putas dolere / Quos tu feris Cupido?" See H-139 and notes for closer renderings.
[2] a roll of lint (soft linen), medicated with balsam (aromatic ointment) put into or on a wound to clean, soothe, and protect it.
[3] stiletto: short, sharp dagger.

H–47 *The* Parcæ,[1] *or, Three dainty*[2] *Destinies. The Armilet.*

THree lovely Sisters working were
(As they were closely set)
Of soft and dainty Maiden-haire,
A curious[3] *Armelet.*
I smiling, ask'd them what they did? 5
(Faire *Destinies* all three)
Who told me, they had drawn a thred
Of Life, and 'twas for me.
They shew'd me then, how fine 'twas spun;
And I reply'd thereto, 10
I care not now how soone 'tis done,
Or cut, if cut by you.

[1] the three Fates who spin the thread of life, mark off each man's portion, and cut it off. Herrick fuses the idea with reference to the

17th-century practice of making a bracelet of hair to be worn by one's beloved. Cf. Donne, "The Funerall" and "The Relique." [2] handsome, choice, delightful; i.e. unlike the classical Fates who were often described as "dreadful." [3] exquisitely contrived.

H–48 *Sorrowes succeed.*

WHen one is past, another care we have,
Thus Woe succeeds a Woe; as wave a Wave.

H–49 *Cherry-pit.*[1]

JUlia, and I did lately sit
Playing for sport, at Cherry-pit:
She threw; I cast; and having thrown,
I got the Pit, and she the Stone.[2]

[1] game in which players try to throw cherry pits into a small hole which, punningly, may also be called a pit. [2] Herrick seems to have in mind a riddling folksong which occurs in numerous versions as early as the 15th century: a girl gives her lover a cherry which has no stone or pit, but ultimately she is herself heavy with consequences.

H–50 *To Robin Red-brest.*

LAid out for dead, let thy last kindnesse be
With leaves and mosse-work for to cover me:
And while the Wood-nimphs my cold corps inter,
Sing thou my Dirge, sweet-warbling Chorister!
For Epitaph, in Foliage, next write this, 5
Here, here the Tomb of Robin Herrick is.

H–51 *Discontents in Devon.*

MOre discontents I never had
Since I was born, then[1] here;
Where I have been, and still am sad,
In this dull *Devon-shire:*
Yet justly too I must confesse; 5

I ne'r invented such
Ennobled numbers for the Presse,
Then[1] where I loath'd so much.

[1] than.

H–52 *To his Paternall Countrey.*

O Earth! Earth! Earth heare thou my voice,[1] and be
Loving, and gentle for to cover me:
Banish'd from thee I live; ne'r to return,
Unlesse thou giv'st my small Remains an Urne.

[1]Herrick echoes Jer. xxii.29, "O earth, earth, earth, hear thou the word of the Lord."

H–53 *Cherrie-ripe.*

CHerrie-Ripe, Ripe, Ripe, I cry,[1]
Full and faire ones; come and buy:
If so be, you ask me where
They doe grow? I answer, There,
Where my *Julia's* lips doe smile; 5
There's the Land, or Cherry-Ile:
Whose Plantations fully show
All the yeere, where Cherries grow.

[1] a street-vendor's cry. With slightly variant words the poem gained popularity as a song with music written by Charles Edward Horn in 1825.

H–54 *To his Mistresses.*

PUt on your silks; and piece by piece
Give them the scent of Amber-Greece:
And for your breaths too, let them smell
Ambrosia-like, or *Nectarell:*[1]
While other Gums[2] their sweets perspire, 5
By your owne jewels set on fire.

[1] like ambrosia, the food of the gods, and like nectar, their drink.
[2] secretions of trees and shrubs used for incense; when burnt such substances exude (perspire) their sweet odors.

H–55 *To* Anthea.

NOw is the time, when all the lights wax dim;
And thou (*Anthea*) must withdraw from him
Who was thy servant. Dearest, bury me
Under that *Holy-oke*, or *Gospel-tree:*[1]
Where (though thou see'st not) thou may'st think upon
Me, when thou yeerly go'st Procession:
Or for mine honour, lay me in that Tombe
In which thy sacred Reliques shall have roome:
For my Embalming (Sweetest) there will be
No Spices wanting, when I'm laid by thee. 10

[1] an oak marking a parish boundary. During Rogation Days (three days before Ascension Day) it was customary to "beat the bounds"; i.e. for a religious procession to move along the parish boundaries, stopping at the oak for the reading of the Gospel.

H–56 *The Vision to* Electra.

I Dream'd we both were in a bed
Of Roses, almost smothered:
The warmth and sweetnes had me there
Made lovingly familiar:
But that I heard thy sweet breath say, 5
Faults done by night, will blush by day:
I kist thee (panting,) and I call
Night to the Record! that was all.
But ah! if empty dreames so please,
Love give me more such nights as these. 10

H–57 *Dreames.*

HEre we are all, by day; By night w'are hurl'd
By dreames, each one, into a sev'rall[1] world.

[1] separate and distinct. According to Plutarch, "Heraclitus was wont to say: That men all the whiles they were awake, enjoyed the benefit of no other world, but that which was common unto all; but when they slept every one had a world to himselfe" (*Morals*, trans. Holland, 1657, p. 215).

H–58 *Ambition.*

IN Man, Ambition is the common'st thing;
Each one, by nature, loves to be a King.

H–59 *His request to* Julia.

JUlia, if I chance to die
Ere I print my Poetry;
I most humbly thee desire
To commit it to the fire:
Better 'twere my Book were dead, 5
Then to live not perfected.

H–60 *Money gets the masterie.*

FIght thou with shafts of silver, and o'rcome,
When no force else can get the masterdome.

H–61 *The Scar-fire.*[1]

WAter, water I desire,
Here's a house of flesh on fire:
Ope' the fountains and the springs,
And come all to Buckittings:
What ye cannot quench, pull downe; 5
Spoile a house, to save a towne:
Better tis that one shu'd fall,
Then by one, to hazard all.

[1] a sudden and dangerous fire or the fire alarm.

H–62 *Upon* Silvia, *a Mistresse.*

WHen some shall say, Faire once my *Silvia* was;
Thou wilt complaine, False now's thy Looking-glasse:
Which renders that quite tarnisht,[1] which was green;[2]

And Priceless[3] now, what Peerless once had been:
Upon thy Forme more wrinkles yet will fall, 5
And comming downe, shall make no noise at all.

[1] withered. [2] youthful and fresh. [3] worthless.

H–63 *Cheerfulnesse in Charitie:* or, *The sweet Sacrifice.*

'TIs not a thousand Bullocks thies
Can please those Heav'nly Deities,
If the Vower don't express
In his Offering, Cheerfulness.

H–64 *Once poore, still penurious.*

GOes the world now, it will with thee goe hard:
The fattest Hogs we grease the more with Lard.
To him that has, there shall be added more;
Who is penurious, he shall still[1] *be poore.*

[1] always—the usual 17th-century meaning.

H–65 *Sweetnesse in Sacrifice.*

'TIs not greatness they require,
To be offer'd up by fire:
But 'tis sweetness that doth please
Those Eternall Essences.

H–66 *Steame in Sacrifice.*

IF meat the Gods give, I the steame
High-towring wil devote to them:
Whose easie natures like it well,
If we the roste have, they the smell.

H–67 *Upon* Julia's *Voice.*

SO smooth, so sweet, so silv'ry is thy voice,
As, could they hear, the Damn'd would make no noise,
But listen to thee, (walking in thy chamber)
Melting melodious words, to Lutes of Amber.[1]

[1] to the accompaniment of lutes inlaid either with amber, the fossilized resin, or with amber, the alloy made of four parts of silver to one of gold. The meaning is discussed in *N&Q,* S9, IX (May 24, 1902), pp. 408–9 and subsequent issues. What Herrick probably intends is that the silver of her voice melts with the golden words to produce musical sounds (like those from lutes), which are thus a musical alloy analogous to metallic amber.

H–68 *Againe.*

WHen I thy singing next shall heare,
Ile wish I might turne all to eare,
To drink in Notes, and Numbers;[1] such
As blessed soules cann't heare too much:
Then melted down, there let me lye 5
Entranc'd, and lost confusedly:
And by thy Musique strucken mute,
Die, and be turn'd into a Lute.

[1] verses or feet in poetry.

H–69 *All things decay and die.*

ALL things decay with Time: The Forrest sees
The growth, and down-fall of her aged trees:
That Timber tall, which three-score *lusters*[1] stood
The proud *Dictator* of the State-like wood:
I meane (the Soveraigne of all Plants) the Oke 5
Droops, dies, and falls without the cleavers stroke.

[1] five-year periods.

H-70 *The succession of the foure sweet months.*

FIrst, *April*, she with mellow showrs
Opens the way for early flowers;
Then after her comes smiling *May*,
In a more rich and sweet aray:
Next enters *June*, and brings us more 5
Jems, then those two, that went before:
Then (lastly) *July* comes, and she
More wealth brings in, then all those three.

H-71
No Shipwrack of Vertue. To a friend.

THou sail'st with others, in this *Argus*[1] here;
Nor wrack, or *Bulging*[2] thou hast cause to feare:
But trust to this, my noble passenger;
Who swims with Vertue, he shall still[3] be sure
(*Ulysses*-like) all tempests to endure; 5
And 'midst a thousand gulfs to be secure.

[1] ship. [2] breaking a hole in the bilge or bottom part of a ship's hull. [3] always.

H-72 *Upon his Sister-in-Law, Mistresse* Elizabeth Herrick.[1]

FIrst, for Effusions due unto the dead,
My solemne Vowes have here accomplished:
Next, how I love thee, that my griefe must tell,
Wherein thou liv'st for ever. Deare farewell.

[1] his brother's widow who kept house for him at Dean Prior and died in April, 1643.

H-73 *Of Love. A Sonet.*[1]

HOw Love came in, I do not know,
Whether by th'eye, or eare, or no:
Or whether with the soule it came

(At first) infused with the same:
Whether in part 'tis here or there, 5
Or, like the soule, whole every where:
This troubles me: but I as well
As any other, this can tell;
That when from hence she does depart,
The out-let then is from the heart. 10

[1] a short lyrical poem, usually about love.

H–74 To Anthea.

AH my *Anthea!* Must my heart still break?
(*Love makes me write, what shame forbids to speak.*)[1]
Give me a kisse, and to that kisse a score;
Then to that twenty, adde an hundred more:
A thousand to that hundred: so kisse on, 5
To make that thousand up a million.
Treble that million, and when that is done,
Let's kisse afresh, as when we first begun.[2]
But yet, though Love likes well such Scenes as these,
There is an Act that will more fully please: 10
Kissing and glancing, soothing, all make way
But to the acting of this private Play:
Name it I would; but being blushing red,
The rest Ile speak, when we meet both in bed.

[1] Ovid, *Heroides,* IV, 10. [2] Lines 3–8 imitate Catullus, V, 7–9.

H–75 *The Rock of Rubies: and The quarrie of Pearls.*

SOme ask'd me where the *Rubies* grew?
And nothing I did say:
But with my finger pointed to
The lips of *Julia.*
Some ask'd how *Pearls* did grow, and where? 5
Then spoke I to my Girle,
To part her lips, and shew'd them there
The Quarelets[1] of Pearl.

[1] little quarries or small quadrangular objects.

H–76 *Conformitie.*

COnformity was ever knowne
A foe to Dissolution:
Nor can we that a ruine call,
Whose crack gives crushing unto all.

H–77

TO THE KING,

Upon his comming with his Army into the West.[1]

WElcome, most welcome to our Vowes and us,
Most great, and universall *Genius!*[2]
The Drooping West, which hitherto has stood
As one, in long-lamented-widow-hood;
Looks like a Bride now, or a bed of flowers, 5
Newly refresh't, both by the Sun, and showers.
War, which before was horrid, now appears
Lovely in you, brave Prince of Cavaliers!
A deale[3] of courage in each bosome springs
By your accesse; (*O you the best of Kings!*) 10
Ride on with all white[4] *Omens;* so, that where
Your Standard's[5] up, we fix a Conquest there.

[1] the western counties of England, particularly Devonshire, where Herrick lived at Dean Prior. Charles I stayed for a short time at Exeter in the summer of 1644 before marching into Cornwall.
[2] tutelary spirit or deity who presides over the destiny of a place.
[3] a large quantity. [4] auspicious. [5] the distinctive ensign of a king.

H–78 *Upon Roses.*

UNder a Lawne, then skyes more cleare,[1]
Some ruffled Roses nestling were:
And snugging[2] there, they seem'd to lye
As in a flowrie Nunnery:
They blush'd, and look'd more fresh then flowers 5
Quickned of late by Pearly showers;

And all, because they were possest
But of the heat of *Julia's* breast:
Which as a warme, and moistned spring,
Gave them their ever flourishing. 10

[1] Under a fine, sheer linen, more pellucid than the skies; but Herrick plays on the other meaning of lawn. [2] nestling closely.

H-79 *To the King and Queene, upon their unhappy distances.*[1]

WOe, woe to them, who (by a ball of strife)[2]
Doe, and have parted here[3] a Man and Wife:
CHARLS the best Husband, while MARIA strives
To be, and is, the very best of Wives:
Like Streams, you are divorc'd; but 'twill come, when 5
These eyes of mine shall see you mix agen.
Thus speaks the *Oke*,[4] here; *C.* and *M.* shall meet,
Treading on *Amber*, with their silver-feet:
Nor wil't be long, ere this accomplish'd be;
The words found true, *C. M.* remember me. 10

[1] The English Civil War caused the separation of Charles I and Queen Henrietta Maria temporarily in 1642 when she went to seek support for him on the Continent, and permanently in 1644 when she went abroad again. [2] probably mixed allusions to the cannonballs of the Civil War and to the golden apple which the goddess of Discord threw into an assembly of gods at a wedding for the greatest beauty there. Juno, Venus, and Minerva claimed it, and their dispute ultimately conduced to the Trojan War. [3] in Devonshire in 1644. [4] The responses of the oracle at Dodona in ancient Epirus were delivered from a sacred oak.

H-80 *Dangers wait on Kings.*[1]

AS oft as Night is banish'd by the Morne,
So oft, we'll think, we see a King new born.

[1] A trans. of Seneca, *Hercules in Œta*, 614–15. The position of the poem after H-79 suggests that Herrick has in mind the successive risings of different parliamentary leaders to power during the Civil War period; e.g. Cromwell's replacement of Fairfax in command of the army.

H–81 *The Cheat of* Cupid: *Or,*
The ungentle guest.[1]

ONe silent night of late,
  When every creature rested,
Came one unto my gate,
  And knocking, me molested.

Who's that (said I) beats there, 5
  And troubles thus the Sleepie?
Cast off (said he) all feare,
  And let not Locks thus keep ye.

For I a Boy am, who
  By Moonlesse nights have swerved;[2] 10
And all with showrs wet through,
  And e'en with cold half starved.[3]

I pittifull arose,
  And soon a Taper lighted;
And did my selfe disclose 15
  Unto the lad benighted.

I saw he had a Bow,
  And Wings too, which did shiver;
And looking down below,
  I spy'd he had a Quiver. 20

I to my Chimney's shine
  Brought him, (as Love professes)
And chaf'd his hands with mine,
  And dry'd his dropping Tresses:

But when he felt him warm'd, 25
  Let's try this bow of ours,
And string if they be harm'd,
  Said he, with these late showrs.

Forthwith his bow he bent,
  And wedded string and arrow, 30
And struck me that it went
  Quite through my heart and marrow.[4]

Then laughing loud, he flew
  Away, and thus said flying,
Adieu, mine Host, Adieu, 35
  Ile leave thy heart a dying.

[1] a version of *Anacreontea,* XXXIII, based chiefly on Estienne's Latin rendering (See H-46), which Martin reprints, p. 501, n. 26.3. Cf. Thomas Stanley's trans. of Anacreon, "Loves Night-walk III," Thomas Stanley's trans. of Anacreon, "Loves Night-walk III," *Poems* (1651): ". . . Love, in this still depth of night, / Lately at my house did light: / Where perceiving all fast lockt, / At the door he boldly knockt: / Who'se that (said I) that does keep / Such a noise, and breaks my sleep? / Ope saith Love, for pity hear; / Tis a Childe, thou need'st not fear, / Wet and weary, from his way / Led by this dark night astray: / With compassion this I heard; / Light I struck; the door unbarr'd : / Where a little Boy appears, / Who wings, bow, and quiver bears; / Near the fire I made him stand; / With my own I chaf't his hand; / And with kindly busie care / Wrung the chill drops from his hair: / When well warm'd he was, and dry, / Now saith he tis time to try / If my bow no hurt did get, / For me thinks the string is wet: / With that, drawing it, a dart / He let fly that pierc'd my heart: / Leaping then, and laughing said, / Come my friend with me be glad; / For my Bow thou seest is sound, / Since my heart hath got a wound." [2] have lost my way because of the lack of moonlight to illuminate it. [3] dead. [4] vital part.

H–82 *To the reverend shade of his religious Father.*[1]

THat for seven *Lusters* I did never come
To doe the *Rites* to thy Religious[2] Tombe:
That neither haire was cut, or true teares shed
By me, o'r thee, (*as justments*[3] *to the dead*)
Forgive, forgive me; since I did not know 5
Whether thy bones had here their Rest,[4] or no.
But now 'tis known, Behold; behold, I bring
Unto thy Ghost, th'Effused Offering:
And look, what Smallage,[5] Night-shade, Cypresse, Yew,
Unto the shades have been, or now are due, 10
Here I devote; And something more then so;
I come to pay a Debt of Birth I owe.
Thou gav'st me life, (but Mortall;) For that one
Favour, Ile make full satisfaction;
For my life mortall, Rise from out thy Herse, 15
And take a life immortall from my Verse.

[1] to the spirit, deeply respected and worthy of honor, of his ven-

erated and scrupulously pious father. Nicholas Herrick made his will on Nov. 7, 1592 and two days later fell from the window of his house and died. The Bishop of Bristol investigated the possibility of suicide (which could have resulted in unsanctified burial and confiscation of the estate), but his report, though leaving unsettled the matter of suicide, granted the estate to the wife and children in accordance with the will. Robert was then 14 months old. His emphasis on *reverend* and *religious* (primarily in the sense of *revered*) indicates that he regarded the death as accidental. [2] If "seven Lusters" is to be taken literally, 35 years had elapsed between the death and the visit and, presumably, the writing of the poem. It was probably composed in 1627 before Herrick went as Buckingham's chaplain on the expedition to the Isle of Rhé. [3] Herrick's use of this word seems to be unique. It may mean *appropriate ceremonies,* but its Latin root is *jus* (right, law, justice), which suggests that the father had been buried with imperfect funeral rites because of the suspicion of suicide, and that Herrick, rejecting this suspicion, felt that an adjustment, a settling of legal and proper claims and liabilities, was due. It is not inconceivable that, as a priest, he himself read the complete and proper funeral service over his father's burial place, although, as is usual in *Hesperides,* he refers to the Graeco-Roman equivalents. [4] The burial took place in St. Vedast's church or churchyard, but it would seem that the exact location was kept secret: a verdict of suicide could have involved disinterment and the disgracing of the corpse. [5] celery or parsley.

H–83 *Delight in Disorder.*

A Sweet disorder[1] in the dresse
Kindles in cloathes a wantonnesse:
A Lawne about the shoulders thrown
Into a fine distraction:
An erring Lace, which here and there 5
Enthralls the Crimson Stomacher:
A Cuffe neglectfull, and thereby
Ribbands to flow confusedly:
A winning wave (deserving Note)
In the tempestuous petticote: 10
A carelesse shooe-string, in whose tye
I see a wilde civility:
Doe more bewitch me, then when Art
Is too precise in every part.

[1] The aesthetic principle that there is beauty in a becoming negligence, in the imitation of nature's "orderly disorder," in an artistically deliberate fine disorder, is an ancient one and Herrick reiter-

ates his delight in disorder, his pleasure with "transgression" (H-175), and the fascinations of "a wild civility" (H-560), or "a civill Wilderness" or "a sweet neglect" (H-665). Ben Jonson anticipated Herrick in the second stanza of the song, "Still to be neat," in *Epicoene,* I, i: "Give me a look, give me a face, / That makes simplicity a grace; / Robes loosely flowing, hair as free: / Such sweet neglect more taketh me, / Than all the adulteries of art." Jonson's poem is a development of one sometimes attributed to Jean de Bonnefon, beginning *Semper munditias.*

H–84 *To his Muse.*

WEre I to give thee *Baptime,* I wo'd chuse
To *Christen* thee, the *Bride,* the *Bashfull Muse,*
Or *Muse* of *Roses:* since that name does fit
Best with those *Virgin-Verses* thou hast writ:
Which are so cleane, so chast, as none may feare 5
Cato the *Censor,*[1] sho'd he scan each here.

[1] See H-8, n.5.

H–85 *Upon Love.*

LOve scorch'd my finger, but did spare
The burning of my heart:
To signifie, in Love my share
Sho'd be a little part.

Little I love; but if that he 5
Wo'd but that heat recall:
That joynt to ashes burnt sho'd be,[1]
Ere I wo'd love at all.

[1] *sho'd be burnt* in *Hesperides,* but in the order printed here in *Wit's Recreations.*

H–86

To Dean-bourn, *a rude River in* Devon, *by which sometimes he lived.*

DEan-Bourn, farewell; I never look to see
Deane, or thy warty incivility.
Thy rockie bottome, that doth teare thy streams,

And makes them frantick, ev'n to all extreames;
To my content, I never sho'd behold,
Were thy streames silver, or thy rocks all gold.
Rockie thou art; and rockie we discover
Thy men; and rockie are thy wayes all over.
O men, O manners;[1] Now, and ever knowne
To be *A Rockie*[2] *Generation!* 10
A people currish;[3] churlish as the seas;
And rude (almost) as rudest Salvages[4]
With whom I did, and may re-sojourne when
Rockes turn to Rivers, Rivers turn to Men.

[1] a reiterated phrase in Cicero's invective against Catiline. [2] Jer. v.3, "they have refused to receive correction: they have made their faces harder than a rock." [3] having the dispositions of curs. [4] savages.

H–87 *Kissing Usurie.*[1]

Blancha, Let
Me pay the debt
I owe thee for a kisse
Thou lend'st to me;
And I to thee 5
Will render ten for this:

If thou wilt say,
Ten will not pay
For that so rich a one;
Ile cleare the summe, 10
If it will come
Unto a Million.

By this I guesse,
Of happinesse
Who has a little measure: 15
He must of right,
To th'utmost mite,
Make payment for his pleasure.

[1] Cf. H-74. Inspired partly by Catullus, V, largely by Johannes Secundus, *Basia,* VI, which is verbosely rendered by Thomas Stanley in "Kisses by Secundus," in his *Poems* (1651).

H–88

To Julia.

HOw rich and pleasing thou my *Julia* art
In each thy dainty, and peculiar part!
First, for thy *Queen-ship* on thy head is set
Of flowers a sweet commingled Coronet:
About thy neck a Carkanet is bound, 5
Made of the *Rubie, Pearle* and *Diamond:*
A golden ring, that shines upon thy thumb:
About thy wrist, the rich **Dardanium.*[1]
Between thy Breasts (then[2] Doune of Swans more white)
There playes the *Saphire* with the *Chrysolite.*
No part besides must of thy selfe be known,
But by the *Topaz, Opal, Calcedon.*[3]

[1]* *A Bracelet from Dardanus so call'd* (Herrick's note). The city of Dardanus was situated near the Hellespont. [2] than. [3] chalcedony: translucent quartz.

H–89

To Laurels.

A Funerall stone,
Or Verse I covet none;
But onely crave
Of you, that I may have
A sacred Laurel springing from my grave: 5
Which being seen,
Blest with perpetuall greene,
May grow to be
Not so much call'd a tree,
As the eternall monument of me. 10

H–90

His Cavalier.

GIve me that man, that dares bestride
The active Sea-horse,[1] and with pride,
Through that huge field of waters ride:
Who, with his looks too, can appease
The ruffling winds and raging Seas, 5

In mid'st of all their outrages.
This, this a virtuous man can doe,
Saile against Rocks, and split them too;
I![2] and a world of Pikes[3] passe through.

[1] a fabulous animal, half horse and half fish, driven by sea-gods, ridden by sea nymphs; the term is sometimes applied to white-capped waves or ships. [2] aye: yea. [3] a pun on the weapons and the fish?

H–91 *Zeal required in Love.*

I'Le doe my best to win, when'ere I wooe:
That man loves not, who is not zealous too.

H–92 *The Bag of the Bee.*

ABout the sweet bag of a Bee,
Two *Cupids* fell at odds;
And whose the pretty prize shu'd be,
They vow'd to ask the Gods.

Which *Venus* hearing; thither came, 5
And for their boldness stript them:
And taking thence from each his flame;
With rods of *Mirtle*[1] whipt them.

Which done, to still their wanton cries,
When quiet grown sh'ad seen them, 10
She kist, and wip'd thir dove-like eyes;[2]
And gave the Bag between them.

[1] Cf. H-40. [2] Song of Sol. i.15, "my love . . . thou hast doves' eyes."

H–93 *Love kill'd by Lack.*

LEt me be warme; let me be fully fed:
Luxurious[1] *Love by Wealth is nourished.*
Let me be leane, and cold, and once grown poore,
I shall dislike, what once I lov'd before.

[1] lascivious. The line is a trans. of Ovid, *De Remedio Amoris,* 746.

H–94A

To his Mistresse.

CHoose me your Valentine;
  Next, let us marry:
Love to the death will pine,
  If we long tarry.

Promise, and keep your vowes, 5
  Or vow you never:[1]
Loves doctrine disallowes
  Troth-breakers ever.

You have broke promise twice
  (Deare) to undoe me; 10
If you prove faithlesse thrice,
  None then will wooe ye.

[1] Eccles. v.4–5, "When thou vowest a vow to God, defer not to pay it: . . . better it is that thou shouldest not vow, than that thou shouldest vow and not pay."

H–94B

His Mistress to him at his Farewell.[1]

You may vow I'll[2] *not forget*
  To pay the debt,
Which to your memory stands as due
  As faith could[3] *seal it you.*
Claim then a tribute[4] *of my tears.* 5
  So long as I have fears
  To prompt me, I shall ever
Languish and look, but your return see never.
  Ah[5] *then, to lessen my despair*
  Print your lips into the air. 10
    So, by this
Means I may kiss your kiss
  Whenas[6] *some kind*
    Wind
Shall hither waft it, as[7] *in lieu* 15
My lips will[8] *send a thousand back to you.*

[1] not in *Hesperides,* but added here as an answer to H-94A. Text: modernized, based chiefly on B (B.M. MS Harl 6918, f.23) and

H (Harvard Eng 626F, f.22v), with variants from A (B.M. Add MS 11811, f.37). In A, *thy* is used instead of *your* throughout the poem. Attributed to Herrick in A. [2] (BH: *I*). [3] (A: *can*). [4] (A: *Take then tribute*). [5] (A: *Oh*). [6] (H: *Whereas*). [7] (H: *and*). [8] (A: *shall*).

H–95 *To the generous Reader.*

SEe, and not see; and if thou chance t'espie
Some Aberrations in my Poetry;
Wink at small faults, the greater, ne'rthelesse
Hide, and with them, their Fathers nakedness.[1]
Let's doe our best, our Watch and Ward[2] to keep: 5
Homer himself, in a long work, may sleep.

[1] So Shem and Japhet hid the nakedness of their father, Noah. (Gen. ix.23). [2] a continuous look-out by a watchman or sentinel.

H–96 *To Criticks.*

ILe write, because Ile give
You Criticks means to live:
For sho'd I not supply
The Cause, th'effect wo'd die.

H–97 *Duty to Tyrants.*

GOod Princes must be pray'd for: for the bad
They must be borne with, and in rev'rence had.
Doe they first pill[1] thee, next, pluck off thy skin?
Good children kisse the Rods, that punish sin.
Touch not the Tyrant; Let the Gods alone 5
To strike him dead, that but usurps a Throne.

[1] make a prey of.

H–98 *Being once blind, his request to* Biancha.

WHen Age or Chance has made me blind,
So that the path I cannot find:
And when my falls and stumblings are

More then the stones i'th'street by farre:
Goe thou afore; and I shall well 5
Follow thy Perfumes by the smell:
Or be my guide; and I shall be
Led by some light that flows from thee.
Thus held, or led by thee, I shall
In wayes confus'd, nor slip or fall. 10

H–99 *Upon* Blanch.

BLanch swears her Husband's lovely; when a scald[1]
Has blear'd his eyes: Besides, his head is bald.
Next, his wilde eares, like Lethern wings full spread,
Flutter to flie, and beare away his head.

[1] an inflammatory disease.

H–100 *No want where there's little.*

TO Bread and Water none is poore;
And having these, what need of more?
Though much from out the Cess[1] be spent,[2]
Nature with little is content.

[1] excess (probably; but assessment, in reference to taxes levied by Parliament during the Civil War may be intended). [2] used up.

H–101 *Barly-Break:*[1] or, *Last in Hell.*

WE two are last in Hell: what may we feare
To be tormented, or kept Pris'ners here?
Alas! If kissing be of plagues the worst,
We'll wish, in Hell we had been Last and First.

[1] a kind of tag game played by couples who, when caught, are taken prisoner and sent to a "den" or place of retreat known as "hell."

H–102 *The Definition of Beauty.*

BEauty, no other thing is, then a Beame
Flasht out between the Middle and Extreame.

H–103 *To Dianeme.*

DEare, though to part it be a Hell,
Yet *Dianeme* now farewell:
Thy frown (last night) did bid me goe;
But whither, onely Grief do's know.
I doe beseech thee, ere we part, 5
(If mercifull, as faire thou art;
Or else desir'st that Maids sho'd tell
Thy pitty by Loves-Chronicle)
O *Dianeme*, rather kill
Me, then to make me languish still! 10
'Tis cruelty in thee to'th'height,
Thus, thus to wound, not kill out-right:
Yet there's a way found (if thou please)
By sudden death to give me ease:
And thus devis'd, doe thou but this, 15
Bequeath to me one parting kisse:
So sup'rabundant joy shall be
The Executioner of me.

H–104 *To* Anthea *lying in bed.*

SO looks *Anthea*, when in bed she lyes,
Orecome, or halfe betray'd by Tiffanies:
Like to a Twi-light, or that simpring Dawn,
That Roses shew, when misted o're with Lawn.
Twilight is yet, till that her Lawnes give way;[1] 5
Which done, that Dawne, turnes then to perfect day.

[1] Anthea's likeness to a "Twi-light" (a light intermediate between darkness and dawn) or to a shyly smiling dawn continues until her sheets of fine linen (tiffany or cobweb lawn) are removed.

H–105 *To* Electra.

MOre white then whitest Lillies far,
Or Snow, or whitest Swans you are:
More white then are the whitest Creames,
Or Moone-light tinselling the streames:

More white then *Pearls*, or *Juno's* thigh; 5
Or *Pelops* Arme[1] of *Yvorie.*
True, I confesse; such Whites as these
May me delight, not fully please:
Till, like *Ixion's* Cloud[2] you be
White, warme, and soft to lye with me. 10

[1] In order to test the divinity of the Greek gods, Tantalus cooked and served his son Pelops to them. All abstained but Ceres who, preoccupied with other matters, ate a shoulder. When the gods reunited and revived him, it was replaced with an ivory one.
[2] When Ixion lusted after Juno, she and Jupiter formed a cloud in her likeness, which Ixion embraced.

H–106 *A Country life: To his Brother, Master* Thomas Herrick.[1]

THrice, and above, blest (my soules halfe) art thou,
In thy both Last, and Better Vow:
Could'st leave the City, for exchange, to see
The Countries sweet simplicity:
And it to know, and practice; with intent 5
To grow the sooner innocent:
By studying to know vertue; and to aime
More at her nature, then her name:
The last is but the least; the first doth tell
Wayes lesse to live, then to live well: 10
And both are knowne to thee, who now can'st live
Led by thy conscience; to give
Justice to soone-pleas'd nature; and to show,
Wisdome and she together goe,
And keep one Centre: This with that conspires, 15
To teach Man to confine desires:
And know, that Riches have their proper stint,[2]
In the contented mind, not mint.[3]
And can'st instruct, that those who have the itch
Of craving more, are never rich. 20
These things thou know'st to'th'height, and dost prevent
That plague; because thou art content
With that Heav'n gave thee with a warie hand,
(More blessed in thy Brasse,[4] then Land)
To keep cheap Nature even, and upright; 25
To coole, not cocker[5] Appetite.

Thus thou canst tearcely[6] live to satisfie
    The belly chiefly; not the eye:
Keeping the barking stomach wisely quiet,
    Lesse with a neat,[7] then needfull diet. 30
But that which most makes sweet thy country life,
    Is, the fruition of a wife:
Whom (Stars consenting with thy Fate)[8] thou hast
    Got, not so beautifull, as chast:
By whose warme side thou dost securely sleep 35
    (While Love the Centinell doth keep)
With those deeds done by day, which n'er affright
    Thy silken slumbers in the night.
Nor has the darknesse power to usher in
    Feare to those sheets, that know no sin. 40
But still thy wife, by chast intentions led,
    Gives thee each night a Maidenhead.
The Damaskt[9] medowes, and the peebly[10] streames
    Sweeten, and make soft your dreames:
The Purling springs, groves, birds, and well-weav'd Bowrs,
    With fields enameled[11] with flowers,
Present their shapes; while fantasie discloses
    Millions of *Lillies* mixt with *Roses*.
Then dream, ye heare the Lamb by many a bleat
    Woo'd to come suck the milkie Teat: 50
While *Faunus*[12] in the Vision comes to keep,
    From rav'ning wolves, the fleecie sheep.
With thousand such enchanting dreams, that meet
    To make sleep not so sound, as sweet:
Nor can these figures[13] so thy rest endeare, 55
    As not to rise when *Chanticlere*
Warnes the last Watch;[14] but with the Dawne dost rise
    To work, but first to sacrifice;
Making thy peace with heav'n, for some late fault,
    With Holy-meale, and spirting-salt.[15]
Which done, thy painfull[16] Thumb this sentence[17] tells us,
    Jove for our labour all things sells us.
Nor are thy daily and devout affaires
    Attended with those desp'rate cares,
Th'industrious Merchant has; who for to find 65
    Gold, runneth to the Western Inde,
And back again, (tortur'd with fears) doth fly,
    Untaught, to suffer Poverty.
But thou at home, blest with securest ease,
    Sitt'st, and beleev'st that there be seas, 70

And watrie dangers; while thy whiter hap,[18]
 But[19] sees these things within thy Map.
And viewing them with a more safe survey,
 Mak'st easie Feare unto thee say,
A heart thrice wall'd with Oke, and Brasse, that man 75
 Had, first,[20] *durst plow the Ocean.*
But thou at home without or tyde or gale,
 Canst in thy Map securely saile:
Seeing those painted Countries; and so guesse
 By those fine Shades, their Substances: 80
And from thy Compasse taking small advice,
 Buy'st Travell at the lowest price.
Nor are thine eares so deafe, but thou canst heare
 (Far more with wonder, then with feare)
Fame[21] tell of States, of Countries, Courts, and Kings; 85
 And beleeve there be such things:
When of these truths, thy happyer knowledge lyes,
 More in thine eares, then in thine eyes.
And when thou hear'st by that too-true-Report,
 Vice rules the Most, or All at Court: 90
Thy pious wishes are, (though thou not there)
 Vertue had, and mov'd[22] her Sphere.
But thou liv'st fearlesse; and thy face ne'r shewes
 Fortune when she comes, or goes.
But with thy equall thoughts, prepar'd dost stand, 95
 To take her by the either hand:
Nor car'st which comes the first, the foule or faire;
 A wise man ev'ry way lies square.[23]
And like a surly *Oke* with storms perplext;
 Growes still the stronger, strongly vext. 100
Be so, bold spirit; Stand Center-like,[24] unmov'd;
 And be not onely thought, but prov'd
To be what I report thee; and inure
 Thy selfe, if want comes to endure:
And so thou dost: for thy desires are 105
 Confin'd to live with private *Larr:*[25]
Not curious whether Appetite be fed,
 Or with the first, or second bread.
Who keep'st no proud mouth for delicious cates:
 Hunger makes coorse meats, delicates. 110
Can'st, and unurg'd, forsake that Larded fare,
 Which Art, not Nature, makes so rare;
To taste boyl'd Nettles, Colworts,[26] Beets, and eate
 These, and sowre herbs, as dainty meat?

While soft Opinion makes thy *Genius*[27] say, 115
Content makes all Ambrosia.
Nor is it, that thou keep'st this stricter size[28]
So much for want, as exercise:
To numb the sence of Dearth, which sho'd sinne haste it,
Thou might'st but onely see't, not taste it.
Yet can thy humble roofe maintaine a Quire
Of singing Crickits by thy fire:
And the brisk Mouse may feast her selfe with crums,
Till that the green-ey'd Kitling comes.
Then to her Cabbin, blest she can escape 125
The sudden danger of a Rape.
And thus thy little-well-kept-stock doth prove,
Wealth cannot make a life, but Love.[29]
Nor art thou so close-handed, but can'st spend
(Counsell concurring with the end) 130
As well as spare: still conning o'r[30] this Theame,
To shun the first, and last extreame.
Ordaining that thy small stock find no breach,
Or to exceed thy Tether's reach:
But to live round,[31] and close, and wisely true 135
To thine owne selfe; and knowne to few.
Thus let thy Rurall Sanctuary be
Elizium to thy wife and thee;
There to disport your selves with golden measure:
For seldome use commends the pleasure. 140
Live, and live blest; thrice happy Paire; Let Breath,
But lost to one, be th'others death.
And as there is one Love, one Faith, one Troth,
Be so one Death, one Grave to both.
Till when, in such assurance live, ye may 145
Nor feare, or wish your dying day.

[1] Thomas, born 1588, left a mercantile life in London and settled on a small farm, probably about 1610. [2] limit. [3] money. [4] possession only of coins of low value; but Herrick may be thinking of the strength and endurance of brass. [5] *Pamper* is the standard dictionary meaning, but in this context Herrick intends a contrast between decreasing appetite with cold and increasing it with heat: apparently he thinks of *cocker* as a derivative from Latin *coquere*, to cook, or to change the nature of something by the application of heat. [6] tersely: freed from excess. [7] glitteringly elegant (Latin, *nitidus*). [8] from Latin *fatum*, literally, *that which has been spoken*—a reference to his brother's decision to live simply in the country—the "Last, and Better Vow" of line 2. [9] variegated like damask, a

figured fabric. [10] pebbly. [11] diversified with smooth, lustrous colors like variegated enamel work. [12] tutelary deity of agriculture and shepherds, later identified with Pan. [13] imaginary forms. [14] a cock whose crowing indicates the last of the three, four, or five periods into which the night was traditionally divided. [15] with a sacrificial offering of barley cakes—sufficient to appease the gods if made with a pure heart. [16] painstaking, hardworking. [17] apothegm. [18] your happier circumstances unsullied by such cares and dangers. [19] only. [20] i.e. who first. [21] public report. [22] had there and kept in motion. [23] According to George Puttenham, Aristotle "termeth a constant minded man even egal [equal] and direct on all sides, and not easily overthrowne by every litle adversitie, *hominem quadratum*, a square man" (*The Arte of English Poesie,* Bk. II, chap. xii, referring to *Ethics,* chap. x). [24] like the point, pivot, or axis around which a body or spheres revolve. [25] tutelary deity of a home. [26] coleworts, plants of the cabbage family, especially kale. [27] the private lar of line 106. [28] regulation or standard. [29] Cf. Prov. xv.17, "Better is a dinner of herbs where love is, than a stalled ox, and hatred therewith" and Luke xii.15, "a man's life consisteth not in the abundance of the things which he possesseth." [30] always studiously remembering. [31] straightforwardly.

H–107 *Divination by a Daffadill.*

WHen a Daffadill I see,
Hanging down his head t'wards me;
Guesse I may, what I must be:
First, I shall decline my head;
Secondly, I shall be dead; 5
Lastly, safely buryed.

H–108 *To the Painter, to draw him a Picture.*[1]

COme, skilfull *Lupo*, now, and take
Thy *Bice*, thy *Umber*, *Pink*, and *Lake*;[2]
And let it be thy Pensils[3] strife,
To paint a Bridgeman[4] to the life:
Draw him as like too, as you can, 5
An old, poore, lying, flatt'ring man:

His cheeks be-pimpled, red and blue;
His nose and lips of mulbrie hiew.
Then for an easie fansie; place
A Burling iron[5] for his face: 10
Next, make his cheeks with breath to swell,
And for to speak, if possible:
But do not so; for feare, lest he
Sho'd by his breathing, poyson thee.

[1] an early example (as is H-133) of the advice-to-a-painter genre. [2] a dull red, a brown or reddish-yellow, a pink, and a purplish-red pigment or color. [3] brush's. [4] official in charge of a bridge. [5] used to remove burls (lumps or knots) from wool or cloth.

H-109 *Upon* Cuffe. *Epigram.*

CUffe comes to Church much; but he keeps his bed
Those Sundayes onely, when as Briefs[1] are read.
This makes *Cuffe* dull; and troubles him the most,
Because he cannot sleep i'th'Church, free-cost.

[1] letters patent from the king as head of the Church of England licensing collections in the churches.

H-110 *Upon* Fone *a School-master.* Epigram.

FOne sayes, those mighty whiskers he do's weare,
Are twigs of Birch, and willow, growing there:
If so, we'll think too, (when he do's condemne
Boyes to the lash) that he do's whip with them.

H-111 *A Lyrick to Mirth.*

WHile the milder Fates consent,
Let's enjoy our merryment:
Drink, and dance, and pipe, and play;
Kisse our *Dollies* night and day:
Crown'd with clusters of the Vine; 5
Let us sit, and quaffe our wine.

Call on *Bacchus;* chaunt his praise;
Shake the *Thyrse,*[1] and bite the *Bayes:*[2]
Rouze *Anacreon* from the dead;
And return him drunk to bed: 10
Sing o're *Horace;* for ere long
Death will come and mar the song:
Then shall *Wilson* and *Gotiere*[3]
Never sing, or play more here.

[1] See H-8, n.2. [2] chew bay (laurel) leaves for inspiration. [3] Dr. John Wilson, Oxford Professor of Music, 1656, who set H-138B to music, and James Gouter or Gualtier, a French lutenist.

H-112 *To the Earle of Westmerland.*[1]

WHen my date's done, and my gray age must die;
Nurse up, great Lord, this my posterity:
Weak though it be; long may it grow, and stand,
Shor'd up by you, (*Brave Earle of Westmerland.*)

[1] Mildmay Fane, d. 1666, second Earl of Westmorland (1628), was a minor poet.

H-113 *Against Love.*

WHen ere my heart, Love's warmth, but entertaines,
O Frost! O Snow! O Haile forbid the Banes.[1]
One drop now deads a spark; but if the same
Once gets a force, Floods cannot quench the flame.
Rather then love, let me be ever lost; 5
Or let me 'gender with eternall frost.

[1] woeful effects.

H-114 *Upon* Julia's *Riband.*

AS shews the Aire, when with a Rain-bow grac'd;
So smiles that Riband 'bout my *Julia's* waste:[1]
Or like——Nay 'tis that *Zonulet*[2] of love,
Wherein all pleasures of the world are wove.

[1] waist. [2] diminutive of *zone;* in dress, an encircling band, belt, or girdle.

H–115

The frozen Zone: or, Julia *disdainfull.*

WHither? Say, whither shall I fly,
To slack these flames wherein I frie?
To the Treasures,[1] shall I goe,
Of the Raine, Frost, Haile, and Snow?
Shall I search the under-ground, 5
Where all Damps, and Mists are found?
Shall I seek (for speedy ease)
All the floods, and frozen seas?
Or descend into the deep,
Where eternall cold does keep? 10
These may coole; but there's a Zone
Colder yet then any one:
That's my *Julia's* breast; where dwels
Such destructive Ysicles;
As that the Congelation will 15
Me sooner starve,[2] then those can kill.

[1] Job xxxviii.22, "Hast thou entered into the treasures of the snow? or hast thou seen the treasures of the hail . . . ?" [2] cause to die.

H–116

An Epitaph upon a sober Matron.[1]

WIth blamelesse carriage, I liv'd here,
To'th' (almost) sev'n and fortieth yeare.
Stout sons I had, and those twice three;
One onely daughter lent to me:
The which was made a happy Bride, 5
But thrice three Moones before she dy'd.
My modest wedlock, that was known
Contented with the bed of one.

[1] based on Martial, X, 63, *Epitaphium nobilis matronæ.*

H–117

To the Patron of Poets, *Master* Endimion Porter.[1]

LEt there be Patrons; Patrons like to thee,
Brave *Porter!* Poets ne'r will wanting be:[2]
Fabius, and *Cotta, Lentulus,*[3] all live
In thee, thou Man of Men! who here do'st give
Not onely subject-matter for our wit, 5
But likewise Oyle of Maintenance to it:
For which, before thy Threshold, we'll lay downe
Our Thyrse, for Scepter; and our Baies for Crown.
For to say truth, all Garlands are thy due;
The *Laurell, Mirtle, Oke,* and *Ivie* too.[4] 10

[1] Endymion Porter, 1587–1649, patron of Jonson, Dekker, Davenant, May, Herrick, and other poets. See his *Life and Letters* by Dorothea Townshend, 1897. [2] Martial, VIII, 56, line 5, tells Flaccus that if there are Maecenases, Virgils will not be lacking. [3] friends of poets mentioned by Juvenal, VII, 95: trans. Holyday (1673), p. 135: "Who's a *Mecenas* Now; A *Fabius,* A *Proculeius, Cotta Lentulus?*" [4] for poetic, amatory, civic and military, and social achievement. Cf. Marvell, "The Garden": "How vainly men themselves amaze / To win the Palm, the Oke, or Bayes."

H–118

The sadnesse of things for Sapho's *sicknesse.*

LIllies will languish; Violets look ill;
Sickly the Prim-rose: Pale the Daffadill:
That gallant Tulip will hang down his head,
Like to a Virgin newly ravished.
Pansies will weep; and Marygolds will wither; 5
And keep a Fast, and Funerall together,
If *Sapho* droop; Daisies will open never,
But bid Good-night, and close their lids for ever.

H–119 Leanders *Obsequies.*

WHen as *Leander* young was drown'd,
No heart by love receiv'd a wound;
But on a Rock himselfe sate by,[1]
There weeping sup'rabundantly.
Sighs numberlesse he cast about, 5
And all his Tapers thus put out:
His head upon his hand he laid;
And sobbing deeply, thus he said,
Ah cruell Sea! and looking on't,
Wept as he'd drowne the Hellespont. 10
And sure his tongue had more exprest,
But that his teares forbad the rest.

[1] Leander's death so grieved Cupid that he sat apart on a rock failing to shoot his arrows; as a result no heart received a wound from him. Cf. Ovid, *Amores,* III, 9, 7–12.

H–120 *Hope heartens.*

NOne goes to warfare, but with this intent;
The gaines must dead the feare of detriment.

H–121 *Foure things make us happy here.*

HEalth is the first good lent to men;
A gentle disposition then:
Next, to be rich by no by-wayes;
Lastly, with friends t'enjoy our dayes.

H–122 *His parting from Mistresse* Dorothy Keneday.[1]

WHen I did goe from thee, I felt that smart,
Which Bodies do, when Souls from them depart.
Thou did'st not mind it; though thou then might'st see

Me turn'd to tears; yet did'st not weep for me.
'Tis true, I kist thee; but I co'd not heare 5
Thee spend a sigh, t'accompany my teare.
Me thought 'twas strange, that thou so hard sho'dst prove,
Whose heart, whose hand, whose ev'ry part spake love.
Prethee (lest Maids sho'd censure thee) but say
Thou shed'st one teare, when as I went away; 10
And that will please me somewhat: though I know,
And Love will swear't, my Dearest did not so.

[1] not identified.

H–123

The Teare sent to her from Stanes.[1]

1. GLide gentle streams, and beare
Along with you my teare
To that coy Girle;
Who smiles, yet slayes
Me with delayes;
And strings my tears as Pearle.

2. See! see she's yonder set,
Making a Carkanet
Of Maiden-flowers!
There, there present
This Orient,
And Pendant Pearle of ours.

3. Then say, I've sent one more
Jem to enrich her store;
And that is all
Which I can send,
Or vainly spend,
For tears no more will fall.

4. Nor will I seek supply
Of them, the spring's once drie;
But Ile devise,
(Among the rest)
A way that's best
How I may save mine eyes.

5. Yet say; sho'd she condemne
Me to surrender them;
Then say; my part
Must be to weep
Out them, to keep
A poore, yet loving heart.

6. Say too, She wo'd[2] have this;
She shall: Then my hope is,
That when I'm poore,
And nothing have
To send, or save;
I'm sure she'll ask no more.

[1] Staines is on the Middlesex bank of the Thames about 7½ miles from Windsor. [2] If she would.

H–124

Upon one Lillie, *who marryed with a maid call'd* Rose.

WHat times of sweetnesse this faire day fore-shows,
When as the Lilly marries with the Rose!
What next is lookt for? but we all sho'd see
To spring from these a sweet Posterity.

H–125

An Epitaph upon a child.

VIrgins promis'd when I dy'd,
That they wo'd each Primrose-tide,
Duely, Morne and Ev'ning, come,
And with flowers dresse my Tomb.
Having promis'd, pay your debts, 5
Maids, and here strew Violets.

H–126

Upon Scobble. *Epigram.*

SCobble for Whoredome whips his wife; and cryes,
He'll slit her nose; But blubb'ring, she replyes,
Good Sir, make no more cuts i'th'outward skin,
One slit's enough to let Adultry in.

H–127 *The Houre-glasse.*

THat Houre-glasse, which there ye see
With Water fill'd, (Sirs, credit me)
The humour[1] was, (as I have read)
But Lovers tears inchristalled.
Which, as they drop by drop doe passe 5
From th'upper to the under-glasse,
Do in a trickling manner tell,
(By many a watrie syllable)
That Lovers tears in life-time shed,
Do restless run when they are dead. 10

[1] moisture.

H–128 *His fare-well to Sack.*

FArewell thou Thing, time-past so knowne, so deare
To me, as blood to life and spirit:[1] Neare,
Nay, thou more neare then kindred, friend, man, wife,
Male to the female, soule to body: Life
To quick action, or the warme soft side 5
Of the resigning, yet resisting Bride.
The kisse of Virgins; First-fruits of the bed;
Soft speech, smooth touch, the lips, the Maiden-head:
These, and a thousand sweets, co'd never be
So neare, or deare, as thou wast once to me. 10
O thou the drink of Gods, and Angels! Wine
That scatter'st Spirit and Lust;[2] whose purest shine,
More radiant then the Summers Sun-beams shows;
Each way illustrious, brave;[3] and like to those
Comets we see by night; whose shagg'd[4] portents 15
Fore-tell the comming of some dire events:
Or[5] some full flame, which with a pride aspires,[6]
Throwing about his wild, and active fires.
'Tis thou, above Nectar, O Divinest soule!
(Eternall in thy self) that canst controule 20
That, which subverts whole nature, grief and care;
Vexation of the mind, and damn'd Despaire.
'Tis thou, alone, who with thy Mistick Fan,[7]
Work'st more then Wisdome, Art, or Nature can,

To rouze the sacred madnesse; and awake
The frost-bound-blood, and spirits; and to make
Them frantick with thy raptures, flashing through
The soule, like lightning, and as active too.
'Tis not *Apollo* can, or those thrice three
Castalian Sisters,[8] sing, if wanting thee. 30
Horace, Anacreon both had lost their fame,
Had'st thou not fill'd them with thy fire and flame.
Phœbean splendour! and thou *Thespian* spring![9]
Of which, sweet Swans[10] must drink, before they sing
Their true-pac'd-Numbers, and their Holy-Layes, 35
Which makes them worthy *Cedar*,[11] and the *Bayes*.
But why? why longer doe I gaze upon
Thee with the eye of admiration?
Since I must leave thee; and enforc'd, must say
To all thy witching beauties, Goe, Away. 40
But if thy whimpring looks doe ask me why?
Then know, that Nature bids thee goe, not I.
'Tis her erroneous self has made a braine
Uncapable of such a Soveraigne,
As is thy powerfull selfe. Prethee not smile;
Or smile more inly; lest thy looks beguile
My vowes denounc'd[12] in zeale, which thus much show thee,
That I have sworn, but by thy looks to know thee.
Let others drink thee freely; and desire
Thee and their lips espous'd; while I admire, 50
And love thee; but not taste thee. Let my Muse
Faile of thy former helps; and onely use
Her inadult'rate strength: what's done by me
Hereafter, shall smell of the Lamp, not thee.

[1] as blood is to the vital spirit and animal spirit. According to 17th-century physiology, blood, phlegm, black bile, and choler are the four primary humors or fluids which govern a person's health and temperament. In the heart, the purest blood is refined into a subtle substance called *vital spirit* because it flows with the blood in the arteries to bring natural heat to all parts of the body, such heat being essential to life. In the brain the vital spirit was further refined into *animal spirit* (Latin *anima*=breath, soul), which is more subtle still. It flows in the nerves and is, like a messenger, the link between mind and body. (For further details and authorities see Lawrence Babb, *The Elizabethan Malady*, 1951, p. 8). During Herrick's lifetime William Harvey was modifying these views: he lectured that "Philosophically" (i.e. scientifically) spirit and blood

are "one thing, as serum and whey in milk" (*Lectures on the Whole of Anatomy,* trans. C. D. O'Malley et al., 1961, p. 203). [2] disperses animal spirit and vital spirit throughout the body as light is thrown back brokenly from a frosted surface. [3] splendid. [4] hairy, referring to comets' tails. [5] or like to. [6] with a magnificent display mounts upward. [7] van, to winnow grain, used as a symbol in ceremonies for Bacchus. [8] the Muses. The Castalian spring on Mt. Parnassus was sacred to them and to Phoebus (Bright) Apollo, god of poetry, music, and the sun. [9] source of dramatic inspiration; Thespis reputedly founded Greek drama. [10] poets. [11] worth preserving: cedar oil was used to preserve papyri. [12] proclaimed. This poem had considerable currency in the 17th century. Martin, pp. 465–7, records variants in 7 MSS and in *Recreation for Ingenious Head-peeces* (1645), f.Z8v. To these may be added the variants in *A*—Rosenbach MS 239/27, pp. 413–15 (formerly Phillipps MS 9536); *Y*—Rosenbach MS 1083/16, pp. 121–23 (formerly Phillipps MS 9549); and Z—Rosenbach MS 1083/17, ff.95r–98v (formerly Phillipps 8270), as follows: 1 time-past / times past *A*. 2 me . . . spirit / come as blood to the life and spiritts *Z*. 4 to body / and body *Y*. 5 quick / quicken *A;* action / actions *Z*. 6 resigning, yet resisting / resistinge yett resigninge *AZ*. 7 Virgins / Maydens *A;* fruits / fruit *Y*. 8 Soft speech, smooth touch, the lips / Sweet speech, sweet touch, the lipp *A;* Swett charminge speach, soft touch *Z;* Sweet Speech, sweet lips, sweet touch *Y*. 9 sweets / such *A*. 10 or / soe *Y;* wast once / was unto *A;* once wast *Y*. 12 Spirit / spiritts *Z;* purest / purer *AY;* pure *Z*. 13 Summers / summer *AZ*. 14 and like to / so like unto *A*. 15 shagg'd / sage *A;* sad *Y*. 16 Fore-tell / Fore show *A;* For-speake *Y;* Foreshewes *Z*. 18 about / abroad *AZ;* active / piercing *Y*. 19 above / lov'd *AZ;* Divinest / diviner *Z*. 23 Fan / flame *Z*. 25 sacred / holy *AYZ;* and / to *Y*. 26 and / in *Z*. 27 flashing / strikinge *AZ;* shining *Y*. 29 or / nor *Z*. 32 thou not / not thou *A*. 34 before / ere that *Y*. 35 Holy / sacred *AYZ*. 38 eye of admiration / eyes of adoration *AYZ*. 39 Since / When *Y*. 41 looks / lips *Y*. 43 made / forg'd *AYZ*. 45 not smile / draw in *AYZ*. 46 ff. READS AS FOLLOWS IN Z AND THE SAME IN *AY* EXCEPT FOR THE PARENTHESIZED WORDS: Thy glaringe (glozinge *A*) fires lest in their sight the sinne | Of fierce Idolatry shoote into (doe shoot *A;* shoote in *Y*) me and | I turne Apostate to the strict command | Of Nature, bide (nature; bidd *A*) me now farewell, or smile | More inly (Lesse kindly *A*) lest they tempting lookes beguile. THE TEXT CONTINUES AS IN LINE 47, EXCEPT FOR THESE VARIANTS: 47 much / must *Z*. 49 and / and with maine *A;* and with vaine (?) *Z*. 50 espous'd / espouse *AZ*. 51 but / yet *AZ*.

H–129 *Upon* Glasco. *Epigram.*

GLasco had none, but now some teeth has got;
Which though they furre, will neither ake, or rot.
Six teeth he has, whereof twice two are known
Made of a Haft, that was a Mutton-bone.
Which not for use, but meerly for the sight, 5
He weares all day, and drawes those teeth at night.

H–130
Upon Mistresse Elizabeth Wheeler,[1] *under the name of Amarillis.*

SWeet *Amarillis,* by a Spring's
Soft and soule-melting murmurings,
Slept; and thus sleeping, thither flew
A *Robin-Red-brest;* who at view,
Not seeing her at all to stir, 5
Brought leaves and mosse to cover her:
But while he, perking, there did prie
About the Arch of either eye;
The lid began to let out day;
At which poore *Robin* flew away: 10
And seeing her not dead, but all disleav'd;
He chirpt for joy, to see himself disceav'd.

[1] The poet's cousin, daughter of his uncle and godfather, Robert Herrick, married a goldsmith, John Wheeler, in 1606.

H–131 *The Custard.*[1]

FOr second course, last night, a Custard came
To th'board, so hot, as none co'd touch the same:
Furze, three or foure times with his cheeks did blow
Upon the Custard, and thus cooled so:
It seem'd by this time to admit the touch; 5
But none co'd eate it, 'cause it stunk so much.

[1] Martial, III, 17, *In Sabidium.*

H–132 *To* Myrrha *hard-hearted.*

FOld now thine armes;[1] and hang the head,
Like to a Lillie withered:
Next, look thou like a sickly Moone;
Or like *Jocasta*[2] in a swoone.
Then weep, and sigh, and softly goe,[3] 5
Like to a widdow drown'd in woe:
Or like a Virgin full of ruth,
For the lost sweet-heart of her youth:
And all because, Faire Maid, thou art
Insensible of all my smart; 10
And of those evill dayes that be
Now posting on to punish thee.
The Gods are easie, and condemne
All such as are not soft like them.

[1] a conventional sign of grief-stricken melancholy. [2] The mother of Oedipus fainted on learning that he was her husband. [3] Cf. Isa. xxxviii.15, "I shall go softly all my years in the bitterness of my soul."

H–133 *The Eye.*[1]

MAke me a heaven; and make me there
Many a lesse and greater spheare.
Make me the straight, and oblique lines;
The Motions, Lations,[2] and the Signes.
Make me a Chariot, and a Sun; 5
And let them through a Zodiac run:
Next, place me Zones, and Tropicks there;
With all the Seasons of the Yeare.
Make me a Sun-set; and a Night:
And then present the Mornings-light 10
Cloath'd in her Chamlets[3] of Delight.
To these, make Clouds to poure downe raine;
With weather foule, then faire againe.
And when, wise Artist, that thou hast,
With all that can be, this heaven grac't; 15
Ah! what is then this curious[4] skie,
But onely my *Corinna's* eye?

[1] like H-108, an advice-to-a-painter poem. [2] transference of a body from one position to another. [3] camlets: garments of rich oriental cloth. [4] artfully elaborate.

H–134 *Upon the much lamented,*
Master J. Warr.[1]

WHat Wisdome, Learning, Wit, or Worth,
Youth, or sweet Nature, co'd bring forth,
Rests here with him; who was the Fame,
The Volumne of himselfe, and Name.
If, Reader, then thou wilt draw neere, 5
And doe an honour to thy teare;
Weep then for him, for whom laments
Not one, but many Monuments.

[1] probably John Warre of Chipley, Somerset. Cf. Thomas Randolph, "An Epitaph upon his Honoured Friend, Master Warre," lines 1–6: "Here lies the knowing head, the honest heart, / Fair blood and courteous hands, and every part / Of gentle Warre, all with one stone content, / Though each deserv'd a several monument. / He was (believe me, reader) for 'tis rare— / Virtuous though young, and learned though an heir."

H–135 *Upon* Gryll.

GRyll eates, but ne're sayes Grace; To speak the troth,
Gryll either keeps his breath to coole his broth;
Or else because *Grill's* roste do's burn his Spit,
Gryll will not therefore say a Grace for it.

H–136

The suspition upon his over-much familiarity with a Gentlewoman.[1]

ANd must we part, because some say,
Loud is our love, and loose our play,
And more then well becomes the day?
Alas for pitty! and for us
Most innocent, and injur'd thus. 5
Had we kept close, or play'd within,
Suspition now had been the sinne,
And shame had follow'd long ere this,

T'ave plagu'd, what now unpunisht is.
But we as fearlesse of the Sunne, 10
As faultlesse; will not wish undone,
What now is done: since *where no sin*
Unbolts the doore, no shame comes in.
Then comely and most fragrant Maid,
Be you more warie, then afraid 15
Of these Reports; because you see
The fairest most suspected be.
The common formes have no one eye,
Or eare of burning jealousie[2]
To follow them: but chiefly, where 20
Love makes the cheek, and chin a sphere
To dance and play in: (Trust me) there
Suspicion questions every haire.
Come, you are faire; and sho'd be seen
While you are in your sprightfull green: 25
And what though you had been embrac't
By me, were you for that unchast?
No, no, no more then[3] is yond' Moone,
Which shining in her perfect Noone;
In all that great and glorious light, 30
Continues cold, as is the night.
Then, beauteous Maid, you may retire;
And as for me, my chast desire
Shall move t'wards you; although I see
Your face no more: So live you free 35
From Fames black lips, as you from me.

[1] See notes on H-979. [2] Cf. Wisd. of Sol. i.10, "For the ear of jealousy heareth all things." [3] than.

H–137 *Single life most secure.*

SUspicion, Discontent, and Strife,
Come in for Dowrie with a Wife.

H–138A *To his false Mistris.*[1]

Whither are all her false oathes blowne,
Or in what region doe they live?
I'me sure no place where faith is knowne
Dare any harbour to them give.

My withered heart, which Love did burne,
Shall venture one sigh with the wind,
Oh may it never home returne
Till one of her false oathes it find.

Then lett them wrestle in the sky
Till they shall both one Lightning prove, 10
And falling may they pierce her eye
That was thus perjurd in her love.

[1] Based on B.M. Add MS 33998, f.82v; not included in *Hesperides.* Martin, pp. 496, 586, records numerous printed and manuscript versions with several ascriptions to Herrick. Cf. H-215. H-138A is frequently followed by H-138B as an answer. It also occurs twice in *A*—Rosenbach MS 239/22, on pp. 37–38 (*A*1) and on p. 156 (*A*2), and in *M*—Rosenbach MS 1083/17, p. 116, with variants as follows: Heading: LACKING *A*1; To his false Mistresse *A*2; Of his perjur'd Mistress *M*. 1 Blowne / flowne *A*2. 3 I'me sure . . . faith is knowne / I knowe . . . love is knowne *A*1. 4 Dare / Will *A*2. 5 which / that *A*2. 8 Till one of her false / Untill one of her *A*1; Till one of those false *A*2. 9 Then lett them / There maie it *A*1; There maie they *A*2; wrestle / grapple *A*2; sky / skies *A*1*A*2. 10 shall both / both *A*1*A*2. 11 may they . . . eye / lett it . . . eies *A*1; lett it blast her Eyes *A*2. 12 was thus / was soe *A*1; is thus *A*2.

H–138B *The Curse. A Song.*[1]

GOe perjur'd man; and if thou ere return
To see the small remainders in mine Urne:
When thou shalt laugh at my Religious dust;
And ask, Where's now the colour, forme and trust
Of Womans beauty? and with hand more rude 5
Rifle the Flowers which the Virgins strew'd:
Know, I have pray'd to Furie, that some wind
May blow my ashes up, and strike thee blind.
[*Reader stay let fall a teare*
For much beauty lyeth here; 10
Thou art if thou sheddest none
As very marble as the stone.]

[1] possibly an answer to H-138A. The 4 bracketed lines did not appear in *Hesperides* (but cf. H-564, lines 4–7); however, they are added in MS Egerton 2421, f.22v. Musical settings of the poem were made by John Blow (Add MS 19759, 22100, 29397,

30382, and 33235), by R. Ramsay (MS Don.c.57 and Add MS 15227), and by John Wilson (MS Mus.b.1). Willa McLung Evans in *Henry Lawes* (New York, 1941), pp. 154–55, conjectures that when, about 1639–40, Herrick took lodgings under the same roof with Lawes, the musician was inspired to imitate this poem with one of his own, "No Constancy in Man," which she prints, or that Herrick may have been the one influenced, or that the same event gave rise to both poems. Martin, pp. 467, 586, records variants in 14 MSS versions. The poem also appears (set to music by John Blow) in *Choice Ayres and Songs* (1683), p. 78, *The Theater of Music* (1687), p. 82, and *The New Treasury of Music* (1695), p. 25. Manuscript variants not noted by Martin occur in *K*–Rosenbach MS 243/4, p. 155; *M*–Rosenbach MS 239/22, f.120v; and *A*–Rosenbach MS 239/27, p. 121, as follows: Heading: A curse to a false love *K;* A forsaken Lady that dyed for Love *M.* 2 the / those *A;* remainders / remainder *M;* mine / my *KM.* 3 laugh / scoff *M.* 5 Of / In *M.* 5–6 with hand more rude Rifle / perhapps with rude Hande, ruffle *A;* perchance with rude Hands scatter *K;* perhaps with rude hand 'stroy *M.* 7 Furie / pittie *AKM.* 8 my ashes up, and / up Ashes, for to *K.* 9–12 LACKING *AKM.*

In *A* this poem is preceded by 14 lines as follows:

A Songe.

Lowe in a vale and here sate a sheaperdesse
Bewailinge to her selfe her great distresse
Her downe cast head upon her knee shee bent
Whilst with her hands her curled haire shee rent
Which carelesly now hunge about her eares
And only served for to dry her teares
But by her face and gesture was exprest
The lively image of a soule distrest.
Her teares that from her redd swolne eyes did flow
Faster then rivers from the mountaines growe
Her heart did heave as though her heartstrings straind
Each part exprest the sorrowe itt sustainde
Only her tongue her sorrowes were soe many
That itt found want of words to utter any.

H-139 *The wounded* Cupid. *Song.*[1]

CUpid as he lay among
Roses, by a Bee was stung.
Whereupon in anger flying
To his Mother, said thus crying;
Help! O help! your Boy's a dying. 5
And why, my pretty Lad, said she?

Then blubbering, replyed he,
A winged Snake has bitten me,
Which Country people call a Bee.
At which she smil'd; then with her hairs 10
And kisses drying up his tears:
Alas! said she, my Wag! if this
Such a pernicious torment is:
Come, tel me then, how great's the smart
Of those, thou woundest with thy Dart! 15

[1] based on *Anacreontea,* XXXV: see H-46. Cf. the rendering, "The Bee XL," by Thomas Stanley (*Poems,* 1651): "Love, a Bee that lurkt among / Roses saw not, and was stung: / Who for his hurt finger crying, / Running sometimes, sometimes flying, / Doth to his fair Mother hie, / And oh help cries he, I dy; / A wing'd Snake hath bitten me, / Called by Countreymen a Bee: / At which *Venus,* if such smart / A bees little sting impart, / How much greater is the pain / They whom thou hast hurt sustain."

H-140 *To Dewes. A Song.*

I Burn, I burn; and beg of you
To quench, or coole me with your Dew.
I frie in fire, and so consume,
Although the Pile[1] be all perfume.
Alas! the heat and death's the same; 5
Whether by choice, or common flame:
To be in Oyle of *Roses* drown'd,
Or water; where's the comfort found?
Both bring one death; and I die here,
Unlesse you coole me with a Teare: 10
Alas! I call; but ah! I see
Ye coole, and comfort all, but me.

[1] funeral pile.

H-141 *Some comfort in calamity.*[1]

TO conquer'd men, some comfort 'tis to fall
By th'hand of him who is the Generall.

[1] Cf. Ovid, *Metamorphoses,* XII, 80–81; trans. Sandys: "O youth, he said, what e'r thou art, rejoyce: / Achilles honours thee with death."

H–142 *The Vision.*

SItting alone (as one forsook)
Close by a Silver-shedding Brook;
With hands held up to Love, I wept;
And after sorrowes spent, I slept:
Then in a Vision I did see 5
A glorious forme[1] appeare to me:
A Virgins face she had; her dresse
Was like a sprightly *Spartanesse.*
A silver bow with green silk strung,
Down from her comely shoulders hung: 10
And as she stood, the wanton Aire
Dandled the ringlets of her haire.
Her legs were such *Diana* shows,
When tuckt up she a hunting goes;
With Buskins shortned to descrie 15
The happy dawning of her thigh:
Which when I saw, I made accesse
To kisse that tempting nakednesse:
But she forbad me, with a wand
Of Mirtle she had in her hand: 20
And chiding me, said, Hence, Remove,
Herrick, thou art too coorse to love.

[1] Venus; lines 7–16 imitate Virgil, *Aeneid,* I, 315–20; trans. John Ogilby (3rd ed., 1675, p. 12): "The *Spartan* Virgins have such Arms, and Weeds, / . . . For, as they us'd, she wore a handsom Bow, / And to the wanton Winds expos'd her Hair; / Tuck'd to her Knee her flowing Garments were."

H–143 *Love me little, love me long.*

YOu say, to me-wards your affection's strong;
Pray love me little, so you love me long.
Slowly goes farre: The meane is best: Desire
Grown violent, do's either die, or tire.

H–144 *Upon a Virgin kissing a Rose.*

'TWas but a single *Rose,*
Till you on it did breathe;
But since (me thinks) it shows
Not so much *Rose,* as Wreathe.[1]

[1] cluster.

H–145 *Upon a Wife that dyed mad with Jealousie.*

IN this little Vault she lyes,
Here, with all her jealousies:
Quiet yet; but if ye make
Any noise, they both will wake,
And such spirits raise, 'twill then 5
Trouble Death to lay agen.

H–146A *Upon the Bishop of* Lincolne's *Imprisonment.*[1]

NEver was Day so over-sick with showres,
But that it had some intermitting houres.
Never was Night so tedious, but it knew
The Last Watch out, and saw the Dawning too.
Never was Dungeon so obscurely deep, 5
Wherein or Light, or Day, did never peep.
Never did Moone so ebbe, or seas so wane,
But they left Hope-seed to fill up againe.
So you, my Lord, though you have now your stay,
Your Night, your Prison, and your Ebbe; you may 10
Spring up afresh; when all these mists are spent,
And Star-like, once more, guild our Firmament.[2]
Let but That Mighty *Cesar* speak,[3] and then,
All bolts, all barres, all gates shall cleave; as when
That Earth-quake shook the house, and gave the stout[4] 15

Apostles, way (unshackled) to goe out.
This, as I wish for, so I hope to see;
Though you (my Lord) have been unkind to me:
To wound my heart, and never to apply
(When you had power) the meanest remedy: 20
Well; though my griefe by you was gall'd, the more;
Yet I bring Balme and Oile to heal your sore.

[1] John Williams, imprisoned in the Tower 1637–40 for revealing secrets of the Privy Council and for subornation of perjury. The nature of his unkindness to Herrick (line 18) is unknown. [2] He became Archbishop of York in 1641. [3] The Star Chamber sentenced him to imprisonment at the king's pleasure. [4] undaunted. Cf. Acts xvi.19–26: Paul and Silas prayed in prison at midnight, and "suddenly there was an earthquake . . . and immediately all the doors were opened, and every one's bands were loosed."

H–146B *A Charroll[1] presented to Dr. Williams, Bishop of Lincolne, as a Newyears guift.[2]*

Fly hence Pale Care, noe more remember
Past Sorrowes with the fled December,[3]
But let each present Cheeke appeare
Smooth as the Childhood of the yeare,
And sing a Caroll here. 5

T'was brave, t'was brave, could we[4] comand the hand
Of Youths swift watch to stand,
As you have done your day;[5]
Then should we not decay.
But all we wither, and our Light 10
Is spilt in everlasting night,
When as your Sight[6]
Shewes like the Heavens above the Moone,
Like an Eternall Noone
That sees noe setting Sunn.[7] 15

Keepe up those flames, and though you shroud
A while your forehead in a Cloude,
Do it like the Sun, to write,
I'th ayre, a greater Text of light.
Welcome to all our vowes, 20

And since you pay
To us the day
Soe long desir'd,
See, we have fyr'd
Our holy Spicknard, and ther's none 25
But brings his stick of Cynamon,
His eager Eye, or Smoother Smyle,
And layes it gently on the Pyle,
Which thus enkindled, we invoke
Your name amidst the sacred smoke. 30

CHORUS

Come then, greate Lord,
And see our Alter burne
With Love of your Returne;
And not a man here but consumes
His soule to glad you in perfumes. 35

[1] H-146B, not in *Hesperides;* from Bodleian Library MS Ashmole 36–37, f.298; italics and some punctuation added; abbreviations expanded. [2] See H-146A. According to the calendar official in 17th-century England, the new year began on March 25, the Feast of the Annunciation, "Lady Day," but Herrick may intend the pagan Roman year which began on Jan. 1. [3] synecdochic for *year,* but Herrick refers particularly to Dec. 1640, when Williams was freed from imprisonment. [4] it would be splendid if we could. [5] a continuation of the conceit in H-146A that the Bishop's imprisonment was like one long night and thus made time or the sun stand still for him. [6] while, on the other hand, the sight of you. [7] according to the old astronomy, change and decay were confined to the sublunar parts of the universe.

H–147 *Disswasions from Idlenesse.*

CYnthius pluck ye by the eare,
That ye may good doctrine heare.[1]
Play not with the maiden-haire;
For each Ringlet there's a snare.
Cheek, and eye, and lip, and chin; 5
These are traps to take fooles in.
Armes, and hands, and all parts else,
Are but Toiles,[2] or Manicles
Set on purpose to enthrall
Men, but Slothfulls most of all. 10

Live employ'd, and so live free
From these fetters; like to me
Who have found, and still can prove,
The lazie man the most doth love.[3]

[1] In Virgil's Eclogue VI, 3, the Cyprian (Phoebus Apollo) twitches the poet's ear to advise him how to use his talents; trans. Ogilby: "*Phoebus* thus, / Nipping my Ear, advis'd." [2] nets or snares. [3] Cf. Burton, *Anatomy,* 3,2,2,1 (6 ed. p. 450): "Idleness overthrows all, *Vacuo pectore regnat amor,* love tyrannizeth in an idle person. . . . For love as *Theophrastus* defines it, is *otiosi animi affectus,* an affection of an idle minde." Cf. Ovid, *De Remedio Amoris,* 139–44.

H–148 *Upon* Strut.

STrut, once a Fore-man of a Shop we knew;
But turn'd a Ladies Usher[1] now, ('tis true:)
Tell me, has *Strut* got ere a title more?
No; he's but Fore-man, as he was before.

[1] attendant who walks before a person of high rank.

H–149A *An Epithalamie to* *Sir* Thomas Southwell *and his Ladie.*[1]

I.

NOw, now's the time; so oft by truth[2]
Promis'd sho'd come to crown your youth.
Then Faire ones, doe not wrong
Your joyes, by staying long:[3]
Or let Love's fire goe out,
By lingring thus in doubt:
But learn, that Time once lost,
Is ne'r redeem'd by cost.
Then away; come, *Hymen* guide
To the bed, the bashfull Bride. 10

II.

Is it (sweet maid) your fault these holy
Bridall-Rites goe on so slowly?
Deare, is it this you dread,
The losse of Maiden-head?
Beleeve me; you will most
Esteeme it when 'tis lost:

Then it no longer keep,
Lest Issue lye asleep.
Then away; come, *Hymen* guide
To the bed, the bashfull Bride. 20

III.

These Precious-Pearly-Purling[4] teares,
But spring from ceremonious feares.
And 'tis but Native shame,
That hides the loving flame:
And may a while controule
The soft and am'rous soule;
But yet, Loves fire will wast[5]
Such bashfulnesse at last.
Then away; come, *Hymen* guide
To the bed, the bashfull Bride. 30

IV.

Night now hath watch'd her self half blind;
Yet not a Maiden-head resign'd!
'Tis strange, ye will not flie
To Love's sweet mysterie.
Might yon Full-Moon the sweets
Have, promis'd to your sheets;
She soon wo'd leave her spheare,
To be admitted there.
Then away; come, *Hymen* guide
To the bed, the bashfull Bride. 40

V.

On, on devoutly, make no stay;
While *Domiduca*[6] leads the way:
And *Genius*[7] who attends
The bed for luckie ends:
With *Juno* goes the houres,[8]
And Graces[9] strewing flowers.
And the boyes with sweet tunes sing,
Hymen, O Hymen bring
Home the Turtles;[10] *Hymen* guide
To the bed, the bashfull Bride. 50

VI.

Behold! how *Hymens* Taper-light
Shews you how much is spent of night.
See, see the Bride-grooms Torch
Halfe wasted in the porch.[11]

And now those Tapers five,[12]
That shew the womb shall thrive:
Their silv'rie flames advance,
To tell all prosp'rous chance
Still shall crown the happy life
Of the good man and the wife. 60

VII.

Move forward then your Rosie feet,
And make, what ere they touch, turn sweet.
May all, like flowrie Meads
Smell, where your soft foot treads;
And every thing assume
To it, the like perfume:
As *Zephirus*[13] when he 'spires
Through *Woodbine,* and *Sweet-bryers.*
Then away; come *Hymen,* guide
To the bed the bashfull Bride. 70

VIII.

And now the yellow Vaile,[14] at last,
Over her fragrant cheek is cast.
Now seems she to expresse
A bashfull willingnesse:
Shewing a heart consenting;
As with a will repenting.
Then gently lead her on
With wise suspicion:
For that, Matrons say, a measure
Of that Passion sweetens Pleasure. 80

IX.

You, you that be of her neerest kin,
Now o're the threshold force her in.
But to avert the worst;
Let her, her fillets first
Knit to the posts:[15] this point
Remembring, to anoint
The sides: for 'tis a charme
Strong against future harme:
And the evil deads,[16] the which
There was hidden by the Witch. 90

X.

O *Venus!* thou, to whom is known
The best way how to loose the Zone[17]
    Of Virgins! Tell the Maid,
    She need not be afraid:
    And bid the Youth apply
    Close kisses, if she cry:
    And charge, he not forbears
    Her, though she wooe with teares.
Tel them, now they must adventer,
Since that Love and Night bid enter. 100

XI.

No Fatal Owle the Bedsted keeps,
With direful notes to fright your sleeps:
    No Furies, here about,
    To put the Tapers out,
    Watch, or did make the bed:
    'Tis *Omen* full of dread:[18]
    But all faire signs appeare
    Within the Chamber here.
Juno here, far off, doth stand
Cooling sleep with charming wand. 110

XII.

Virgins, weep not; 'twill come, when,
As she, so you'l be ripe for men.
    Then grieve her not, with saying
    She must no more a Maying:
    Or by Rose-buds devine,
    Who'l be her Valentine.
    Nor name those wanton reaks[19]
    Y'ave had at Barly-breaks.
But now kisse her, and thus say,
Take time[20] Lady while ye may. 120

XIII.

Now barre the doors, the Bride-groom puts
The eager Boyes to gather Nuts.[21]
    And now, both Love and Time
    To their full height doe clime:
    O! give them active heat
    And moisture, both compleat:
    Fit Organs for encrease,
    To keep, and to release

That, which may the honour'd Stem[22]
Circle with a Diadem.[23] 130

XIV.

And now, Behold! the Bed or Couch
That ne'r knew Brides, or Bride-grooms touch,
Feels in it selfe a fire;
And tickled with Desire,
Pants with a Downie brest,
As with a heart possest:
Shrugging as[24] it did move,
Ev'n with the soule of love.
And (oh!) had it but a tongue,
Doves, 'two'd say, yee bill too long. 140

XV.

O enter then! but see ye shun
A sleep, untill the act be done.
Let kisses, in their close,
Breathe as the Damask Rose:
Or sweet, as is that gumme
Doth from *Panchaia*[25] come.
Teach Nature now to know,
Lips can make Cherries grow
Sooner, then she, ever yet,
In her wisdome co'd beget. 150

XVI.

On your minutes, hours, dayes, months, years,
Drop the fat blessing of the sphears.
That good, which Heav'n can give
To make you bravely live;
Fall, like a spangling dew,
By day, and night on you.
May Fortunes Lilly-hand
Open at your command;
With all luckie Birds[26] to side
With the Bride-groom, and the Bride. 160

XVII.

Let bounteous Fate your spindles full
Fill, and winde up with whitest wooll.
Let them not cut the thred
Of life, untill ye bid.
May Death yet come at last;
And not with desp'rate hast:

But when ye both can say,
Come, Let us now away.
Be ye to the Barn then born,
Two, like two ripe shocks of corn.[27] 170

[1] Margaret Fuller. The marriage took place on March 27, 1618 and did not prove successful. The poem has some echoes of lines 445–564 of the epithalamion in Jonson's masque *Hymenaei;* the marriage customs described are not accurately classical: Herrick seems to have sought the universality of imprecision in such matters. [2] troth: pledging to marry. [3] Urging the bridal couple to lose no time is conventional in epithalamia. [4] *Purling:* flowing circuitously. [5] consume. [6] the spirit that leads a bride to the bridegroom's house. [7] the spirit which gives a man generative power; the corresponding spirit for a woman was called Juno. [8] the Horae, who had charge of seasons and parts of the day. [9] divine bestowers of beauty and charm, the goddesses Aglaia (Splendor), Thalia (Joy), and Euphrosyne (Pleasure). [10] turtledoves: i.e. lovers. [11] The man stood on the porch, torch in hand, awaiting the bride. [12] five tapers of virgin wax carried by servants and symbolic of the binding force of marriage (since five cannot be divided into equal parts). [13] west wind. [14] symbolizing modesty. [15] Before entering the groom's home, the bride ties woollen strips to the doorposts and anoints them with oil to drive off evil influences and the effects of sorcery. [16] deadens the efficacy of potions buried by a witch to destroy sexual potency. [17] girdle. [18] It is a dreadful omen if any of these happen. [19] pranks during the game of barley break; cf. H-101. [20] *carpe diem:* seize the opportunity. [21] thrown to the torchbearers as the bride approaches, in the belief that they conduced to fertility. [22] the begetter of a family. [23] a crown. Cf. Prov. xvii.6, "Children's children are the crown of old men." [24] as if. [25] fabulous isle invented by Euhemerus but later confused with Arabia Felix, a source of incense, gums, and spices. Cf. Virgil, *Georgics,* II, 139; trans. Ogilby: "not *Panchaians* dare / With all their Myrrhe and Frankincense compare." [26] birds of good omen, in contrast to the "Owle" of line 101. [27] Job v.26, "Thou shalt come to thy grave in a full age, like as a shock of corn cometh in in his season."

H–149B *An Epithalamium:*[1]

Now, now's the time soe oft by truth
promised should come to crowne your youth;
then faire ones doe not wrong
your Joyes by staying long;
or let your fires goe out
by lingring still in doubt

love not admitts delay,
then haste and come away,
night with all her children starres
waite to light you to the warres: 10

Faire virgin enter Cupids field
and though you doe resist, yet yeeld:
It is noe shame at all
for you to take the fall,
When thousands like to you
could nere the foyle eschew,
nor in their strict defence
depart unconquerd hence:
then faire Maide now adventer
Since Time and Love bidds enter: 20

Is it your fault, that these soe holy
Bridall Rites goe on soe slowly?
or is it that you dread
the losse of maydenhead?
Know virgin you will most
love it when it is lost;
then it noe longer keepe
Least issue lye asleepe;
Come, come Hymen, Hymen guide
to the bedd the bashfull Bride: 30

These pretious pearly purling teares
but spring from Ceremonious feares,
and tis but native shame
that hides the loving flame;
Loves fire, faire maide, will waste
all bashfullnesse at last,
then trust that night will cover
what the Rosy Cheekes discover:

Night now hath watcht her selfe halfe blinde
yet not a maydenhead resigned; 40
tis strange yee will not trye
Loves sacred mistery;
might yon full moone the sweetes
have, promis'd to your sheetes
Shee soone would leave her spheare
to be admitted there;
Then away faire virgin come,
haste least Luna take your roome:

Behold the Bridegroome in the porch
Expects you with his pinie Torch, 50
and Hymens Taper light
tells what is spent of night;
five Boyes with torches five,
that shew the wombe shall thrive,
their golden flames advance,
and tell all prosperous Chance,
still shall Crowne the happy life
of the Goodman, and the wife:

Now forward then your Rosy feete
to make each thing you touch turne sweete; 60
and where your shooe you sett
there spring a Violet;
Let all the Balmy meades
Smell, where your soft foote treades,
make Earth as flourishing,
as in the painted spring,
when Zephirus, and warme May
pranke the fields in sweete arraye:

Now on devoutly, make noe stay
for domiduca leades the way, 70
and Genius that attends
the bedd for lucky ends;
with Juno goe thy howers
And Graces scattering flowers,
while Boyes with soft tunes singe
Hymen, oh Hymen bringe,
bring oh Hymen, bringe the Bride,
or the winged Boy will Chide:

See, see the yellow Vayle at last
ore her fragrant Cheeke is cast, 80
now seemes she to expresse
a bashfull willingnesse,
and hath a will thereto
without a minde to doe,
then softly leade her on
with wise suspition,
wise matrons say a measure
of it, will sweeten pleasure:

You, you that bee her nearest Kinne
ore the Threshold force her in, 90
But to avert the worst
let her, her fillets first
knitt to the post, this poynt
remembering to annoynt
the last, for tis a Charme
strong against future harme;
and poyson kills, the which
there was hidden by the witch:

Now quickly Venus leade them to it,
and then instruct them how to doe it 100
first let them meete with kisses,
then shew them other blisses;
fullnesse of pleasure give and Joy,
may Comfort never cloye
Thou mistrisse of these games
double in them their flames;
oh bidd thou them undresse,
and tell them nakednesse,
suits thy sports, bidd them venter
for Love, Time, place bids enter: 110

Noe fatall owle the Bedsted keepes
with direfull note to fright your sleepes,
nor furies full of dread
made this your Bridall bedd,
nor with their Brands doe watch
the lights away to snatch;
but all good omen there
doth at the bedd appeare;
Juno here, aloofe doth stand
soft sleepe with his Charming wand: 120

Oh now behold the longing Couch
that nere yet felt a virgins touch,
feeles in it selfe a fire,
and tickled with desire,
pants with its downy breast
as with a heart possest;
shrugging as if it moved
with passions as it loved,
Then undoe your selves and venter
for the dimpling bedd bidds enter: 130

Virgins weepe not, twill come when
as she, soe you'll be ripe for men;
then grieve her not with saying
she must noe more a maying;
or by her dreame divine
who'll be her valentine,
or kisse a Rose budd over,
And wish it were her Lover;
But kisse her, and embrace her,
and twixt the soft sheets place her: 140

Now shutt the doores, the husband putts
the eager boyes to gather nutts,
and now both Love and Time
to their full height doe climbe,
give them both active heate,
with moisture good and neate,
and organs for encrease,
to keepe and to release,
that may the honourd stemme
Circle with a diadem: 150

Oh Venus thou to whom the Zone
of virgins is soe truly knowne,
cherish, and blesse this deede,
and with a mellow speede,
bring to the parents Joy,
their first fruite bee a Boy
soe sprightfull, that the Earth
may swell with such a birth;
and her time of reckoning come
thou Lucina helpe the wombe: 160

Not a slumber, much more shunne
a sleepe, untill the act be done;
not the least breath expire
but let it urge desire;
flye slowly, slowly howers
Now while their lipps make flowers;
Each kisse in its warme Close
smells like a damaske Rose,
or like that pretious Gumme
doth from Panchaia come; 170
soules, and breaths, and lipps excite
sweetes, to rouze up appetite:

On you minuts, howers, dayes, moneths, yeares
dropp the full blessing of the spheares,
what good to man, and wife
to build an happy life
benignant heaven allowes
follow your prayers and vowes;
may fortunes Lilly hand
open at your command: 180

Oh Venus thou to whom is knowne
the best way how to loose the Zone
of virgins; tell the maide
she neede not be afraid;
and teach the youth to apply
close kisses if she crye;
and Charge hee not forbeares
although she wooe with teares
Then tell them now they must adventer
while yet Time and Love bidds enter: 190

May bounteous fates your spindle full-
fill, and winde up with whiter wooll;
let them not cutt the thread
of life, untill you bidd;
Let Death yet come at last
with slow, not desperate haste,
But when yee both can say
fate wee will now away;
Bee yee to the Barne then borne
Two, like two ripe shocks of Corne. 200

[1] H-149B, not in *Hesperides;* a variant version of H-149A from British Museum, MS Harl 6918, f.43v.

H-150 *Teares are Tongues.*

WHen *Julia* chid, I stood as mute the while,
As is the fish, or tonguelesse Crocadile.
Aire coyn'd to words, my *Julia* co'd not heare;
But she co'd see each eye to stamp a teare:
By which, mine angry Mistresse might descry,
Teares are the noble language of the eye.
And when true love of words is destitute,
The Eyes by tears speak, while the Tongue is mute.

H–151

Upon a young mother of many children.

LEt all chaste Matrons, when they chance to see
My num'rous issue: Praise, and pitty me.
Praise me, for having such a fruitfull wombe;
Pity me too, who found so soone a Tomb.

H–152

To Electra.

ILe come to thee in all those shapes
As *Jove* did, when he made his rapes:
Onely, Ile not appeare to thee,
As he did once to *Semele.*[1]
Thunder and Lightning Ile lay by, 5
To talk with thee familiarly.
Which done, then quickly we'll undresse
To one and th'others nakednesse.
And ravisht, plunge into the bed,
(Bodies and souls commingled) 10
And kissing, so as none may heare,
We'll weary all the Fables there.

[1] She prayed to have Jove visit her in all his splendor; when he did so, his lightning consumed her.

H–153

His wish.

IT is sufficient if we pray
To *Jove,* who gives, and takes away:
Let him the Land and Living finde;
Let me alone to fit the mind.

H–154

His Protestation to Perilla.[1]

NOone-day and Midnight shall at once be seene:
Trees, at one time, shall be both sere and greene:
Fire and water shall together lye
In one-self-sweet-conspiring sympathie:

Summer and Winter shall at one time show 5
Ripe eares of corne, and up to th'eares in snow:
Seas shall be sandlesse; Fields devoid of grasse;
Shapelesse the world, (as when all *Chaos* was)
Before, my deare *Perilla*, I will be
False to my vow, or fall away from thee. 10

[1] See H-198, n.1.

H–155 *Love perfumes all parts.*

IF I kisse *Anthea's* brest,
There I smell the Phenix nest:
If her lip, the most sincere
Altar of Incense, I smell there.
Hands, and thighs, and legs, are all 5
Richly Aromaticall.
Goddesse *Isis* cann't transfer
Musks and Ambers[1] more from her:
Nor can *Juno* sweeter be,
When she lyes with *Jove*, then she. 10

[1] See H-15, n.4.

H–156 *To* Julia.

PErmit me, *Julia*, now to goe away;
Or by thy love, decree me here to stay.
If thou wilt say, that I shall live with thee;
Here shall my endless Tabernacle be:
If not, (as banisht) I will live alone 5
There, where no language ever yet was known.

H–157 *On himselfe.*

LOve-sick I am, and must endure
A desp'rate grief, that finds no cure.
Ah me! I try; and trying, prove,
No Herbs have power to cure Love.
Only one Soveraign salve, I know, 5
And that is Death, the end of Woe.

H–158 *Vertue is sensible of suffering.*

THough a wise man all pressures can sustaine;
His vertue still is sensible of paine:
Large shoulders though he has, and well can beare,
He feeles when Packs do pinch him; and the where.

H–159 *The cruell Maid.*

ANd Cruell Maid, because I see
You scornfull of my love, and me:
Ile trouble you no more; but goe
My way, where you shall never know
What is become of me: there I 5
Will find me out a path to die;
Or learne some way how to forget
You, and your name, for ever: yet
Ere I go hence; Know this from me,
What will, in time, your Fortune be: 10
This to your coynesse I will tell;
And having spoke it once, Farewell.
The Lillie will not long endure;
Nor the Snow continue pure:
The Rose, the Violet, one day 15
See, both these Lady-flowers decay:
And you must fade, as well as they.
And it may chance that Love may turn,
And (like to mine) make your heart burn
And weep to see't; yet this thing doe, 20
That my last Vow commends to you:
When you shall see that I am dead,
For pitty let a teare be shed;
And (with your Mantle o're me cast)
Give my cold lips a kisse at last: 25
If twice you kisse, you need not feare,
That I shall stir, or live more here.
Next, hollow out a Tombe to cover
Me; me, the most despised Lover:
And write thereon, *This, Reader, know,* 30
Love kill'd this man. No more but so.

H–160

To Dianeme.

SWeet, be not proud of those two eyes,
Which Star-like sparkle in their skies:
Nor be you proud, that you can see
All hearts your captives; yours, yet free:
Be you not proud of that rich haire, 5
Which wantons with the Love-sick aire:
When as that *Rubie,* which you weare,
Sunk from the tip of your soft eare,
Will last to be a precious Stone,
When all your world of Beautie's gone. 10

H–161

TO THE KING,

To cure the Evill.[1]

TO find that Tree of Life, whose Fruits did feed,
And Leaves did heale, all sick of humane seed:[2]
To finde *Bethesda,* and an Angel there,
Stirring the waters,[3] I am come; and here,
At last, I find, (after my much to doe) 5
The Tree, Bethesda, and the Angel too:
And all in Your Blest Hand, which has the powers
Of all those suppling-healing herbs and flowers.
To that soft *Charm,* that *Spell,* that *Magick Bough,*
That high Enchantment I betake me now: 10
And to that Hand, (the Branch of Heavens faire Tree)
I kneele for help; O! lay that hand on me,
Adored *Cesar!* and my Faith is such,
I shall be heal'd, if that my *KING* but touch.
The Evill is not Yours: my sorrow sings, 15
Mine is the Evill, but the Cure, the KINGS.

[1] scrofula was believed curable by a king's touch. [2] Rev. xxii.1–2: the Angel showed John "a pure river of water of life" and "the tree of life, which bare twelve manner of fruits . . . and the leaves of the tree were for the healing of the nations." [3] John v.2–4: "there is at Jerusalem . . . a pool . . . Bethesda, having five

porches. In these lay a multitude of impotent folk . . . waiting for the movement of the water. For an angel . . . at a certain season . . . troubled the water: whosoever then first . . . stepped in, was made whole of whatsoever disease he had."

H–162 *His misery in a Mistresse.*

WAter, Water I espie:
Come, and coole ye; all who frie
In your loves; but none as I.

Though a thousand showres be
Still a falling, yet I see 5
Not one drop to light on me.

Happy you, who can have seas
For to quench ye, or some ease
From your kinder Mistresses.

I have one, and she alone, 10
Of a thousand thousand known,
Dead to all compassion.

Such an one, as will repeat
Both the cause, and make the heat
More by Provocation great. 15

Gentle friends, though I despaire
Of my cure, doe you beware
Of those Girles, which cruell are.

H–163 *Upon* Jollies *wife.*

FIrst, *Jollies* wife is lame; then next, loose-hipt:
Squint-ey'd, hook-nos'd; and lastly, Kidney-lipt.

H–164A

To a Gentlewoman, objecting to him his gray haires.[1]

AM I despis'd, because you say,
And I dare sweare, that I am gray?
Know, Lady, you have but your day:
And time will come when you shall weare
Such frost and snow upon your haire: 5

And when (though long it comes to passe)
You question with your Looking-glasse;
And in that sincere *Christall* seek,
But find no Rose-bud in your cheek:
Nor any bed to give the shew 10
Where such a rare Carnation grew.
Ah! then too late, close in your chamber keeping,
It will be told
That you are old;
By those true teares y'are weeping. 15

[1] Cf. Horace, *Carmina,* IV, 10 and *Anacreontea,* VII, 1–5 and Stanley's trans. of Anacreon (*Poems,* 1651), "The Old Lover XI": "By the women I am told / 'Lasse *Anacreon* thou grow'st old, / Take thy glasse and look else, there / Thou wilt see thy temples bare; / Whether I be bald or no / That I know not, this I know, / Pleasures, as lesse time to try / Old men have, they more should ply." Cf. H-527.

H–164B

[An earlier version of H–164A][1]

Am I dispised, because you saie
And I beleive that I am graie[?]
Knowe Lady, you have but your daye
And Night will come, when men will sweare
Tyme has spilt snowe upon your haire[.] 5
Then when in your glasse you seeke
But find noe rose budd in your cheeke[,]
Noe[,] *nor the bed to give the showe*
Where such a rare carnation grewe[,]
And such a smileing Tulipp too[,] 10
Ah then too late, close in your chamber keeping
It willbee told that you are old
By those true teares y'are weepinge.

[1] Text based on A—Rosenbach MS 239/22, p. 11—except for variants noted below. The poem must have been written before 1640 when it appeared in William Shakespeare, *Poems;* it occurs also in Henry Lawes, *Ayres and Dialogues* (1653); *Wits Interpreter* (1655); Playford, *Select Ayres and Dialogues,* 1669. Martin, pp. 468–9, collates these and four manuscripts, but not *A*, which is followed above except for the following readings in other sources: 6 seeke / shall seeke *A.* 8 bed / Budd *A.*

H–165 *To Cedars.*

IF 'mongst my many Poems, I can see
One, onely, worthy to be washt by thee:[1]
I live for ever; let the rest all lye
In dennes of Darkness, or condemn'd to die.

[1] by cedar oil, a preservative.

H–166 *Upon* Cupid.

LOve, like a Gypsie, lately came;
And did me much importune
To see my hand; that by the same
He might fore-tell my Fortune.

He saw my Palme; and then, said he, 5
I tell thee, by this score here;
That thou, within few months, shalt be
The youthfull Prince *D'Amour* here.

I smil'd; and bade him once more prove,
And by some crosse-line show it; 10
That I co'd ne'r be Prince of Love,
Though here the Princely Poet.

H–167 *How Primroses came green.*[1]

VIrgins, time-past, known were these,
Troubled with Green-sicknesses,[2]
Turn'd to flowers: Stil the hieu,
Sickly Girles, they beare of you.

[1] pale. [2] anemic diseases frequent in puberty.

H–168

To Joseph *Lord Bishop of* Exeter.[1]

WHom sho'd I feare to write to, if I can
Stand before you, my learn'd *Diocesan*?
And never shew blood-guiltinesse,[2] or feare
To see my Lines *Excathedrated*[3] here.

Since none so good are, but you may condemne; 5
Or here so bad, but you may pardon them.
If then, (my Lord) to sanctifie my Muse
One onely Poem out of all you'l chuse;
And mark it for a Rapture nobly writ,
'Tis Good Confirm'd; for you have Bishop't[4] it. 10

[1] Joseph Hall, Lord Bishop of the Diocese of Exeter 1627–41, utopist, satirist, character-writer, author of numerous works of biblical scholarship; later, a defender of Anglicanism against "Smectymnuus" and Milton. See the *Life* by T. F. Kinloch. [2] shame which causes blood to redden cheeks. [3] authoritatively condemned. [4] confirmed; formally sanctioned.

H–169

Upon a black Twist, rounding the Arme of the Countesse of Carlile.[1]

I Saw about her spotlesse wrist,
Of blackest silk, a curious twist;
Which, circumvolving gently, there
Enthrall'd her Arme, as Prisoner.
Dark was the Jayle;[2] but as if light 5
Had met t'engender with the night;
Or so, as Darknesse made a stay
To shew at once, both night and day.
I fancie more![3] but if there be
Such Freedome in Captivity; 10
I beg of Love, that ever I
May in like Chains of Darknesse[4] lie.

[1] Lucy Percy, daughter of the 9th Earl of Northumberland and second wife of James Hay, Earl of Carlisle (d. March, 1636), was renowned for beauty, wit, and social graces. Davenant, Cartwright, Suckling, and Voiture addressed poems to her; and Waller's tributes to her include "The Countess of Carlisle in Mourning," in which, like Herrick, he plays with the contrast of darkness and light ("Such was th'appearance of new-formed Light, / While yet it struggled with Eternal Night"). She is the subject of a laudatory prose *character* in *A Collection of Letters, made by Sir Tobie Mathews Kt* (1660); e.g. "Amongst men her person is both considered and admired; and her wit, being most eminent, among the rest of her abilities, She affects [desires] the conversation of the persons, who are most famed for it." [2] fetter. [3] Grosart regards "I"

as an error for "One"; Martin replaces "more" with "none"; but the 1648 wording probably means *I fancy (or like) more freedom than there could ever be in captivity; but if there is such freedom in captivity, then I beg*, etc. [4] II Pet. ii.4.

H–170 *On himselfe.*[1]

I Feare no Earthly Powers;
But care for crowns of flowers:
And love to have my Beard
With Wine and Oile besmear'd.
This day Ile drowne all sorrow; 5
Who knowes to live to morrow?

[1] based on *Anacreontea,* VIII, 1–10. Cf. Thomas Stanley's version (*Poems,* 1651), Anacreon XV: "I care not for *Gyges* sway, / Or the *Lydian* scepter weigh; / Nor am covetous of gold, / Nor with envy Kings behold: / All my care is to prepare / Fragrant unguents for my hair: / All my care is where to get / Roses for a Coronet; / All my care is for to day; / What's to morrow who can say? / Come then, let us drink and dice / And to *Bacchus* sacrifice, / Ere death come and take us off, / Crying, hold! th'hast drunk enough."

H–171 *Upon* Pagget.

PAgget, a School-boy, got a Sword, and then
He vow'd Destruction both to Birch, and Men:
Who wo'd not think this Yonker[1] fierce to fight?
Yet comming home, but somewhat late, (last night)
Untrusse, his Master bade him; and that word 5
Made him take up his shirt, lay down his sword.

[1] lordly youngster.

H–172 *A Ring presented to* Julia.

JUlia, I bring
To thee this Ring,
Made for thy finger fit;
To shew by this,
That our love is 5
(Or sho'd be) like to it.

Close though it be,
The joynt is free:
So when Love's yoke is on,
It must not gall, 10
Or fret at all
With hard oppression.

But it must play
Still either way;
And be, too, such a yoke, 15
As not too wide,
To over-slide;
Or be so strait to choak.

So we, who beare,
This beame, must reare 20
Our selves to such a height:
As that the stay
Of either may
Create the burden light.

And as this round 25
Is no where found
To flaw, or else to sever:
So let our love
As endless prove;
And pure as Gold for ever. 30

H–173 *To the Detracter.*

WHere others love, and praise my Verses; still
Thy long-black-Thumb-nail marks 'em out for ill:
A fellon[1] take it, or some Whit-flaw[2] come
For to unslate, or to untile that thumb!
But cry thee Mercy: Exercise thy nailes 5
To scratch or claw, so that thy tongue not railes:
Some numbers prurient are,[3] and some of these
Are wanton with their itch; scratch, and 'twill please.

[1] an inflamed sore. [2] whitlow: a white flaw inflaming the finger.
[3] Some verses are prurient—i.e. lascivious and itchy.

H–174 *Upon the same.*[1]

I Ask't thee oft, what Poets thou hast read,
And lik'st the best? Still thou reply'st, The dead.
I shall, ere long, with green turfs cover'd be;
Then sure thou't like, or thou wilt envie me.

[1] partially based on Martial, VIII, 69.

H–175 Julia's *Petticoat.*

THy Azure Robe, I did behold,
As ayrie as the leaves of gold;[1]
Which erring here, and wandring there,
Pleas'd with transgression ev'ry where:
Sometimes 'two'd pant, and sigh, and heave, 5
As if to stir it scarce had leave:
But having got it; thereupon,
'Two'd make a brave expansion.
And pounc't with Stars, it shew'd to me
Like a *Celestiall Canopie.* 10
Sometimes 'two'd blaze, and then abate,
Like to a flame growne moderate:
Sometimes away 'two'd wildly fling;
Then to thy thighs so closely cling,
That some conceit[2] did melt me downe, 15
As Lovers fall into a swoone:
And all confus'd, I there did lie
Drown'd in Delights; but co'd not die.
That Leading Cloud,[3] I follow'd still,
Hoping t'ave seene of it my fill; 20
But ah! I co'd not: sho'd it move
To Life Eternal, I co'd love.

[1] attached to the bright blue skirt. [2] a thought or fanciful notion.
[3] Exod. xiii.21: the Lord led the Israelites in "a pillar of a cloud."

H–176 *To Musick.*

BEgin to charme, and as thou stroak'st mine eares
With thy enchantment, melt me into tears.
Then let thy active hand scu'd o're thy Lyre:
And make my spirits frantick with the fire.
That done, sink down into a silv'rie straine; 5
And make me smooth as Balme, and Oile againe.

H–177 *Distrust.*

TO safe-guard Man from wrongs, there nothing must
Be truer to him, then a wise Distrust.
And to thy selfe be best this sentence knowne,
Heare all men speak; but credit few or none.

H–178 Corinna's *going a Maying.*

GEt up, get up for shame, the Blooming Morne
Upon her wings presents the god unshorne.[1]
See how *Aurora* throwes her faire
Fresh-quilted colours through the aire:
Get up, sweet-Slug-a-bed, and see 5
The Dew-bespangling Herbe and Tree.
Each Flower has wept, and bow'd toward the East,
Above an houre since; yet you not drest,
Nay! not so much as out of bed?
When all the Birds have Mattens seyd, 10
And sung their thankfull Hymnes: 'tis sin,
Nay, profanation to keep in,
When as a thousand Virgins on this day,
Spring, sooner then the Lark, to fetch in May.

Rise; and put on your Foliage, and be seene 15
To come forth, like the Spring-time, fresh and greene;
And sweet as *Flora*. Take no care
For Jewels for your Gowne, or Haire:
Feare not; the leaves will strew
Gemms in abundance upon you: 20

Besides, the childhood of the Day has kept,
Against you come, some *Orient Pearls* unwept:
Come, and receive them while the light
Hangs on the Dew-locks of the night:[2]
And *Titan*[3] on the Eastern hill 25
Retires himselfe, or else stands still
Till you come forth. Wash, dresse, be briefe in praying:
Few Beads[4] are best, when once we goe a Maying.

Come, my *Corinna*, come; and comming, marke
How each field turns a street; each street a Parke
Made green, and trimm'd with trees: see how
Devotion gives each House a Bough,
Or Branch: Each Porch, each doore, ere this,
An Arke a Tabernacle[5] is
Made up of white-thorn[6] neatly enterwove; 35
As if here were those cooler shades of love.
Can such delights be in the street,
And open fields, and we not see't?
Come, we'll abroad; and let's obay
The Proclamation made for May:[7] 40
And sin no more, as we have done, by staying;
But my *Corinna*, come, let's goe a Maying.

There's not a budding Boy, or Girle, this day,
But is got up, and gone to bring in May.
A deale of Youth, ere this, is come
Back, and with *White-thorn* laden home.
Some have dispatcht their Cakes and Creame,
Before that we have left to dreame:
And some have wept, and woo'd, and plighted Troth,
And chose their Priest, ere we can cast off sloth: 50
Many a green-gown has been given;[8]
Many a kisse, both odde and even:
Many a glance too has been sent
From out the eye, Loves Firmament:
Many a jest told of the Keyes betraying 55
This night, and Locks pickt, yet w'are not a Maying.

Come, let us goe, while we are in our prime;
And take the harmlesse follie of the time.
We shall grow old apace, and die
Before we know our liberty. 60
Our life is short; and our dayes run
As fast away as do's the Sunne:

And as a vapour, or a drop of raine
Once lost, can ne'r be found againe:
So when or you or I are made 65
A fable, song, or fleeting shade;
All love, all liking, all delight
Lies drown'd with us in endlesse night.[9]
Then while time serves, and we are but decaying;
Come, my *Corinna*, come, let's goe a Maying. 70

[1] a stock epithet for the sun-god Apollo. Herrick thinks of the sun emerging like a divine being over the horizon, with rays of light streaming like hair. [2] Night, personified, has dew, like jewels, on the locks of her hair. [3] the sun or sun-god. [4] prayers. [5] Cf. Lev. xxiii.40–42, "ye shall take you on the first day the boughs of goodly trees, branches of palm trees . . . and ye shall rejoice before the Lord. . . . Ye shall dwell in booths seven days." [6] symbolizing joy and pain. [7] either a particular local proclamation of May Day festivities or possibly a reference to Charles I's "declaration to his subjects concerning lawful sports," 1633, which forbade interference on Sundays after divine service with "any lawful recreation, such as dancing" or with "having of May-games . . . and the setting up of May-poles and other sports therewith used." Order was also given that "women shall have leave to carry rushes to the church for the decorating of it, according to their old custom." [8] the result of rolling a woman, in sport, on the grass so that her dress was stained with green. [9] Cf. Wisd. of Sol. ii.1–8, "For the ungodly said . . . Our life is short and tedious, and in the death of a man there is no remedy: neither was there any man known to have returned from the grave . . . for the breath of our nostrils is as smoke, and a little spark . . . which being extinguished, our body shall be turned to ashes, and our spirit shall vanish as the soft air . . . and our life shall pass away as the trace of a cloud . . . and after our end there is no returning. . . . Come on therefore, let us enjoy the good things that are present: and let us speedily use the creatures like as in youth . . . and let no flower of the spring pass by us. Let us crown ourselves with rose buds, before they be withered." Prov. vii.18, "Come, let us take our fill of love until the morning, let us solace ourselves with loves." This *carpe diem* sentiment is also reiterated in classical literature.

H–179 *On* Julia's *breath.*

BReathe, *Julia*, breathe, and Ile protest,
Nay more, Ile deeply sweare,
That all the Spices of the East
Are circumfused[1] there.

[1] blended and encompassed.

H–180 *Upon a Child. An Epitaph.*

BUt borne, and like a short Delight,
I glided by my Parents sight.
That done, the harder Fates deny'd
My longer stay, and so I dy'd.
If pittying my sad Parents Teares, 5
You'l spil a tear, or two with theirs:
And with some flowrs my grave bestrew,
Love and they'l thank you for't. Adieu.

H–181
A Dialogue betwixt Horace *and* Lydia, *Translated*[1] Anno 1627. *and set by Master* Robert Ramsey.[2]

Hor. WHile, *Lydia*, I was lov'd of thee,
Nor any was preferr'd 'fore me
To hug thy whitest neck: Then[3] I,
The Persian King liv'd not more happily.

Lyd. While thou no other didst affect,[4] 5
Nor *Cloe* was of more respect;
Then *Lydia*, far-fam'd *Lydia*,
I flourish't more then Roman *Ilia*.

Hor. Now *Thracian Cloe* governs me,
Skilfull i'th'Harpe, and Melodie: 10
For whose affection, *Lydia*, I
(So Fate spares her) am well content to die.

Lyd. My heart now set on fire is
By *Ornithes* sonne, young *Calais;*
For whose commutuall flames here I 15
(To save his life) twice am content to die.

Hor. Say our first loves we sho'd revoke,
And sever'd, joyne in brazen yoke:
Admit I *Cloe* put away,
And love againe love-cast-off *Lydia*? 20

Lyd. Though mine be brighter then the Star;
Thou lighter then the Cork by far:
Rough as th'*Adratick sea,* yet I
Will live with thee, or else for thee will die.[5]

[1] from Horace, Odes, III, ix. [2] organist of Trinity College, Cambridge; he also set to music H-138B. Cf. Jonson's version, *Underwoods,* 87. [3] than. [4] desire. [5] Cf. Thomas Stanley's translation (Cambridge University Library: Add MS 7514), dated 1646; some punctuation added: "Whilst thy affection I possest, / Nor any youth before me grac'd / Thy neck with his fair armes embrac'd, / The Persian King was not so blest. // Whilst to no other thou wert kind, / Nor Lydia lesse then Cloë went, / Lydia a name of proud extent; / The Roman Ilia I outshind. // Now Thracian Cloë is my care, / Whose hand and voice alike are sweet; / For whom I death would fearlesse meet, / Would Fates my soule surviving spare. // Me Calaïs, Thurine Orniths heire, / Kindly consumes in mutuall fire; / For whom I doubly would expire, / Would Fates the boy surviving spare. // What if old Love return and chaine / The severd to his brazen yoak; / If fair-haird Cloë I revile / And slighted Lydia entertain? // Though fairer then a star is he, / Lighter then aery cork art thou / Rougher then Adria's stormy brow, / Ide choose to live and dy with thee."

H-182

The captiv'd Bee: or, *The little Filcher.*

AS *Julia* once a slumb'ring lay,
It chanc't a Bee did flie that way,
(After a dew, or dew-like shower)
To tipple freely in a flower.
For some rich flower, he took the lip 5
Of *Julia,* and began to sip;
But when he felt he suckt from thence
Hony, and in the quintessence:

He drank so much he scarce co'd stir;
So *Julia* took the Pilferer.
And thus surpiz'd (as Filchers use)
He thus began himselfe t'excuse:
Sweet *Lady-Flower*, I never brought
Hither the least one theeving thought:
But taking those rare lips of yours 15
For some fresh, fragrant, luscious flowers:
I thought I might there take a taste,
Where so much sirrop ran at waste.
Besides, know this, I never sting
The flower that gives me nourishing: 20
But with a kisse, or thanks, doe pay
For Honie, that I beare away.
This said, he laid his little *scrip*[1]
Of hony, 'fore her Ladiship:
And told her, (as some tears did fall) 25
That, that he took, and that was all.
At which she smil'd; and bade him goe
And take his bag; but thus much know,
When next he came a pilfring so,
He sho'd from her full lips derive, 30
Hony enough to fill his hive.

[1] bag.

H–183 *Upon* Prig.

PRig now drinks Water, who before drank Beere:
What's now the cause? we know the case is cleere:
Look in *Prigs's* purse, the chev'rell[1] there tells you
Prig mony wants, either to buy, or brew.

[1] cheveral: a flexible kid leather; hence, flexibility.

H–184 *Upon* Batt.

BAtt he gets children, not for love to reare 'em;
But out of hope his wife might die to beare 'em.

H–185

An Ode to Master Endymion Porter, *upon his Brothers death.*[1]

NOt all thy flushing Sunnes are set,
Herrick, as yet:
Nor doth this far-drawn Hemisphere
Frown, and look sullen ev'ry where.
Daies may conclude in nights; and Suns may rest, 5
As dead, within the West;
Yet the next Morne, re-guild the fragrant East.

Alas for me! that I have lost
E'en all almost:
Sunk is my sight; set is my Sun; 10
And all the loome[2] of life undone:
The staffe, the Elme, the prop, the shelt'ring wall
Whereon my Vine did crawle,
Now, now, blowne downe; needs must the old stock fall.

Yet, *Porter*, while thou keep'st alive, 15
In death I thrive:
And like a *Phenix* re-aspire
From out my *Narde*,[3] and Fun'rall fire:
And as I prune[4] my feather'd youth, so I
Doe mar'l[5] how I co'd die, 20
When I had Thee, my chiefe Preserver, by.

I'm up, I'm up, and blesse that hand,
Which makes me stand
Now as I doe; and but for thee,
I must confesse, I co'd not be. 25
The debt is paid: for he who doth resigne
Thanks to the gen'rous Vine;
Invites fresh Grapes to fill his Presse with Wine.

[1] a soliloquy by Herrick almost certainly about the death of his brother William in the early 1630's (See H-186), and addressed to Endymion Porter (See H-117, n.1 and H-662 and H-1071, also addressed to him). However, the poem may be about Porter's brother Edmund, d. 1628, or Gyles, d. ca. 1645; Grosart suggests that the speaker at the beginning was supposed to be Porter himself. [2] the frame a weaver works on, or the fabric itself. [3] spike-

nard, an aromatic substance derived from an Eastern plant. Cf. John xii.2–7, "Then took Mary a pound of ointment of spikenard, very costly, and anointed the feet of Jesus. . . . Then saith one of his disciples . . . Why was not this ointment sold for three hundred pence, and given to the poor? . . . Then said Jesus, Let her alone: against the day of my burying hath she kept this." [4] preen. [5] marvel.

H–186

To his dying Brother, Master William Herrick.[1]

LIfe of my life, take not so soone thy flight,
But stay the time till we have bade Good night.
Thou hast both Wind and Tide with thee; Thy way
As soone dispatcht is by the Night, as Day.
Let us not then so rudely henceforth goe 5
Till we have wept, kist, sigh't, shook hands, or so.
There's paine in parting; and a kind of hell,
When once true-lovers take their last Fare-well.
What? shall we two our endlesse leaves take here
Without a sad looke, or a solemne teare? 10
He knowes not Love, that hath not this truth proved,
Love is most loth to leave the thing beloved.
Pay we our Vowes, and goe; yet when we part,
Then, even then, I will bequeath my heart
Into thy loving hands: For Ile keep none 15
To warme my Breast, when thou my Pulse art gone.
No, here Ile last, and walk (a harmless shade)
About this Urne, wherein thy Dust is laid,
To guard it so, as nothing here shall be
Heavy, to hurt those sacred seeds of thee. 20

[1] See H-185, n.1.

H–187

The Olive Branch.

SAdly I walk't within the field,
To see what comfort it wo'd yeeld:
And as I went my private way,
An Olive-branch before me lay:
And seeing it, I made a stay. 5

And took it up, and view'd it; then
Kissing the *Omen,* said Amen:
Be, be it so, and let this be
A Divination unto me:
That in short time my woes shall cease; 10
And Love shall crown my End with Peace.

H–188 *Upon* Much-more. *Epigram.*

MUch-more, provides, and hoords up like an Ant;
Yet *Much-more* still complains he is in want.
Let *Much-more* justly pay his tythes; then try
How both his Meale and Oile will multiply.

H–189 *To Cherry-blossomes.*

YE may simper, blush, and smile,
And perfume the aire a while:
But (sweet things) ye must be gone;
Fruit, ye know, is comming on:
Then, Ah! Then, where is your grace, 5
When as Cherries come in place?

H–190 *How Lillies came white.*

WHite though ye be; yet, Lillies, know,
From the first ye were not so:
But Ile tell ye
What befell ye;
Cupid and his Mother lay 5
In a Cloud; while both did play,
He with his pretty finger prest
The rubie niplet of her breast;
Out of the which, the creame of light,
Like to a Dew, 10
Fell downe on you,
And made ye white.

H–191

To Pansies.

AH, cruell Love! must I endure
Thy many scorns, and find no cure?
Say, are thy medicines made to be
Helps to all others, but to me?
Ile leave thee, and to *Pansies* come; 5
Comforts you'l afford me some:
You can ease my heart, and doe
What Love co'd ne'r be brought unto.

H–192

On Gelli-flowers[1] begotten.

WHat was't that fell but now
From that warme kisse of ours?
Look, look, by Love I vow
They were two *Gelli-flowers.*

Let's kisse, and kisse agen; 5
For if so be our closes[2]
Make *Gelli-flowers,* then
I'm sure they'l fashion *Roses.*

[1] gillyflowers: several varieties of clove-scented flowers. [2] junctions.

H–193

The Lilly in a Christal.

YOu have beheld a smiling *Rose*
When Virgins hands have drawn
O'r it a Cobweb-Lawne:
And here, you see, this Lilly shows,
Tomb'd in a *Christal* stone, 5
More faire in this transparent case,
Then when it grew alone;
And had but single grace.

You see how *Creame* but naked is;
Nor daunces in the eye 10
Without a Strawberrie:
Or some fine tincture, like to this,

Which draws the sight thereto,
More by that wantoning with it;
Then when the paler hieu 15
No mixture did admit.

You see how *Amber* through the streams
More gently stroaks the sight,
With some conceal'd delight;
Then when he darts his radiant beams 20
Into the boundlesse aire:
Where either too much light his worth
Doth all at once impaire,
Or set it little forth.

Put Purple Grapes, or Cherries in- 25
To Glasse, and they will send
More beauty to commend
Them, from that cleane and subtile skin,
Then if they naked stood,
And had no other pride at all, 30
But their own flesh and blood,
And tinctures naturall.

Thus Lillie, Rose, Grape, Cherry, Creame,
And Straw-berry do stir
More love, when they transfer 35
A weak, a soft, a broken beame;
Then if they sho'd discover
At full their proper excellence;
Without some Scean[1] cast over,
To juggle with the sense. 40

Thus let this *Christal'd Lillie* be
A Rule, how far to teach,
Your nakednesse must reach:
And that, no further, then we see
Those glaring colours laid 45
By Arts wise hand, but to this end
They sho'd obey a shade;
Lest they too far extend.

So though y'are white as Swan, or Snow,
And have the power to move 50
A world of men to love:
Yet, when your Lawns and Silks shal flow;

And that white cloud divide
Into a doubtful Twi-light; then,
Then will your hidden Pride 55
Raise greater fires in men.[2]

[1] veil or curtain. [2] When your semi-transparent fine linens and silks move over your white complexion and break its light into a mysterious twilight, then your hidden splendor or glory will arouse greater ardor in men.

H–194 *To his Booke.*

LIke to a Bride, come forth my Book, at last,
With all thy richest jewels over-cast:
Say, if there be 'mongst many jems here; one
Deservelesse of the name of *Paragon*:[1]
Blush not at all for that; since we have set 5
Some *Pearls* on *Queens*, that have been counterfet.

[1] jewelers' term for a perfect diamond.

H–195 *Upon some women.*

THou who wilt not love, doe this;
Learne of me what Woman is.
Something made of thred and thrumme;[1]
A meere Botch of all and some.
Pieces, patches, ropes of haire; 5
In-laid Garbage ev'ry where.
Out-side silk, and out-side Lawne;
Sceanes[2] to cheat us neatly drawne.
False in legs, and false in thighes;
False in breast, teeth, haire, and eyes: 10
False in head, and false enough;
Onely true in shreds and stuffe.

[1] thrum: odds and ends of thread. [2] veil or curtain.

H–196 *Supreme fortune falls soonest.*

WHile leanest Beasts in Pastures feed,
The fattest Oxe the first must bleed.

H–197 *The Welcome to Sack.*

SO soft streams meet, so springs with gladder smiles
Meet after long divorcement by the Iles:
When Love (the child of likenesse) urgeth on
Their Christal natures to an union.
So meet stolne kisses, when the Moonie nights 5
Call forth fierce Lovers to their wisht Delights:
So *Kings and Queens* meet, when Desire convinces[1]
All thoughts, but such as aime at getting Princes,
A[s] I meet thee. Soule of my life, and fame!
Eternall Lamp of Love! whose radiant flame 10
Out-glares the Heav'ns **Osiris;*[2] and thy gleams
Out-shine the splendour of his mid-day beams.
Welcome, O welcome my illustrious Spouse;
Welcome as are the ends unto my Vowes:
I! far more welcome then the happy soile, 15
The Sea-scourg'd Merchant, after all his toile,
Salutes with tears of joy; when fires betray
The smoakie chimneys of his *Ithaca*.
Where hast thou been so long from my embraces,
Poore pittyed Exile? Tell me, did thy Graces 20
Flie discontented hence, and for a time
Did rather choose to blesse another clime?
Or went'st thou to this end, the more to move me,
By thy short absence, to desire and love thee?
Why frowns my Sweet? Why won't my Saint confer 25
Favours on me, her fierce Idolater?
Why are Those Looks, Those Looks the which have been
Time-past so fragrant, sickly now drawn in
Like a dull Twi-light? Tell me; and the fault
Ile expiate with[3] Sulphur, Haire, and Salt: 30
And with the Christal humour[4] of the spring,
Purge hence the guilt, and kill this quarrelling.
Wo't thou not smile, or tell me what's amisse?
Have I been cold to hug thee, too remisse,
Too temp'rate in embracing? Tell me, ha's desire 35
To thee-ward dy'd i'th'embers, and no fire
Left in this rak't-up Ash-heap, as a mark
To testifie the glowing of a spark?

Have I divorc't thee onely to combine
In hot Adult'ry with another Wine?
True, I confesse I left thee, and appeale
'Twas done by me, more to confirme my zeale,
And double my affection on thee; as doe those,
Whose love growes more enflam'd, by being Foes.
But to forsake thee ever, co'd there be 45
A thought of such like possibilitie?
When thou thy selfe dar'st say, thy Iles shall lack
Grapes, before *Herrick* leaves Canarie Sack.
Thou mak'st me ayrie, active to be born,
Like *Iphyclus*,[5] upon the tops of Corn. 50
Thou mak'st me nimble, as the winged howers,[6]
To dance and caper on the heads of flowers,
And ride the Sun-beams. Can there be a thing
Under the heavenly **Isis*,[7] that can bring
More love unto my life, or can present 55
My *Genius* with a fuller blandishment?
Illustrious Idoll! co'd th'*Ægyptians* seek
Help from the *Garlick, Onyon*, and the *Leek*,
And pay no vowes to thee? who wast their best
God, and far more transcendent then the rest? 60
Had *Cassius*,[8] that weak Water-drinker, known
Thee in thy Vine, or had but tasted one
Small Chalice of thy frantick liquor; He
As the wise *Cato*[9] had approv'd of thee.
Had not **Joves* son,[10] that brave *Tyrinthian* Swain, 65
(Invited to the *Thesbian* banquet) ta'ne
Full goblets of thy gen'rous blood; his spright
Ne'r had kept heat for fifty Maids that night.
Come, come and kisse me; Love and lust commends
Thee, and thy beauties; kisse, we will be friends 70
Too strong for Fate to break us: Look upon
Me, with that full pride of complexion,
As *Queenes*, meet *Queenes;* or come thou unto me,
As *Cleopatra* came to *Anthonie;*
When her high carriage did at once present 75
To the *Triumvir*, Love and Wonderment.
Swell up my nerves with spirit; let my blood
Run through my veines, like to a hasty flood.
Fill each part full of fire, active to doe
What thy commanding soule shall put it to. 80
And till I turne Apostate to thy love,
Which here I vow to serve, doe not remove

Thy Fiers from me; but *Apollo's* curse
Blast these-like actions, or a thing that's worse;
When these Circumstants[11] shall but live to see 85
The time that I prevaricate from thee.
Call me *The sonne of Beere*, and then confine
Me to the Tap, the Tost, the Turfe;[12] Let Wine
Ne'r shine upon me; May my Numbers all
Run to a sudden Death, and Funerall. 90
And last, when thee (deare Spouse) I disavow,
Ne'r may Prophetique *Daphne*[13] crown my Brow.

[1] overpowers. [2]* The Sun (Herrick's note). [3] I'll atone for the fault by making propitiatory offerings of. [4] the clear water. [5] to be borne or supported as was this Greek hero: he was so fleet of foot that he ran on the tops of growing grain in fields. [6] goddesses of the seasons. See H-149A, n.8. [7]* The Moon (Herrick's note). [8] the conspirator against Caesar; he drank only water. [9] The elder Cato, known as the Censor, wrote a treatise on agriculture which included rules for grape-growing and recipes for wine. [10]* Hercules (Herrick's note). He regained possession of Tirynthus, a city of Argolis, where his father had ruled. Thespius, King of Thespia, had fifty daughters. [11] bystanders. [12] i.e. confine me to beer tapped from the kegs, to the bits of toasted bread put into it as sops, and to the earth—the earth because beer lacks the power of wine to exalt him; cf. lines 49 ff., "Thou mak'st me ayrie," etc. [13] Daphne, pursued by Phoebus Apollo, god of music and poetry, was changed to a bay tree or laurel: winners of poetic contests were crowned with laurel. Martin, pp. 469–73, records variants in ten manuscripts and *Parnassus Biceps,* 1656. There are also versions in *Y* (Rosenbach MS 1083/16, pp. 123–6) and Z (Rosenbach MS 1083/17, f.96v), but only variants not recorded by Martin are given here. Heading: A welcome to sacke *Y;* His Returne Z. 2 by / from Z. 3 likenesse / liking *Y*. 6 fierce / hot *Y*. 6 wisht / stolne *Y*. 7 *Kings and Queens* meet / Kings meets Queenes Z. 16 The / Then *Y*. 22 Did / Didst *Y*. 30 and / or *Y*. 34 cold / to cold Z. 40 In . . . Wine / Or quench my thirst uppon some other wine Z. 41 left / lost Z. 47 dar'st / shall *Y*. FOLLOWING LINE 48: Thou art my life, my lover, salt to all, My boast of Dainties, navell, principall, *Y;* Thou art my life, my leaven, salt to all My dearer dainties, Navell, Principall, Fire to all my functions, givst me blood Shine, Marrow, Spiritt, and what else is good Z. 49 ayrie, active / active, easy *Y*. 50 *Iphyclus* . . . Corn / Ixions uppon the top of Corne *Y;* . . . the topps of the corne Z. FOLLOWING LINE 50: Fire to all my functions, givest me blood, Cheere, spirit, and marrow, and what else is good *Y*. 52 on the heads of / on the head of *Y;* one the Z. 53 And ride / Amid Z. 54 *Isis* / Iles *Y*. 58 *Garlick, Onyon,* and / Onions, garlicke, or *Y*. 65 *Joves . . . Tyrinthian* /

Juno's sonne that vast Ternithean Y. 66 banquet / banquetts Z. 68 fifty / forty Z. 81 till / while Z.

H–198 *Impossibilities to his friend.*[1]

MY faithful friend, if you can see
The Fruit to grow upon the Tree:
If you can see the colour come
Into the blushing Peare, or Plum:
If you can see the water grow 5
To cakes of Ice, or flakes of Snow:
If you can see, that drop of raine
Lost in the wild sea, once againe:
If you can see, how Dreams do creep
Into the Brain by easie sleep: 10
Then there is hope that you may see
Her love me once, who now hates me.

[1] The differing treatments of the impossibility theme could almost be classed as a minor literary genre. Cf. H-154, H-720; N-3; Esdras iv.5–11 and v.36–40; Donne's "Goe, and catche a falling starre"; and Marvell's "To his Coy Mistress."

H–199 *Upon* Luggs. *Epigram.*

LUggs, by the Condemnation of the Bench,
Was lately whipt for lying with a Wench.
Thus Paines and Pleasures turne by turne succeed:
He smarts at last, who do's not first take heed.

H–200 *Upon* Gubbs. *Epigram.*

GUbbs call's his children *Kitlings:* and wo'd bound
(Some say) for joy, to see those Kitlings drown'd.

H–201 *To live merrily, and to trust to Good Verses.*

NOw is the time for mirth,
Nor cheek, or tongue be dumbe:
For with the flowrie earth,
The golden pomp is come.

The golden Pomp is come;[1] 5
For now each tree do's weare
(Made of her Pap and Gum)
Rich beads of *Amber* here.

Now raignes the *Rose*,[2] and now
Th'*Arabian* Dew[3] besmears 10
My uncontrolled brow,[4]
And my retorted[5] haires.

Homer, this Health to thee,
In Sack of such a kind,
That it wo'd make thee see, 15
Though thou wert ne'r so blind.

Next, *Virgil*, Ile call forth,
To pledge this second Health
In Wine, whose each cup's worth
An Indian Common-wealth. 20

A Goblet next Ile drink
To *Ovid;* and suppose,
Made he the pledge, he'd think
The world had all *one Nose*.[6]

Then this immensive cup 25
Of *Aromatike* wine,
Catullus, I quaffe up
To that Terce Muse of thine.

Wild I am now with heat;
O *Bacchus!* coole thy Raies! 30
Or frantick I shall eate
Thy *Thyrse*, and bite the *Bayes*.

Round, round, the roof do's run;
And being ravisht thus,
Come, I will drink a Tun 35
To my *Propertius*.

Now, to *Tibullus*, next,
This flood I drink to thee:
But stay; I see a Text,[7]
That this presents to me. 40

Behold, *Tibullus* lies
Here burnt, whose smal return
Of ashes, scarce suffice
To fill a little Urne.

Trust to good Verses then;
They onely will aspire,
When Pyramids, as men,
Are lost, i'th'funerall fire.

And when all Bodies meet
In *Lethe* to be drown'd; 50
Then onely Numbers sweet,
With endless life are crown'd.

[1] This line and the last half of the title echo Ovid, *Amores,* III, 2, 44 and III, 9, 39. [2] "Now reigns (*regnat*) the rose" is frequent in Martial and others, but Herrick seems to intend wordplay on *rain* as well. [3] Ovid, *Heroides,* XV, 76. [4] my ungoverned countenance, the brow being the seat of facial expressions of boldness, joy, sorrow, etc. [5] bent backwards. [6] Ovid's family name was *Naso:* nose. He would find the aroma so rich that he would think the world had one nose and that he was smelling with it. [7] Ovid, *Amores,* III, 9, 39–40, translated in the next stanza.

H–202

Faire dayes: or, *Dawnes deceitfull.*

FAire was the Dawne; and but e'ne now the Skies
Shew'd like to Creame, enspir'd with Strawberries:
But on a sudden, all was chang'd and gone
That smil'd in that first-sweet complexion.
Then Thunder-claps and Lightning did conspire 5
To teare the world, or set it all on fire.
What trust to things, below, when as we see,
As Men, the Heavens have their Hypocrisie?

H–203

Lips Tonguelesse.

FOr my part, I never care
For those lips, that tongue-ty'd are:
Tell-tales I wo'd have them be
Of my Mistresse, and of me.
Let them prattle how that I 5
Sometimes freeze, and sometimes frie:
Let them tell how she doth move
Fore- or backward in her love:
Let them speak by gentle tones,
One and th'others passions: 10

How we watch, and seldome sleep;
How by Willowes we doe weep:
How by stealth we meet, and then
Kisse, and sigh, so part agen.
This the lips we will permit 15
For to tell, not publish it.

H–204

To the Fever, not to trouble Julia.

TH'ast dar'd too farre; but Furie now forbeare
To give the least disturbance to her haire:
But lesse presume to lay a Plait upon
Her skins most smooth, and cleare expansion.
'Tis like a Lawnie-Firmament as yet 5
Quite dispossest of either fray, or fret.[1]
Come thou not neere that Filmne so finely spred,
Where no one piece is yet unlevelled.
This if thou dost, woe to thee Furie, woe,
Ile send such Frost, such Haile, such Sleet, and Snow, 10
Such Flesh-quakes, Palsies, and such fears as shall
Dead thee to th'most, if not destroy thee all.
And thou a thousand thousand times shalt be
More shak't thy selfe, then she is scorch't by thee.

[1] either a blemish caused by chafing or a small pimple.

H–205

To Violets.

1. WElcome Maids of Honour,
You doe bring
In the Spring;
And wait upon her.

2. She has Virgins many,
Fresh and faire;
Yet you are
More sweet then any.

3. Y'are the Maiden Posies,
And so grac't,
To be plac't,
'Fore Damask Roses.

4. Yet though thus respected,
By and by
Ye doe lie,
Poore Girles, neglected.

H–206 *Upon* Bunce. *Epigram.*

MOny thou ow'st me; Prethee fix a day
For payment promis'd, though thou never pay:
Let it be Doomes-day; nay, take longer scope;
Pay when th'art honest; let me have some hope.

H–207 *To Carnations. A Song.*

1. STay while ye will, or goe;
And leave no scent behind ye:[1]
Yet trust me, I shall know
The place, where I may find ye.

2. Within my *Lucia's* cheek,
(Whose Livery ye weare)
Play ye at *Hide* or *Seek*,
I'm sure to find ye there.

[1] Cf. H-1068, st. 1.

H–208

To the Virgins, to make much of Time.[1]

1. GAther ye Rose-buds while ye may,
Old Time is still a flying:
And this same flower that smiles today,
To morrow will be dying.

2. The glorious Lamp of Heaven, the Sun,
The higher he's a getting;
The sooner will his Race be run,
And neerer he's to Setting.

3. That Age is best, which is the first,
When Youth and Blood are warmer;
But being spent, the worse, and worst
Times, still succeed the former.

4. Then be not coy, but use your time;
And while ye may, goe marry:
For having lost but once your prime,
You may for ever tarry.

[1] Cf. H-178, lines 57–70 and n.9; Burton, 3,2,5,5 (misnumbered 3,2,6,5 in eds. 6 and 7; in eds. 6 and 7, the two unnumbered pp. following p. 577): "Virgins must be provided for in season. . . . For if they tarry longer . . . they are past date. . . . A virgin, as the Poet [Ausonius *Idyl.* 14] holds . . . is like a flowre, a Rose withered on a sudden. . . . *She that was erst a maid as fresh as May, / Is now an old Crone, time so steals away.* Let them take time then while they may, make advantage of youth, and as he prescribes. . . . *Fair maids go gather Roses in the prime, / And think that as a flowre so goes on time.* Let's all love . . . whiles we are in the flower of yeers, fit for love matters, and while time serves: for . . . *Suns that set may rise again, / But if once we lose this light, / 'Tis with us perpetual night* [Catullus, V, 4–6, trans. Ben Jonson] . . . time past cannot be recal'd." Cf. also Fairfax, *Tasso,* XVI, 15; Seneca, *Hippolytus,* 773–6 and 446–51 and *Ep.* CVIII, 24; Tibullus, I, 8, 47–48; Propertius, IV, 5; and what Martin (p. 518) calls "perhaps the nearest anticipation provided by a single work . . . that of Philostratus in his *Letters,* No. 17 (Loeb, *Alciphron,* etc.)"

H–209 *Safety to look to ones selfe.*

FOr my neighbour Ile not know,
Whether high he builds or no:
Onely this Ile look upon,
Firm be my foundation.
Sound, or unsound, let it be; 5
'Tis the lot ordain'd for me.
He who to the ground do's fall,
Has not whence to sink at all.

H–210

To his Friend, on the untuneable Times.

PLay I co'd once; but (gentle friend) you see
My Harp hung up, here on the Willow tree.[1]
Sing I co'd once; and bravely too enspire
(With luscious Numbers) my melodious Lyre.
Draw I co'd once (although not stocks or stones, 5

Amphion-like)[2] men made of flesh and bones,
Whether I wo'd; but (ah!) I know not how,
I feele in me, this transmutation now.
Griefe, (my deare friend) has first my Harp unstrung;
Wither'd my hand, and palsie-struck my tongue. 10

[1] Psalm cxxxvii.1–2, "we wept, when we remembered Zion. We hanged our harps upon the willows." [2] Amphion's harp playing attracted stones to move into their places to build Thebes' walls.

H–211 *His Poetrie his Pillar.*

1. ONely a little more
   I have to write,
   Then Ile give o're,
   And bid the world Good-night.

2. 'Tis but a flying minute,
   That I must stay,
   Or linger in it;
   And then I must away.

3. O time that cut'st down all!
   And scarce leav'st here
   Memoriall
   Of any men that were.

4. How many lye forgot
   In Vaults beneath?
   And piece-meale rot
   Without a fame in death?

5. Behold this living stone,
   I reare for me,
   Ne'r to be thrown
   Downe, envious Time by thee.

6. Pillars let some set up,
   (If so they please)
   Here is my hope,
   And my *Pyramides*.

H–212 *Safety on the Shore.*

WHat though the sea be calme? Trust to the shore:
Ships have been drown'd, where late they danc't before.

H–213A

A Pastorall upon the birth of Prince Charles,[1] *Presented to the King, and Set by Master* Nicholas Laniere.[2]

The Speakers, Mirtillo, Amintas, *and* Amarillis.

Amint: GOod day, *Mirtillo.*
Mirt: And to you no lesse:
And all faire Signs lead on our Shepardesse.
Amar: With all white luck to you.
Mirt: But say, What news
Stirs in our Sheep-walk?
Amint: None, save that my Ewes,
My Weathers,[3] Lambes, and wanton Kids are well,
Smooth, faire, and fat, none better I can tell:
Or that this day *Menalchas* keeps a feast
For his Sheep-shearers.
Mirt: True, these are the least.
But dear *Amintas,* and sweet *Amarillis,*
Rest but a while here, by this bank of Lillies, 10
And lend a gentle eare to one report
The Country has.
Amint: From whence?
Amar: From whence?
Mirt: The Court.

Three dayes before the shutting in of *May,*
(With whitest Wool be ever crown'd that day!)
To all our joy, a sweet-fac't child was borne, 15
More tender then the childhood of the Morne.
Chor: *Pan* pipe to him, and bleats of lambs and sheep,
Let Lullaby the pretty Prince asleep!
Mirt: And that his birth sho'd be more singular,
At Noone of Day, was seene a silver Star,
Bright as the Wise-mens Torch, which guided them
To Gods sweet Babe, when borne at *Bethlehem;*
When Golden Angels (some have told to me)
Sung out his Birth with Heav'nly Minstralsie.

Amint: O rare! But is't a trespasse if we three
Sho'd wend along his Baby-ship to see?
Mirt: Not so, not so.
Chor: But if it chance to prove
At most a fault, 'tis but a fault of love.
Amar: But deare *Mirtillo*, I have heard it told,
Those learned men brought *Incense, Myrrhe,* 30
[and *Gold,*
From Countries far, with store of Spices, (sweet)
And laid them downe for Offrings at his feet.
Mirt: 'Tis true indeed; and each of us will bring
Unto our smiling, and our blooming King,
A neat, though not so great an Offering. 35
Amar: A Garland for my Gift shall be
Of flowers, ne'r suckt by th'theeving Bee:
And all most sweet; yet all lesse sweet then he.[4]
Amint: And I will beare along with you
Leaves dropping downe the honyed dew, 40
With oaten pipes, as sweet, as new.
Mirt: And I a Sheep-hook will bestow,
To have his little King-ship know,
As he is Prince, he's Shepherd too.
Chor: Come let's away, and quickly let's be drest, 45
And quickly give, *The swiftest Grace is best.*
And when before him we have laid our treasures,
We'll blesse the Babe, Then back to Countrie
[pleasures.

[1] May 29, 1630. In the 1648 folio, the speakers' names are crowded into the text without spacing for separate speeches; but for the sake of clarity, we depart here from our principle of approximating the appearance of the original printing and separate the names from the text and isolate each speech. [2] Nicholas Lanier, Master of the King's Music in 1625. [3] wethers: rams. [4] Cf. N-97, line 10.

H–213B

[*A dialogue on Prince Charles his birth betweene 3 Shepherds:*]

Mirtillo. Aminta, and Amarillis[1]

Amint: *Good daie Mirtillo.*
Mirt: *And to you noe lesse*
Ambo: *And crownes of wheate fall on our Shepherdesse*
Amar: *And mirrthfull pipes to you.*
Mirt: *But saye what newes?*
Stirres in our Sheepewalks?
Ambo: *None.*
Amar: *Save that myne Ewes*
My weathers, lambs and kidds are well 5
I noething els can tell.
Amar: *Or that this daie, Menalcas mak's a feast*
To his Sheepeshearers.
Mirt: *These are the least*
But deare Amynta *and faire* Amaryllis
List but a while here on this Banke of Lillies
And lend an Eare to a report
The Countrey has.
Ambo: *From whence?*
Mirt: *The Court.*
Twoe dayes before the shutting upp of Maye.
(With whiter wooll becladd the daie)
To Englands *joye a* Prince *was borne* 15
Softe as the Childhood of the Morne
Ambo: Pan *pipe to him, and bleats of lambes and sheepe*
Lett Lullabie *this preettie* Prince *asleepe*
Mirt: *And that his* Birth *might bee more singular*
Att Noone of daie appear'd a starre 20
Bright as the Wisemens *torch that guided them*
To Gods Babe borne att Bethelem
Amar: *But is't a sinne if wee*
Should goe this Child to see
Mirt: *Not soe, not soe: But if soe bee it prove* 25
Allmost a fault, 'tis but a fault of love.

Amynta: *Yea but* Mirtillo *I have heard it tould*
Those Learned *men brought* Incense, Myrrh,
[*and gold.*
And Spices *sweete*
And lay'd them downe att their Kings feete
Amar: *'Tis true.*
Mirt: *is true.*
Omnes: *And each of us will bring*
Unto our Blooming Kinge
A Neat
Though not soe great
An Offeringe 35
Amar: *A* Garland *for my guifte shalbee*
Of flowers ne're suckt by Theeving Bee
And all most Sweete, yett all lesse sweete then hee
Amynta: *And I will laye before his viewe*
Leaves dropping downe the honey dewe 40
Mirt: *And I a* Sheehooke *will bestowe*
To make his little Kingshipp *knowe*
As hee's a Prince *hee's* Shepheard *too.*
Chorus: *Come letts make hast and tymely letts be drest*
And quickly give the swiftest Grace is best
And when before him wee have lay'd our
[*treasures*
Weele blesse his face, then backe to
[*Countrey pleasures*

[1] Not included in this form in *Hesperides;* from Rosenbach MS 293/23 (formerly 188), pp. 94–95; not previously recorded by Herrick's editors. The main text is italicized here to distinguish it from the poems in *Hesperides.* The abbreviations for the speakers' names in the MS appear internally in lines 1, 3, 4, 8, 12 as "M:" or "Am:" but are here expanded. A variant text of this early version occurs in Rosenbach MS 293/27 (formerly 189), pp. 250–1 and is printed on pp. 460–1 in Martin's edition; it is the source of the bracketed title. Ambo—both—refers to Aminta and Amarillis.

H-214 *To the Lark.*

GOod speed, for I this day
Betimes my Mattens say:
Because I doe
Begin to wooe:
Sweet singing Lark, 5
Be thou the Clark,
And know thy when
To say, *Amen.*
And if I prove
Blest in my love; 10
Then thou shalt be
High-Priest to me,
At my returne,
To Incense burne;
And so to solemnize 15
Love's, and my Sacrifice.

H-215 *The Bubble. A Song.*

TO my revenge, and to her desp'rate feares,
Flie thou madd[1] Bubble of my sighs, and tears.
In the wild aire, when thou hast rowl'd about,
And (like a blasting Planet) found her out;
Stoop, mount, passe by to take her eye, then glare 5
Like to a dreadfull Comet in the Aire:
Next, when thou dost perceive her fixed sight,
For thy revenge to be most opposite;
Then like a Globe, or Ball of Wild-fire,[2] flie,
And break thy self in shivers on her eye. 10

[1] misprinted as *made.* [2] spontaneously ignited marsh gas; *ignis fatuus.*

H-216 *A Meditation for his Mistresse.*

1. YOu are a *Tulip* seen to day,
But (Dearest) of so short a stay;
That where you grew, scarce man can say.

2. You are a lovely *July-flower,*
Yet one rude wind, or ruffling shower,
Will force you hence, (and in an houre.)

3. You are a sparkling *Rose* i'th'bud,
Yet lost, ere that chast flesh and blood
Can shew where you or grew, or stood.

4. You are a full-spread faire-set Vine,
And can with Tendrills love intwine,
Yet dry'd, ere you distill your Wine.

5. You are like Balme inclosed (well)
In *Amber,* or some *Chrystall* shell,
Yet lost ere you transfuse your smell.

6. You are a dainty *Violet,*
Yet wither'd, ere you can be set
Within the Virgins Coronet.

7. You are the *Queen* all flowers among,
But die you must (faire Maid) ere long,
As He, the maker of this Song.

H–217

The bleeding hand: or, *The sprig of Eglantine given to a maid.*

FRom this bleeding hand of mine,
Take this sprig of *Eglantine.*
Which (though sweet unto your smell)
Yet the fretfull bryar will tell,
He who plucks the sweets shall prove 5
Many thorns to be in Love.

H–218

Lyrick for Legacies.

GOld I've none, for use or show,
Neither Silver to bestow[1]
At my death; but thus much know,
That each Lyrick here shall be
Of my love a Legacie, 5
Left to all posterity.

Gentle friends, then doe but please,
To accept such coynes as these;
As my last Remembrances.

[1] Acts iii.6, "Silver and gold have I none; but such as I have give I thee."

H–219

A Dirge upon the Death of the Right Valiant Lord, Bernard Stuart.[1]

1. HEnce, hence, profane; soft silence let us have;
While we this *Trentall*[2] sing about thy Grave.

2. Had Wolves or Tigers seen but thee,
They wo'd have shew'd civility;
And in compassion of thy yeeres, 5
Washt those thy purple wounds with tears.
But since th'art slaine; and in thy fall,
The drooping Kingdome suffers all.

Chorus.

This we will doe; we'll daily come
And offer Tears upon thy Tomb: 10
And if that they will not suffice,
Thou shalt have soules for sacrifice.

Sleepe in thy peace, while we with spice perfume thee,
And *Cedar*[3] wash thee, that no times consume thee.

3. Live, live thou dost, and shalt; for why? 15
Soules doe not with their bodies die:
Ignoble off-springs, they may fall
Into the flames of Funerall:
When as the chosen seed shall spring
Fresh, and for ever flourishing. 20

Chorus.

And times to come shall, weeping, read thy glory,
Lesse in these Marble stones, then in thy story.

[1] the 3rd Duke of Lennox's 6th son, killed near Chester Sept. 24, 1645. [2] in Roman Catholic usage a set of 30 requiem masses; here a dirge or month of daily dirges; cf. line 9. [3] preservative cedar oil.

H–220 *To* Perenna, *a Mistresse.*

DEare *Perenna*, prethee come,
And with *Smallage*[1] dresse my Tomb:
Adde a *Cypresse*-sprig thereto,
With a teare; and so *Adieu*.

[1] celery or parsley.

H–221 *Great boast, small rost.*

OF Flanks and Chines of Beefe doth *Gorrell* boast
He has at home; but who tasts boil'd or rost?
Look in his Brine-tub, and you shall find there
Two stiffe-blew-Pigs-feet, and a sow's cleft eare.

H–222 *Upon a Bleare-ey'd woman.*

WIther'd with yeeres, and bed-rid *Mumma* lyes;
Dry-rosted all, but raw yet in her eyes.

H–223
The Fairie Temple: or, Oberons *Chappell.*[1] *Dedicated to Master* John Merrifield, *Counsellor at Law.*

RAre Temples thou hast seen, I know,
And rich for in and outward show:
Survey this Chappell, built, alone,
Without or Lime, or Wood, or Stone:
Then say, if one th'ast seene more fine 5
Then this, the Fairies once, now *Thine*.

The Temple.

A Way enchac't with glasse and beads
There is, that to the Chappel leads:
Whose structure (for his holy rest)
Is here the *Halcion's* curious nest:[2]

Into the which who looks shall see 5
His *Temple of Idolatry:*
Where he of *God-heads* has such store,
As *Rome's Pantheon* had not more.
His house of *Rimmon,*[3] this he calls,
Girt with small bones, instead of walls. 10
First, in a *Neech,*[4] more black then jet,
His Idol-Cricket there is set:
Then in a Polisht Ovall by
There stands his *Idol-Beetle-flie:*
Next in an Arch, akin to this, 15
His *Idol-Canker*[5] seated is:
Then in a Round, is plac't by these,
His golden god, *Cantharides.*[6]
So that where ere ye look, ye see,
No *Capitoll,* no *Cornish*[7] free, 20
Or *Freeze,* from this fine Fripperie.
Now this the Fairies wo'd have known,
Theirs is a mixt Religion.
And some have heard the Elves it call
Part Pagan, part Papisticall. 25
If unto me all Tongues were granted,
I co'd not speak the Saints here painted.
Saint *Tit,* Saint *Nit,* Saint *Is,* Saint *Itis,*
Who 'gainst *Mabs-state*[8] plac't here right is.
Saint *Will o'th'Wispe* (of no great bignes) 30
But *alias* call'd here *Fatuus ignis.*
Saint *Frip,* Saint *Trip,* Saint *Fill,* Saint *Fillie,*[9]
Neither those other-Saint-ships will I
Here goe about for to recite
Their number (almost) infinite, 35
Which one by one here set downe are
In this most curious Calendar.
First, at the entrance of the gate,
A little-Puppet-Priest doth wait,
Who squeaks to all the commers there, 40
Favour your tongues,[10] *who enter here.*
Pure hands bring hither, without staine.
A second pules, *Hence, hence, profane.*
Hard by, i'th'shell of halfe a nut,
The Holy-water there is put: 45
A little brush of Squirrils haires,
(Compos'd of odde, not even paires)
Stands in the Platter, or close by,

To purge the Fairie Family.
Neere to the Altar stands the Priest,
There off'ring up the Holy-Grist:[11]
Ducking in Mood,[12] and perfect Tense,
With (much-good-do't him) reverence.
The Altar is not here foure-square,
Nor in a forme Triangular; 55
Nor made of glasse, or wood, or stone,[13]
But of a little Transverce bone;
Which boyes, and Bruckel'd[14] children call
(Playing for Points and Pins) *Cockall.*[15]
Whose Linnen-Drapery is a thin 60
Subtile and ductile Codlin's skin;[16]
Which o're the board is smoothly spred,
With little Seale-work Damasked.
The Fringe that circumbinds it too,
Is Spangle-work of trembling dew, 65
Which, gently gleaming, makes a show,
Like Frost-work glitt'ring on the Snow.
Upon this fetuous[17] board doth stand
Something for *Shew-bread,*[18] and at hand[19]
(Just in the middle of the Altar) 70
Upon an end, the *Fairie-Psalter,*
Grac't with the Trout-flies curious wings,
Which serve for watched[20] Ribbanings.
Now, we must know, the Elves are led
Right by the Rubrick, which they read. 75
And if Report of them be true,
They have their Text for what they doe;
I, and their Book of Canons too.
And, as Sir *Thomas Parson* tells,
They have their Book of Articles: 80
And if that Fairie Knight not lies,
They have their Book of Homilies:
And other Scriptures, that designe
A short, but righteous discipline.
The Bason stands the board upon 85
To take the Free-Oblation:
A little Pin-dust; which they hold
More precious, then we prize our gold:
Which charity they give to many
Poore of the Parish, (if there's any) 90
Upon the ends of these neat Railes
(Hatcht,[21] with the Silver-light of snails)

The Elves, in formall manner, fix
Two pure, and holy *Candlesticks:*
In either which a small tall bent[22] 95
Burns for the Altars ornament.
For sanctity, they have, to these,
Their curious *Copes* and *Surplices*
Of cleanest *Cobweb,* hanging by
In their *Religious Vesterie.* 100
They have their *Ash-pans,* and their *Brooms*
To purge the Chappel and the rooms:
Their many *mumbling Masse-priests* here,
And many a dapper *Chorister.*
Their ush'ring *Vergers,* here likewise, 105
Their *Canons,* and their *Chaunteries:*
Of *Cloyster-Monks* they have enow,
I, and their *Abby-Lubbers* too:
And if their Legend doe not lye,
They much affect the *Papacie:* 110
And since the last is dead, there's hope,
Elve Boniface shall next be Pope.
They have their *Cups* and *Chalices;*
Their *Pardons* and *Indulgences:*
Their *Beads* of Nits,[23] *Bels, Books,* and *Wax* 115
Candles (forsooth) and other knacks:
Their *Holy Oyle,* their *Fasting-Spittle;*[24]
Their *sacred Salt* here, (not a little.)
Dry *chips,* old *shooes, rags, grease,* and *bones;*
Beside their *Fumigations,* 120
To drive the Devill from the Cod-piece[25]
Of the Fryar, (of work an odde-piece.)
Many a trifle too, and trinket,
And for what use, scarce man wo'd think it.
Next, then, upon the *Chanters* side 125
An *Apples-core* is hung up dry'd,
With ratling Kirnils, which is rung
To call to Morn, and Even-Song.
The Saint, to which the most he prayes
And offers *Incense* Nights and dayes, 130
The *Lady*[26] of the *Lobster* is,
Whose foot-pace[27] he doth stroak and kisse;
And, humbly, chives[28] of Saffron brings,
For his most cheerfull offerings.
When, after these, h'as paid his vows, 135
He lowly to the Altar bows:

And then he dons the Silk-worms shed,[29]
(Like a *Turks Turbant* on his head)
And reverently departeth thence,
Hid in a cloud of *Frankincense:* 140
And by the glow-worms light wel guided,
Goes to the Feast[30] that's now provided.

[1] H-293, H-443, H-638 are also fairy poems, all probably composed about the same time as Sir Simeon Steward, *A Description of the King of Faeries Clothes,* 1626, and Drayton, *Nymphidia,* 1627. See Drayton's *Works,* ed. Hebel, V, 202, 222–23; M. W. Latham, *The Elizabethan Fairies* (1930), pp. 208–11. [2] The elaborately contrived nest of the halcyon or kingfisher was fabled to charm winds and waves to rest. [3] Syrian god; see II Kings v.18. [4] niche. [5] canker worm. [6] venomous green flies used, when dried, to raise blisters; the term is also applied to beetles. [7] cornice. [8] the Fairy Queen's canopied throne. [9] *Tit, Nit,* and *Trip* also occur in *Nymphidia,* lines 162–68; Grosart suggests that the imaginary saints' names correspond with those of Saints Titus, Neot, Idus, Fridian, Trypho, Felan, and Felix. [10] i.e. keep silent—*Favete linguis,* Horace, Odes, III, 2, 2. This and other italicized Latin tags occur in Jonson's *Sejanus,* V, 171–77; his notes reveal their sources. [11] grain or meal. [12] in a manner appropriate to the grammatical mood (predication, wish, command, etc.) of the words used in the service. [13] refers to theologians' disputes about the proper shape and material of an altar. [14] begrimed. [15] knuckle-bone; four are used for the game. [16] apple skin, here used as altarcloth. [17] featous: artistically fashioned, handsome. [18] unleavened bread placed by Israelite priests before Yahweh on a table beside the altar of incense. [19] within reach of the priest. The 1549 Anglican Prayerbook instructed priests to stand before the middle of the altar at the beginning of the communion service. [20] watchet: light blue or green. [21] inlaid. [22] grass. [23] rosaries of nuts. [24] the saliva of a person who is fasting. [25] a flap or bag in the front of breeches. Cf. the fumigation to drive away the devil in Tobit vi.16–17. [26] part of a lobster's digestive apparatus slightly resembling a seated female figure. [27] raised portion of a floor, or a mat. [28] shreds. [29] cocoon. [30] described in H-293.

H–224

To Mistresse Katherine Bradshaw, *the lovely, that crowned him with Laurel.*

MY Muse in Meads has spent her many houres,
Sitting, and sorting severall sorts of flowers,
To make for others garlands; and to set
On many a head here, many a Coronet:
But, amongst All encircled here, not one 5
Gave her a day of Coronation;
Till you (sweet Mistresse) came and enterwove
A *Laurel* for her, (ever young as love)
You first of all crown'd her; she must of due,
Render for that, a crowne of life[1] to you. 10

[1] phrase from Rev. ii.10.

H–225 *The Plaudite,[1] or end of life.*

IF after rude and boystrous seas,
My wearyed Pinnace here finds ease:[2]
If so it be I've gain'd the shore
With safety of a faithful Ore:
If having run my Barque on ground, 5
Ye see the aged Vessell crown'd:
What's to be done? but on the Sands
Ye dance, and sing, and now clap hands.
The first Act's doubtfull, (but we say)
It is the last commends the Play. 10

[1] appeal for applause at the end of a performance. [2] based on Ovid, *De Remedio Amoris,* 811–2; cf. H-1127.

H–226

To the most vertuous Mistresse Pot, *who many times entertained him.*

WHen I through all my many Poems look,
And see your selfe to beautifie my Book;
Me thinks that onely lustre doth appeare
A Light ful-filling all the Region here.

Guild still with flames this Firmament, and be 5
A Lamp Eternall to my Poetrie.
Which if it now, or shall hereafter shine,
'Twas by your splendour (Lady) not by mine.
The Oile was yours; and that I owe for yet:
He payes the halfe, who do's confesse the Debt.[1] 10

[1] If Mistress Pot is a pot to hold liquor, *vertuous* refers to the efficacy of its contents: they *beautifie* the book by inspiring the poems: their *Light, flames, Lamp,* and *splendour* find parallels in H-197, lines 10–12; however, the *Oile* is not the *Oyle of Maintenance* of H-117. But the use of the proverb at the end may indicate that the poem is addressed to a real person.

H–227

To Musique, to becalme his Fever.

1. CHarm me asleep, and melt me so
With thy Delicious Numbers;
That being ravisht, hence I goe
Away in easie slumbers.
Ease my sick head,
And make my bed,
Thou Power that canst sever
From me this ill:[1]
And quickly still:
Though thou not kill 10
My Fever.

2. Thou sweetly canst convert the same
From a consuming fire,
Into a gentle-licking flame,
And make it thus expire.
Then make me weep
My paines asleep;
And give me such reposes,
That I, poore I,
May think, thereby, 20
I live and die
'Mongst Roses.

3. Fall on me like a silent dew,
Or like those Maiden showrs,
Which, by the peepe of day, doe strew
A Baptime o're the flowers.

Melt, melt my paines,
With thy soft straines;
That having ease me given,
With full delight, 30
I leave this light;
And take my flight
For Heaven.

[1] Cf. Psalm xli.3, "The Lord will strengthen him upon the bed of languishing; thou wilt make all his bed in his sickness."

H–228

Upon a Gentlewoman with a sweet Voice.

SO long[1] you did not sing, or touch your Lute,
We knew 'twas Flesh and Blood, that there sate mute.
But when your Playing, and your Voice came in,
'Twas no more you then, but a *Cherubin.*

[1] So long as.

H–229

Upon Cupid.[1]

AS lately I a Garland bound,
'Mongst Roses, I there *Cupid* found:
I took him, put him in my cup,
And drunk with Wine, I drank him up.
Hence then it is, that my poore brest 5
Co'd never since find any rest.

[1] based on *Anacreontea,* VI.

H–230

Upon Julia's *breasts.*

DIsplay thy breasts, my *Julia,* there let me
Behold that circummortall[1] purity:
Betweene whose glories, there my lips Ile lay,
Ravisht, in that faire *Via Lactea.*[2]

[1] more than mortal. [2] Milky Way.

H–231 *Best to be merry.*

FOoles are they, who never know
How the times away doe goe:
But for us, who wisely see
Where the bounds of black Death be:
Let's live merrily, and thus 5
Gratifie the *Genius.*

H–232 *The Changes to* Corinna.

BE not proud, but now encline
Your soft eare to Discipline.
You have changes in your life,
Sometimes peace, and sometimes strife:
You have ebbes of face and flowes, 5
As your health or comes, or goes;
You have hopes, and doubts, and feares
Numberlesse, as are your haires.
You have Pulses that doe beat
High, and passions lesse of heat. 10
You are young, but must be old,
And, to these, ye must be told,
Time, ere long, will come and plow
Loathed Furrowes in your brow:
And the dimnesse of your eye 15
Will no other thing imply,
But you must die
As well as I.

H–233 *No Lock against Letcherie.*

BArre close as you can, and bolt fast too your doore,
To keep out the Letcher, and keep in the whore:
Yet, quickly you'l see by the turne of a pin,[1]
The Whore to come out, or the Letcher come in.

[1] bolt.

H–234 *Neglect.*

ARt quickens Nature; Care will make a face:
Neglected beauty perisheth apace.[1]

[1] Cf. Burton, 3,2,3,3 (6 ed. p. 474): "why is all this labour, all this cost, preparation, riding, running, far fetched, and dear bought stuffe? *Because forsooth they would be fair and fine, and where nature is defective, supply it by art.*"

H–235 *Upon himselfe.*

MOp-ey'd[1] I am, as some have said,
Because I've liv'd so long a maid:
But grant that I sho'd wedded be,
Sho'd I a jot the better see?
No, I sho'd think, that Marriage might, 5
Rather then mend, put out the light.

[1] shortsighted.

H–236 *Upon a Physitian.*

THou cam'st to cure me (Doctor) of my cold,
And caught'st thy selfe the more by twenty fold:
Prethee goe home; and for thy credit be
First cur'd thy selfe;[1] then come and cure me.

[1] Luke iv.23, "Physician, heal thyself."

H–237 *Upon* Sudds *a Laundresse.*

SUdds Launders Bands[1] in pisse; and starches them
Both with her Husband's, and her own tough fleame.

[1] neckbands; collars. Cf. Martial, VI, 93, 1–2. Pliny, XXVIII, 8, remarks on the use of camels' urine for washing clothes; in Colonial America urine was used to wash the filth and lanolin off raw wool.

H–238 *To the Rose. Song.*

1. GOe happy Rose, and enterwove
With other Flowers, bind my Love.[1]
Tell her too, she must not be,
Longer flowing, longer free,
That so oft has fetter'd me.

2. Say (if she's fretfull) I have bands
Of Pearle, and Gold, to bind her hands:
Tell her, if she struggle still,
I have Mirtle rods, (at will)
For to tame, though not to kill.

3. Take thou my blessing, thus, and goe,
And tell her this, but doe not so,
Lest a handsome anger flye,
Like a Lightning, from her eye,
And burn thee'up, as well as I.

[1] Martial, VII, 89, inspired the opening lines and probably also Waller's "Go, lovely Rose."

H–239 *Upon* Guesse. *Epigram.*

GUesse cuts his shooes, and limping, goes about
To have men think he's troubled with the Gout:
But 'tis no Gout (beleeve it) but hard Beere,
Whose acrimonious humour bites him here.[1]

[1] In Martial, VII, 39, Caelius pretends to have gout in order to avoid working in the early morning.

H–240 *To his Booke.*

THou art a plant sprung up to wither never,
But like a Laurell, to grow green for ever.

H-241 *Upon a painted Gentlewoman.*

MEn say y'are faire; and faire ye are, 'tis true;
But (Hark!) we praise the Painter now, not you.[1]

[1] Cf. Donne's epigram "Phryne," which, according to Drummond was often quoted by Jonson: "Thy flattering picture, *Phryne*, is like thee, / Onely in this, that you both painted be."

H-242 *Upon a crooked Maid.*

CRooked you are, but that dislikes not me;
So you be straight, where Virgins straight sho'd be.

H-243 *Draw Gloves.*

AT Draw-Gloves[1] we'l play,
And prethee, let's lay
A wager, and let it be this;
Who first to the Summe
Of twenty shall come, 5
Shall have for his winning a kisse.

[1] a game won by being the first to remove gloves from the twenty fingers of himself and his partner.

H-244 *To Musick, to becalme a sweet-sick-youth.*

CHarms, that call down the moon from out her sphere,
On this sick youth work your enchantments here:
Bind up his senses with your numbers, so,
As to entrance his paine, or cure his woe.
Fall gently, gently, and a while him keep 5
Lost in the civill Wildernesse[1] of sleep:
That done, then let him, dispossest of paine,
Like to a slumbring Bride, awake againe.[2]

[1] Cf. H-83, line 12: "wilde civility" and H-665, line 6, "civill Wilderness." [2] Cf. the song "Care charming sleep" in John Fletcher's

Valentinian, V, ii.13–22, especially "fall like a Cloud / in gentle showres . . . / Passe by his troubled senses; sing his paine / Like hollow murmuring winde, or silver Rayne? / Into his senses gently, Oh gently slide, / And kisse him into slumbers like a Bride."

H–245

To the High and Noble Prince, GEORGE, *Duke, Marquesse, and Earle of* Buckingham.[1]

NEver my Book's perfection did appeare,
Til I had got the name of VILLARS here.
Now 'tis so full, that when therein I look,
I see a Cloud of Glory fills my Book.
Here stand it stil to dignifie our Muse, 5
Your sober Hand-maid; who doth wisely chuse,
Your Name to be a *Laureat Wreathe* to Hir,
Who doth both love and feare you *Honour'd Sir.*

[1] George Villiers. Herrick was one of his chaplains during the expedition to the Isle of Rhé, 1627.

H–246

His Recantation.

LOve, I recant,
And pardon crave,
That lately I offended,
But 'twas,
Alas, 5
To make a brave,[1]
But no disdaine intended.

No more Ile vaunt,
For now I see,
Thou onely hast the power, 10
To find,
And bind
A heart that's free,
And slave it in an houre.

[1] to act the bravo.

H–247 *The comming of good luck.*

SO Good-luck came, and on my roofe did light,
Like noyse-lesse Snow; or as the dew of night:
Not all at once, but gently, as the trees
Are, by the Sun-beams, tickel'd by degrees.

H–248 *The Present:* or, *The Bag of the Bee.*

FLy to my Mistresse, pretty pilfring Bee,
And say, thou bring'st this Hony-bag from me:
When on her lip, thou hast thy sweet dew plac't,
Mark, if her tongue, but slily, steale a taste.
If so, we live; if not, with mournfull humme, 5
Tole forth my death; next, to my buryall come.

H–249 *On Love.*

LOve bade me aske a gift,
And I no more did move,
But this, that I might shift
Still with my clothes, my Love:[1]
That favour granted was; 5
Since which, though I love many,
Yet so it comes to passe,
That long I love not any.

[1] I asked only this: that I might change the object of my love every time I changed my clothes.

H–250 *The Hock-cart,* or *Harvest home: To the Right Honourable,* Mildmay, *Earle of* Westmorland.[1]

COme Sons of Summer, by whose toile,
We are the Lords of Wine and Oile:
By whose tough labours, and rough hands,
We rip up first, then reap our lands.

Crown'd with the eares of corne, now come, 5
And, to the Pipe, sing Harvest home.
Come forth, my Lord, and see the Cart
Drest up with all the Country Art.
See, here a *Maukin*,[2] there a sheet,
As spotlesse pure, as it is sweet: 10
The Horses, Mares, and frisking Fillies,
(Clad, all, in Linnen, white as Lillies.)
The Harvest Swaines, and Wenches bound
For joy, to see the *Hock-cart* crown'd.
About the Cart, heare, how the Rout 15
Of Rurall Younglings raise the shout;
Pressing before, some coming after,
Those with a shout, and these with laughter.
Some blesse the Cart; some kisse the sheaves;
Some prank them up with Oaken leaves: 20
Some crosse the Fill-horse;[3] some with great
Devotion, stroak the home-borne wheat:
While other Rusticks, lesse attent
To Prayers, then to Merryment,
Run after with their breeches rent. 25
Well, on, brave boyes, to your Lords Hearth,
Glitt'ring with fire; where, for your mirth,
Ye shall see first the large and cheefe
Foundation of your Feast, Fat Beefe:
With Upper Stories, Mutton, Veale 30
And Bacon,[4] (which makes full the meale)
With sev'rall dishes standing by,
As here a Custard, there a Pie,
And here all tempting Frumentie.[5]
And for to make the merry cheere, 35
If smirking Wine be wanting here,
There's that, which drowns all care, stout Beere;
Which freely drink to your Lords health,
Then to the Plough, (the Common-wealth)
Next to your Flailes, your Fanes,[6] your Fatts;[7] 40
Then to the Maids with Wheaten Hats:
To the rough Sickle, and crookt Sythe,
Drink frollick boyes, till all be blythe.
Feed, and grow fat; and as ye eat,
Be mindfull, that the lab'ring Neat 45
(As you) may have their fill of meat.
And know, besides, ye must revoke[8]
The patient Oxe unto the Yoke,

And all goe back unto the Plough
And Harrow, (though they'r hang'd up now.) 50
And, you must know, your Lords word's true,
Feed him ye must, whose food fils you.
And that this pleasure is like raine,
Not sent ye for to drowne your paine,
But for to make it spring againe.[9] 55

[1] See H-112, n.1. [2] malkin: a pole with cloth bound around one end, used as a sort of broom or as a scarecrow or effigy. [3] Some sit astride the shaft-horse. [4] pork. [5] wheat boiled in milk, sweetened, and flavored with cinnamon or the like. [6] fans for winnowing grain. [7] vats, barrels, and the like—presumably for storing grain. [8] bring back. [9] For a similar classical poem, see Tibullus, II, 1.

H–251 *The Perfume.*

TO morrow, *Julia,* I betimes must rise,
For some small fault, to offer sacrifice:
The Altar's ready; Fire to consume
The fat; breathe thou, and there's the rich perfume.

H–252 *Upon her Voice.*

LEt but thy voice engender with the string,
And Angels will be borne, while thou dost sing.

H–253 *Not to love.*

HE that will not love, must be
My Scholar, and learn this of me:
There be in Love as many feares,
As the Summers Corne has eares:
Sighs, and sobs, and sorrowes more 5
Then the sand, that makes the shore:
Freezing cold, and firie heats,
Fainting swoones, and deadly sweats;
Now an Ague, then a Fever,
Both tormenting Lovers ever. 10
Wod'st thou know, besides all these,
How hard a woman 'tis to please?

How crosse, how sullen, and how soone
She shifts and changes like the Moone.
How false, how hollow she's in heart; 15
And how she is her owne least part:
How high she's priz'd, and worth but small;
Little thou't love, or not at all.

H–254 *To Musick. A Song.*

MUsick, thou *Queen of Heaven,* Care-charming-spel,
That strik'st a stilnesse into hell:
Thou that tam'st *Tygers,* and fierce storms (that rise)
With thy soule-melting Lullabies:
Fall down, down, down, from those thy chiming spheres,
To charme our soules, as thou enchant'st our eares.

H–255 *To the Western wind.*

1. SWeet Western Wind, whose luck it is,
(Made rivall with the aire)
To give *Perenn'as* lip a kisse,
And fan her wanton haire.

2. Bring me but one, Ile promise thee,
Instead of common showers,
Thy wings shall be embalm'd by me,
And all beset with flowers.

H–256 *Upon the death of his Sparrow. An Elegie.*

WHy doe not all fresh maids appeare
To work Love's Sampler onely here,
Where spring-time smiles throughout the yeare?
Are not here *Rose-buds, Pinks,* all flowers,
Nature begets by th'Sun and showers, 5
Met in one Hearce-cloth, to ore-spred
The body of the under-dead?[1]

Phill, the late dead, the late dead Deare,
O! may no eye distill a Teare
For you once lost, who weep not here! 10
Had *Lesbia* (too-too-kind) but known
This Sparrow, she had scorn'd her own:
And for this dead which under-lies,
Wept out her heart, as well as eyes.
But endlesse Peace, sit here, and keep 15
My *Phill*, the time[2] he has to sleep,
And thousand Virgins come and weep,
To make these flowrie Carpets show
Fresh, as their blood; and ever grow,
Till passengers shall spend their doome, 20
Not *Virgil's* Gnat had such a Tomb.[3]

[1] The flowers resemble a hearse-cloth spread over the grave of the pet sparrow. Poems on such deaths constitute a minor genre. Cf. Catullus, III, where Lesbia mourns for her sparrow and Marvell, "The Nymph complaining for the death of her Faun." [2] guard him during the time that. [3] In *Culex*, attributed to Virgil, a gnat stings a shepherd to warn him of a serpent. The shepherd kills both, is reproached for ingratitude by the ghost of the gnat, and, in contrition, erects a monument to it. See the translation by Spenser.

H–257

To Primroses fill'd with morning-dew.

1. WHy doe ye weep, sweet Babes? can Tears
Speak griefe in you,
Who were but borne
Just as the modest Morne
Teem'd[1] her refreshing dew? 5
Alas you have not known that shower,
That marres a flower;
Nor felt th'unkind
Breath of a blasting wind;
Nor are ye worne with yeares; 10
Or warpt, as we,
Who think it strange to see,
Such pretty flowers, (like to Orphans young)
To speak by Teares, before ye have a Tongue.

2. Speak, whimp'ring Younglings, and make known
The reason, why
Ye droop, and weep;
Is it for want of sleep?
Or childish Lullabie?
Or that ye have not seen as yet 20
The *Violet*?
Or brought a kisse
From that Sweet-heart, to this?
No, no, this sorrow shown
By your teares shed, 25
Wo'd have this Lecture read,
That things of greatest, so of meanest worth,
Conceiv'd with grief are, and with teares brought forth.

[1] gave birth to.

H–258 *How Roses came red.*[1]

1. ROses at first were white,
Till they co'd not agree,
Whether my *Sapho's* breast,
Or they more white sho'd be.

2. But being vanquisht quite,
A blush their cheeks bespred;
Since which (beleeve the rest)
The *Roses* first came red.

[1] partly based on Horace, *Carmina*, II, 9.

H–259

Comfort to a Lady upon the Death of her Husband.

DRy your sweet cheek, long drown'd with sorrows raine;
Since Clouds disperst, Suns guild the Aire again.
Seas chafe and fret, and beat, and over-boile;
But turne soone after calme, as Balme, or Oile.
Winds have their time to rage; but when they cease, 5
The leavie-trees nod in a still-born peace.

Your storme is over; Lady, now appeare
Like to the peeping-spring-time of the yeare.
Off then with grave clothes; put fresh colours on;
And flow, and flame, in your *Vermillion*. 10
Upon your cheek sate *Ysicles* awhile;
Now let the Rose raigne like a Queene, and smile.

H–260 *How Violets came blew.*

LOve on a day (wise Poets tell)
Some time in wrangling spent,
Whether the Violets sho'd excell,
Or she, in sweetest scent.

But *Venus* having lost the day, 5
Poore Girles, she fell on you;
And beat ye so, (as some dare say)
Her blowes did make ye blew.

H–261 *Upon* Groynes.[1] *Epigram.*

GRoynes, for his fleshly *Burglary* of late,
Stood in the *Holy-Forum*[2] *Candidate:*[3]
The word[4] is *Roman;* but in English knowne:
Penance, and standing so, are both but one.

[1] the groin is, figuratively, the seat of lust. [2] i.e. in Church, as a penitent. [3] Candidates (from *candidatus*, clothed in white) running for public office in ancient Rome stood in the Forum wearing white togas; *candidate* may also be used as an adjective (from the past participle of *candidare*, to make glittering white); Herrick puns on *holey* and *fore-room.* [4] penance, *penitentia*—another play on words.

H–262 *To the Willow-tree.*

1. THou art to all lost love the best,
The onely true plant found,
Wherewith young men and maids distrest,
And left of love, are crown'd.

2. When once the Lovers Rose is dead,
   Or laid aside forlorne;
Then Willow-garlands, 'bout the head,
   Bedew'd with teares, are worne.

3. When with Neglect, (the Lovers bane)
   Poore Maids rewarded be,
For their love lost; their onely gaine
   Is but a Wreathe from thee.

4. And underneath thy cooling shade,
   (When weary of the light)
The love-spent Youth, and love-sick Maid,
   Come to weep out the night.

H–263

Mistresse Elizabeth Wheeler,[1] *under the name of the lost Shepardesse.*

AMong the *Mirtles*, as I walkt,
Love and my sighs thus intertalkt:
Tell me, said I, in deep distresse,
Where I may find my Shepardesse.
Thou foole, said Love, know'st thou not this? 5
In every thing that's sweet, she is.
In yond' *Carnation* goe and seek,
There thou shalt find her lip and cheek:
In that ennamel'd *Pansie* by,
There thou shalt have her curious[2] eye: 10
In bloome of *Peach*, and *Roses* bud,
There waves the Streamer of her blood.
'Tis true, said I, and thereupon
I went to pluck them one by one,
To make of parts an union; 15
But on a sudden all were gone.
At which I stopt; Said Love, these be
The true resemblances of thee;
For as these flowers, thy joyes must die,
And in the turning of an eye; 20
And all thy hopes of her must wither,
Like those short sweets ere knit together.

[1] the poet's cousin; see H-130. [2] delicate, excellent.

H–264

TO THE KING.

IF when these Lyricks (CESAR) You shall heare,
And that *Apollo* shall so touch Your eare,
As for to make this, that, or any one
Number, Your owne, by free Adoption;
That Verse, of all the Verses here, shall be 5
The Heire to This *great Realme of Poetry.*

H–265

TO THE QUEENE.

GOddesse of Youth, and Lady of the Spring,
(Most fit to be the Consort to a King)
Be pleas'd to rest you in *This Sacred Grove,*[1]
Beset with *Mirtles;* whose each leafe drops Love.
Many a sweet-fac't *Wood-Nymph* here is seene, 5
Of which chast *Order You* are now the *Queene:*
Witness their *Homage,* when they come and strew
Your Walks with Flowers, and give their Crowns to you.
Your Leavie-Throne (with *Lilly*-work) possesse;
And be both *Princesse* here, and *Poetresse.* 10

[1] probably the Garden of the Hesperides and, by extension, this volume of poems.

H–266

The Poets good wishes for the most hopefull and handsome Prince, the Duke of Yorke.[1]

MAy his pretty Duke-ship grow
Like t'a Rose of *Jericho:*
Sweeter far, then ever yet
Showrs or Sun-shines co'd beget.
May the Graces, and the Howers 5
Strew his hopes, and Him with flowers:

And so dresse him up with Love,
As to be the Chick of *Jove*.[2]
May the thrice-three-Sisters[3] sing
Him the Soveraigne of their Spring:[4] 10
And entitle none to be
Prince of *Hellicon*, but He.
May his soft foot, where it treads,
Gardens thence produce and Meads:
And those Meddowes full be set 15
With the Rose, and Violet.
May his ample Name be knowne
To the last succession:
And his actions high be told
Through the world, but writ in gold. 20

[1] the future James II, born Oct. 14, 1633, and immediately declared Duke of York. The poem was probably written to celebrate the birth or an early birthday. [2] Heaven's darling. [3] the Muses. [4] The Castalian spring on Mt. Parnassus and the springs of Aganippe and Hippocrene on Mt. Helicon were sacred to the Muses.

H–267

To Anthea, *who may command him any thing.*

BId me to live, and I will live
Thy Protestant[1] to be:
Or bid me love, and I will give
A loving heart to thee.

2. A heart as soft, a heart as kind,
A heart as sound and free,
As in the whole world thou canst find,
That heart Ile give to thee.

3. Bid that heart stay, and it will stay,
To honour thy Decree:
Or bid it languish quite away,
And't shall doe so for thee.

4. Bid me to weep, and I will weep,
While I have eyes to see:
And having none, yet I will keep
A heart to weep for thee.

5. Bid me despaire, and Ile despaire,
   Under that *Cypresse* tree:
   Or bid me die, and I will dare
   E'en Death, to die for thee.

6. Thou art my life, my love, my heart,
   The very eyes of me:
   And hast command of every part,
   To live and die for thee.

[1] a suitor; one who solemnly declares his love. Cf. H-154, title.

H–268 *Prevision, or Provision.*

THat Prince takes soone enough the Victors roome,
Who first provides, not to be overcome.[1]

[1] The prince who first makes provision not to be defeated in battle soon enough achieves the place of victor: based on Suetonius Paulinus in Tacitus, *Histories,* II, 25: *satis cito incipi,* etc.

H–269 *Obedience in Subjects.*[1]

THe Gods to Kings the Judgement give to sway:
The Subjects onely glory to obay.

[1] Tacitus, *Annals,* VI, 8, M. Terentius to Tiberius: *tibi summum,* etc.

H–270 *More potent, lesse peccant.*[1]

HE that may sin, sins least; Leave to transgresse
Enfeebles much the seeds of wickednesse.

[1] Ovid, *Amores,* III, 4, 9–10: *Cui peccare licet,* etc.

H-271 *Upon a maid that dyed the day she was marryed.*

THat Morne which saw me made a Bride,
The Ev'ning witnest that I dy'd.
Those holy lights, wherewith they guide
Unto the bed the bashfull Bride;
Serv'd, but as Tapers, for to burne, 5
And light my Reliques to their Urne.
This *Epitaph*, which here you see,
Supply'd the *Epithalamie*.

H-272 *Upon* Pink *an ill-fac'd Painter. Epigram.*

TO paint the Fiend, *Pink* would the Devill see;
And so he may, if he'll be rul'd by me:
Let but *Pink's* face i'th'Looking-glasse be showne,
And *Pink* may paint the Devill's by his owne.

H-273 *Upon* Brock. *Epigram.*

TO clense his eyes, *Tom Brock* makes much adoe,
But not his mouth (the fouler of the two.)
A clammie Reume makes loathsome both his eyes:
His mouth worse furr'd with oathes and blasphemies.

H-274 *To Meddowes.*

1. YE have been fresh and green,
 Ye have been fill'd with flowers:
And ye the Walks have been
 Where Maids have spent their houres.

2. You have beheld, how they
 With *Wicker Arks* did come
To kisse, and beare away
 The richer Couslips home.

3. Y'ave heard them sweetly sing,
And seen them in a Round:
Each Virgin, like a Spring,
With Hony-succles crown'd.

4. But now, we see, none here,
Whose silv'rie feet did tread,
And with dishevell'd Haire,
Adorn'd this smoother Mead.

5. Like Unthrifts, having spent,
Your stock, and needy grown,
Y'are left here to lament
Your poore estates, alone.

H–275 *Crosses.*

THough good things answer many good intents;
Crosses doe still bring forth the best events.[1]

[1] Cf. Ovid, *Metamorphoses*, VI, 574–5; trans. Sandys: "Great sorrow addes a quicknesse to conceit."

H–276 *Miseries.*

THough hourely comforts from the Gods we see,
No life is yet life-proofe from miserie.

H–277 *Laugh and lie downe.*[1]

Y'Ave laught enough (sweet) vary now your Text;
And laugh no more; or laugh, and lie down next.

[1] the name of a card game in which a loser was supposed to laugh and lay down his cards.

H–278 *To his Houshold gods.*

RIse, Houshold-gods, and let us goe;
But whither, I my selfe not know.
First, let us dwell on rudest seas;
Next, with severest Salvages;[1]

Last, let us make our best abode, 5
Where humane foot, as yet, ne'r trod:
Search worlds of Ice; and rather there
Dwell, then in lothed *Devonshire.*

[1] savages.

H–279 *To the Nightingale, and Robin-Red-brest.*

WHen I departed am, ring thou my knell,
Thou pittifull, and pretty *Philomel:*
And when I'm laid out for a Corse; then be
Thou *Sexton* (*Red-brest*) for to cover me.

H–280 *To the Yew and Cypresse to grace his Funerall.*

1. BOth you two have
Relation to the grave:
And where
The *Fun'rall-Trump* sounds, you are there.

2. I shall be made
Ere long a fleeting shade:
Pray come,
And doe some honour to my Tomb.

3. Do not deny
My last request; for I
Will be
Thankfull to you, or friends, for me.

H–281 *I call and I call.*

I Call, I call, who doe ye call?
The Maids to catch this Cowslip-ball:
But since these Cowslips fading be,
Troth, leave the flowers, and Maids, take me.
Yet, if that neither you will doe, 5
Speak but the word, and Ile take you.

H–282 *On a perfum'd Lady.*

YOu say y'are sweet; how sho'd we know
Whether that you be sweet or no?
From *Powders* and *Perfumes* keep free;
Then we shall smell how sweet you be.

H–283

A Nuptiall Song, or Epithalamie, on Sir Clipseby Crew *and his Lady.*[1]

1. WHat's that we see from far? the spring of Day
Bloom'd from the East, or faire Injewel'd May
Blowne out of April; or some New-
Star fill'd with glory to our view,
Reaching at heaven,
To adde a nobler Planet to the seven?
Say, or doe we not descrie
Some Goddesse, in a cloud of Tiffanie
To move, or rather the
Emergent *Venus* from the Sea? 10

2. 'Tis she! 'tis she! or else some more Divine
Enlightned substance; mark how from the Shrine
Of holy Saints she paces on,
Treading upon *Vermilion*
And *Amber;* Spice-
ing the Chafte[2] Aire with fumes of Paradise.
Then come on, come on, and yeeld
A savour like unto a blessed field,[3]
When the bedabled Morne
Washes the golden eares of corne. 20

3. See where she comes; and smell how all the street
Breathes Vine-yards and Pomgranats: O how sweet!
As a fir'd Altar, is each stone,
Perspiring pounded Cynamon.
The Phenix nest,
Built up of odours, burneth in her breast.
Who therein wo'd not consume
His soule to Ash-heaps in that rich perfume?
Bestroaking Fate the while
He burnes to Embers on the Pile. 30

4. *Himen, O Himen!* Tread the sacred ground;[4]
Shew thy white feet, and head with Marjoram crown'd:
Mount up thy flames, and let thy Torch[5]
Display the Bridegroom in the porch,
In his desires
More towring, more disparkling[6] then thy fires:
Shew her how his eyes do turne
And roule about, and in their motions burne
Their balls to Cindars: haste,
Or else to ashes he will waste. 40

5. Glide by the banks of Virgins then, and passe
The Shewers of Roses, lucky-foure-leav'd grasse:[7]
The while the cloud of younglings sing,
And drown yee with a flowrie Spring:
While some repeat
Your praise, and bless you, sprinkling you with Wheat:
While that others doe divine;[8]
Blest is the Bride, on whom the Sun doth shine;
And thousands gladly wish
You multiply, as doth a Fish. 50

6. And beautious Bride we do confess y'are wise,
In dealing forth these bashfull jealousies:[9]
In Lov's name do so; and a price
Set on your selfe, by being nice:[10]
But yet take heed;
What now you seem, be not the same indeed,
And turne *Apostate:* Love will
Part of the way be met; or sit stone-still.
On then, and though you slow-
ly go, yet, howsoever, go. 60

7. And now y'are enter'd; see the Codled[11] Cook
Runs from his *Torrid Zone,* to prie, and look,
And blesse his dainty Mistresse: see,
The Aged point out, This is she,
Who now must sway
The House (Love shield her) with her Yea and Nay:
And the smirk Butler thinks it
Sin, in's Nap'rie, not to express his wit;
Each striving to devise
Some gin,[12] wherewith to catch your eyes. 70

8. To bed, to bed, kind Turtles, now, and write
This the short'st day, and this the longest night;
But yet too short for you: 'tis we,
Who count this night as long as three,
Lying alone,
Telling the Clock strike Ten, Eleven, Twelve, One.
Quickly, quickly then prepare;
And let the Young-men and the Bride-maids share
Your Garters; and their joynts
Encircle with the Bride-grooms Points.[13] 80

9. By the Brides eyes, and by the teeming life
Of her green hopes, we charge ye, that no strife
(Farther then Gentlenes tends) gets place
Among ye, striving for her lace:
O doe not fall
Foule in these noble pastimes, lest ye call
Discord in, and so divide
The youthfull Bride-groom, and the fragrant Bride:
Which Love fore-fend; but spoken,
Be't to your praise, no peace was broken. 90

10. Strip her of Spring-time, tender-whimpring-maids,
Now *Autumne's* come, when all those flowrie aids
Of her Delayes must end; Dispose
That *Lady-smock*, that *Pansie*, and that *Rose*
Neatly apart;
But for *Prick-madam*, and for *Gentle-heart;*
And soft-*Maidens-blush*, the Bride
Makes holy these, all others lay aside:
Then strip her, or unto her
Let him come, who dares undo her. 100

11. And to enchant yee more, see every where
About the Roofe a *Syren* in a Sphere;
(As we think) singing to the dinne
Of many a warbling *Cherubim:*
O marke yee how
The soule of Nature melts in numbers: now
See, a thousand *Cupids* flye,
To light their Tapers at the Brides bright eye.
To Bed; or her they'l tire,
Were she an Element of fire. 110

12. And to your more bewitching, see, the proud
Plumpe Bed beare up, and swelling like a cloud,
Tempting the two too modest; can
Yee see it brusle[14] like a Swan,
And you be cold
To meet it, when it woo's and seemes to fold
The Armes to hugge it? throw, throw
Your selves into the mighty over-flow
Of that white Pride, and Drowne
The night, with you, in floods of Downe. 120

13. The bed is ready, and the maze of Love
Lookes for the treaders; every where is wove
Wit and new misterie;[15] read,[16] and
Put in practise, to understand
And know each wile,
Each hieroglyphick of a kisse or smile;
And do it to the full; reach
High in your own conceipt,[17] and some way teach
Nature and Art, one more
Play, then they ever knew before. 130

14. If needs we must for Ceremonies-sake,
Blesse a *Sack-posset;*[18] Luck go with it; take
The Night-Charme quickly; you have spells,
And magicks for to end, and hells,
To passe; but such
And of such Torture as no one would grutch[19]
To live therein for ever: Frie
And consume, and grow again to die,
And live, and in that case,
Love the confusion of the place. 140

15. But since It must be done, dispatch, and sowe
Up in a sheet your Bride, and what if so
It be with Rock, or walles of Brasse,
Ye Towre her up, as *Danae*[20] was;
Thinke you that this,
Or hell it selfe a powerfull Bulwarke is?
I tell yee no; but like a
Bold bolt of thunder he will make his way,
And rend the cloud, and throw
The sheet about, like flakes of snow. 150

16. All now is husht in silence; *Midwife-moone,*
With all her *Owle-ey'd* issue begs a boon
Which you must grant; that's entrance; with
Which extract, all we can call pith
And quintiscence
Of Planetary bodies; so commence
All faire *Constellations*
Looking upon yee, that two Nations[21]
Springing from two such Fires,
May blaze the vertue of their Sires. 160

[1] Clipsby Crewe, 1599–1649; attended St. John's College, Cambridge, and Lincoln's Inn; knighted 1620; Member of Parliament 1624–26; married Jane Pulteney July 7, 1625. Cf. H-149. [2] made warm. [3] Gen. xxvii.27, "the smell of a field which the Lord hath blessed." [4] In Exod. iii.5 God tells Moses, "put off thy shoes . . . for the place whereon thou standest, is holy ground." Cf. Josh. v.15 and Acts vii.33. [5] The god of marriage (or a youth impersonating him in wedding celebrations) carried a torch of pine or white hawthorn. [6] I.e. the flames of the bridegroom's desires mount higher than Hymen's torches and are more disparpling or widespreading. (*Disparkling* is usually regarded as a corrupt form of *disparpling,* but Herrick may well intend the idea of spark-scattering). [7] showers of roses and four-leaved clovers. [8] practice divination. [9] Cf. H-149A, st. viii. [10] fastidious. [11] parboiled. [12] artifice or device. [13] tagged cords or ties used to lace parts of clothing together. [14] raise its feathers. [15] mystery—in standard meanings but including the now outmoded one of *art* or *skill.* [16] make out the meaning of. [17] conceit: inventiveness. [18] spiced hot milk curdled by sack. [19] would be unwilling to allow. [20] Danae's father hid her from males in a brazen tower, but Zeus intruded as a shower of gold. [21] Herrick hopes for propitious influences from the stars upon the children of this union, and he remembers that in Gen. xxv.23 the Lord informed Rebekah that she carried "Two nations" as yet unborn. (Most copies of the 1648 *Hesperides* read "that, That".)

H-284 *The silken Snake.*

FOr sport my *Julia* threw a Lace
Of silke and silver at my face:
Watchet[1] the silke was; and did make
A shew, as if't'ad been a snake:

The suddenness did me affright;
But though it scar'd, it did not bite.

[1] light blue or green.

H–285 *Upon himselfe.*

I Am Sive-like, and can hold
Nothing hot, or nothing cold.
Put in Love, and put in too
Jealousie, and both will through:
Put in Feare, and hope, and doubt; 5
What comes in, runnes quickly out:
Put in secrecies withall,
What ere enters, out it shall:
But if you can stop the Sive,
For mine own part I'de as lieve, 10
Maides sho'd say, or Virgins sing,
Herrick keeps, as holds nothing.

H–286 *Upon Love.*

LOve's a thing, (as I do heare)
Ever full of pensive feare;
Rather then to which I'le fall,
Trust me, I'le not like at all:
If to love I should entend, 5
Let my haire then stand an[1] end:
And that terrour likewise prove,
Fatall to me in my love.
But if horrour cannot slake
Flames, which wo'd an entrance make; 10
Then the next thing I desire,
Is to love, and live i'th fire.

[1] on.

H–287 *Reverence to Riches.*

LIke to the Income must be our expence;
Mans Fortune must be had in reverence.[1]

[1] Ausonius, Epigram VIII, 7: *Fortunam reverenter habe.*

H–288 *Devotion makes the Deity.*[1]

WHo formes a Godhead out of Gold or Stone,
Makes not a God; but he that prayes to one.

[1] based on Martial, VIII, 24, 5–6.

H–289 *To all young men that love.*

I Could wish you all, who love,
That ye could your thoughts remove
From your Mistresses, and be,
Wisely wanton (like to me.)
I could wish you dispossest 5
Of that *Fiend that marres your rest;*
And with Tapers comes to fright
Your weake senses in the night.
I co'd wish, ye all, who frie
Cold as Ice, or coole as I. 10
But if flames best like ye, then
Much good do't ye Gentlemen.
I a merry heart will keep,
While you wring your hands and weep.

H–290 *The Eyes.*

'TIs a known principle in War,
The eies be first, that conquer'd are.[1]

[1] Tacitus, *Germania,* 43: *nam primi in omnibus proeliis oculi vincuntur.* Cf. Burton, 3,2,2,2 (ed. 6, pp. 452 ff.); e.g. "But the most familiar and usual cause of Love, is that which comes by sight." On pp. 465–7 Burton quotes passages on the eyes' power to conquer from Scaliger, Castilio, Propertius, Petronius, Tibullus, Musaeus, etc., concluding, "The strongest beams of beauty, are still darted from the eyes."

H–291 *No fault in women.*

NO fault in women to refuse
The offer, which they most wo'd chuse.
No fault in women, to confesse
How tedious they are in their dresse.
No fault in women, to lay on 5
The tincture of *Vermillion:*
And there to give the cheek a die
Of white, where nature doth deny.
No fault in women, to make show
Of largeness, when th'are nothing so: 10
(When true it is, the out-side swels
With inward Buckram,[1] little else.)
No fault in women, though they be
But seldome from suspition free:
No fault in womankind, at all, 15
If they but slip, and never fall.

[1] stiffened cloth.

H–292 *Upon* Shark. *Epigram.*[1]

SHark, when he goes to any publick feast,
Eates to ones thinking, of all there, the least.
What saves the master of the House thereby?
When if the servants search, they may descry
In his wide Codpeece,[2] (dinner being done) 5
Two Napkins cram'd up, and a silver Spoone.

[1] Similar pilferings are treated in Catullus, XII, XXV; Martial, XII, 29. [2] breeches' front.

H–293A Oberons *Feast.*[1]

SHapcot![2] To thee the Fairy State
I with discretion, dedicate.
Because thou prizest things that are
Curious, and un-familiar.
Take first the feast; these dishes gone; 5
Wee'l see the Fairy-Court *anon.*[3]

A Little mushroome table spred,
After short prayers, they set on bread;
A Moon-parcht grain of purest wheat,
With some small glit'ring gritt,[4] to eate 10
His choyce bitts with; then in a trice
They make a feast lesse great then nice.
But all this while his eye is serv'd,
We must not thinke his eare was sterv'd:
But that there was in place to stir 15
His Spleen,[5] the chirring Grashopper;
The merry Cricket, puling Flie,
The piping Gnat for minstralcy.
And now, we must imagine first,
The Elves present to quench his thirst 20
A pure seed-Pearle of Infant dew,
Brought and besweetned in a blew
And pregnant[6] violet; which done,
His kitling[7] eyes begin to runne
Quite through the table, where he spies 25
The hornes of paperie Butterflies,
Of which he eates, and tastes a little
Of that we call the Cuckoes spittle.[8]
A little Fuz-ball[9]-pudding stands
By, yet not blessed by his hands, 30
That was too coorse; but then forthwith
He ventures boldly on the pith
Of sugred Rush, and eates the sagge
And well bestrutted[10] Bees sweet bagge:
Gladding his pallat with some store 35
Of Emits[11] eggs; what wo'd he more?
But Beards of Mice, a Newt's stew'd thigh,
A bloated Earewig, and a Flie;
With the Red-capt worme, that's shut
Within the concave of a Nut, 40
Browne as his Tooth. A little Moth,
Late fatned in a piece of cloth:
With withered cherries; Mandrakes eares;
Moles eyes; to these, the slain-Stags teares:
The unctuous dewlaps of a Snaile; 45
The broke-heart of a Nightingale
Ore-come in musicke;[12] with a wine,
Ne're ravisht from the flattering Vine,
But gently prest from the soft side
Of the most sweet and dainty Bride,[13] 50

Brought in a dainty daizie, which
He fully quaffs up to bewitch
His blood to height; this done, commended
Grace by his Priest; *The feast is ended.*

[1] a sequel to H-223. [2] Herrick's close friend, Thomas Shapcott, a lawyer; see H-444. [3] The promised sequel poem is H-443. [4] husked, coarsely ground grain. [5] a ductless organ near the stomach believed to be the seat of either happy or morose feelings. [6] full. [7] morose. [8] a frothy secretion in which some insects' larvae are enveloped on leaves, stems, etc. [9] the fungus called puffball. [10] eats the laden and well swollen. [11] emmet's or ant's. [12] Contests between a nightingale and a musician or singer are frequently mentioned in literature; e.g. in Coryat's *Crudities* (1611), p. 253. Famianus Strada's poem on a contest with a lutenist appeared in his *Prolusiones* (1617), and was paraphrased by John Ford in *The Lover's Melancholy* (1629), I, ii, where the bird, having failed to imitate the sounds, "for grief dropped . . . on his lute, / And brake her heart." Other versions were written by William Strode (*Poetical Works*, ed. B. Dobell, 1907, pp. 16–18) and later poets. Crashaw expanded 14 lines of Strada's original in "Musick's Duell." [13] bridewort or meadowsweet?

H–293B *A Description of his Dyet.*[1]

Now they the Elves within a trice,
Prepar'd a feast lesse great than nice.
Where you may imagine first,
The Elves prepare to quench his thirst,
In pure seed pearle of infant dew 5
Brought and sweetned with a blew
And pregnant Violet; which done,
His killing eyes begin to runne
Quite ore the table, where he spyes
The hornes of waterd Butter-flies. 10
Of which he eates, but with a little
Neat coole allay of Cuckows spittle.
Next this the red cap worme thats shut
Within the concave of a nut.
Moles eyes he tastes, then Adders eares; 15
To these for sauce the slaine stagges teares
A bloted earewig, and the pith
Of sugred rush he glads him with.
Then he takes a little Mothe,
Late fatted in a scarlet cloth, 20

A spinners[2] ham, the beards of mice,
Nits carbonaded,[3] a device
Before unknowne; the blood of fleas
Which gave his Elveships stomacke ease.
The unctious dew lops[4] of a Snaile, 25
The broake heart of a Nightingale:
Ore come in musicke, with the sagge
And well bestrowted[5] Bees sweet bagge.
Conserves of Atomes, and the mites,
The stike wormes sperme, and the delights 30
Of all that ever yet hath blest
Fayrie land: so ends his feast.

[1] A variant, early version of H-293A, probably the second work of Herrick's to be printed (H-376 was the first) is here reprinted for the first time from the unique copy in the Rosenbach Foundation Library of *A Description Of the King and Queene of Fayries, their habit, fare, their abode, pompe, and state. Being very delightfull to the sense, and full of mirth.* London: Printed for *Richard Harper,* and are to be sold at his shop, at the Hospitall gate in Smithfield. 1634. The prefatory *To the Reader* by R. S. begins as follows: "*Courteous Reader,* I Present thee here with the description of the King of *Fayries,* of his attendants, apparell, gesture, and victuals, which though comprehended in the brevity of so short a volume yet as the Proverbe truely averres, it hath as mellifluous and pleasing discourse, as that whose ampliture containes the fulnesse of a bigger composition." There follows a poem by Sir Simeon Steward, "A Description of the King of *Fayries* Clothes, brought to him on New-yeares day in the morning, 1626 by his Queenes Chambermaids." Herrick's poem appears on pp. 4–5 (misprinted 6). It is italicized here to distinguish it from the contents of *Hesperides.* [2] spider's. [3] scored and broiled or grilled. [4] printed as *tops.* [5] bestrutted: swollen.

H–294

Event of things not in our power.

BY Time, and Counsell, doe the best we can,
Th'event[1] is never in the power of man.

[1] the way things work out.

H–295

Upon her blush.

WHen *Julia* blushes, she do's show
Cheeks like to Roses, when they blow.

H-296 *Merits make the man.*

OUr Honours, and our Commendations be
Due to the Merits, not Authoritie.

H-297 *To Virgins.*

HEare ye Virgins, and Ile teach,
What the times of old did preach.
Rosamond was in a Bower[1]
Kept, as *Danae* in a Tower:[2]
But yet Love (who subtile is) 5
Crept to that, and came to this.
Be ye lockt up like to these,
Or the rich *Hesperides;*[3]
Or those Babies[4] in your eyes,
In their Christall Nunneries; 10
Notwithstanding Love will win,
Or else force a passage in:
And as coy be, as you can,
Gifts will get ye, or the man.

[1] dwelling. The Fair Rosamond, daughter of Walter de Clifford, was the mistress of Henry II. According to legend he had a labyrinthine dwelling like a maze built for her. Thomas Deloney wrote a ballad on the subject, Samuel Daniel a poem, "The Complaint of Rosamond," and Joseph Addison an opera, *Rosamond.* [2] See H-283, n.20. [3] The garden of the Hesperides was remote and was guarded by a dragon. [4] Latin *pupillae:* little girls or pupils; or, reflections of other persons in the eyes. Cf. Burton, 3,2,6,5 (ed. 6, p. 574): "they may then kiss and coll, lye and look babies in one anothers eyes."

H-298 *Vertue.*

EAch must, in vertue, strive for to excell;
That man lives twice, that lives the first life well.[1]

[1] Martial, X, 23, 7–8, on Antonius Primus; one of the most frequently translated distiches by Martial; e.g. W. J. Courthope: "T'enjoy the past in life is twice to live"; Sir Henry Newbolt: "He lives twice, who can at once employ / The present well, and ev'n the past enjoy."

H–299

The Bell-man.[1]

FRom noise of Scare-fires[2] rest ye free,
From Murders *Benedicitie.*[3]
From all mischances, that may fright
Your pleasing slumbers in the night:
Mercie secure ye all, and keep
The Goblin from ye, while ye sleep.
Past one aclock, and almost two,
My Masters all, *Good day to you.*

[1] night watchman or town crier. [2] sudden conflagrations; fire alarms. [3] *benedicite:* bless you!

H–300

Bashfulnesse.

OF all our parts, the eyes expresse
The sweetest kind of bashfulnesse.

H–301

To the most accomplisht Gentleman, Master Edward Norgate, *Clark of the Signet*[1] *to His Majesty. Epigram.*

FOr one so rarely[2] tun'd to fit all parts;
For one to whom espous'd are all the Arts;
Long have I sought for: but co'd never see
Them all concenter'd in one man, but Thee.
Thus, thou, that man art, whom the Fates conspir'd
To make but One (and that's thy selfe) admir'd.

[1] clerk in charge of the seal used to authenticate royal letters and official documents. [2] exceptionally well.

H–302

Upon Prudence Baldwin *her sicknesse.*

PRue, my dearest Maid, is sick,
Almost to be Lunatick:

Æsculapius![1] come and bring
Means for her recovering;
And a gallant Cock shall be
Offer'd up by Her, to Thee.

[1] god of medicine. The traditional offering to him was a cock. The maid lived until 1678.

H–303 *To* Apollo. *A short Hymne.*

PHœbus! when that I a Verse,
Or some numbers more rehearse;
Tune my words, that they may fall,
Each way smoothly Musicall:
For which favour, there shall be
Swans devoted unto thee.

H–304 *A Hymne to* Bacchus.

BAcchus, let me drink no more;
Wild are Seas, that want a shore.
When our drinking has no stint,
There is no one pleasure in't.
I have drank up for to please
Thee, that great cup *Hercules:*[1]
Urge no more; and there shall be
Daffadills g'en up to Thee.

[1] Herculean: huge.

H–305 *Upon* Bungie.

BUngie do's fast; looks pale; puts Sack-cloth on;
Not out of Conscience, or Religion:
Or that this Yonker keeps so strict a Lent,
Fearing to break the Kings Commandement:[1]
But being poore, and knowing Flesh is deare,
He keeps not one, but many Lents i'th'yeare.

[1] to restrain meat-eating during Lent.

H–306 *On himselfe.*

HEre down my wearyed limbs Ile lay;
My Pilgrims staffe; my weed[1] of gray:
My Palmers hat; my Scallops shell;[2]
My Crosse; my Cord; and all farewell.
For having now my journey done, 5
(Just at the setting of the Sun)
Here I have found a Chamber fit,
(God and good friends be thankt for it)
Where if I can a lodger be
A little while from Tramplers free; 10
At my up-rising next, I shall,
If not requite, yet thank ye all.
Meane while, the *Holy-Rood* hence fright
The fouler Fiend, and evill Spright,
From scaring you or yours this night. 15

[1] garment. [2] Pilgrims returning from the shrine of St. James of Campostella wore shell badges. Cf. Ralegh, "The Passionate Mans Pilgrimage": "Give me my Scallop shell of quiet, / My staffe of Faith to walke upon, / . . . My Gowne of Glory, hopes true gage, / And thus Ile take my pilgrimage."

H–307 *Casualties.*

GOod things, that come of course, far lesse doe please,
Then those, which come by sweet contingences.

H–308 *Bribes and Gifts get all.*

DEad falls the Cause, if once the Hand be mute;
But let that speak, the Client gets the suit.

H–309 *The end.*

IF well thou hast begun, goe on fore-right;
It is the End that crownes us, not the Fight.

H–310 *Upon a child that dyed.*

HEre she lies, a pretty bud,
Lately made of flesh and blood:
Who, as soone, fell fast asleep,
As her little eyes did peep.
Give her strewings; but not stir
The earth, that lightly covers her.

H–311 *Upon* Sneape. *Epigram.*

SNeape has a face so brittle, that it breaks
Forth into blushes, whensoere he speaks.

H–312 *Content, not cates.*[1]

'TIs not the food, but the content
That makes the Tables merriment.
Where Trouble serves the board, we eate
The Platters there, as soone as meat.
A little Pipkin[2] with a bit
Of Mutton, or of Veale in it,
Set on my Table, (Trouble-free)
More then a Feast contenteth me.[3]

[1] choice viands, delicacies. [2] small pot or pan. [3] Prov. xv.17, "Better is a dinner of herbs where love is, than a stalled ox, and hatred therewith"; xvii.1, "Better is a dry morsel, and quietness therewith, than a house full of sacrifices [or *good cheer*] with strife."

H–313

The Entertainment: or, *Porch-verse, at the Marriage of Master* Henry Northly, *and the most witty Mistresse* Lettice Yard.[1]

WEelcome! but yet no entrance, till we blesse
First you, then you, and both for white[2] successe.
Profane no Porch young man and maid, for fear
Ye wrong the *Threshold-god*, that keeps peace here:

Please him, and then all good-luck will betide 5
You, the brisk Bridegroome, you the dainty Bride.
Do all things sweetly, and in comely wise;
Put on your Garlands first, then Sacrifice:
That done; when both of you have seemly fed,
We'll call on Night, to bring ye both to Bed: 10
Where being laid, all Faire signes looking on,
Fish-like, encrease then to a million:
And millions of spring-times may ye have,
Which spent, on[e][3] death, bring to ye both one Grave.

[1] Henry Northleigh of Devonshire married Lettice Yard in 1639; *witty* refers to her wisdom, intelligence, and capability; the *Porch* appears to be that of his house. [2] propitious, auspicious. [3] "on" in the 1648 *Hesperides*.

H–314 *The good-night or Blessing.*

BLessings, in abundance come,
To the Bride, and to her Groome;
May the Bed, and this short night,
Know the fulness of delight!
Pleasures, many here attend ye, 5
And ere long, a Boy Love send ye
Curld and comely, and so trimme,
Maides (in time) may ravish him.
Thus a dew of Graces fall
On ye both; Goodnight to all. 10

H–315 *Upon* Leech.

LEech boasts, he has a Pill, that can alone,
With speed give sick men their salvation:
'Tis strange, his Father long time has been ill,
And credits Physick, yet not trusts his Pill:
And why? he knowes he must of Cure despaire,
Who makes the slie Physitian his Heire.

H–316

To Daffadills.

1. FAire Daffadills, we weep to see
You haste away so soone:
As yet the early-rising Sun
Has not attain'd his Noone.
Stay, stay,
Untill the hasting day
Has run
But to the Even-song;
And, having pray'd together, we
Will goe with you along.

2. We have short time to stay, as you,
We have as short a Spring;
As quick a growth to meet Decay,
As you, or any thing.
We die,
As your hours doe, and drie
Away,
Like to the Summers raine;
Or as the pearles of Mornings dew
Ne'r to be found againe.

H–317

To a Maid.

YOu say, you love me; that I thus must prove;
If that you lye, then I will sweare you love.

H–318

Upon a Lady that dyed in child-bed, and left a daughter behind her.

AS Gilly flowers do but stay
To blow,[1] and seed, and so away;
So you sweet Lady (sweet as May)
The gardens-glory liv'd a while,
To lend the world your scent and smile. 5

But when your own faire print was set
Once in a Virgin *Flosculet,*[2]
(Sweet as your selfe, and newly blown)
To give that life, resign'd your own:
But so, as still the mothers power 10
Lives in the pretty Lady-flower.

[1] blossom. [2] a little flower.

H–319

A New-yeares gift sent to Sir Simeon Steward.[1]

NO newes of Navies burnt at Seas;[2]
No noise of late spawn'd *Tittyries:*[3]
No closset plot, or open vent,
That frights men with a Parliament:[4]
No new devise, or late found trick, 5
To read by th' Starres, the Kingdoms sick:
No ginne to catch the State, or wring
The free-born Nosthrills of the King,
We send to you; but here a jolly
Verse crown'd with *Yvie,* and with *Holly:* 10
That tels of Winters Tales and Mirth,
That Milk-maids make about the hearth,
Of Christmas sports, the *Wassell-boule,*
That['s] tost up, after *Fox-i'th'hole:*[5]
Of *Blind-man-buffe,* and of the care 15
That young men have to shooe the *Mare:*[6]
Of Twelf-tide Cakes, of Pease, and Beanes
Wherewith ye make those merry Sceanes,
When as ye chuse your King and Queen,[7]
And cry out, *Hey,*[8] *for our town green.* 20
Of Ash-heapes,[9] in the which ye use
Husbands and Wives by streakes to chuse:
Of crackling Laurell, which fore-sounds,
A Plentious harvest to your grounds:
Of these, and such like things, for shift, 25
We send in stead of New-yeares gift.
Read then, and when your faces shine
With bucksome[10] meat and capring Wine:
Remember us in Cups full crown'd,
And let our Citie-health go round, 30

Quite through the young maids and the men,
To the ninth number, if not tenne;
Untill the fired Chesnuts leape
For joy, to see the fruits ye reape,
From the plumpe Challice, and the Cup, 35
That tempts till it be tossed up:
Then as ye sit about your embers,
Call not to mind those fled Decembers;[11]
But think on these, that are t'appeare,
As Daughters to the instant yeare: 40
Sit crown'd with Rose-buds, and carouse,
Till *Liber Pater*[12] twirles the house
About your eares; and lay upon
The yeare (your cares) that's fled and gon.
And let the russet Swaines the Plough 45
And Harrow hang up resting now;
And to the Bag-pipe all addresse;
Till sleep takes place of wearinesse.
And thus, throughout, with Christmas playes
Frolick the full twelve Holy-dayes. 50

[1] See H-223, n.1 and H-293B. Sir Simeon and Herrick probably knew each other at Trinity Hall. [2] Martin notes that such rumors were rife in 1623, citing two play passages and one about setting fire to the navy—but not at sea. Such reports were recurrent, especially in the Civil War period. [3] Yonge, *Diary* (Camden Soc., 1848, p. 70), relates that a great number of tavern-haunters including knights, noblemen, and gentlemen, swore mutual assistance and secrecy to each other in a brotherhood known as the *Tytere tues* (from the opening of Virgil's *Eclogues*) in Dec. 1623. They identified each other by wearing a black "bugle"—a tube-shaped black bead. According to a letter of Dec. 6, 1623 (*C.S.P.Dom.*, XXI, 125), this secret society first began in the Netherlands. Herrick probably had some connection with what seems to have been a revival or continuation of this society, an *Order of the Black Ribband* initiated probably by Thomas Stanley about 1646. H-169 may be connected with it; also Shirley's "On a Black Ribband." There are references to it in John Hall's poem "Armilla Negra." See Margaret Flower's bibliography of Stanley in *Trans. Camb. Bibliog. Soc.* (1950), I, ii, 140–41, and G. M. Crump's Introd. to his ed. of Stanley's *Poems* (1962), pp. xxvi–xxvii. [4] Elections took place in Jan. 1624 and Parliament met on Feb. 19, 1624. [5] game played hopping on one foot. [6] a game. [7] for the Twelfth-day celebrations, Jan. 6; see H-1035, n.1. [8] hurrah. The town green was often used as a trysting place. [9] tub in which alkaline salts are dissolved from wood ashes. [10] buxom, tender. [11] past years. [12] Bacchus.

H–320 *Mattens, or morning Prayer.*

WHen with the Virgin morning thou do'st rise,
Crossing thy selfe; come thus to sacrifice:
First wash thy heart in innocence, then bring
Pure hands, pure habits, pure, pure every thing.
Next to the Altar humbly kneele, and thence, 5
Give up thy soule in clouds of frankinsence.
Thy golden Censors fil'd with odours sweet,[1]
Shall make thy actions with their ends to meet.

[1] Cf. Rev. v.8, "golden vials full of odours, which are the prayers of the saints."

H–321 *Evensong.*

BEginne with *Jove;* then is the worke halfe done;
And runnes most smoothly, when tis well begunne.
Jove's is the first and last:[1] The Morn's his due,
The midst is thine; But *Joves* the Evening too;
As sure a[s] *Mattins* do's to him belong, 5
So sure he layes claime to the *Evensong.*

[1] Rev. xxii.13, "I am Alpha and Omega, the beginning and the end, the first and the last."

H–322 *The Braclet*[1] *to* Julia.

WHy I tye about thy wrist,
Julia, this my silken twist;
For what other reason is't,
But to shew thee how in part,
Thou my pretty Captive art? 5
But thy Bondslave is my heart:
'Tis but silke that bindeth thee,
Knap[2] the thread, and thou art free:
But 'tis otherwise with me;
I am bound, and fast bound so, 10
That from thee I cannot go;
If I co'd, I wo'd not so.

[1] bracelet. [2] break.

H-323 *The Christian Militant.*

A Man prepar'd against all ills to come,
That dares to dead the fire of martirdome:
That sleeps at home; and sayling there at ease,
Feares not the fierce sedition of the Seas:
That's counter-proofe against the Farms mis-haps, 5
Undreadfull too of courtly thunderclaps:
That weares one face (like heaven) and never showes
A change, when Fortune either comes, or goes:
That keepes his own strong guard, in the despight
Of what can hurt by day, or harme by night:[1] 10
That takes and re-delivers every stroake
Of Chance, (as made up all of rock, and oake:)
That sighs at others death; smiles at his own
Most dire and horrid crucifixion.
Who for true glory suffers thus; we grant 15
Him to be here our *Christian militant.*

[1] Psalm xci.5, "Thou shalt not be afraid for the terror by night; nor for the arrow that flieth by day."

H-324 *A short Hymne to* Larr.[1]

THough I cannot give thee fires
Glit'ring to my free desires:
These accept, and Ile be free,
Offering *Poppy* unto thee.

[1] household god. Cf. H-333.

H-325 *Another to* Neptune.

MIghty *Neptune*, may it please
Thee, the *Rector* of the Seas,
That my Barque may safely runne
Through thy watrie-region;
And a *Tunnie-fish* shall be 5
Offer'd up, with thanks to thee.

H–326 *Upon* Greedy. *Epigram.*

AN old, old widow *Greedy* needs wo'd wed,
Not for affection to her, or her Bed;
But in regard, 'twas often said, this old
Woman wo'd bring him more then co'd be told,
He tooke her; now the jest in this appeares, 5
So old she was, that none co'd tell her yeares.

H–327 *His embalming to* Julia.

FOr my embalming, *Julia*, do but this,
Give thou my lips but their supreamest kiss:
Or else trans-fuse thy breath into the chest,
Where my small reliques must for ever rest:
That breath the *Balm*, the *myrrh*, the *Nard* shal be, 5
To give an *incorruption* unto me.

H–328 *Gold, before Goodnesse.*

HOw rich a man is, all desire to know;[1]
But none enquires if good he be, or no.[2]

[1] Cf. Burton, 1,2,4,6 (ed. 6, p. 154): "so that he be rich . . . he shall be honoured. . . . He shall be befriended: *for, riches gather many friends*, Prov. 19.4." [2] Ibid., p. 161: "we see men commonly respected according to their means (*an dives sit omnes quaerunt, nemo an bonus*)" (Seneca, *Ep.* CXV, 14, wrongly attributed by Burton to Euripides).

H–329 *The* Kisse. *A Dialogue.*

1. AMong thy Fancies, tell me this,
What is the thing we call a kisse?
2. I shall resolve ye, what it is.

It is a creature born and bred
Between the lips, (all cherrie-red,)
By love and warme desires fed,
Chor. And makes more soft the Bridall Bed.

2. It is an active flame, that flies,
First, to the Babies of the eyes;
And charmes them there with lullabies; 10
Chor. And stils the Bride too, when she cries.

2. Then to the chin, the cheek, the eare,
It frisks, and flyes, now here, now there,
'Tis now farre off, and then tis nere;
Chor. And here, and there, and every where.

1. Ha's it a speaking virtue? 2. Yes;
1. How speaks it, say? 2. Do you but this,
Part your joyn'd lips, then speaks your kisse;
Chor. And this loves sweetest language is.

1. Has it a body? 2. I, and wings 20
With thousand rare encolourings:
And as it flyes, it gently sings,
Chor. Love, honie yeelds; but never stings.

H-330 *The admonition.*

SEest thou those *Diamonds* which she weares
In that rich Carkanet;
Or those on her dishevel'd haires,
Faire *Pearles* in order set?
Beleeve young man all those were teares 5
By wretched Wooers sent,
In mournfull *Hyacinths* and *Rue,*
That figure[1] discontent;
Which when not warmed by her view,
By cold neglect, each one, 10
Congeal'd to Pearle and stone;
Which precious spoiles upon her,
She weares as trophees of her honour.
Ah then consider! What all this implies;
She that will weare thy teares, wo'd weare thine eyes. 15

[1] represent.

H–331

To his honoured kinsman Sir William Soame.[1] *Epigram.*

I Can but name thee, and methinks I call
All that have been, or are canonicall
For love and bountie, to come neare, and see,
Their many vertues volum'd up in thee;
In thee Brave Man! Whose incorrupted fame, 5
Casts forth a light like to a Virgin flame:
And as it shines, it throwes a scent about,
As when a Rain-bow in perfumes goes out.
So vanish hence, but leave a name, as sweet,
As *Benjamin,* and *Storax,*[2] when they meet. 10

[1] of Great Thurlow, Suffolk, eldest son of the poet's maternal aunt, Anne Stone of London, by her marriage with Sir Stephen Soame (d. 1619), grocer, alderman, Lord Mayor, and M.P. for London, a wealthy trader in the East India, Virginia, and other trading companies. According to *C.S.P.Dom. 1619–23,* p. 48, Sir William was summoned before the Privy Council for not contributing his assessment to the Palatine wars. See H-466 (to his brother) and n.1. [2] benzoin and storax, fragrant gum resins.

H–332

On himselfe.

ASke me, why I do not sing
To the tension of the string,
As I did, not long ago,
When my numbers full did flow?
Griefe (ay me!) hath struck my Lute, 5
And my tongue at one time mute.

H–333

To Larr.

NO more shall I, since I am driven hence,
Devote to thee my graines of Frankinsence:
No more shall I from mantle-trees hang downe,
To honour thee, my little Parsly crown:

No more shall I (I feare me) to thee bring 5
My chives of Garlick for an offering:
No more shall I, from henceforth, heare a quire
Of merry Crickets by my Country fire.
Go where I will, thou luckie *Larr* stay here,
Warme by a glit'ring chimnie all the yeare. 10

H-334

The departure of the good Dæmon.

WHat can I do in Poetry,
Now the good Spirit's gone from me?
Why nothing now, but lonely sit,
And over-read what I have writ.

H-335

Clemency.

FOr punishment in warre, it will suffice,
If the chiefe author of the faction dyes;
Let but few smart, but strike a feare through all:
Where the fault springs, there let the judgement fall.

H-336

His age,[1] *dedicated to his peculiar friend, Master* John Wickes,[2] *under the name of* Posthumus.

1. AH *Posthumus!* Our yeares hence flye,
And leave no sound; nor piety,
Or prayers, or vow
Can keepe the wrinkle from the brow:
But we must on, 5
As Fate do's lead or draw us; none,
None, *Posthumus,* co'd ere decline
The doome of cruell *Proserpine.*[3]

2. The pleasing wife, the house, the ground
Must all be left, no one plant found 10
To follow thee,
Save only the *Curst-Cipresse* tree:

A merry mind
Looks forward, scornes what's left behind:
Let's live, my *Wickes,* then, while we may, 15
And here enjoy our Holiday.

3. W'ave seen the past-best Times, and these
Will nere return, we see the Seas,
And Moons to wain;
But they fill up their Ebbs again: 20
But vanisht man,
Like to a Lilly-lost, nere can,
Nere can repullulate,[4] or bring
His dayes to see a second Spring.

4. But on we must, and thither tend, 25
Where *Anchus* and rich *Tullus*[5] blend
Their sacred seed:
Thus has *Infernall Jove* decreed;
We must be made,
Ere long, a song, ere long, a shade. 30
Why then, since life to us is short,
Lets make it full up, by our sport.

5. Crown we our Heads with Roses then,[6]
And 'noint with *Tirian Balme;*[7] for when
We two are dead, 35
The world with us is buried.
Then live we free,
As is the Air, and let us be
Our own fair wind, and mark each one
Day with the white and Luckie stone. 40

6. We are not poore; although we have
No roofs of Cedar, nor our brave
Baiæ,[8] nor keep
Account of such a flock of sheep;
Nor Bullocks fed 45
To lard the shambles:[9] Barbels[10] bred
To kisse our hands, nor do we wish
For *Pollio's*[11] Lampries in our dish.

7. If we can meet, and so conferre,
Both by a shining Salt-seller; 50
And have our Roofe,
Although not archt, yet weather proofe,

And seeling free,
From that cheape *Candle baudery:*[12]
We'le eate our Beane with that full mirth, 55
As we were Lords of all the earth.

8. Well then, on what Seas we are tost,
Our comfort is, we can't be lost.
Let the winds drive
Our Barke; yet she will keepe alive 60
Amidst the deepes;
'Tis constancy (my *Wickes*) which keepes
The Pinnace up; which though she erres
I'th'Seas, she saves her passengers.

9. Say, we must part (sweet mercy blesse 65
Us both i'th'Sea, Camp, Wildernesse)
Can we so farre
Stray, to become lesse circular,[13]
Then we are now?
No, no, that selfe same heart, that vow, 70
Which made us one, shall ne'r undoe;
Or ravell so, to make us two.

10. Live in thy peace; as for my selfe,
When I am bruised on the Shelfe
Of Time, and show 75
My locks behung with frost and snow:
When with the reume,
The cough, the ptisick,[14] I consume[15]
Unto an almost nothing; then,
The Ages fled, Ile call agen: 80

11. And with a teare compare these last
Lame, and bad times, with those are past,
While *Baucis* by,
My old leane wife, shall kisse it dry:
And so we'l sit 85
By'th'fire, foretelling snow and slit,
And weather by our aches, grown
Now old enough to be our own

12. True Calenders, as Pusses eare
Washt o're, to tell what change is neare:[16] 90
Then to asswage
The gripings of the chine[17] by age;

I'le call my young
Iülus[18] to sing such a song
I made upon my *Julia's* brest; 95
And of her blush at such a feast.

13. Then shall he read that flowre[19] of mine
Enclos'd within a christall shrine:
A Primrose[20] next;
A piece, then of a higher text: 100
For to beget
In me a more transcendant heate,
Then that insinuating fire,
Which crept into each aged Sire.

14. When the faire *Hellen*, from her eyes, 105
Shot forth her loving Sorceries:
At which I'le reare
Mine aged limbs above my chaire:
And hearing it,
Flutter and crow, as in a fit 110
Of fresh concupiscence, and cry,
No lust theres like to Poetry.

15. Thus frantick crazie man (God wot)
Ile call to mind things half forgot:
And oft between, 115
Repeat the Times that I have seen!
Thus ripe with tears,
And twisting my *Iülus* hairs;
Doting, Ile weep and say (In Truth)
Baucis, these were my sins of youth. 120

16. Then next Ile cause my hopefull Lad
(If a wild Apple[21] can be had)
To crown the Hearth,
(*Larr* thus conspiring with our mirth)
Then to infuse 125
Our browner Ale into the cruse:
Which sweetly spic't, we'l first carouse
Unto the *Genius* of the house.

17. Then the next health to friends of mine
(Loving the brave *Burgundian wine*) 130
High sons of Pith,[22]
Whose fortunes I have frolickt with:

Such as co'd well
Bear up the Magick bough, and spel:
And dancing 'bout the Mystick *Thyrse*, 135
Give up the just applause to verse:

18. To those, and then agen to thee
We'l drink, my *Wickes*, untill we be
Plump as the cherry,
Though not so fresh, yet full as merry 140
As the crickit;
The untam'd Heifer, or the Pricket,[23]
Untill our tongues shall tell our ears,
W'are younger by a score of years.

19. Thus, till we see the fire lesse shine 145
From th'embers, then the kitlings eyne,
We'l still sit up,
Sphering[24] about the wassail cup,
To all those times,
Which gave me honour for my Rhimes, 150
The cole once spent, we'l then to bed,
Farre more then night bewearied.

[1] i.e. a poem on his old age. [2] or Weeks, whom Anthony à Wood described as "This doctor, a jocular person" (*Fasti*, ed. Bliss, II, 68). Along with Herrick he was ordained as deacon and priest, April 24–25, 1623; both were friends of Endymion Porter (H-1071). Posthumus is addressed by Horace in *Carmina*, II, 14, 1–4, translated here in lines 1–4. [3] the sentence imposed by the queen of the underworld whose Greek name, Persephone, was interpreted to mean *bearer of destruction or death.* [4] sprout and germinate again. [5] kings of ancient Rome. [6] Wisd. of Sol. ii.8, "Let us crown ourselves with rose-buds, before they be withered." [7] purple balm-wine. [8] Campanian seaside resort resplendent with villas; its hot springs attracted invalids. [9] slaughterhouse or meat-market. [10] fish. [11] In anger Vedius Pollo had a slave thrown into a pond to be eaten by lampreys. [12] the dirt of candlesmoke accumulated on the ceiling. Cf. Marvell, "The last Instructions to a Painter," lines 10–11: "The Aly roof, with snuff of Candle dimm, / Sketching in shady smoke prodigious tools." [13] perfectly complementary, self-sufficing, complete. [14] phthisic: consumption. [15] burn up my substance. [16] as some soft and furry object is rubbed over us to tell what change in the weather is near (by the effect of static electricity on the nap). [17] spinal area. [18] son. Iülus was the mythical name of Ascanius, son of Áeneas. [19] the poem H-193. [20] the poem H-580. [21] i.e. the log of the wild-apple tree. [22] mettle, vigor, strength. In a manuscript version, the names are specified: Hind was probably Richard Hinde, a fellow

student at St. John's, later Vicar of Higham, Kent. *Goderiske* or *Godderick* could be Henry or John Goodrick, students at Cambridge in the 1610's. Smith was almost certainly the poet-priest James Smith who, with Sir John Mennes, edited *Recreation for Ingenious Head-peeces* (1650) in which 75 poems by Herrick were printed. *Nansagge* or *Nansogg* was Martin Nansogg, a Fellow at Trinity Hall when Herrick studied there. [23] a buck in his 2nd year. [24] circling. For variants in seven manuscripts and Poole's *The English Parnassus* (1657), see Martin, pp. 482–84. The poem also occurs in Rosenbach MS 239/22, pp. 48–55, with the following variants from our text: Heading: His old Age to Master Weekes. 2 nor / Noe. 3 Or prayers, or / Nor pray'r nor. 6 do's / doth. 14 Looks . . . left / Dislikes to csre for what's. 16 here / thus. 22 Lilly-lost / lost *Maidenhead.* 26 *Anchus . . . Tullus / Tullus . . . Anchus.* 28 Thus has / This. 29 must / should. 33 Roses / Rosebudds. 39 wind / winds. 40 white and Luckie / best and whitest. 41 We are not / Wee'le not bee. 42 roofs / roofe. 43 *Baiæ* / Baies. 47 do / will.

Two stanzas not in our text follow line 48:

Wee have noe Vyneyards, which doe beare
Their lustfull Clusters all the yeare
Nor odoriferous
Orchards like *Alcinous*
Nor gale the Seas
Our wittie Appetits to please
With *Mullett, Turbett, Guilt heads* bought
Att a highe rate, and further brought

Nor can wee glorie of a Great
And strutted *Magazine* of wheat
We have noe Bath
Of Oyle, but onely rich in *Faith,*
Ore which the hand
Of *Fortune* can have noe commaund
For what shee gives not, shee not takes
But of her owne a Spoile shee makes

52 Although not archt / Though not of gold. 54 that cheape / open. 55 that / the. 57 then . . . Seas / on what Seas then. 60 she / they. 61 Amidst / Midd'st. 62 which / that. 63 she / it. 64 she / yett. 66 i'th'Sea, Camp / in the Campe and. 75 show / read. 76 My . . . snow / Eternall daielight on my head. 78 ptisick / *Fisique.* 79 Unto . . . nothing / Into an heape of Sindars. 82 Lame . . . with / And cold tymes to. 84 My . . . it / With her leane lipps shall kisse them. 85 And so we'l / Then will wee. 89 Calenders / *Kallendar.* 90 Washt . . . tell / Is, for to knowe. 92 gripings of / Gripeinge in. 95 *Julia's* / Mistress. 96 And of her / Or such a. 97 that flowre of mine / my *Lillie* fine. 98 Enclos'd / Entomb'd. 104 aged / reverend. 105 faire . . . eyes / highe *Helen,* her faire

cheekes. 106 / Shew'd to the *Armie* of the *Greekes.* 107 reare / rise. 108 / Blind, though att Midnight in myne Eyes. 111 fresh . . . cry / younge . . . feele. 112 / Newe flames within the aged Steele. 116 Repeat . . . I / Sighe att the tymes, that wee. 117 / And shedd a teare. 118 hairs / haire. 121 Then / next. 126 browner Ale / better beare. 127 sweetly / neatly. 128 *Genius* / *Vesta.* 130 Loving the brave / In Oysters, and. 131 / *Hind, Godderick, Smith.* 132 / And *Nansocke,* Sonnes of *Chyne* and *Pith.* 133 as co'd / who knowes. 134 Bear . . . spel / To beare . . . spill. 135 / All-mightie bloud, that can'st doe more. 136 / Then *Jove* and *Chaios* him before. 140 yet full / but yett. 141 As / As is. 150 for / from.

H-337 *A short hymne to* Venus.

GOddesse, I do love a Girle
Rubie-lipt, and tooth'd with *Pearl:*
If so be, I may but prove
Luckie in this Maide I love:
I will promise there shall be 5
Mirtles offer'd up to Thee.

H-338 *To a Gentlewoman on just dealing.*

TRue to your self, and sheets, you'l have me swear,
You shall; if righteous dealing I find there.
Do not you fall through frailty; Ile be sure
To keep my Bond still free from forfeiture.

H-339 *The hand and tongue.*

TWo parts of us successively command;
The tongue in peace; but then in warre the hand.

H-340 *Upon a delaying Lady.*

1. COme come away,
Or let me go;
Must I here stay,
Because y'are slow;
And will continue so?
Troth Lady, no.

2. I scorne to be
A slave to state:
And since I'm free,
I will not wait,
Henceforth at such a rate,
For needy Fate.

3. If you desire
My spark sho'd glow,
The peeping fire
You must blow;
Or I shall quickly grow,
To Frost or Snow.

H–341

To the Lady Mary Villars,[1] *Governesse to the Princesse* Henretta.

WHen I of *Villars* doe but heare the name,
It calls to mind, that mighty *Buckingham,*
Who was your brave exalted Uncle here,
(Binding the wheele of Fortune to his Sphere)
Who spurn'd at Envie; and co'd bring, with ease, 5
An end to all his stately purposes.
For his love then, whose sacred Reliques show
Their Resurrection, and their growth in you:
And for my sake, whoever did prefer
You, above all Those *Sweets* of *Westminster:* 10
Permit my Book to have a free accesse
To kisse your hand, most Dainty Governesse.

[1] Mary Villiers was the Duke of Buckingham's daughter. As line 3 indicates, Herrick intended the poem for her cousin Anne, daughter of the Duke's brother, Sir Edward Villiers. She married Robert Douglas, Lord Dalkeith, and was governess to Princess Henrietta Anne, 5th daughter of Charles I, from the time of Anne's birth at Exeter in 1644. The poem was probably written before 1646, when Lady Dalkeith took the Princess abroad.

H–342 *Upon his* Julia.

WIll ye heare, what I can say
Briefly of my *Julia*?
Black and rowling is her eye,[1]
Double chinn'd,[2] and forehead high:[3]
Lips she has, all Rubie red, 5
Cheeks like Creame Enclarited:
And a nose that is the grace
And *Proscenium* of her face.
So that we may guesse by these,
The other parts will richly please. 10

[1] Cf. Burton, 3,2,2,2 (ed. 6, p. 466): "Of all eyes . . . black are the most amiable, enticing and, fairer . . . a round black eye is the best"; 3,2,3,3 (p. 470): "it is not the eye of it self that entiseth to lust, but an adulterous eye, as *Peter* terms it, 2.2.14. a wanton, a rolling, lascivious eye: A wandring eye, which *Isaiah* taxeth, 3.16." [2] Burton, 3,2,2,2 (p. 463): "dimple in the chin." [3] ibid., "An high brow like unto the bright heavens . . . white and smooth like polished alabaster."

H–343 *To Flowers.*

IN time of life, I grac't ye with my Verse;
Doe now your flowrie honours to my Herse.
You shall not languish, trust me: Virgins here
Weeping, shall make ye flourish all the yeere.

H–344 *To my ill Reader.*[1]

THou say'st my lines are hard;
And I the truth will tell;
They are both hard, and marr'd,
If thou not read'st them well.

[1] based on Martial, I, 38: "What you're reciting is my book, O Fidentinus; but when you recite it badly, it begins to be yours."

H–345 *The power in the people.*

LEt Kings Command, and doe the best they may,
The saucie Subjects still will beare the sway.

H–346 *A Hymne to* Venus, *and* Cupid.

SEa-born Goddesse, let me be,
By thy sonne thus grac't, and thee;
That when ere I wooe, I find
Virgins coy, but not unkind.
Let me when I kisse a maid, 5
Taste her lips, so over-laid
With Loves-sirrop; that I may,
In your Temple, when I pray,
Kisse the Altar, and confess
Ther's in love, no bitterness. 10

H–347 *On* Julia's *Picture.*

HOw am I ravisht! When I do but see,
The Painters art in thy *Sciography*?[1]
If so, how much more shall I dote thereon,
When once he gives it incarnation?

[1] in a rough sketch of thee. Phillips' Dictionary (1706) defines *sciagraphy* as "the first rude Draught of a thing," but Herrick seems to intend a shadow picture (traced around the outline of a shadow) in contrast to a true-to-the-life painting.

H–348 *Her Bed.*

SEe'st thou that Cloud as silver cleare,
Plump, soft, & swelling every where?
Tis *Julia's* Bed, and she sleeps there.

H-349 *Her Legs.*

FAin would I kiss my *Julia's* dainty Leg,
Which is as white and hair-less as an egge.

H-350 *Upon her Almes.*

SEe how the poore do waiting stand,
For the expansion of thy hand.
A wafer Dol'd by thee, will swell
Thousands to feed by miracle.[1]

[1] Cf. Christ's miracle of the loaves and fishes, Matt. xv.33–38.

H-351 *Rewards.*

STill to our gains our chief respect is had;
Reward it is, that makes us good or bad.

H-352 *Nothing new.*

NOthing is New:[1] we walk where others went.
Ther's no vice now, but has his president.

[1] Eccles. i.9–10.

H-353 *The Rainbow.*

LOok, how the *Rainbow* doth appeare
But in one onely *Hemisphere:*
So likewise after our disseace,
No more is seen the Arch of Peace.
That Cov'nant's[1] here; The under-bow, 5
That nothing shoots, but war and woe.

[1] Cf. Gen. ix.13–14 and H-687.

H–354A

The meddow verse or Aniversary to Mistris Bridget Lowman.[1]

COme with the Spring-time, forth Fair Maid, and be
This year again, the *medows Deity.*
Yet ere ye enter, give us leave to set
Upon your Head this flowry Coronet:
To make this neat distinction from the rest; 5
You are the Prime, and Princesse of the Feast:
To which, with silver feet lead you the way,
While sweet-breath Nimphs, attend on you this Day.
This is your houre; and best you may command,
Since you are Lady of this Fairie land. 10
Full mirth wait on you; and such mirth as shall
Cherrish the cheek, but make none blush at all.

[1] daughter of Philip Lowman, niece of Sir Edward Giles. See next poem.

H–354B

[*Epitaph.*]

No trust to Metals nor to Marbles, when[1]
These have their Fate, and wear away as Men;
Times, Titles, Trophies may be lost and Spent;
But Vertue Rears the eternal Monument.
What more than these can Tombes or Tomb-stones Say 5
But here's the Sun-set of a Tedious day:
These Two asleep are: I'll but be Undrest
And so to Bed: Pray wish us all Good Rest.[2]

[1] An epitaph on the tomb of Sir Edward and Lady Mary Giles in the south aisle of Dean Prior Church, attributed to Herrick by John Prince, *Danmonii Orientales Illustres* (1701), p. 334, who states that Herrick was "very Aged" when he composed the epitaph; however, Sir Edward died in 1637. Not in *Hesperides.*
[2] Cf. the ending of Milton's first epitaph "On the University Carrier": "If any ask for him, it shall be sed, / *Hobson* has supt, and's newly gon to bed."

H-355

The parting verse, the feast there ended.

LOth to depart, but yet at last, each one
Back must now go to's habitation:
Not knowing thus much, when we once do sever,
Whether or no, that we shall meet here ever.
As for my self, since time a thousand cares 5
And griefs hath fil'de upon my silver hairs;
'Tis to be doubted whether I next yeer,
Or no, shall give ye a re-meeting here.
If die I must, then my last vow shall be,
You'l with a tear or two, remember me, 10
Your sometime Poet; but if fates do give
Me longer date, and more fresh springs to live:
Oft as your field, shall her old age renew,
Herrick shall make the meddow-verse for you.

H-356

Upon Judith. *Epigram.*[1]

JUdith has cast her old-skin, and got new;
And walks fresh varnisht to the publick view.
Foule *Judith* was; and foule she will be known,
For all this fair *Transfiguration.*

[1] Cf. Burton, 3,2,3,3 (ed. 6, p. 477), quoting Tertullian, *De cultu foeminarum: "Let whores and queanes prank up themselves, let them paint their faces with minion and cerusse, they are but fuels of lust and signs of a corrupt soul."*

H-357

Long and lazie.

THat was the Proverb. Let my mistresse be
Lasie to others, but be long to me.

H-358

Upon Ralph. *Epigram.*

CUrse not the mice, no grist of thine they eat:
But curse thy children, they consume thy wheat.

H–359

To the right honourable, Philip, *Earle of Pembroke, and Montgomerie.*[1]

HOw dull and dead are books, that cannot show
A *Prince* [of[2]] *Pembroke*, and that *Pembroke*, you!
You, who are High born, and a Lord no lesse
Free by your fate, then Fortunes mightinesse,
Who hug our Poems (Honourd Sir) and then 5
The paper gild, and Laureat the pen.
Nor suffer you the Poets to sit cold,
But warm their wits, and turn their lines to gold.
Others there be, who righteously will swear
Those smooth-pac't Numbers, amble every where; 10
And these brave Measures go a stately trot;
Love those, like these; regard, reward them not.
But you my Lord, are One, whose hand along
Goes with your mouth, or do's outrun your tongue;
Paying before you praise; and cockring wit, 15
Give both the Gold and Garland unto it.

[1] Philip Herbert, 1584–1650, nephew of Sir Philip Sidney. The Shakespeare folio of 1623 was dedicated to him and his brother William. [2] possibly a misprint for "or".

H–360

An hymne to Juno.

STately Goddesse, do thou please,
Who art chief at marriages,
But to dresse the Bridall-Bed,
When my Love and I shall wed:
And a *Peacock* proud shall be 5
Offerd up by us, to thee.

H–361

Upon Mease. *Epigram.*

MEase brags of Pullets which he eats: but *Mease*
Ne'r yet set tooth in stump, or rump of these.

H–362

Upon Sapho, *sweetly playing, and sweetly singing.*

WHen thou do'st play, and sweetly sing,
Whether it be the voice or string,
Or both of them, that do agree
Thus to en-trance and ravish me:
This, this I know, I'm oft struck mute; 5
And dye away upon thy Lute.

H–363

Upon Paske *a Draper.*

PAske, though his debt be due upon the day
Demands no money by a craving way;
For why sayes he, all debts and their arreares,
Have reference to the shoulders, not the eares.[1]

[1] i.e. debtors should be arrested (tapped on the shoulders or grasped there by an officer of the law) rather than merely asked for repayment.

H–364

Chop-Cherry.[1]

THou gav'st me leave to kisse;
Thou gav'st me leave to wooe;
Thou mad'st me thinke by this,
And that, thou lov'dst me too.

2. But I shall ne'r forget,
How for to make thee merry;
Thou mad'st me chop, but yet,
Another snapt the Cherry.

[1] game of snatching with the mouth at cherries in water or hanging on strings.

H–365

To the most learned, wise, and Arch-Antiquary, Master John Selden.[1]

I Who have favour'd many, come to be
Grac't (now at last) or glorifi'd by thee.
Loe, I, the Lyrick Prophet, who have set
On many a head the Delphick Coronet,
Come unto thee for Laurell, having spent, 5
My wreaths on those, who little gave or lent.
Give me the *Daphne*,[2] that the world may know it,
Whom they neglected, thou hast crown'd a Poet.
A City here of *Heroes* I have made,
Upon the rock, whose firm foundation laid, 10
Shall never shrink, where making thine abode,
Live thou a *Selden*, that's a Demi-god.

[1] 1584–1654, author of *De Dis Syris; The Historie of Tithes;* a book on the Arundel marbles; now best known for his legal works and *Table-Talk*. [2] laurel.

H–366

Upon himself.

THou shalt not All die; for while Love's fire shines
Upon his Altar, men shall read thy lines;
And learn'd Musicians shall to honour *Herricks*
Fame, and his Name, both set, and sing his Lyricks.

H–367

Upon wrinkles.

WRinkles no more are, or no lesse,
Then beauty turn'd to sowernesse.

H–368

Upon Prigg.

PRigg, when he comes to houses, oft doth use
(Rather then fail) to steal from thence old shoes:
Sound or unsound, be they rent or whole,
Prigg bears away the body and the sole.

H–369 *Upon Moon.*

MOon is an Usurer, whose gain,
Seldome or never, knows a wain,
Onely Moons conscience, we confesse,
That ebs from pittie lesse and lesse.

H–370 *Pray and prosper.*

FIrst offer Incense, then thy field and meads
Shall smile and smell the better by thy beads.[1]
The spangling Dew dreg'd[2] o're the grasse shall be
Turn'd all to Mell,[3] and Manna there for thee.
Butter of *Amber, Cream,* and *Wine,* and *Oile* 5
Shall run, as rivers, all throughout thy soyl.
Wod'st thou to sincere-silver[4] turn thy mold?
Pray once, twice pray; and turn thy ground to gold.

[1] as a result of thy prayers. [2] dredged: sprinkled. [3] honey.
[4] pure silver.

H–371 *His Lachrimæ or Mirth, turn'd to mourning.*[1]

1. CAll me no more,
As heretofore,
The musick of a Feast;
Since now (alas)
The mirth, that was
In me, is dead or ceast.

2. Before I went
To banishment
Into the loathed West;
I co'd rehearse
A Lyrick verse,
And speak it with the best.

3. But time (Ai me)
Has laid, I see
My Organ fast asleep;
And turn'd my voice
Into the noise
Of those that sit and weep.[2]

[1] Cf. Lam. v.15, "The joy of our heart is ceased; our dance is turned into mourning." [2] Cf. Job xxx.31, "My harp also is turned to mourning, and my organ into the voice of them that weep."

H–372 *Upon Shift.*

SHift now has cast his clothes: got all things new;
Save but his hat, and that he cannot mew.[1]

[1] moult or shed.

H–373 *Upon Cuts.*

IF wounds in clothes, *Cuts* calls his rags, 'tis cleere,
His linings are the matter running there.

H–374 *Gain and Gettings.*

WHen others gain much by the present cast,[1]
The coblers getting time, is at the Last.

[1] stroke of fortune or throw of the dice.

H–375

To the most fair and lovely Mistris, Anne Soame, *now Lady* Abdie.[1]

SO smell those odours that do rise
From out the wealthy spiceries:
So smels the flowre of *blooming Clove;*
Or *Roses* smother'd in the stove:[2]
So smells the Aire of spiced wine; 5
Or *Essences* of *Jessimine:*[3]

So smells the Breath about the hives,
When well the work of hony thrives;
And all the *busie Factours*[4] come
Laden with wax and hony home: 10
So smell those neat and woven Bowers,
All over-archt with *Oringe flowers,*
And *Almond blossoms,* that do mix
To make rich these *Aromatikes:*
So smell those bracelets, and those bands 15
Of *Amber*[5] chaf't between the hands,
When thus enkindled they transpire
A noble perfume from the fire.
The wine of cherries, and to these,
The cooling breath of Respasses;[6] 20
The smell of mornings milk, and cream;
Butter of *Cowslips* mixt with them;
Of rosted warden,[7] or bak'd peare,
These are not to be reckon'd here;
When as the meanest part of her, 25
Smells like the maiden-Pomander.
Thus sweet she smells, or what can be
More lik'd by her, or lov'd by mee.

[1] daughter of Herrick's mother's sister Anne and Sir Thomas Soame (H-466); 2nd wife of Thomas Abdy who was created a baronet in 1641, which makes it probable that "*now Lady* Abdie" was added to a poem already written. [2] an air-tight cabinet containing several rows of wire shelves on which sweetmeats and the like were dried. [3] jasmine. [4] workers. [5] ambergris. [6] raspberries. [7] winter pears.

H-376 *Upon his kinswoman Mistris* Elizabeth Herrick.[1]

SWeet virgin, that I do not set
The pillars up of weeping *Jet,*
Or mournfull *Marble;* let thy shade
Not wrathfull seem, or fright the Maide,
Who hither at her wonted howers 5
Shall come to strew thy earth with flowers.
No, know (Blest Maide) when there's not one
Remainder left of Brasse or stone,

Thy living Epitaph shall be,
Though lost in them, yet found in me. 10
Dear, in thy *bed of Roses*, then,
Till this world shall dissolve as men,
Sleep, while we hide thee from the light,
Drawing thy curtains round: *Good night*.

[1] 1619–30, daughter of Herrick's brother William. This was probably the first poem by Herrick to be printed. It appears in Stow's *Survey of London* (1633), p. 812, as taken from a memorial tablet in St. Margaret's, Westminster, headed "In Memory of the late deceased Virgin Mistris Elizabeth Hereicke." Variants: 2 / The Grave-verse up in mournfull Jet. 3 mournfull / dapl'd. 5 wonted / weeping.

H–377

A Panegerick to Sir Lewis Pemberton.[1]

TIll I shall come again, let this suffice,
I send my salt, my sacrifice
To Thee, thy Lady, younglings, and as farre
As to thy *Genius* and thy *Larre;*
To the worn Threshold, Porch, Hall, Parlour, Kitchin, 5
The fat-fed smoking Temple, which in
The wholsome savour of thy mighty Chines[2]
Invites to supper him who dines,
Where laden spits, warp't with large Ribbs of Beefe,
Not represent, but give reliefe 10
To the lanke-Stranger, and the sowre Swain;
Where both may feed, and come againe:
For no black-bearded *Vigil*[3] from thy doore
Beats with a button'd-staffe the poore:
But from thy warm-love-hatching gates each may 15
Take friendly morsels, and there stay
To Sun his thin-clad members, if he likes,
For thou no Porter keep'st who strikes.
No commer to thy Roofe his *Guest-rite* wants;
Or staying there, is scourg'd with taunts
Of some rough Groom, who (yirkt with Corns) sayes, Sir
Y'ave dipt too long i'th Vinegar;[4]
And with our Broth and bread, and bits; Sir, friend,
Y'ave farced[5] well, pray make an end;
Two dayes y'ave larded here; a third, yee know, 25
Makes guests and fish smell strong; pray go

You to some other chimney, and there take
Essay of other giblets; make
Merry at anothers hearth; y'are here
Welcome as thunder to our beere: 30
Manners knowes distance, and a man unrude
Wo'd soon recoile, and not intrude
His Stomach to a second Meale. No, no,
Thy house, well fed and taught, can show
No such crab'd vizard: Thou hast learnt thy Train, 35
With heart and hand to entertain:
And by the Armes-full (with a Brest unhid)
As the old Race of mankind did,
When eithers heart, and eithers hand did strive
To be the nearer Relative: 40
Thou do'st redeeme those times; and what was lost
Of antient honesty, may boast
It keeps a growth in thee; and so will runne
A course in thy Fames-pledge, *thy Sonne.*
Thus, like a *Roman Tribune,* thou thy gate 45
Early setts ope to feast, and late:
Keeping no *currish Waiter* to affright,
With blasting eye, the appetite,
Which fain would waste upon thy Cates, but that[6]
The *Trencher-creature*[7] marketh what 50
Best and more suppling piece he cuts, and by
Some private pinch tels danger's nie
A hand too desp'rate, or a knife that bites
Skin deepe into the Porke, or lights
Upon some part of Kid, as if mistooke, 55
When checked by the Butlers look.
No, no, thy bread, thy wine, thy jocund Beere
Is not reserv'd for *Trebius*[8] here,
But all, who at thy table seated are,
Find equall freedome, equall fare; 60
And Thou, like to that *Hospitable God,*
Jove, joy'st when guests make their abode
To eate thy Bullocks thighs, thy Veales, thy fat
Weathers, and never grudged at.
The *Phesant, Partridge, Gotwit,*[9] *Reeve,*[10] *Ruffe, Raile,* 65
The *Cock,* the *Curlew,* and the *quaile;*
These, and thy choicest viands do extend
Their taste unto the lower end
Of thy glad table: not a dish more known
To thee, then unto any one: 70

But as thy meate, so thy *immortall wine*
Makes the smirk face of each to shine,
And spring fresh *Rose-buds,* while the salt, the wit
Flowes from the Wine, and graces it:
While Reverence, waiting at the bashfull board, 75
Honours my Lady and my Lord.
No scurrile jest; no open Sceane is laid
Here, for to make the face affraid;
But temp'rate mirth dealt forth, and so discreet-
ly that it makes the meate more sweet; 80
And adds perfumes unto the Wine, which thou
Do'st rather poure forth, then allow
By cruse and measure; thus devoting Wine,
As the *Canary* Isles were thine:
But with that wisdome, and that method, as 85
No One that's there his guilty glasse
Drinks of distemper,[11] or ha's cause to cry
Repentance to his liberty.
No, thou know'st order, Ethicks, and ha's read
All Oeconomicks, know'st to lead 90
A House-dance neatly, and can'st truly show,
How farre a Figure[12] ought to go,
Forward, or backward, side-ward, and what pace
Can give, and what retract a grace;
What Gesture, Courtship; Comliness agrees, 95
With those thy primitive decrees,
To give subsistance to thy house, and proofe,
What *Genii* support thy roofe,
Goodnes and *Greatnes;* not the oaken Piles;
For these, and marbles have their whiles 100
To last, but not their ever: Vertues Hand
It is, which builds, 'gainst Fate to stand.
Such is thy house, whose firme foundations trust
Is more in thee, then in her dust,
Or depth, these last may yeeld, and yearly shrinke, 105
When what is strongly built, no chinke
Or yawning rupture can the same devoure,
But fixt it stands, by her own power,
And well-laid bottome, on the iron and rock,
Which tryes, and counter-stands the shock, 110
And *Ramme* of time and by vexation growes
The stronger: *Vertue dies when foes*
Are wanting to her exercise, but great
And large she spreads by dust, and sweat[.]

Safe stand thy Walls, and Thee, and so both will,
Since neithers height was rais'd by th'ill
Of others; since no Stud, no Stone, no Piece,
Was rear'd up by the Poore-mans fleece:
No Widowes Tenement was rackt to guild
Or fret thy Seeling, or to build 120
A *Sweating-Closset,* to annoint the silke-
soft-skin, or bath in *Asses milke:*
No *Orphans* pittance, left him, serv'd to set
The Pillars up of *lasting Jet,*
For which their cryes might beate against thine eares, 125
Or in the dampe Jet read their Teares.
No *Planke* from *Hallowed* Altar, do's appeale
To yond' *Star-chamber,*[13] or do's seale
A curse to Thee, or Thine; but all things even
Make for thy peace, and pace to heaven. 130
Go on directly so, as just men may
A thousand times, more sweare, then say,
This is that *Princely Pemberton,* who can
Teach man to keepe a God in man:
And when wise Poets shall search out to see 135
Good men, *They find them all in Thee.*

[1] Sheriff of Northamptonshire in 1621; knighted 1617; died 1640. The theme of hospitality and its decay is frequent in literature, especially of the 17th century; cf. Joseph Hall, *Virgidemiarum,* V, 2 (ed. A. Davenport, p. 79), which begins, "Hous-keping's dead." Herrick's panegyric also belongs to the minor genre of Country House Poems which, in their 17th-century forms, tended to characterize their owners in terms of their environments and are thus related to the character genre; e.g. Marvell's "Upon Appleton House." Herrick here shows the influence of Martial, III, 58, Jonson's "To Penshurst," and possibly Carew's "To Saxham" as well as the satire by Hall mentioned above. [2] backbone cuts of meat. Cf. *Servingmans Comfort* (1598), Shakespeare Assoc. Facs. 3, sig. G4v: "Where are the great Chines of staulled Beefe? . . . and the multitude of good fellowes assembling to the houses of Potentates and men of worth? In a worde, they are all banyshed with the spirit of the Butterie, they are as rare in this age, as common in former tymes." [3] guard. [4] Cf. Ruth ii.14, "eat of the bread, and dip thy morsel in the vinegar." [5] crammed. [6] which willingly would diminish itself upon your delicacies but for the fact that. [7] base servant who carves meat. [8] a friend of the epicure Lucullus: Juvenal's Satire V attacks him: *"The Poet here strives to disswade / Vile* Trebius *from his Table-trade"* ("Argument," trans. Holyday). [9] godwit: a marsh bird, "the daintiest dish in

England" according to Sir Thomas Browne. [10] female of the ruff, a bird of the sandpiper family. [11] intemperately to the point of intoxication. [12] evolutions (or sets of them) in dancing. [13] The Court of Star Chamber was a judicial body of the King's Council, but Herrick refers to such a high court in heaven, where divine judgments are given.

H-378

To his Valentine, *on* S. Valentines *day.*

OFt have I heard both Youths and Virgins say,
Birds chuse their Mates, and couple too, this day:
But by their flight I never can divine,
When I shall couple with my Valentine.

H-379 *Upon* Doll. *Epigram.*

DOll she so soone began the wanton trade;
She ne'r remembers that she was a maide.

H-380 *Upon* Skrew. *Epigram.*

SKrew lives by shifts; yet sweares by no small oathes;
For all his shifts, he cannot shift his clothes.

H-381 *Upon Linnit. Epigram.*

LInnit playes rarely on the Lute, we know;
And sweetly sings, but yet his breath sayes no.

H-382

Upon Master Ben. Johnson. *Epigram.*

AFter the rare Arch-Poet[1] JOHNSON dy'd,
The Sock grew loathsome, and the Buskins pride,[2]
Together with the Stages glory stood
Each like a poore and pitied widowhood.
The Cirque[3] prophan'd was; and all postures rackt: 5
For men did strut, and stride, and stare, not act.

Then temper flew from words; and men did squeake,
Looke red, and blow, and bluster, but not speake:
No Holy-Rage, or frantick-fires did stirre,
Or flash about the spacious Theater. 10
No clap of hands, or shout, or praises-proofe
Did crack the Play-house sides, or cleave her roofe.
Artlesse the Sceane was; and that monstrous sin
Of deep and *arrant ignorance* came in;
Such ignorance as theirs was, who once hist 15
At thy unequal'd Play, the *Alchymist:*[4]
Oh fie upon 'em! Lastly too, all witt
In utter darkenes did, and still will sit
Sleeping the locklesse Age out, till that she
Her Resurrection ha's again with Thee. 20

[1] "*B. Johnson,* our arch Poet," Burton, 3,2,4,1 (margin of p. 506 in 2 ed., 1624, and 6 ed.). [2] *soccus:* low-heeled boot worn for comedies; *cothurnus:* thick-soled boot for tragedies. [3] circus: theater. [4] No other report of hissing at this play is known, but cf. Thomas Randolph, "*An answer to* Mr Ben Johnson's *Ode to perswade him not to leave the stage*" (*Poems,* 1638, p. 71): "Their hisse is thy applause."

H-383 *Another.*

THou had'st the wreath before, now take the Tree;
That henceforth none be *Laurel crown'd but Thee.*

H-384 *To his Nephew,[1] to be prosperous in his art of Painting.*

ON, as thou hast begunne, brave youth, and get
The Palme from *Urbin, Titian, Tintarret,*
Brugel and *Coxie,*[2] and the workes out-doe,
Of *Holben,* and That mighty *Ruben* too.
So draw, and paint, as none may do the like, 5
No, not the glory of the World, *Vandike.*

[1] Herrick probably used "nephew" to include cousins; cf. "Neice" applied to Mary Stone in H-764. He may refer to one of the sons of his 3 brothers and 3 sisters who grew to maturity; but if his mother's family was related to Nicholas Stone of Devon, the out-

standing mason-sculptor of the period before his death in 1647, then the "nephew" may be Stone's son Henry, an independent painter who is also credited with some copies of Van Dyck's paintings. [2] Raphael, Titian, Tintoretto, Bruegel, and the Flemish painter Michiel van Coxcyen. (*Coxu,* the misprint in the 1648 *Hesperides* is here changed to the form of the name which was used in 17th-century England.)

H–385 *Upon* Glasse. *Epigram.*

GLasse, out of deepe, and out of desp'rate want,
Turn'd, from a Papist here, a Predicant.[1]
A Vicarige at last *Tom Glasse* got here,
Just upon five and thirty pounds a yeare.[2]
Adde to that thirty five, but five pounds more, 5
He'l turn a Papist, rancker then before.

[1] preacher. [2] The figure probably approximates Herrick's own income.

H–386 *A Vow to* Mars.[1]

STore of courage to me grant,
Now I'm turn'd a combatant:
Helpe me so, that I my *shield,*
(Fighting) lose not in the field.
That's the greatest shame of all, 5
That in warfare can befall.
Do but this; and there shall be
Offer'd up a Wolfe to thee.

[1] Possibly written before going as Buckingham's chaplain on the expedition to the Isle of Rhé. There is no evidence that Herrick was ever a combatant in the Civil Wars.

H–387 *To his maid* Prew.[1]

THese *Summer-Birds* did with thy Master stay
The times of warmth; but then they flew away;
Leaving their Poet (being now grown old)
Expos'd to all the comming Winters cold.

But thou *kind Prew* did'st with my Fates abide, 5
As well the Winters, as the Summers Tide:
For which thy Love, live with thy Master here,
Not two, but all the seasons of the yeare.

[1] See H-302.

H–388

A Canticle to Apollo.

PLay *Phœbus* on thy Lute;
And we will all sit mute:
By listning to thy Lire,
That sets all eares on fire.

2. Hark, harke, the God do's play!
And as he leads the way
Through heaven, the very Spheres,
As men, turne all to eares.

H–389

A just man.

A Just man's like a Rock that turnes the wroth
Of all the raging Waves, into a froth.

H–390

Upon a hoarse singer.

SIng me to death; for till thy voice be cleare,
'Twill never please the pallate of mine eare.

H–391

How Pansies *or* Hearts-ease *came first.*

FRollick Virgins once these were,
Over-loving, (living here:)
Being here their ends deny'd
Ranne for Sweet-hearts mad, and dy'd.
Love in pitie of their teares, 5
And their losse in blooming yeares;
For their restlesse here-spent houres,
Gave them *Hearts-ease* turn'd to Flow'rs.

H–392

To his peculiar[1] *friend Sir* Edward Fish, *Knight Baronet.*

SInce for thy full deserts (with all the rest
Of these chaste spirits, that are here possest
Of Life eternall) Time has made Thee one,
For growth in this my rich Plantation:[2]
Live here: But know 'twas vertue, and not chance, 5
That gave Thee this so high inheritance.
Keepe it for ever; grounded with the good,
Who hold fast here an endlesse lively-hood.

[1] special, personal. Sir Edward lived in Chertsey, Surrey and died in 1638. [2] i.e. Herrick's garden of *Hesperides.*

H–393

Larr's *portion, and the* Poets *part.*

AT my homely Country-seat,
I have there a little wheat;
Which I worke to Meale, and make
Therewithall a *Holy-cake:*
Part of which I give to *Larr,* 5
Part is my peculiar.[1]

[1] personal property.

H–394

Upon Man.

MAn is compos'd here of a two-fold part;
The first of Nature, and the next of Art:
Art presupposes Nature; Nature shee
Prepares the way to mans docility.[1]

[1] aptness for being taught.

H-395 *Liberty.*

THose ills that mortall men endure,
So long are capable of cure,
As they of freedome may be sure:
But that deni'd; a griefe, though small,
Shakes the whole Roofe, or ruines all. 5

H-396 *Lots to be liked.*

LEarn this of me, where e'r thy Lot doth fall;
Short lot, or not, to be content with all.

H-397 *Griefes.*

JOve may afford us thousands of reliefs;
Since man expos'd is to a world of griefs.

H-398 *Upon* Eeles. *Epigram.*[1]

EEles winds and turnes, and cheats and steales; yet *Eeles*
Driving these sharking trades, is out at heels.

[1] Martial's Vacerra (XI, 66), though an informer, blackmailer, perjurer, pimp, profligate, and master of gladiators, still lacks wealth. Cf. H-1025.

H-399 *The Dreame.*

BY Dream I saw, one of the three
Sisters of Fate appeare to me.
Close to my Beds side she did stand
Shewing me there a fire brand;[1]
She told me too, as that did spend, 5
So drew my life unto an end.

Three quarters were consum'd of it;
Onely remaind a little bit,
Which will be burnt up by and by,
Then *Julia* weep, for I must dy. 10

[1] The Fates similarly appeared at the birth of Meleager declaring that his life would end when a piece of wood, then burning on the fire, was consumed.

H–400 *Upon* Raspe *Epigram.*

RAspe playes at Nine-holes;[1] and 'tis known he gets
Many a Teaster[2] by his game, and bets:
But of his gettings there's but little sign;
When one hole wasts more then he gets by Nine.

[1] game of throwing small balls into nine holes. [2] a coin.

H–401 *Upon* Center *a Spectacle-maker with a flat nose.*

CEnter is known weak sighted, and he sells
To others store of helpfull spectacles.
Why weres he none? Because we may suppose,
Where *Leaven* wants, there *Levill* lies the nose.[1]

[1] I Cor. v.6, "a little leaven leaveneth the whole lump."

H–402 *Clothes do but cheat and cousen us.*

AWay with silks, away with Lawn,
Ile have no Sceans,[1] or Curtains drawn:
Give me my Mistresse, as she is,
Drest in her nak't simplicities:
For as my Heart, ene so mine Eye 5
Is wone with flesh, not *Drapery.*

[1] hangings.

H-403 *To* Dianeme.

SHew me thy feet; shew me thy legs, thy thighes;
Shew me Those *Fleshie Principalities;*
Shew me that Hill (where smiling Love doth sit)
Having a living Fountain under it.
Shew me thy waste; Then let me there withall, 5
By the *Assention* of thy Lawn, see All.

H-404 *Upon* Electra.

WHen out of bed my Love doth spring,
'Tis but as day a kindling:
But when She's up and fully drest,
'Tis then *broad Day throughout the East.*

H-405 *To his Booke.*

HAve I not blest Thee? Then go forth; nor fear
Or spice, or fish, or fire, or close-stools[1] here.
But with thy fair Fates leading thee, Go on
With thy most white[2] *Predestination.*
Nor thinke these Ages that do hoarcely sing 5
The *farting Tanner*, and *familiar King;*[3]
The *dancing Frier*, tatter'd in the bush;[4]
Those monstrous lies of little *Robin Rush:*[5]
Tom Chipperfeild, and pritty-*lisping Ned*,
That doted on a Maide of *Gingerbred:* 10
The *flying Pilcher*, and the *frisking Dace,*[6]
With all the rabble of *Tim-Trundells*[7] race,
(Bred from the dung-hils, and adulterous rhimes,)
Shall live, and thou not superlast all times?
No, no, thy Stars have destin'd Thee to see 15
The whole world die, and turn to dust with thee.
He's greedie of his life, who will not fall,
When as a publick ruine bears down All.[8]

[1] commodes. Herrick remembers the uses of paper for wrapping spices or fish, burning, etc. [2] auspicious. [3] the ballad "King Edward the Fourth and the Tanner of Tamworth" (F. R. Child, *Popular Ballads,* 1898, V, 75–77). [4] In "Fryar and Boys"

(*Percy's Folio Manuscript,* ed. J. W. Hales and F. J. Furnivall, 1867–69, III, Appen. pp. 9–28), the boy gets the friar into a bush and by means of a magic flute makes him dance there. [5] Friar Rush (the devil in disguise) became cook in a monastery in order to mislead the brothers, according to a German folk legend. [6] The ballads referred to have not been identified. [7] There was a publisher of ballads named *John* Trundle. [8] reference to the Civil Wars?

H–406 *Of Love.*

I Do not love, nor can it be
Love will in vain spend shafts on me:
I did this God-head once defie;
Since which I freeze, but cannot frie.
Yet out alas! the deaths the same, 5
Kil'd by a frost or by a flame.

H–407 *Upon himself.*

I Dislikt but even now;
Now I love I know not how.
Was I idle, and that while
Was I fier'd with a smile?
Ile to[1] work, or pray; and then 5
I shall quite dislike agen.[2]

[1] "too" in the 1648 edition, but "to" in *Wit's Recreations.* [2] Cf. Burton, 3,2,5 (misnumbered 6 in ed. 6), 1 (ed. 6. p. 545): "Take idleness away, and put to flight / Are *Cupids* Arts, his Torches give no light. . . . 'Tis in vain to set upon those that are busie. . . . Magninus adds, *Never to be idle, but at hours of sleep.*"

H–408 *Another.*

LOve he that will; it best likes me,
To have my neck from Loves yoke-free.

H–409 *Upon* Skinns. *Epigram.*

SKinns he din'd well to day; how do you think?
His Nails they were his meat, his Reume the drink.

H–410 *Upon Pievish. Epigram.*

PIevish doth boast, that he's the very first
Of English Poets, and 'tis thought the Worst.

H–411 *Upon* Jolly *and* Jilly, *Epigram.*

JOlly and *Jillie*, bite and scratch all day,
But yet get children (as the neighbours say.)
The reason is, though all the day they fight,
They cling and close, some minutes of the night.

H–412 *The mad Maids song.*

1. GOod morrow to the Day so fair;
   Good morning Sir to you:
   Good morrow to mine own torn hair
   Bedabled with the dew.

2. Good morning to this Prim-rose too;
   Good morrow to each maid;
   That will with flowers the *Tomb* bestrew,
   Wherein my Love is laid.

3. Ah woe is me, woe, woe is me,
   Alack and welladay!
   For pitty, Sir, find out that Bee,
   Which bore my Love away.

4. I'le seek him in your *Bonnet* brave;
   Ile seek him in your eyes;
   Nay, now I think th'ave made his grave
   I'th'bed of strawburies.

5. Ile seek him there; I know, ere this,
   The cold, cold Earth doth shake him;
   But I will go, or send a kisse
   By you, Sir, to awake him.

6. Pray hurt him not; though he be dead,
   He knowes well who do love him,
   And who with green-turfes reare his head,
   And who do rudely move him.

7. He's soft and tender (Pray take heed)
With bands of Cow-slips bind him;
And bring him home, but 'tis decreed,
That I shall never find him.

H–413 *To Springs and Fountains.*

I Heard ye co'd coole heat; and came
With hope you would allay the same:
Thrice I have washt, but feel no cold,
Nor find that true, which was foretold.
Me thinks like mine, your pulses beat;
And labour with unequall heat:
Cure, cure your selves, for I discrie,
Ye boil with Love, as well as I.

H–414 *Upon* Julia's *unlacing her self.*

TEll, if thou canst, (and truly) whence doth come
This *Camphire, Storax, Spiknard, Galbanum:*
These *Musks,* these *Ambers,* and those other smells
(Sweet as the *Vestrie of the Oracles.*)
Ile tell thee; while my *Julia* did unlace 5
Her silken bodies, but a breathing space:
The passive Aire such odour then assum'd,
As when to *Jove* Great *Juno* goes perfum'd.
Whose pure-Immortall body doth transmit
A scent, that fills both Heaven and Earth with it. 10

H–415 *To* Bacchus, *a Canticle.*

WHither dost thou whorry[1] me,
Bacchus, being full of thee?[2]
This way, that way, that way, this,
Here, and there a fresh Love is.
That doth like me, this doth please;
Thus a thousand Mistresses,
I have now; yet I alone,
Having All, injoy not *One.*

[1] impel or carry hurriedly. [2] So Horace begins *Carmina,* III, 25: "Whither, O Bacchus, do you hurry (*rapis*) me, full of you?"

H–416 *The Lawne.*

WO'd I see Lawn, clear as the Heaven, and thin?
It sho'd be onely in my *Julia's* skin:[1]
Which so betrayes her blood, as we discover
The blush of cherries, when a Lawn's cast over.

[1] i.e. the "fabric" of such transparency and fineness that I would find would be her skin.

H–417 *The Frankincense.*

WHen my off'ring next I make,
Be thy hand the hallowed Cake:
And thy brest the Altar, whence
Love may smell the *Frankincense.*

H–418

Upon Patrick *a footman, Epigram.*

NOw *Patrick* with his footmanship has done,
His eyes and ears strive which sho'd fastest run.

H–419 *Upon* Bridget. *Epigram.*[1]

OF foure teeth onely *Bridget* was possest;
Two she spat out, a cough forc't out the rest.

[1] based on Martial, I, 19. Cf. Crashaw's version (*"Out of* Martiall," *The Delights of the Muses,* 1646): "Foure Teeth thou had'st that ranck'd in goodly state / Kept thy Mouthes Gate. / The first blast of thy cough left two alone, / The second none. / This last cough *Ælia,* cought out all thy feare, / Th'hast left the third cough now no businesse here."

H–420 *To* Sycamores.

I'M sick of Love;[1] O let me lie
Under your shades, to sleep or die!
Either is welcome; so I have
Or here my Bed, or here my Grave.
Why do you sigh, and sob, and keep 5
Time with the tears, that I do weep?
Say, have ye sence,[2] or do you prove[3]
What *Crucifixions* are in Love?
I know ye do; and that's the why,
You sigh for Love, as well as I. 10

[1] Song of Sol. ii.5 and v.8, "I am sick of love." [2] the faculties of physical sensation and perception. [3] experience.

H–421

A Pastorall sung to the King: Montano, Silvio, *and* Mirtillo, *Shepheards.*

Mon. BAd are the times. *Sil.* And wors then they are we.
Mon. Troth, bad are both; worse fruit, and ill the tree:
The feast of Shepheards fails.[1] *Sil.* None crowns the cup
Of *Wassaile* now, or sets the *quintell*[2] up:
And He, who us'd to leade the Country-round, 5
Youthfull *Mirtillo,* Here he comes, Grief drownd.[3]
Ambo Lets cheer him up. *Sil.* Behold him weeping ripe.[4]
Mirt. Ah! *Amarillis,* farewell mirth and pipe;
Since thou art gone,[5] no more I mean to play,
To these smooth Lawns, my mirthfull Roundelay. 10
Dear *Amarillis! Mon.* Hark! *Sil.* mark: *Mir.* this earth [grew sweet
Where, *Amarillis,* Thou didst set thy feet.
Ambo. Poor pittied youth! *Mir.* And here the breth of kine
And sheep, grew more sweet, by that breth of Thine.
This flock of wooll, and this rich lock of hair, 15
This ball of *Cow-slips,* these she gave me here.
Sil. Words sweet as Love it self. *Montano,* Hark.
Mirt. This way she came, and this way too she went;
How each thing smells divinely redolent!

Like to a field of beans, when newly blown; 20
Or like a medow being lately mown.
Mont. A sweet-sad passion.——
Mirt. In dewie-mornings when she came this way,
Sweet Bents[6] wode bow, to give my Love the day:
And when at night, she folded had her sheep, 25
Daysies wo'd shut, and closing, sigh and weep.
Besides (Ai me!) since she went hence to dwell,
The voices Daughter[7] nea'r spake syllable.
But she is gone. *Sil. Mirtillo,* tell us whether,[8]
Mirt. Where she and I shall never meet together. 30
Mont. Fore-fend it *Pan,* and *Pales*[9] do thou please
To give an end: *Mir.* To what? *Scil.* such griefs as these.
Mirt. Never, O never! Still I may endure
The wound I suffer, never find a cure.
Mont. Love for thy sake will bring her to these hills 35
And dales again: *Mir.* No I will languish still;
And all the while my part shall be to weepe;
And with my sighs, call home my bleating sheep:
And in the Rind of every comely tree
Ile carve thy name, and in that name kisse thee: 40
Mont. Set with the Sunne, thy woes: *Scil.* The day grows old:
And time it is our full-fed flocks to fold.

Chor. The shades grow great; but greater growes our sorrow,
But lets go steepe
Our eyes in sleepe; 45
And meet to weepe
To morrow.

[1] The Parilia or Palilia, the festival of Pales (line 31) fails ("fail" in 1648 ed. of *Hesperides*) to be celebrated. In Roman religion it took place on April 21. She was the goddess who presided over cattle and pastures. [2] quintain: a post (or some object on it) tilted at with poles or lances. [3] Cf. H-77. [4] Cf. I Sam. xxx.4, "until they had no more power to weep." [5] probably a reference to Queen Henrietta Maria and her departure from England. See H-79. [6] grasses. [7] echo. [8] whither. [9] See n.1.

H–422

The Poet loves a Mistresse, but not to marry.

1. I Do not love to wed,
Though I do like to wooe;
And for a maidenhead
Ile beg, and buy it too.

2. Ile praise, and Ile approve
Those maids that never vary;
And fervently Ile love;
But yet I would not marry.

3. Ile hug, Ile kisse, Ile play,
And Cock-like Hens Ile tread:
And sport it any way;
But in the Bridall Bed:

4. For why? that man is poore,
Who hath but one of many;
But crown'd he is with store,
That single may have any.

5. Why then, say, what is he
(To freedome so unknown)
Who having two or three,
Will be content with one?

H–423

Upon Flimsey. *Epigram.*

WHy walkes *Nick Flimsey* like a Male-content?
Is it because his money all is spent?
No, but because the Ding-thrift[1] now is poore,
And knowes not where i'th world to borrow more.

[1] spendthrift.

H–424 *Upon* Shewbread. *Epigram.*

LAst night thou didst invite me home to eate;
And shew'st me there much Plate, but little meate.
Prithee, when next thou do'st invite, barre State,[1]
And give me meate, or give me else thy Plate.

[1] eliminate ceremoniousness. The epigram is based on "In Varum," attributed to Martial (Loeb Library, II, 520).

H–425 *The* Willow Garland.

A Willow Garland thou did'st send
Perfum'd (last day) to me:
Which did but only this portend,
I was forsooke by thee.

Since so it is; Ile tell thee what, 5
To morrow thou shalt see
Me weare the Willow; after that,
To dye upon the Tree.

As Beasts unto the Altars go
With Garlands drest, so I 10
Will, with my Willow-wreath also,
Come forth and sweetly dye.

H–426 *A Hymne to Sir* Clipseby Crew.[1]

'TWas not Lov's Dart;
Or any blow
Of want, or foe,
Did wound my heart
With an eternall smart: 5

But only you,
My sometimes known
Companion,
(My dearest *Crew,*)
That me unkindly slew.[2] 10

May your fault dye,
And have no name
In Bookes of fame;
Or let it lye
Forgotten now, as I. 15

We parted are,
And now no more,
As heretofore,
By jocund Larr,
Shall be familiar. 20

But though we Sever
My *Crew* shall see,
That I will be
Here faithlesse never;
But love my *Clipseby* ever. 25

[1] See H-283. [2] Psalm lv.12–14, "it was not an enemy that reproached me; then I could have borne it: neither was it he that hated me, that did magnify himself against me; then I would have hid myself from him: But it was thou, a man, mine equal, my guide, and mine acquaintance. We took counsel together."

H–427 *Upon* Roots. *Epigram.*

ROots had no money; yet he went o'th score[1]
For a wrought[2] Purse; can any tell wherefore?
Say, What sho'd *Roots* do with a Purse in print,[3]
That h'ad nor Gold or Silver to put in't?

[1] on tick. [2] manufactured, probably of silk ornamented with needlework. [3] in precisely the proper manner.

H–428 *Upon* Craw.

CRaw cracks in sirrop;[1] and do's stinking say,
Who can hold that (my friends) that will away?

[1] Sugar syrup reaches the crackling stage when a finger plunged into it and then into cold water is covered with hardened sugar which, when rubbed, breaks off with a crackling sound. But the syrup here is fluid faeces.

H–429 *Observation.*

WHo to the North, or South, doth set
His Bed, Male children shall beget.[1]

[1] based on J[ohn] G[regory], *Notes and Observations upon some Passages of Scripture* (Oxford, 1646), p. 92: "whoever . . . shall set his Bed *North* and *South* shall beget male children. *Ps.* 17.14 *&c.* Therefore the Jewes hold this Rite of Collocation." Herrick frequently versifies passages from Gregory: N-193 is a continuation of this one.

H–430 *Empires.*

EMpires of Kings, are now, and ever were,
(As *Salust*[1] saith) co-incident to feare.

[1] *Ad Caesarem Oratio,* III, 2: *Equidem ego cuncta imperia crudelia . . . metu agites.*

H–431 *Felicity, quick of flight.*

EVery time seemes short to be,
That's measur'd by felicity:
But one halfe houre, that's made up here
With griefe; seemes longer then a yeare.

H–432 *Putrefaction.*

PUtrefaction is the end
Of all that Nature doth entend.

H–433 *Passion.*

WEre there not a Matter known,
There wo'd be no Passion.

H–434 Jack *and* Jill.[1]

SInce *Jack* and *Jill* both wicked be;
It seems a wonder unto me,
That they no better do agree.

[1] Martial, VIII, 35.

H–435 *Upon Parson* Beanes.

OLd Parson *Beanes* hunts six dayes of the week,
And on the seaventh, he has his Notes to seek.
Six dayes he hollows so much breath away,
That on the seaventh, he can nor preach, or pray.

H–436 *The crowd and company.*

IN holy meetings, there a man may be
One of the crowd, not of the companie.[1]

[1] Bacon, "Of Friendship": "a crowd is not company."

H–437 *Short and long both likes.*

THis Lady's short, that Mistresse she is tall;
But long or short, I'm well content with all.

H–438 *Pollicie in Princes.*

THat Princes may possesse a surer seat,
'Tis fit they make no One with them too great.

H–439 *Upon Rook, Epigram.*

ROok he sells feathers, yet he still doth crie
Fie on this pride, this Female vanitie.
Thus, though the Rooke do's raile against the sin,
He loves the gain that vanity brings in.

H–440

Upon the Nipples of Julia's *Breast.*

HAve ye beheld (with much delight)
A red-Rose peeping through a white?
Or else a Cherrie (double grac't)
Within a Lillie? Center plac't?
Or ever mark't the pretty beam, 5
A Strawberry shewes halfe drown'd in Creame?
Or seen rich Rubies blushing through
A pure smooth Pearle, and Orient too?
So like to this, nay all the rest,
Is each neate Niplet of her breast. 10

H–441

To Daisies, *not to shut so soone.*

1. SHut not so soon; the dull-ey'd night
 Ha's not as yet begunne
To make a seisure on the light,
 Or to seale up the Sun.

2. No Marigolds yet closed are;
 No shadowes great appeare;
Nor doth the early Shepheards Starre
 Shine like a spangle here.

3. Stay but till my *Julia* close
 Her life-begetting eye;
And let the whole world then dispose
 It selfe to live or dye.

H–442

To the little Spinners.[1]

YEe pretty Huswives, wo'd ye know
The worke that I wo'd put ye to?
This, this it sho'd be, for to spin,
A Lawn for me, so fine and thin,
As it might serve me for my skin. 5
For cruell Love ha's me so whipt,
That of my skin, I all am stript;

And shall dispaire, that any art
Can ease the rawnesse, or the smart;
Unlesse you skin again each part. 10
Which mercy if you will but do,
I call all Maids to witnesse too[2]
What here I promise, that no Broom
Shall now, or ever after come
To wrong a *Spinner* or her Loome. 15

[1] spiders. [2] to.

H–443 Oberons *Palace.*

AFter the Feast (my *Shapcot*)[1] see,
The Fairie Court I give to thee:
Where we'le present our *Oberon* led
Halfe tipsie to the Fairie Bed,
Where *Mab* he finds; who there doth lie 5
Not without mickle majesty.
Which, done; and thence remov'd the light,
We'l wish both Them and Thee, good night.

Full as a Bee with Thyme, and Red,
As Cherry harvest, now high fed 10
For Lust and action; on he'l go,
To lye with *Mab,* though all say no.
Lust ha's no eares; He's sharpe as thorn;
And fretfull, carries Hay in's horne,[2]
And lightning in his eyes; and flings 15
Among the Elves, (if mov'd) the stings
Of peltish[3] wasps; we'l know his Guard[.]
Kings though th'are hated, will be fear'd.
Wine lead him on. Thus to a Grove
(Sometimes devoted unto Love) 20
Tinseld with *Twilight,* He, and They
Lead by the shine of Snails; a way
Beat with their num'rous feet, which by
Many a neat perplexity,
Many a turn, and man' a crosse- 25
Track they redeem[4] a bank of mosse
Spungie and swelling, and farre more
Soft then the finest Lemster Ore.[5]
Mildly disparkling, like those fiers,
Which break from the Injeweld tyres 30

Of curious Brides;[6] or like those mites
Of Candi'd dew in Moony nights.
Upon this *Convex*, all the flowers,
(Nature begets by th'Sun, and showers,)
Are to a wilde digestion brought, 35
As if Loves *Sampler* here was wrought:
Or *Citherea's Ceston*,[7] which
All with temptation doth bewitch.
Sweet Aires move here; and more divine
Made by the breath of great ey'd kine, 40
Who as they lowe empearl with milk
The four-leav'd grasse, or mosse like silk.
The breath of *Munkies*[8] met to mix
With *Musk-flies*, are th'*Aromaticks*,
Which cense this Arch; and here and there, 45
And farther off, and every where,
Throughout that *Brave Mosaick* yard
Those Picks[9] or Diamonds in the Card:
With peeps[10] of Harts, of Club and Spade
Are here most neatly inter-laid. 50
Many a Counter,[11] many a Die,
Half rotten, and without an eye,
Lies here abouts; and for to pave
The excellency of this Cave,
Squirrils and childrens teeth late shed, 55
Are neatly here enchequered[12]
With brownest *Toadstones*,[13] and the Gum
That shines upon the blewer Plum.
The nails faln off by Whit-flawes:[14] Art's
Wise hand enchasing here those warts, 60
Which we to others (from our selves)
Sell, and brought hither by the Elves.
The tempting Mole, stoln from the neck
Of the shie Virgin, seems to deck
The holy Entrance; where within 65
The roome is hung with the blew skin
Of shifted Snake: enfreez'd throughout
With eyes of Peacocks Trains, and Trout-
flies curious wings; and these among
Those silver-pence, that cut the tongue 70
Of the red infant,[15] neatly hung.
The glow-wormes eyes; the shining scales
Of silv'rie fish; wheat-strawes, the snailes

Soft Candle-light; the Kitling's eyne;
Corrupted wood; serve here for shine. 75
No glaring light of bold-fac't Day,
Or other over radiant Ray
Ransacks this roome; but what weak beams
Can make reflected from these jems,
And multiply; Such is the light, 80
But ever doubtfull Day, or night.
By this quaint Taper-light he winds
His Errours up;[16] and now he finds
His Moon-tann'd *Mab,* as somewhat sick,
And (Love knowes) tender as a chick. 85
Upon six plump *Dandillions,* high-
Rear'd, lyes her Elvish-majestie:
Whose woollie-bubbles seem'd to drowne
Hir *Mab-ship* in obedient Downe.
For either sheet, was spread the Caule 90
That doth the Infants face enthrall,
When it is born: (by some enstyl'd
The luckie *Omen* of the child)
And next to these two blankets ore-
Cast of the finest *Gossamore.* 95
And then a Rug of carded wooll,
Which, *Spunge-like* drinking in the dull-
Light of the Moon, seem'd to comply,[17]
Cloud-like, the *daintie Deitie.*
Thus soft she lies: and over-head 100
A *Spinners* circle is bespread,
With Cob-web-curtains: from the roof
So neatly sunck, as that no proof
Of any tackling can declare
What gives it hanging in the Aire. 105
The Fringe about this, are those *Threds*
Broke at the Losse of *Maiden-heads:*
And all behung with these pure Pearls,
Dropt from the eyes of *ravisht Girles*
Or writhing Brides; when, (panting) they 110
Give unto Love the straiter way.
For Musick now; He has the cries
Of fained-lost-Virginities;
The which the *Elves* make to excite
A more unconquer'd appetite. 115
The Kings undrest; and now upon
The Gnats-watch-word the *Elves* are gone.

And now the bed, and *Mab* possest
Of this great-little-kingly-Guest.
We'll nobly think, what's to be done, 120
He'll do no doubt; *This flax is spun.*

H-293A, n.2. [2] he is dangerously ill-tempered. Hay was fastened o a dangerous ox's horns. [3] frettingly angry. [4] reach. [5] wool rom the market of Leominster (pronounced *Lemster*) in Hereordshire. Cf. Drayton, Poly-Olbion, VII, 189–91: "Where lives he man so dull, on Britains furthest shore, / To whom did never ound the name of Lemster ore? / That with the silkworms web or smalness doth compare." [6] the bejewelled headdresses of exuisitely elegant brides. [7] Venus's girdle. [8] monkey-flowers or gworts? [9] another word for the diamonds on playing cards. [0] pips: figures or "spots." [11] many of the chips (of metal, ivory, r the like) used in games of cards, etc.; *counter* is also used for piece or man in chess and checkers. [12] fitted into a checkered attern. [13] tiny stones shaped or colored like a toad. Cf. *As You ike It*, II, i.13–14: "the toad, ugly and venomous, / Wears yet a recious jewel in his head." [14] because of whitlows (finger inammations). [15] a sharp-edged silver coin was sometimes used o cut the ligament which made an infant tongue-tied. [16] he rings his wanderings to an end. [17] enfold.

I–444

To his peculiar friend Master Thomas Shapcott, *Lawyer.*

I'Ve paid Thee, what I promis'd; that's not All;
Besides I give Thee here a Verse that shall
(When hence thy Circum-mortall-part is gon)
Arch-like, hold up, *Thy Name's Inscription.*
Brave men can't die; whose Candid Actions are 5
Writ in the Poets Endlesse-Kalendar:
Whose *velome,* and whose *volumne* is the Skie,
And the pure Starres the praising Poetrie.
Farewell.

I–445

To Julia *in the Temple.*

BEsides us two, i'th'Temple here's not one
To make up now a Congregation.

Let's to the *Altar of perfumes* then go,
And say short Prayers; and when we have done so,
Then we shall see, how in a little space,
Saints will come in to fill each Pew and Place.

H–446 *To* Oenone.

1. WHat Conscience,[1] say, is it in thee
   When I a Heart had one,[2]
   To Take away that Heart from me,
   And to retain thy own?

2. For shame or pitty now encline
   To play a loving part;
   Either to send me kindly thine,
   Or give me back my heart.

3. Covet not both; but if thou dost
   Resolve to part with neither;
   Why! yet to shew that thou art just,
   Take me and mine together.

[1] What sense of right, reason, or fairness. [2] i.e. *only one*, in contrast with *both* in line 9. (The notion that *one* = *won*, and Martin's suggestion that *one* = the past participle of *owe*, to possess seem uncalled for).

H–447 *His weaknesse in woes.*

I Cannot suffer; And in this, my part
Of Patience wants.[1] *Grief breaks the stoutest Heart.*

[1] is defective.

H–448 *Fame makes us forward.*

TO Print our Poems, the propulsive cause
Is Fame, (the breath of popular applause.)

H–449 *To Groves.*

YEe silent shades, whose each tree here
Some Relique of a Saint doth weare:
Who for some sweet-hearts sake, did prove
The fire, and martyrdome of love.
Here is the Legend of those Saints 5
That di'd for love; and their complaints:
Their wounded hearts; and names we find
Encarv'd upon the Leaves and Rind.
Give way, give way to me, who come
Scorch't with the selfe-same martyrdome: 10
And have deserv'd as much (Love knowes)
As to be canoniz'd 'mongst those,
Whose deeds, and deaths here written are
Within your *Greenie-Kalendar:*
By all those Virgins Fillets hung 15
Upon your Boughs, and Requiems sung
For Saints and Soules departed hence,
(Here honour'd still with Frankincense)
By all those teares that have been shed,
As a *Drink-offering,* to the dead: 20
By all those True-love-knots, that be
With Motto's carv'd on every tree,
By sweet *Saint Phillis;*[1] pitie me:
By deare *Saint Iphis;*[2] and the rest,
Of all those other Saints now blest; 25
Me, me, forsaken, here admit
Among your Mirtles to be writ:
That my poore name may have the glory
To live remembred in your story.

[1] "Saint" Phillis, a Thracian princess hanged herself for love of Demophoön when he failed to return to her on the promised day. According to Hyginus, *Fabulae,* LIX, the trees around her tomb periodically dropped their leaves in mourning. In other accounts she changed to a leafless almond tree which, when embraced by her belated lover, put forth leaves. [2] When Anaxarete slighted his wooing, he hanged himself. When she watched his funeral without emotion, she turned to stone (Ovid, *Metamorphoses,* XIV, 698–764).

H–450 *An Epitaph upon a Virgin.*

HEre a solemne Fast we keepe,
While all beauty lyes asleep
Husht be all things; (no noyse here)
But the toning of a teare:
Or a sigh of such as bring 5
Cowslips for her covering.

H–451

To the right gratious Prince, Lodwick, *Duke of* Richmond *and* Lenox.[1]

OF all those three-brave-brothers, faln i'th'Warre,
(Not without glory) Noble Sir, you are,
Despite of all concussions left the Stem
To shoot forth Generations like to them.
Which may be done, if (Sir) you can beget 5
Men in their substance, not in counterfeit.
Such Essences as those Three Brothers; known
Eternall by their own production.
Of whom, from Fam[e]'s white Trumpet, This Ile Tell,
Worthy their everlasting Chronicle, 10
Never since first *Bellona* us'd a Shield,
Such Three brave Brothers fell in Mars *his Field.*
These were those Three *Horatii*[2] *Rome* did boast,
Rom's where[3] these *Three Horatii* we have lost.
One *Cordelion*[4] had that Age long since; 15
This, Three; which Three, you make up Foure *Brave Prince.*

[1] Herrick is confused. Ludovick, 2nd Duke of Lennox, died in 1624, and also his brother, Esme, the 3rd Duke. Esme's son, James Stuart, the 4th Duke, had three brothers who were killed in the wars: George in 1642, John in 1644, and Bernard in 1645 (See H-219). Another brother named Ludovick became an ecclesiastic but never succeeded to the ducal title. [2] three brothers whose victories in single combats with three Latin brothers, the Curatii, decided a struggle between Rome and Alba. [3] Martin changes "where" to "were". [4] Coeur-de-lion: Richard I, the Lion-Hearted.

H–452 *To Jealousie.*

O *Jealousie,* that art
The Canker of the heart:
And mak'st all hell
Where thou do'st dwell;[1]
For pitie be
No *Furie,* or no *Fire-brand* to me.

2. Farre from me Ile remove
All thoughts of irksome Love:
And turn to snow,
Or Christall grow;
To keep still free
(O! Soul-tormenting Jealousie,) from Thee.

[1] Cf. Burton, 3,3,1,1 (ed. 6, p. 596), on jealousy: "A most violent passion it is where it taketh place, an unspeakable torment, an hellish torture, an infernal plague, as *Ariosto* cals it, *A fury, a continual fever.*"

H–453 *To live Freely.*[1]

LEt's live in hast; use pleasures while we may:
Co'd life return, 'twod never lose a day.

[1] Martial, VII, 47, 11–12.

H–454 *Upon* Spunge. *Epigram.*

SPunge makes his boasts that he's the onely man
Can hold of Beere and Ale an Ocean;
Is this his Glory? then his Triumph's Poore;
I know the *Tunne* of *Hidleberge*[1] holds more.

[1] a cask at Heidelberg renowned for its size.

H–455 *His Almes.*

HEre, here I live,
And somewhat give,
Of what I have,
To those, who crave.
Little or much, 5
My Almnes is such:
But if my deal[1]
Of Oyl and Meal
Shall fuller grow,
More Ile bestow: 10
Mean time be it
E'en but a bit,
Or else a crum,
The scrip[2] hath some.

[1] portion. [2] wallet.

H–456 *Upon himself.*

COme, leave this loathed Country-life, and then
Grow up to be a Roman *Citizen.*
Those mites of Time, which yet remain unspent,
Waste[1] thou in that most Civill Government.
Get their comportment, and the gliding tongue 5
Of those mild Men, thou art to live among:
Then being seated in that smoother *Sphere,*
Decree thy everlasting *Topick*[2] there.
And to the Farm-house nere return at all;
Though Granges do not love thee, Cities shall. 10

[1] pass or spend. [2] place. Cf. Ps. cxlviii.6, "He hath also established them for ever and ever: he hath made a decree which shall not pass." In Job xxxviii.10 God states that he broke up His "decreed place" for the sea.

H–457 *To enjoy the Time.*

WHile Fate[1] permits us, let's be merry;
Passe all we must the fatall Ferry:[2]
And this our life too whirles away,
With the Rotation of the Day.

[1] "Fates" in the 1648 text. [2] Charon's ferry across the river Styx.

H–458 *Upon Love.*

1. LOve, I have broke
Thy yoke;
The neck is free:
But when I'm next
Love vext,
Then shackell me.

2. 'Tis better yet
To fret
The feet or hands;
Then to enthrall,
Or gall
The neck with bands.

H–459

To the right Honourable Mildmay,[1] *Earle of* Westmorland.

YOu are a Lord, an Earle, nay more, a Man,
Who writes sweet Numbers well as any can:
If so, why then are not These Verses hurld,
Like *Sybels* Leaves, throughout the ample world?[2]
What is a Jewell if it be not set 5
Forth by a Ring, or some rich Carkanet?
But being so; then the beholders cry,
See, see a Jemme (as rare as *Bælus* eye.)[3]
Then publick praise do's runne upon the Stone,
For a most rich, a rare, a precious One. 10
Expose your jewels then unto the view,
That we may praise Them, or themselves prize You.

Vertue conceal'd (with *Horace* you'l confesse)
Differs not much from drowzie slothfullnesse.[4]

[1] Mildmay Fane, d. 1665, minor dramatist and poet. He failed to print his works other than *Otia Sacra* (1648); a copy of this poem sent to him in manuscript may have conduced to this one publication. [2] The Sibyl or Prophetess of Cumae wrote predictions on leaves and placed them at the entrance to her cave. Winds often scattered them, making their meaning unintelligible, before they could be gathered by those who wanted to consult her. [3] a white stone within which a black circle glitters like gold; the ancient Assyrians dedicated it to their god Belus. See Pliny, Natural History, XXXVII, 55. [4] Horace, *Carmina*, IV, 9, 29–30.

H–460

The Plunder.[1]

I Am of all bereft;
Save but some few Beanes left,
Whereof (at last) to make
For me, and mine a Cake:
Which eaten, they and I 5
Will say our grace, and die.

[1] Cf. I Kings xvii.12, "I have not a cake, but an handful of meal in a barrel, and a little oil in a cruse: and behold, I am gathering two sticks, that I may go in, and dress it for me and my son, that we may eat it, and die."

H–461

Littlenesse no cause of Leannesse.

ONe feeds on Lard, and yet is leane;
And I but feasting with a Beane,
Grow fat and smooth: The reason is,
Jove prospers my meat, more then his.

H–462

Upon one who said she was alwayes young.

YOu say y'are young; but when your Teeth are told[1]
To be but three, Black-ey'd, wee'l thinke y'are old.

[1] counted.

H-463 *Upon* Huncks. *Epigram.*

HUncks ha's no money (he do's sweare, or say)
About him, when the Taverns shot's to pay.
If he ha's none in's pockets, trust me, *Huncks*
Ha's none at home, in Coffers, Desks, or Trunks.[1]

[1] Cf. Martial's one-line epigram (VIII, 19), *Pauper videri Cinna vult, et est pauper,* which Lovelace rendered with more neatness than accuracy: "Cinna seems poor in show, / And he is so."

H-464

The Jimmall Ring,[1] or True-love-knot.

THou sent'st to me a True-love-knot; but I
Return'd a Ring of Jimmals, to imply
Thy Love had one knot, mine a triple tye.

[1] a gimmal: a finger-ring divisible into two or three rings.

H-465

The parting Verse, or charge to his supposed Wife when he travelled.[1]

GO hence, and with this parting kisse,
Which joyns two souls, remember this;
Though thou beest young, kind, soft, and faire,
And may'st draw thousands with a haire:
Yet let these glib temptations be 5
Furies to others, Friends to me.
Looke upon all; and though on fire
Thou set'st their hearts, let chaste desire
Steere Thee to me; and thinke (me gone)
In having all, that thou hast none. 10
Nor so immured wo'd I have
Thee live, as dead and in thy grave;
But walke abroad, yet wisely well
Stand for my comming, Sentinell.
And think (as thou do'st walke the street) 15
Me, or my shadow thou do'st meet.

I know a thousand greedy eyes
Will on thy Feature[2] tirannize,[3]
In my short absence; yet behold
Them like some Picture, or some Mould 20
Fashion'd like Thee; which though 'tave eares
And eyes, it neither sees or heares.
Gifts will be sent, and Letters, which
Are the expressions of that itch,
And salt,[4] which frets thy Suters; fly 25
Both, lest thou lose thy liberty:
For that once lost, thou't fall to one,
Then prostrate to a million.
But if they wooe thee, do thou say,
(As that chaste Queen of *Ithaca*[5] 30
Did to her suitors) this web done
(Undone as oft as done) I'm wonne;
I will not urge Thee, for I know,
Though thou art young, thou canst say no,
And no again, and so deny, 35
Those thy Lust-burning *Incubi*.[6]
Let them enstile Thee Fairest faire,
The Pearle of Princes,[7] yet despaire
That so thou art, because thou must
Believe, Love speaks it not, but Lust; 40
And this their Flatt'rie do's commend
Thee chiefly for their pleasures end.
I am not jealous of thy Faith,
Or will be; for the Axiome saith,
He that doth suspect, do's haste 45
A gentle mind to be unchaste.
No, live thee to thy selfe, and keep
Thy thoughts as cold, as is thy sleep:
And let thy dreames be only fed
With this, that I am in thy bed. 50
And thou then turning in that Sphere,
Waking shalt find me sleeping there.
But yet if boundlesse Lust must skaile
Thy Fortress, and will needs prevaile;
And wildly force a passage in, 55
Banish consent, and 'tis no sinne
Of Thine; so *Lucrece* fell, and the
Chaste *Syracusian Cyane*.
So *Medullina*[8] fell, yet none
Of these had imputation 60

For the least trespasse; 'cause the mind
Here was not with the act combin'd.
The body sins not, 'tis the Will
That makes the Action, good, or ill.[9]
And if thy fall sho'd this way come, 65
Triumph in such a Martirdome.
I will not over-long enlarge
To thee, this my religious charge.
Take this compression,[10] so by this
Means I shall know what other kisse 70
Is mixt with mine; and truly know,
Returning, if't be mine or no:
Keepe it till then; and now my Spouse,
For my wisht safety pay thy vowes,
And prayers to *Venus;* if it please 75
The *Great-blew-ruler*[11] of the Seas;
Not many full-fac't-moons shall waine,
Lean-horn'd, before I come again
As one triumphant; when I find
In thee, all faith of Woman-kind. 80
Nor wo'd I have thee thinke, that Thou
Had'st power thy selfe to keep this vow;
But having scapt temptations shelfe,
Know vertue taught thee, not thy selfe.

[1] There is a long tradition of literary works on imaginary wives, mistresses, and children; e.g. Crashaw's "Wishes. To his (supposed) Mistresse" and Lamb's "Dream Children." This poem also belongs to a tradition of poems on partings from loved ones; cf. Donne's "Valediction Forbidding Mourning." [2] comeliness. [3] have the power of gazing without restraint. [4] sexual desire. [5] Odysseus' wife, Penelope. [6] adulterous demons. [7] The title was applied to females as well as males. [8] All three were victims of rape but, not having consented, remained chaste. [9] This doctrine is a commonplace in law, theology, and classical literature. [10] Possibly (a) this succinct injunction—referring to the preceding statement that he will not be needlessly verbose in explaining to her the dutiful responsibility entrusted to her by him. (b) an embrace. (c) a ring which has the magic property of turning pale if its wearer is unfaithful: this meaning is suggested by MS variants. [11] Neptune.

H–466

To his Kinsman, Sir Thomas Soame.[1]

SEeing Thee *Soame*, I see a Goodly man,
And in that Good, a great *Patrician*.[2]
Next to which Two; among the City-Powers,
And Thrones, thy selfe one of Those Senatours:[3]
Not wearing Purple only for the show; 5
(As many Conscripts of the Citie do)
But for True Service, worthy of that Gowne,
The *Golden* chain too, and the *Civick* Crown.[4]

[1] son of Herrick's mother's sister Anne, brother of William Soame (H-331), father of Anne who became Lady Abdy (H-375). He was a prominent member of the Grocer's Company, had interests in the Russia and East India Companies, and served as an alderman and colonel in London. He and his family had close connections with puritan groups. As a member of Parliament, though knighted in 1641, he was loyal to the parliamentary side but was removed from his aldermanship and secluded from the House of Commons in 1648. His several residences included a fine house in Soper Lane, London. [2] In calling Soame "*Patrician*" because of his noble character, Herrick may refer to Soame's imprisonment in 1640 for refusing to list men in his aldermannic ward able to advance money for a loan demanded by the king. When examined in Star Chamber, Soame bluntly asserted that he thought the duty required of him to be dishonest. [3] Sir Thomas is placed among the civic equivalents of the angelic orders of Powers and Thrones because, as an alderman, his position is loosely equivalent to the *Patres Conscripti* (enrolled or elected civic fathers) or Senators of ancient Rome. [4] worthy of the alderman's gown, the Lord Mayor's golden chain of office, and the garland of oak leaves conferred by the ancients upon those who served the state with distinction. In Sept. 1640 Sir Thomas was the leading candidate for Lord Mayor of London and probably would have been declared elected had he been *persona grata* to the king. The poem must have been written after Soame was knighted in December, 1641, but probably before the outbreak of the Civil War in 1642.

H–467

To Blossoms.

1. FAire pledges of a fruitfull Tree,
Why do yee fall so fast?
Your date is not so past;

But you may stay yet here a while,
To blush and gently smile;
And go at last.

2. What, were yee borne to be
An houre or half's delight;
And so to bid goodnight?
'Twas pitie Nature brought yee forth
Meerly to shew your worth,
And lose you quite.

3. But you are lovely Leaves, where we
May read how soon things have
Their end, though ne'r so brave:
And after they have shown their pride,
Like you a while: They glide
Into the Grave.

H-468 *Mans dying-place uncertain.*

MAn knowes where first he ships himselfe; but he
Never can tell, where shall his Landing be.

H-469 *Nothing Free-cost.*

NOthing comes Free-cost here; *Jove* will not let
His gifts go from him; if not bought with sweat.

H-470 *Few fortunate.*

MAny we are, and yet but few possesse
Those Fields of everlasting happinesse.

H-471 *To* Perenna.

HOw long, *Perenna*, wilt thou see
Me languish for the love of Thee?
Consent and play a friendly part
To save; when thou may'st kill a heart.

H–472 *To the Ladyes.*

TRust me Ladies, I will do
Nothing to distemper you;
If I any fret or vex,
Men they shall be, *not your sex.*

H–473 *The old Wives Prayer.*

HOly-Rood come forth and shield
Us i'th'Citie, and the Field:
Safely guard us, now and aye,
From the blast that burns by day;
And those sounds that us affright
In the dead of dampish night.[1]
Drive all hurtfull Feinds us fro,
By the Time the Cocks first crow.

[1] Cf. Ps. xci.5–6, "Thou shalt not be afraid for the terror by night; nor for the arrow that flieth by day; Nor for the pestilence that walketh in darkness."

H–474

Upon a cheap Laundresse. Epigram.

FEacie (some say) doth wash her clothes i'th'Lie
That sharply trickles from her either eye.
The *Laundresses,* They envie her good-luck,
Who can with so small charges *drive the buck.*[1]
What needs she fire and ashes to consume,
Who can scoure Linnens with her own salt *reeume?*

[1] who can so cheaply buck-wash, i.e. boil dirty linen in a lye solution and then beat and rinse it in water.

H–475 *Upon his departure hence.*

THus I
Passe by,
And die:
As One,

Unknown,
And gon:
I'm made
A shade,
And laid
I'th grave, 10
There have
My Cave.
Where tell
I dwell,
Farewell.

H–476 *The Wassaile.*[1]

1. GIve way, give way ye Gates, and win
An easie blessing to your Bin,
And Basket, by our entring in.

2. May both with manchet[2] stand repleat;
Your Larders too so hung with meat,
That though a thousand, thousand eat;

3. Yet, ere twelve *Moones* shall whirl about
Their silv'rie Spheres, ther's none may doubt,
But more's sent in, then was serv'd out.

4. Next, may your Dairies Prosper so,
As that your pans no Ebbe may know;
But if they do, the more to flow.

5. Like to a solemne sober Stream
Bankt all with Lillies, and the Cream
Of sweetest *Cow-slips* filling Them.

6. Then, may your Plants be prest[3] with Fruit,
Nor Bee, or Hive you have be mute;
But sweetly sounding like a Lute.

7. Next may your Duck and teeming Hen
Both to the Cocks-tread say *Amen;*
And for their two egs render ten.

8. Last, may your Harrows, Shares and Ploughes,
Your Stacks, your Stocks, your sweetest Mowes,[4]
All prosper by your Virgin-vowes.

9. Alas! we blesse, but see none here,
That brings us either Ale or Beere;
In a drie-house all things are neere.[5]

10. Let's leave[6] a longer time to wait,
Where Rust and Cobwebs bind the gate;
And all live here with *needy Fate.*

11. Where Chimneys do for ever weepe,
For want of warmth, and Stomachs keepe
With noise, the servants eyes from sleep.

12. It is in vain to sing, or stay
Our free-feet here; but we'l away:
Yet to the Lares this we'l say,

13. The time will come, when you'l be sad,
And reckon this for fortune bad,
T'ave lost the good ye might have had.

[1] literally "Health to you," but here the term is extended to the song of blessing sung by a group who went from house to house in the Christmas season. Their singing was customarily rewarded with drink or small gifts. [2] small rolls or loaves made of the finest wheat flour. [3] laden. [4] haymows and heaps of grain. [5] niggardly, penurious. [6] cease.

H–477

Upon a Lady faire, but fruitlesse.

TWice has *Pudica* been a Bride, and led
By holy *Himen* to the Nuptiall Bed.
Two Youths sha's known, thrice two, and twice 3. yeares;
Yet not a Lillie from the Bed appeares;
Nor will; for why, *Pudica*, this may know,
Trees never beare, unlesse they first do blow.[1]

[1] blossom.

H–478

How Springs came first.

THese Springs were Maidens once that lov'd,
But lost to that they most approv'd:
My Story tells, by Love they were
Turn'd to these Springs, which wee see here:

The pretty whimpering that they make,
When of the Banks their leave they take;
Tels ye but this, they are the same,
In nothing chang'd but in their name.

H–479 *To Rosemary and Baies.*

MY wooing's ended: now my wedding's neere;
When Gloves are giving,[1] *Guilded be you there.*[2]

[1] a wedding custom. [2] Rosemary and laurel were sometimes gilded for display at weddings.

H–480 *Upon* Skurffe.

SKurffe by his Nine-bones[1] sweares, and well he may,
All know a Fellon eate[2] the Tenth away.

[1] A common oath was to swear "by these ten bones," i.e. the fingers. [2] a finger infection (whitlow) ate.

H–481 *Upon a Scarre in a* Virgins *Face.*

'TIs Heresie in others: In your face
That Scarr's no *Schisme,*[1] but the *sign of grace.*

[1] from Greek *schisma,* cleft or division.

H–482 *Upon his eye-sight failing him.*

I Beginne to waine in sight;
Shortly I shall bid goodnight:
Then no gazing more about,
When the Tapers once are out.

H-483 *To his worthy Friend, Master* Thomas Falconbirge.

STand with thy Graces forth, Brave man, and rise
High with thine own *Auspitious Destinies:*
Nor leave the search, and proofe,[1] till Thou canst find
These, or those ends, to which Thou wast design'd.
Thy lucky *Genius,* and thy guiding *Starre,* 5
Have made Thee prosperous in thy wayes, thus farre:
Nor will they leave Thee, till they both have shown
Thee to the World a *Prime* and *Publique One.*
Then, when Thou see'st thine Age all turn'd to gold,
Remember what thy *Herrick* Thee foretold, 10
When at the holy Threshold of thine house,
He Boded good-luck to thy Selfe and Spouse.
Lastly, be mindfull (when thou art grown great)
That Towrs high rear'd dread most the lightnings threat:[2]
When as the humble Cottages not feare 15
The cleaving Bolt of Jove *the Thunderer.*

[1] testing, examining, putting to trial. Falconbridge's only known public offices were those of an auditor of excise accounts and a receiver general at Westminster. [2] Burton, 2,3,3 (ed. 6, p. 321) quotes Horace, *Carmina,* II, 10, 10–12, and adds a loose paraphrase: "the lightning commonly sets on fire the highest towers; in the more eminent place he is, the more subject to fall."

H-484

Upon Julia's *haire fill'd with Dew.*

DEw sate on *Julia's* haire,
And spangled too,
Like Leaves that laden are
With trembling Dew:
Or glitter'd to my sight,
As when the Beames
Have their reflected light,
Daunc't by the Streames.

H–485 *Another on her.*

HOw can I choose but love, and follow her,
Whose shadow smels like milder *Pomander!*
How can I chuse but kisse her, whence do's come
The *Storax, Spiknard, Myrrhe,* and *Ladanum.*

H–486 *Losse from the least.*

GReat men by small meanes oft are overthrown:
He's Lord of thy life, who contemnes his own.[1]

[1] trans. from Seneca, *Epistolae,* IV, 8.

H–487 *Reward*[s] *and punishments.*

ALl things are open to these two events,[1]
Or to Rewards, or else to Punishments.

[1] eventualities.

H–488 *Shame, no Statist.*

SHame is a bad attendant to a State:[1]
He rents his Crown, That feares the Peoples hate.

[1] trans. from Seneca, *Hippolytus,* 430.

H–489 *To Sir* Clisebie Crew.[1]

SInce to th'Country first I came,
I have lost my former flame:
And, methinks, I not inherit,[2]
As I did, my ravisht spirit.
If I write a Verse, or two, 5
'Tis with very much ado;

In regard I want that Wine,
Which sho'd conjure up a line.
Yet, though now of Muse bereft,
I have still the manners left 10
For to thanke you (Noble Sir)
For those gifts you do conferre
Upon him, who only can
Be in Prose a *gratefull man.*

[1] See H-426, H-544, H-620. [2] possess.

H-490 *Upon himselfe.*

I Co'd never love indeed;
Never see mine own heart bleed:
Never crucifie my life;
Or for Widow, Maid, or Wife.

2. I co'd never seeke to please
One, or many Mistresses:
Never like their lips, to sweare
Oyle of Roses still smelt there.

3. I co'd never breake my sleepe,
Fold mine Armes, sob, sigh, or weep:
Never beg, or humbly wooe
With oathes, and lyes, (as others do.)

4. I co'd never walke alone;
Put a shirt of sackcloth on:
Never keep a fast, or pray
For good luck in love (that day.)

5. But have hitherto liv'd free,
As the aire that circles me:
And kept credit with my heart,
Neither broke i'th whole, or part.

H-491 Fresh Cheese and Cream.

WO'd yee have fresh Cheese and Cream?
Julia's Breast can give you them:
And if more; Each *Nipple* cries,
To your *Cream,* her[e]'s *Strawberries.*

H–492

An Eclogue, or Pastorall between Endimion Porter[1] *and* Lycidas Herrick, *set and sung.*

1.

Endym. AH! *Lycidas,* come tell me why
Thy whilome merry Oate
By thee doth so neglected lye;
And never purls a Note?

2.

I prithee speake: *Lyc.* I will. *End.* Say on:
Lyc. 'Tis thou, and only thou,
That art the cause *Endimion;*
End. For Loves-sake, tell me how.

3.

Lyc. In this regard, that thou do'st play
Upon an other Plain:
And for a Rurall Roundelay,
Strik'st now a Courtly strain.

4.

Thou leav'st our Hills, our Dales, our Bowers,
Our finer fleeced sheep:
(Unkind to us) to spend thine houres,
Where Shepheards sho'd not keep.

5.

I meane the Court: Let *Latmos*[2] be
My lov'd *Endymions* Court;
End. But I the Courtly State wo'd see:
Lyc. Then see it in report.

6.

What ha's the Court to do with Swaines,
Where *Phillis* is not known?
Nor do's it mind the Rustick straines
Of us, or *Coridon.*

7.

Breake, if thou lov'st us, this delay;
End. Dear *Lycidas,* e're long,
I vow by *Pan,* to come away
And Pipe unto thy Song.

8.

Then *Jessimine*, with *Florabell;*
And dainty *Amarillis,*
With handsome-handed *Drosomell*
Shall pranke[3] thy Hooke with Lillies.

9.

Lyc. Then *Tityrus*, and *Coridon*,
And *Thyrsis*, they shall follow
With all the rest; while thou alone
Shalt lead, like young *Apollo.*

10.

And till thou com'st, thy *Lycidas,*
In every *Geniall* Cup,
Shall write in Spice, *Endimion* 'twas
That kept his Piping up.

And my most luckie Swain, when I shall live to see
Endimions Moon to fill up full, remember me:
Mean time, let *Lycidas* have leave to Pipe to thee.

[1] See H-117, H-185, H-662. [2] mountain in Caria where Endymion kept flocks and loved the moon goddess. [3] adorn.

H–493 *To a Bed of Tulips.*

1. BRight Tulips, we do know,
You had your comming hither;
And Fading-time do's show,
That Ye must quickly wither.

2. Your *Sister-hoods* may stay,
And smile here for your houre;
But dye ye must away:
Even as the meanest Flower.

3. Come Virgins then, and see
Your frailties; and bemone ye;
For lost like these, 'twill be,
As Time had never known ye.

H-494 *A Caution.*

THat Love last long; let it thy first care be
To find a Wife, that is most fit for Thee.
Be She too wealthy, or too poore; be sure,
Love in extreames, can never long endure.

H-495 *To the Water Nymphs, drinking at the Fountain.*[1]

1. REach, with your whiter hands, to me,
   Some Christall of the Spring;
   And I, about the Cup shall see
   Fresh Lillies flourishing.

2. Or else sweet Nimphs do you but this;
   To'th'Glasse your lips encline;
   And I shall see by that one kisse,
   The Water turn'd to Wine.

[1] The poem may be sung to the tune of Jonson's "Drink to me only with thine eyes."

H-496 *To his Honoured Kinsman, Sir* Richard Stone.[1]

TO this *white Temple* of my *Heroes,*[2] here
Beset with stately Figures (every where)
Of such rare *Saint-ships,* who did here consume
Their lives in sweets, and left in death perfume.
Come thou *Brave*[3] *man!* And bring with Thee a Stone 5
Unto thine own *Edification.*[4]
High are These Statues here, besides no lesse
Strong then the Heavens for everlastingnesse:
Where build aloft; and being fixt by These,
Set up Thine own *eternall Images.* 10

[1] of Stukeley, Huntingdonshire; son of Herrick's mother's brother John; knighted 1642. Her brother Richard and his son of the same name seem not to have been knighted. [2] Herrick's imaginary hall of fame containing statues of patrons, relatives, and friends. [3] splendid and superior. [4] building or erection as a statue.

H-497 *Upon a Flie.*

A Golden Flie one shew'd to me,
Clos'd in a Box of Yvorie:
Where both seem'd proud; the Flie to have
His buriall in an yvory grave:
The yvorie tooke State to hold 5
A Corps as bright as burnisht gold.
One Fate had both; both equall Grace;
The Buried, and the Burying-place.
Not *Virgils Gnat,*[1] to whom the Spring
All Flowers sent to'is burying. 10
Not *Marshals Bee,* which in a Bead
Of *Amber* quick was buried.[2]
Nor that fine Worme that do's interre
Her selfe i'th'*silken Sepulchre.*
Nor my rare ***Phil,*[3] that lately was 15
With Lillies Tomb'd up in a Glasse;
More honour had, then this same *Flie;*
Dead, and clos'd up in *Yvorie.*

[1] See H-256; *Culex,* 397–410. [2] Martial, IV, 32; trans. Lovelace: "Both lurks and shines, hid in an amber tear, / The bee, in her own nectar prisoner; / So she, who in her life time was contemn'd, / Ev'n in her very funerals is gemm'd." Cf. Martial, VI, 15 (on an ant). [3]* Sparrow (Herrick's note). See H-256.

H-498 *Upon* Jack *and* Jill. *Epigram.*

WHen *Jill* complaines to *Jack* for want of meate;
Jack kisses *Jill,* and bids her freely eate:
Jill sayes, of what? sayes *Jack,* on that sweet kisse,
Which full of Nectar and Ambrosia is,
The food of Poets; so I thought sayes *Jill,* 5
That makes them looke so lanke, so Ghost-like still.
Let Poets feed on aire, or what they will;
Let me feed full, till that I fart, sayes *Jill.*

H-499 *To* Julia.

JUlia, when thy *Herrick* dies,
Close thou up thy Poets eyes:
And his last breath, let it be
Taken in by none but Thee.

H-500 *To Mistresse* Dorothy Parsons.[1]

IF thou aske me (Deare) wherefore
I do write of thee no more:
I must answer (Sweet) thy part
Lesse is here, then in my heart.

[1] daughter of John Parsons, organist of Westminster Abbey; sister of Thomasine (H-979).

H-501 *Upon* Parrat.

PArrat protests 'tis he, and only he
Can teach a man the *Art of memory:*
Believe him not; for he forgot it quite,
Being drunke, who 'twas that Can'd his Ribs last night.

H-502 *How he would drinke his Wine.*

FIll me my Wine in Christall; thus, and thus
I see't in's *puris naturalibus:*
Unmixt. I love to have it smirke and shine,
'Tis sin I know, 'tis sin to throtle Wine.[1]
What Mad-man's he, that when it sparkles so, 5
Will coole his flames, or quench his fires with snow?

[1] Martial, I, 18, 5, declares that it is a crime to adulterate Falernum.

H–503 *How* Marigolds *came yellow.*

JEalous Girles these sometimes were,
While they liv'd, or lasted here:
Turn'd to *Flowers,* still they be
Yellow, markt for Jealousie.

H–504 *The broken Christall.*

TO Fetch me Wine my *Lucia* went,
Bearing a Christall *continent:*[1]
But making haste, it came to passe,
She brake in two the purer Glasse,
Then smil'd, and sweetly chid her speed; 5
So with a blush, beshrew'd the deed.

[1] a glass container or holder in which the crystal glass or goblet ("the purer Glasse") was placed.

H–505 *Precepts.*

GOod Precepts we must firmly hold,
By daily *Learning* we wax old.

H–506 *To the right Honourable* Edward *Earle of* Dorset.[1]

IF I dare write to You, my Lord, who are,
Of your own selfe, a *Publick Theater.*
And sitting, see the wiles, wayes, walks of wit,
And give a righteous judgement upon it.
What need I care, though some dislike me sho'd, 5
If *Dorset* say, what *Herrick* writes, is good?
We know y'are learn'd i'th'Muses, and no lesse
In our *State-sanctions,*[2] deep, or bottomlesse.
Whose smile can make a Poet; and your glance
Dash all bad Poems out of countenance. 10

So, that an Author needs no other Bayes
For Coronation, then Your onely Praise.
And no one mischief greater then your frown,
To null his Numbers, and to blast his Crowne.
Few live the life immortall. He ensures 15
His Fame's long life, who strives to set up Yours.

[1] Sir Edward Sackville, 4th Earl of Dorset, 1591–1652, a staunch Anglican and Loyalist; in 1644, Lord Chamberlain of the King's Household, Lord Privy Seal, President of the Privy Council. The Venetian Ambassador called him "one of the most active and generous persons of the kingdom; Clarendon observed that he gave full scope to the vices of the period but had a "pleasant, sparkling, and sublime" wit. [2] laws, politics, etc.

H–507 *Upon himself.*

TH'art hence removing, (like a Shepherds Tent)[1]
And walk thou must the way that others went:
Fall thou must first, then rise to life with These,
Markt in thy Book for faithfull Witnesses.[2]

[1] Isa. xxxviii.12, "Mine age is departed, and is removed from me as a shepherd's tent." [2] Ps. xl.7, "Lo, I come: in the volume of the book it is written of me." Dan. xii.1, "thy people shall be delivered, every one that shall be found written in the book." Herrick echoes these passages when he refers to his heroes (H-496) and his roll of their names in an imaginary book, or in *Hesperides*, or possibly in an actual MS volume which he kept for his eulogies. Cf. H-510.

H–508 *Hope well and Have well: or, Faire after Foule weather.*

WHat though the Heaven be lowring now,
And look with a contracted brow?
We shall discover, by and by,
A Repurgation of the Skie:
And when those clouds away are driven, 5
Then will appeare a cheerfull Heaven.

H–509 *Upon Love.*

I Held Love's head while it did ake;
But so it chanc't to be;
The cruell paine did his forsake,
And forthwith came to me.

2. Ai me! How shal my griefe be stil'd?
Or where else shall we find
One like to me, who must be kill'd
For being too-too-kind?

H–510 *To his Kinswoman,*
Mistresse Penelope Wheeler.[1]

NExt is your lot (Faire) to be number'd one,
Here, in my Book's Canonization:
Late you come in; but you a Saint shall be,
In Chiefe, in this Poetick Liturgie.

[1] probably a daughter or sister of John Wheeler, goldsmith, who married the daughter of Robert Herrick, the poet's uncle and godfather.

H–511 *Another upon her.*

FIrst, for your shape, the curious cannot shew
Any one part that's dissonant in you:
And 'gainst your chast behaviour there's no Plea,
Since you are knowne to be *Penelope*.[1]
Thus faire and cleane you are, although there be 5
A mighty strife 'twixt Forme and Chastitie.[2]

[1] Odysseus' faithful wife. [2] Ovid, *Heroides*, XVI (Paris to Helen), 288; trans. by Burton, 3,3,1,2 (ed. 6, p. 601): "Beautie and honesty have ever been at oddes." Cf. *Hamlet*, III. i.111–14: "the power of beauty will sooner transform honesty from what it is to a bawd than the force of honesty can translate beauty into his likeness."

H–512 *Kissing and Bussing.*

KIssing and bussing differ both in this;
We busse our Wantons, but our Wives we kisse.

H–513 *Crosse and Pile.*[1]

FAire and foule dayes trip Crosse and Pile; The faire
Far lesse in number, then our foule dayes are.

[1] head or tail; a toss-up.

H–514

To the Lady Crew,[1] *upon the death of her Child.*

WHy, Madam, will ye longer weep,
When as your Baby's lull'd asleep?
And (pretty Child) feeles now no more
Those paines it lately felt before.
All now is silent; groanes are fled: 5
Your Child lyes still, yet is not dead:
But rather like a flower hid here
To spring againe another yeare.

[1] See H-283, H-426.

H–515 *His Winding-sheet.*

COme thou, who art the Wine, and wit
Of all I've writ:
The Grace, the Glorie, and the best
Piece of the rest.
Thou art of what I did intend 5
The All, and End.
And what was made, was made to meet
Thee, thee my sheet.
Come then, and be to my chast side
Both Bed, and Bride. 10

We two (as Reliques left) will have
One Rest, one Grave.
And, hugging close, we will not feare
Lust entring here:
Where all Desires are dead, or cold 15
As is the mould:
And all Affections are forgot,
Or Trouble not.
Here, here the Slaves and Pris'ners be
From Shackles free:[1] 20
And weeping Widowes long opprest
Doe here find rest.
The wronged Client ends his Lawes
Here, and his Cause.
Here those long suits of Chancery[2] lie 25
Quiet, or die:
And all Star-chamber-Bils[3] doe cease,
Or hold their peace.
Here needs no Court for our Request,[4]
Where all are best; 30
All wise; all equall; and all just
Alike i'th'dust.
Nor need we here to feare the frowne
Of Court, or Crown.
Where Fortune bears no sway o're things, 35
There all are Kings.
In this securer place we'l keep,
As lull'd asleep;
Or for a little time we'l lye,
As Robes laid by; 40
To be another day re-worne,
Turn'd, but not torn:
Or like old Testaments ingrost,[5]
Lockt up, not lost:
And for a while lye here conceal'd, 45
To be reveal'd
Next, at that great Platonick yeere,[6]
And then meet here.

[1] Job iii.17–18, "There the wicked cease from troubling; and there the weary be at rest. There the prisoners rest together; they hear not the voice of the oppressor." [2] lawsuits in the Lord Chancellor's court, the 2nd highest in England. [3] written statements of pleas tried by the Court of Star Chamber, which developed from the

judicial sittings of the King's Council and was abolished in 1641. [4] The Court of Requests was instituted to hear "all poor men's suits"; it was abolished in 1641. [5] wills written out in proper legal form. [6] a period of about 30,000 years, at the end of which the heavenly bodies were supposed to return to their original positions.

H–516 *To Mistresse* Mary Willand.[1]

ONe more by Thee, Love, and Desert have sent,
T'enspangle this expansive Firmament.
O Flame of Beauty! come, appeare, appeare
A Virgin Taper, ever shining here.

[1] relative of Leonard Willan? See H-955.

H–517 *Change gives content.*

WHat now we like, anon we disapprove:
The new successor drives away old Love.[1]

[1] Ovid, *De Remedio Amoris*, 462.

H–518 *Upon* Magot *a frequenter of Ordinaries.*[1]

MAgot frequents those houses of good-cheere,
Talkes most, eates most, of all the Feeders there.
He raves through leane, he rages through the fat;
(What gets the master of the Meal by that?)
He who with talking can devoure so much, 5
How wo'd he eate, were not[2] his hindrance such?

[1] eating houses or taverns providing meals at fixed prices. [2] "nor" in the 1648 ed.

H–519 *On himselfe.*

BOrne I was to meet with Age,
And to walke Life's pilgrimage.
Much I know of Time is spent,
Tell I can't, what's Resident.[1]

Howsoever, cares, adue; 5
Ile have nought to say to you:
But Ile spend my comming houres,
Drinking wine, and crown'd with flowres.

[1] remaining.

H–520 *Fortunes favours.*

FOrtune did never favour one
Fully, without exception;
Though free she be, ther's something yet
Still wanting to her Favourite.

H–521

To Phillis *to love, and live with him.*[1]

LIve, live with me, and thou shalt see
The pleasures Ile prepare for thee:
What sweets the Country can afford
Shall blesse thy Bed, and blesse thy Board.
The soft sweet Mosse shall be thy bed, 5
With crawling Woodbine over-spread:
By which the silver-shedding streames
Shall gently melt thee into dreames.
Thy clothing next, shall be a Gowne
Made of the Fleeces purest Downe. 10
The tongues of Kids shall be thy meate;
Their Milke thy drinke; and thou shalt eate
The Paste of Filberts for thy bread
With Cream of Cowslips buttered:
Thy Feasting-Tables shall be Hills 15
With *Daisies* spread, and *Daffadils;*
Where thou shalt sit, and *Red-brest* by,
For meat, shall give thee melody.
Ile give thee Chaines and Carkanets
Of *Primroses* and *Violets.* 20
A Bag and Bottle thou shalt have;
That richly wrought, and This as brave;
So that as either shall expresse
The Wearer's no meane Shepheardesse.

At Sheering-times, and yearely Wakes,
When *Themilis* his pastime makes,
There thou shalt be; and be the wit,
Nay more, the Feast, and grace of it.
On Holy-dayes, when Virgins meet
To dance the Heyes[2] with nimble feet; 30
Thou shalt come forth, and then appeare
The *Queen of Roses* for that yeere.
And having danc't ('bove all the best)
Carry the Garland from the rest.
In Wicker-baskets Maids shal bring 35
To thee, (my dearest Shepharling)
The blushing Apple, bashfull Peare,
And shame-fac't Plum, (all simp'ring there) [.]
Walk in the Groves, and thou shalt find
The name of *Phillis* in the Rind 40
Of every straight, and smooth-skin tree;
Where kissing that, Ile twice kisse thee.
To thee a Sheep-hook I will send,
Be-pranckt with Ribbands, to this end,
This, this alluring Hook might be 45
Lesse for to catch a sheep, then me.
Thou shalt have Possets, Wassails fine,
Not made of Ale, but spiced Wine;
To make thy Maids and selfe free mirth,
All sitting neer the glitt'ring Hearth. 50
Thou sha't have Ribbands, Roses, Rings,
Gloves, Garters, Stockings, Shooes, and Strings
Of winning Colours, that shall move
Others to Lust, but me to Love.
These (nay) and more, thine own shal be, 55
If thou wilt love, and live with me.

[1] on the Passionate Shepherd theme in a tradition to which Marlowe, Ralegh, Donne, and others contributed. See the article by R. S. Forsythe, *PMLA*, XL (1925), 692–742. [2] country dances with serpentine movements.

H–522 *To his Kinswoman, Mistresse* Susanna Herrick.[1]

WHen I consider (Dearest) thou dost stay
But here awhile, to languish and decay;

Like to these Garden-glories, which here be
The Flowrie-sweet resemblances of Thee:
With griefe of heart, methinks, I thus doe cry, 5
Wo'd thou hast ne'r been born, or might'st not die.

[1] Suzan, daughter of the poet's brother Nicholas and his wife Susanna (H-977); or the daughter of his uncle John; she married John Nurse in 1630.

H–523

Upon Mistresse Susanna Southwell[1] *her cheeks.*

RAre are thy cheeks *Susanna*, which do show
Ripe Cherries smiling, while that others blow.

[1] presumably a relative of Thomas Southwell (H-149A), but none of his known four daughters bore this name.

H–524

Upon her Eyes.

CLeere are her eyes,
Like purest Skies.
Discovering from thence
A Babie there
That turns each Sphere, 5
Like an Intelligence.[1]

[1] one of the order of angels who moved the spheres or hollow globes which carried with them the sun, planets, and fixed stars. See H-38, n.1.

H–525

Upon her feet.

HEr pretty feet
Like snailes did creep
A little out, and then,
As if they started at Bo-peep,[1]
Did soon draw in agen. 5

[1] moved suddenly in a game in which one person hides, peeps out, and hides again. Cf. Suckling, "A Ballad upon a Wedding," 43–45:

"Her feet beneath her petticoat / Like little mice stole in and out, / As if they fear'd the light." Some copies of the 1648 ed. have "played" instead of "started."

H–526

To his honoured friend, Sir John Mynts.[1]

FOr civill, cleane, and circumcised[2] wit,
And for the comely carriage of it;
Thou art The Man, the onely Man best known,
Markt for the *True-wit*[3] of a Million:
From whom we'l reckon. Wit came in, but since 5
The *Calculation* of thy Birth, *Brave Mince.*

[1] or Mennes ("Mince" in some copies); knighted 1642; naval commander 1645; collaborated with James Smith in editing *Wit's Recreations,* etc. in which some of Herrick's poems appeared. [2] neat, trim, pure. [3] Cf. Truewit in Jonson's *Epicoene.*

H–527

Upon his gray haires.[1]

FLy me not, though I be gray,
Lady, this I know you'l say;
Better look the Roses red,
When with white commingled.
Black your haires are; mine are white; 5
This begets the more delight,
When things meet most opposite:
As in Pictures we descry,
Venus standing *Vulcan* by.

[1] *Anacreontea,* LI; for Stanley's version see H-43, notes. Cf. Edward Sherburne's rendering (*Poems,* 1651, p. 107): "Scorn me not Fair because you see / My Hairs are white; what if they be? / Think not 'cause in your Cheeks appear / Fresh springs of Roses all the year, / And mine, like Winter, wan and cold, / My Love like Winter should be cold: / See in the Garland which you wear / How the sweet blushing Roses there / With pale-hu'd Lillies do combine? / Be taught by them; so let us joyn."

H–528 *Accusation.*

IF Accusation onely can draw blood,[1]
None shall be guiltlesse, be he ne'r so good.

[1] if a mere accusing someone of something can cause his blood to flow. In trial by combat or dueling, bleeding was a sign of guilt.

H–529 *Pride allowable in Poets.*

AS thou deserv'st, be proud; then gladly let
The Muse give thee the Delphick[1] Coronet.

[1] sacred to Apollo, god of poetry.

H–530 *A Vow to* Minerva.

GOddesse, I begin an Art;
Come thou in, with thy best part,
For to make the Texture lye
Each way smooth and civilly:
And a broad-fac't Owle[1] shall be 5
Offer'd up with Vows to Thee.

[1] sacred to Minerva because of its appearance of wisdom, her "best part."

H–531 *On* Jone.

JOne wo'd go tel[1] her haires; and well she might,
Having but seven in all; three black, foure white.

[1] count.

H–532 *Upon* Letcher. *Epigram.*

LEtcher was Carted first about the streets,
For false Position in his neighbours sheets:
Next, hang'd for Theeving: Now the people say,
His Carting was the *Prologue* to this Play.

H–533 *Upon* Dundrige.[1]

DUndrige his Issue[2] hath; but is not styl'd
For all his Issue, Father of one Child.

[1] The name occurs in the Dean Prior Parish Register. [2] pun on issue in the sense of a running sore.

H–534 *To* Electra.

'TIs Ev'ning, my Sweet,
And dark; let us meet;
Long time w'ave here been a toying:
And never, as yet,
That season co'd get,
Wherein t'ave had an enjoying.

2. For pitty or shame,
Then let not Love's flame,
Be ever and ever a spending;
Since now to the Port
The path is but short;
And yet[1] our way has no ending.

3. Time flyes away fast;
Our houres doe waste:
The while we never remember,
How soone our life, here,
Growes old with the yeere,
That dyes with the next *December*.

[1] as yet; so far.

H–535 *Discord not disadvantageous.*

FOrtune no higher Project can devise,
Then to sow Discord 'mongst the Enemies.

H–536 *Ill Government.*

PReposterous is that Government, (and rude)
When Kings obey the wilder Multitude.

H–537 *To Marygolds.*

GIve way, and be ye ravisht by the Sun,
(And hang the head when as the Act is done)
Spread as He spreads; wax lesse as He do's wane;
And as He shuts, close up to Maids again.

H–538 *To* Dianeme.

GIve me one kisse,
And no more;
If so be, this
Makes you poore;
To enrich you,
Ile restore
For that one, two
Thousand score.

H–539 *To* Julia, *the* Flaminica Dialis, *or* Queen-Priest.

THou know'st, my *Julia,* that it is thy turne
This Mornings Incense to prepare, and burne.
The Chaplet, and **Inarculum*[1] here be,
With the white Vestures, all attending Thee.
This day, the *Queen-Priest,* thou art made t'appease 5
Love for our very-many Trespasses.
One chiefe transgression is among the rest,
Because with Flowers her Temple was not drest:
The next, because her Altars did not shine
With daily Fyers: The last, neglect of Wine: 10
For which, her wrath is gone forth to consume
Us all, unlesse preserv'd by thy Perfume.
Take then thy Censer; Put in Fire, and thus,
O *Pious-Priestresse!* make a Peace for us.
For our neglect, Love did our Death decree,[2] 15
That we escape. *Redemption comes by Thee.*

[1]* A twig of Pomgranat, which the queen-priest did use to weare on her head at sacrificing (Herrick's note). [2] Cf. Num. xvi.44–46, "And the Lord spake unto Moses, saying, Get you up from among

this congregation that I may consume them as in a moment . . . and Moses said unto Aaron, Take a censer, and put fire therein . . . and make an atonement for them."

H–540 *Anacreontike.*[1]

BOrn I was to be old,
   And for to die here:
After that, in the mould
   Long for to lye here.
But before that day comes,
   Still I be Bousing;
For I know, in the Tombs
   There's no Carousing.

[1] echoes *Anacreontea,* VII, VIII, XL, as does H-519.

H–541 *Meat without mirth.*

EAten I have; and though I had good cheere,
I did not sup, because no friends were there.
Where Mirth and Friends are absent when we Dine
Or Sup, there wants the Incense and the Wine.

H–542 *Large Bounds doe but bury us.*

ALl things o'r-rul'd are here by Chance;
The greatest mans Inheritance,
Where ere the luckie Lot doth fall,
Serves but for place of Buriall.

H–543 *Upon* Ursley.

URsley, she thinks those Velvet Patches[1] grace
The Candid[2] Temples of her comely face:
But he will say, who e'r those Circlets seeth,
They be but signs of *Ursleys* hollow teeth.

[1] stuck on the face to enhance beauty or hide blemishes. [2] white.

H-544 *An Ode to Sir* Clipsebie Crew.[1]

1. HEre we securely[2] live, and eate
The Creame of meat;
And keep eternal fires,
By which we sit, and doe Divine
As Wine
And Rage[3] inspires.

2. If full we charme; then call upon
Anacreon
To grace the frantick Thyrse:[4]
And having drunk, we raise a shout
Throughout
To praise his Verse.

3. Then cause we *Horace* to be read,
Which sung, or seyd,
A Goblet, to the brim,
Of Lyrick Wine, both swell'd and crown'd,
A Round
We quaffe to him.

4. Thus, thus, we live, and spend the houres
In Wine and Flowers:
And make the frollick yeere,
The Month, the Week, the instant Day
To stay
The longer here.

5. Come then, brave Knight, and see the Cell
Wherein I dwell;
And my Enchantments too;
Which Love and noble freedome is;
And this
Shall fetter you.

6. Take Horse, and come; or be so kind,
To send your mind
(Though but in Numbers few)
And I shall think I have the heart,
Or part
Of *Clipseby Crew*.

[1] See H-283, H-426. [2] free from care. [3] poetic inspiration. [4] See Herrick's note to H-8.

H–545 *To his worthy Kinsman, Master* Stephen Soame.[1]

NOr is my Number full, till I inscribe
Thee sprightly *Soame*, one of my righteous Tribe:
A Tribe of one Lip,[2] Leven,[3] and of One
Civil Behaviour, and Religion.
A stock of Saints; where ev'ry one doth weare 5
A stole of white, (and Canonized here)
Among which Holies, be Thou ever known,
Brave Kinsman, markt out with the whiter stone:
Which seals Thy Glorie; since I doe prefer
Thee here in my eternall Calender.[4] 10

[1] Herrick had two second cousins so named, sons of Sir Stephen and Sir William Soame, grandsons of the poet's mother's sister Anne. [2] language; i.e., who understood each other. Cf. Gen. xi.1, "the whole earth was of one language, and one speech." [3] leaven, i.e. batch; alike in nature and character. A semicolon separates "Lip" and "Leven" in the 1648 ed. [4] list of saints.

H–546 *To his Tomb-maker.*

GO I must; when I am gone,
Write but this upon my Stone;
Chaste I liv'd, without a wife,
That's the Story of my life.
Strewings need none, every flower 5
Is in this word, Batchelour.

H–547 *Great Spirits supervive.*

OUr mortall parts may wrapt in Seare-cloths lye:
Great Spirits never with their bodies dye.

H–548 *None free from fault.*

OUt of the world he must, who once comes in:
No man exempted is from Death, or sinne.

H–549 *Upon himselfe being buried.*

LEt me sleep this night away,
Till the Dawning of the day:
Then at th'opening of mine eyes,
I, and all the world shall rise.

H–550 *Pitie to the prostrate.*

TIs worse then barbarous cruelty to show
No part of pitie on a conquer'd foe.

H–551 *Way in a crowd.*

ONce on a Lord-Mayors day, in Cheapside, when
Skulls co'd not well passe through that scum of men.
For quick dispatch, *Sculls* made no longer stay,
Then but to breath, and every one gave way:
For as he breath'd, the People swore from thence 5
A Fart flew out, or a *Sir-reverence.*[1]

[1] a respectful salutation and obeisance (with wordplay on *irreverence*); also a cant term for breaking wind.

H–552 *His content in the Country.*

HEre, here I live with what my Board,
Can with the smallest cost afford.
Though ne'r so mean the Viands be,
They well content my *Prew*[1] and me.
Or Pea, or Bean, or Wort,[2] or Beet, 5
What ever comes, content makes sweet:
Here we rejoyce, because no Rent
We pay for our poore Tenement:
Wherein we rest, and never feare
The Landlord, or the Usurer. 10
The Quarter-day[3] do's ne'r affright
Our Peacefull slumbers in the night.

We eate our own, and batten[4] more,
Because we feed on no mans score:[5]
But pitie those, whose flanks grow great, 15
Swel'd with the Lard of others meat.
We blesse our Fortunes, when we see
Our own beloved privacie:
And like our living, where w'are known
To very few, or else to none. 20

[1] Herrick's housekeeper. [2] new drink, either ale or beer. [3] when rents were due. [4] eat to the full and thrive on. [5] accounts of debts owed.

H–553 *The credit of the Conquerer.*

HE who commends the vanquisht, speaks the Power,
And glorifies the worthy Conquerer.

H–554 *On himselfe.*

SOme parts may perish; dye thou canst not all:
The most of Thee shall scape the funerall.

H–555 *Upon one-ey'd* Broomsted. *Epigram.*

BRoomsted a lamenesse got by cold and Beere;
And to the *Bath* went, to be cured there:
His feet were helpt, and left his Crutch behind:
But home return'd, as he went forth, halfe blind.

H–556 *The Fairies.*

IF ye will with *Mab* find grace,
Set each Platter in his place:
Rake the Fier up, and get
Water in, ere Sun be set.
Wash your Pailes, and clense your Dairies; 5
Sluts are loathsome to the Fairies:
Sweep your house: Who doth not so,
Mab will pinch her by the toe.

H-557 *To his honoured friend, Master* John Weare, *Councellour.*[1]

DId I or love, or could I others draw
To the indulgence of the rugged Law:
The first foundation of that zeale sho'd be
By Reading all her *Paragraphs* in Thee.
Who dost so fitly with the Lawes unite, 5
As if You Two, were one *Hermophrodite:*
Nor courts[2] thou Her because she's well attended
With wealth, but for those ends she was entended:
Which were, (and still her offices are known)
Law is to give to ev'ry one his owne. 10
To shore the Feeble up, against the strong;
To shield the Stranger, and the Poore from wrong:
This was the Founders grave and good intent,
To keepe the out-cast in his Tenement:
To free the Orphan from that Wolfe-like-man, 15
Who is his *Butcher* more then *Guardian.*
To drye the Widowes teares; and stop her Swoones,
By pouring Balme and Oyle into her wounds.
This was the old way; and 'tis yet thy course,
To keep those pious Principles in force. 20
Modest I will be; but one word Ile say
(Like to a sound that's vanishing away)
Sooner the in-side of thy hand shall grow
Hisped,[3] and hairie, ere thy Palm shall know
A *Postern*[4]*-bribe* tooke, or a *Forked-Fee*[5] 25
To fetter Justice, when She might be free.
Eggs Ile not shave:[6] But yet brave man, if I
Was destin'd forth to golden Soveraignty:
A Prince I'de be, that I might Thee preferre
To be my Counsell both, and Chanceller. 30

[1] John Were of Silverton, counsellor-at-law—one who gave legal advice to clients and conducted their court cases. [2] courtest. [3] rough with hairs (Latin *hispidus*). [4] back door. [5] a fee from both sides in a lawsuit. [6] a proverbial way of saying, "I'll not attempt the impossible."

H–558 *The Watch.*

MAn is a Watch, wound up at first, but never
Wound up again: Once down, He's down for ever.
The Watch once downe, all motions then do cease;
And Mans Pulse stopt, *All passions sleep in Peace.*

H–559 *Lines have their Linings, and Bookes their Buckram.*

AS in our clothes, so likewise he who lookes,
Shall find much farcing[1] Buckram in our Books.

[1] padding or stuffing.

H–560 *Art above Nature, to* Julia.

WHen I behold a Forrest spread
With silken trees upon thy head;
And when I see that other Dresse
Of flowers set in comlinesse:
When I behold another grace 5
In the ascent of curious Lace,
Which like a Pinacle doth shew
The top, and the top-gallant[1] too.
Then, when I see thy Tresses bound
Into an Ovall, square, or round; 10
And knit in knots far more then I
Can tell by tongue; or true-love tie:
Next, when those Lawnie Filmes I see
Play with a wild civility:
And all those airie silks to flow, 15
Alluring me, and tempting so:
I must confesse, mine eye and heart
Dotes less on Nature, then on Art.

[1] shows the platforms at the heads of the second-highest and highest masts.

H–561 *Upon* Sibilla.

WIth paste of Almonds, *Syb* her hands doth scoure;
Then gives it to the children to devoure.
In Cream she bathes her thighs (more soft then silk)
Then to the poore she freely gives the milke.

H–562 *Upon his kinswoman Mistresse* Bridget Herrick.[1]

SWeet *Bridget* blusht, and therewithall,
Fresh blossoms from her cheekes did fall.
I thought at first 'twas but a dream,
Till after I had handled them;
And smelt them, then they smelt to me,
As Blossomes of the *Almond* Tree.

[1] probably the daughter of Herrick's brother Nicholas and sister to the Suzan of H-522.

H–563 *Upon Love.*

I Plaid with Love, as with the fire
The wanton Satyre did;[1]
Nor did I know, or co'd descry
What under there was hid.

2. That Satyre he but burnt his lips;
(But min's the greater smart)
For kissing Loves dissembling chips,
The fire scorcht my heart.

[1] According to legend, when Prometheus stole fire from heaven, a satyr, attracted by it, kissed it and was burned.

H–564

Upon a comely, and curious Maide.

IF Men can say that beauty dyes;
Marbles will sweare that here it lyes.

If Reader then thou canst forbeare,
In publique loss to shed a Teare:
The Dew of griefe upon this stone
Will tell thee *Pitie* thou hast none.

H–565 *Upon the losse of his Finger.*

ONe of the five straight branches of my hand
Is lopt already; and the rest but stand
Expecting when to fall: which soon will be;
First dyes the Leafe, the Bough next, next the Tree.

H–566 *Upon* Irene.

ANgry if *Irene* be
But a Minutes life with me:
Such a fire I espie
Walking in and out her eye,
As at once I freeze, and frie.

H–567 *Upon* Electra's *Teares.*

UPon her cheekes she wept, and from those showers
Sprang up a sweet *Nativity* of Flowres.

H–568 *Upon* Tooly.

THe Eggs of Pheasants wrie-nos'd *Tooly* sells;
But ne'r so much as licks the speckled shells:
Only, if one prove addled, that he eates
With superstition, (as the Cream of meates.)
The Cock and Hen he feeds; but not a bone
He ever pickt (as yet) of any one.

H-569 *A Hymne to the Graces.*

WHen I love, (as some have told,
Love I shall when I am old)
O ye Graces! Make me fit
For the welcoming of it.
Clean my Roomes, as Temples be, 5
T'entertain that Deity.
Give me words wherewith to wooe,
Suppling and successefull too:
Winning postures; and withall,
Manners each way musicall: 10
Sweetnesse to allay my sowre
And unsmooth behaviour.
For I know you have the skill
Vines to prune, though not to kill,
And of any wood ye see, 15
You can make a *Mercury*.[1]

[1] a herm or herma, a four-cornered pillar surmounted by a bust of the god Mercury or Hermes, inventor of the lyre and god of eloquence. Herrick varies the proverb, "Every block will not make a Mercury."

H-570 *To* Silvia.

NO more my *Silvia*, do I mean to pray
For those good dayes that ne'r will come away.
I want beliefe; O gentle *Silvia*, be
The patient Saint, and send up vowes for me.

H-571 *Upon* Blanch. *Epigram.*

I Have seen many Maidens to have haire;
Both for their comely need, and some to spare:
But *Blanch* has not so much upon her head,
As to bind up her chaps when she is dead.

H-572 *Upon* Umber. *Epigram.*

UMber was painting of a Lyon fierce,
And working it, by chance from *Umbers* Erse
Flew out a crack, so mighty, that the Fart,
(As *Umber* sweares) did make his Lyon start.

H-573 *The Poet hath lost his pipe.*

I Cannot pipe as I was wont to do,
Broke is my Reed, hoarse is my singing too:
My wearied Oat Ile hang upon the Tree,
And give it to the *Silvan Deitie.*

H-574 *True Friendship.*

WIlt thou my true Friend be?
Then love not mine, but me.

H-575 *The Apparition of his Mistresse calling him to* Elizium.[1]

Desunt nonnulla——[2]

COme then, and like two Doves with silv'rie wings,[3]
Let our soules flie to'th'shades, where ever springs
Sit smiling in the Meads; where Balme and Oile,
Roses and Cassia crown the untill'd soyle.
Where no disease raignes, or infection comes 5
To blast the Aire, but *Amber-greece* and *Gums.*
This, that, and ev'ry Thicket doth transpire[4]
More sweet, then *Storax*[5] from the hallowed fire:
Where ev'ry tree a wealthy issue beares
Of fragrant Apples, blushing Plums, or Peares: 10
And all the shrubs, with sparkling spangles, shew
Like Morning-Sun-shine tinsilling the dew.
Here in green Meddowes sits eternall May,
Purfling the Margents,[6] while perpetuall Day
So double gilds the Aire, as that no night 15
Can ever rust th'Enamel of the light.

Here, naked Younglings, handsome Striplings run
Their Goales for Virgins kisses; which when done,
Then unto Dancing forth the learned Round
Commixt they meet, with endlesse Roses crown'd. 20
And here we'l sit on Primrose-banks, and see
Love's *Chorus* led by *Cupid;* and we'l be
Two loving followers too unto the Grove,
Where Poets sing the stories of our love.
There thou shalt hear Divine *Musæus*[7] sing 25
Of *Hero,* and *Leander;* then Ile bring
Thee to the Stand, where honour'd *Homer* reades
His *Odisees,* and his high *Iliades.*
About whose Throne the crowd of Poets throng
To heare the incantation of his tongue: 30
To *Linus,*[8] then to *Pindar;* and that done,
Ile bring thee *Herrick* to *Anacreon,*
Quaffing his full-crown'd bowles of burning Wine,
And in his Raptures speaking Lines of Thine,
Like to His subject; and as his Frantick- 35
Looks, shew him truly *Bacchanalian* like,[9]
Besmear'd with Grapes; welcome he shall thee thither,
Where both may rage, both drink and dance together.
Then stately *Virgil,* witty *Ovid,* by
Whom faire *Corinna* sits, and doth comply[10] 40
With Yvorie wrists, his Laureat head, and steeps
His eye in dew of kisses, while he sleeps.
Then soft *Catullus,* sharp-fang'd *Martial,*
And towring *Lucan, Horace, Juvenal,*
And Snakie[11] *Perseus,* these, and those, whom Rage 45
(Dropt from[12] the jarres of heaven) fill'd t'engage
All times unto their frenzies; Thou shalt there
Behold them in a spacious Theater.
Among which glories, (crown'd with sacred Bayes,
And flatt'ring Ivie) Two recite their Plaies, 50
Beumont and *Fletcher,* Swans, to whom all eares
Listen, while they (like Syrens in their Spheres)[13]
Sing their *Evadne;*[14] and still more for thee
There yet remaines to know, then thou can'st see
By glim'ring of a fancie: Doe but come, 55
And there Ile shew thee that capacious roome
In which thy Father *Johnson* now is plac't,[15]
As in a Globe of Radiant fire, and grac't
To be in that Orbe crown'd (that doth include
Those Prophets of the former Magnitude) 60

And he one[16] chiefe; But harke, I heare the Cock,
(The Bell-man of the night) proclaime the clock
Of late struck one; and now I see the prime
Of Day break from the pregnant East, 'tis time
I vanish; more I had to say; 65
But Night determines here, Away.

[1] Tibullus in I, 3, 57–66 asks Venus to escort him to the Elysian fields where the untilled field bears cassia, scented roses bloom, and young men sport with maidens. Delattre, pp. 425–6, finds some resemblances to Johannes Secundus, *Basia,* II. [2] Some things are lacking. [3] Ps. lxviii.13, "the wings of a dove covered with silver." [4] breathe an exhalation. [5] sweet-scented gum of a Syrian tree. [6] adorning and richly embroidering the meadows' edges. [7] Greek poet, 4th or 5th century A.D. Herrick confuses him with the legendary pre-Homeric Musaeus. [8] supposed to be the first Greek to invent verse and music; the ancient Greeks annually sang a harvest dirge for him. [9] like a follower of the god of wine. [10] embrace. [11] The meaning, "Venomous," suggested by Martin is hardly apt for Persius's work or character; *tortuous,* referring to his involved style is probably intended. [12] "from" occurs in MSS, "for" in the 1648 ed. [13] Musical beings, one on each of the eight celestial spheres (Plato, *Republic,* X). [14] in *The Maid's Tragedy.* [15] Herrick regarded himself as a poetic son of Jonson. In *Poems: Written by Wil. Shake-speare* (1640), the reading "shall be plac'd" suggests composition before Jonson's death in 1637. [16] Martin changes *he one* to *be our;* but Herrick's mistress's shade would hardly call Jonson *her* chief.

H–576 *Life is the Bodies Light.*

LIfe is the Bodies light; which once declining,
Those crimson clouds i'th'cheeks and lips leave shining.
Those counter-changed[1] *Tabbies*[2] in the ayre,
(The Sun once set) all of one colour are.
So, when Death comes, *Fresh tinctures* lose their place, 5
And dismall Darknesse then doth smutch the face.

[1] diversified in color. [2] striped silk taffetas.

H-577 *Upon* Urles. *Epigram.*[1]

URles had the Gout so, that he co'd not stand;
Then from his Feet, it shifted to his Hand:
When 'twas in's Feet, his Charity was small;
Now tis in's Hand, he gives no Almes at all.

[1] Martial, I, 98.

H-578 *Upon* Franck.

FRanck ne'r wore silk she sweares; but I reply,
She now weares silk to hide her blood-shot eye.

H-579 *Love lightly pleased.*[1]

LEt faire or foule my Mistresse be,
Or low, or tall, she pleaseth me:
Or let her walk, or stand, or sit,
The posture hers, I'm pleas'd with it.
Or let her tongue be still, or stir,
Gracefull is ev'ry thing from her.
Or let her Grant, or else Deny,
My Love will fit each Historie.[2]

[1] Cf. H-21; Thomas Beedome, "The Choyce" (*Poems Divine and Humane,* 1641): "Be she faire, or foule, or either, / Or made up of both together, / Be her heart mine, or hand or eye / Be what it will, why, what care I?"; Donne, "The Indifferent"; Suckling, "Verses" and "Sonnets: II." [2] each subject for discourse. Ovid, *Amores,* II, 44, states that his love suits itself to all histories. Cf. the last line of H-750.

H-580 *The Primrose.*[1]

ASke me why I send you here
This sweet *Infanta*[2] of the yeere?
Aske me why I send to you
This Primrose, thus bepearl'd with dew?
I will whisper to your eares, 5
The sweets of Love are mixt with tears.

2. Ask me why this flower do's show
So yellow-green, and sickly too?
Ask me why the stalk is weak
And bending, (yet it doth not break?) 10
I will answer, These discover
What fainting hopes are in a Lover.

[1] Cf. H-336, st. 4. [2] infant and princess.

H–581 *The Tythe. To the Bride.*

IF nine times you your Bride-groome kisse;
The tenth you know the Parsons is.
Pay then your Tythe; and doing thus,
Prove in your Bride-bed numerous.
If children you have ten, Sir *John*[1] 5
Won't for his tenth part ask you one.

[1] the parson.

H–582 A Frolick.

BRing me my Rose-buds, Drawer[1] come;
So, while I thus sit crown'd;
Ile drink the aged *Cecubum*,[2]
Untill the roofe turne round.

[1] waiter. [2] a Roman wine.

H–583 Change common to all.

ALl things subjected are to Fate;
Whom this Morne sees most fortunate,
The Ev'ning sees in poore estate.[1]

[1] Seneca, *Thyestes*, 613–14.

H–584 To Julia.

THe Saints-bell calls; and, *Julia,* I must read
The Proper[1] Lessons for the Saints now dead:
To grace which Service, *Julia,* there shall be
One *Holy Collect,*[2] said or sung for Thee.
Dead when thou art, Deare *Julia,* thou shalt have 5
A *Trentall*[3] sung by Virgins o're thy Grave:
Meane time we two will sing the Dirge of these;
Who dead, deserve our best remembrances.

[1] appointed for a particular occasion. [2] opening prayer. [3] elegy or dirge; misprinted "Tentrall" in the 1648 ed.

H–585 *No luck in Love.*

I Doe love I know not what;
Sometimes this, and sometimes that:
All conditions I aime at.

2. But, as lucklesse, I have yet
Many shrewd disasters met,
To gaine her whom I wo'd get.

3. Therefore now Ile love no more,
As I've doted heretofore:
He who must be, shall be poore.

H–586 *In the darke none dainty.*

NIght hides our thefts;[1] all faults then pardon'd be:
All are alike faire, when no spots we see.
Lais[2] and *Lucrece,* in the night time are
Pleasing alike; alike both singular:
Jone, and my *Lady* have at that time one, 5
One and the selfe-same priz'd complexion.
Then please alike the Pewter and the Plate;
The chosen *Rubie,* and the *Reprobate.*[3]

[1] amorous intrigues. [2] famous courtesan; a type of incontinence in contrast to Lucrece's purity. [3] the one rejected because inferior or impure.

H–587 *A charme, or an allay for Love.*

IF so be a Toad be laid
In a Sheeps-skin newly flaid,
And that ty'd to man 'twil sever
Him and his affections ever.

H–588
Upon a free[1] Maid, with a foule breath.

YOu say you'l kiss me, and I thanke you for it:
But stinking breath, I do as hell abhorre it.

[1] ready to grant favors or take liberties.

H–589 *Upon* Coone. *Epigram.*

WHat is the reason *Coone* so dully smels?
His Nose is over-cool'd with Isicles.

H–590
To his Brother in Law Master John Wingfield.[1]

FOr being comely, consonant,[2] and free
To most of men, but most of all to me:
For so decreeing, that thy clothes expence
Keepes still within a just circumference:
Then for contriving so to loade thy Board, 5
As that the Messes[3] ne'r o'r-laid the Lord:[4]
Next for Ordaining, that thy words not swell
To any one unsober *syllable.*
These I co'd praise thee for beyond another,
Wert thou a *Winckfield* onely, not a Brother. 10

[1] The poem must have been written between 1611 when he married Herrick's sister Mercy and 1619 when he was knighted. [2] agreeable. [3] servings of food. [4] the head of the household.

H–591 *The Head-ake.*

MY head doth ake,
O *Sappho!* take
Thy fillit,[1]
And bind the paine;
Or bring some bane
To kill it.

2. But lesse that part,
Then my poore heart,
Now is sick:
One kisse from thee
Will counsell be,
And Physick.

[1] fillet: headband.

H–592 *On himselfe.*

LIve by thy Muse thou shalt; when others die
Leaving no Fame to long Posterity:
When Monarchies trans-shifted are, and gone;
Here shall endure thy vast Dominion.

H–593 *Upon a Maide.*

HEnce a blessed soule is fled,
Leaving here the body dead:
Which (since here they can't combine)
For the Saint, we'l keep the Shrine.

H–594 *Upon* Spalt.

OF Pushes[1] *Spalt* has such a knottie race,
He needs a Tucker[2] for to burle his face.

[1] pimples, pustules, boils. [2] a cloth finisher: he stretches the cloth, uses a fuller's teasel to raise its naps, and burls it, i.e. removes knots and lumps.

H–595 *Of* Horne *a Comb-maker.*

HOrne sells to others teeth; but has not one
To grace his own Gums, or of Box,[1] or bone.

[1] boxwood.

H–596 *Upon the troublesome times.*

O! Times most bad,
Without the scope
Of hope
Of better to be had!

2. Where shall I goe,
Or whither run
To shun
This publique overthrow?

3. No places are
(This I am sure)
Secure
In this our wasting Warre.

4. Some storms w'ave past;
Yet we must all
Down fall,
And perish at the last.

H–597 *Cruelty base in Commanders.*

NOthing can be more loathsome, then to see
Power conjoyn'd with Natures *Crueltie.*

H–598 *Upon a sowre-breath Lady. Epigram.*

FIe, (quoth my Lady) what a stink is here?
When 'twas her breath that was the *Carrionere.*[1]

[1] that which has the characteristics of putrefied flesh.

H–599

Upon Lucia.

I Askt my *Lucia* but a kisse;
And she with scorne deny'd me this:
Say then, how ill sho'd I have sped,
Had I then askt her Maidenhead?

H–600

Little and loud.

LIttle you are; for Womans sake be proud;
For my sake next, (though little) *be not loud.*

H–601

Ship-wrack.

HE, who has suffer'd Ship-wrack, feares to saile
Upon the Seas, though with a gentle gale.

H–602

Paines without profit.

A Long-lifes-day I've taken paines
For very little, or no gaines:
The Ev'ning's come; here now Ile stop,
And work no more; but shut up Shop.

H–603

To his Booke.

BE bold my Booke, nor be abasht, or feare
The cutting Thumb-naile, or the Brow severe.
But by the *Muses* sweare, all here is good,
If but well read; or ill read, understood.

H–604

His Prayer to Ben. Johnson.

WHen I a Verse shall make,
Know I have praid thee,
For old *Religions*[1] sake,
Saint *Ben* to aide me.

2. Make the way smooth for me,
When I, thy *Herrick*,
Honouring thee, on my knee
Offer my *Lyrick*.

3. Candles Ile give to thee,
And a new Altar;
And thou Saint *Ben*, shalt be
Writ in my *Psalter*.

[1] *Religion* may mean *the sacredness of an oath;* i.e. for the sake of our former vows of friendship; but Herrick may refer to the ancient form of *pietas*, the duty, honesty, conscientiousness, and good dealing due to God and then to relatives and friends. Cf. H-870, 3; Ovid, *Fasti*, III, 264, *antiqua religione*.

H–605 *Poverty and Riches.*

GIve *Want* her welcome if she comes; we find,
Riches to be but burthens to the mind.

H–606 *Again.*

WHo with a little cannot be content,
Endures an everlasting punishment.

H–607 *The Covetous still Captives.*

LEt's live with that smal pittance that we have;
Who covets more, is evermore a slave.[1]

[1] Horace, *Ep.* I, 10, 41.

H–608 *Lawes.*

WHen Lawes full power have to sway, we see
Little or no part there of Tyrannie.

H–609

Of Love.

ILe get me hence,
Because no fence,
Or Fort that I can make here;
But Love by charmes,
Or else by Armes 5
Will storme, or starving take here.

H–610

Upon Cock.

COck calls his Wife his Hen: when *Cock* goes too't,
Cock treads his Hen, but treads her under-foot.

H–611

To his Muse.

GO wooe young *Charles*[1] no more to looke,
Then but to read this in my Booke:
How *Herrick* beggs, if that he can-
Not like the Muse; to love the man,
Who by the Shepheards, sung (long since)
The Starre-led-birth of Charles the *Prince.*[2]

[1] the Prince of Wales, later Charles II. See prefatory poem to *Hesperides.* [2] to love Herrick who, by means of the shepherds (in H-213) sang, long ago, about the birth of Prince Charles (May 29, 1630), and the appearance of the star Hesperus in the sky that noon.

H–612

The bad season makes the Poet sad.

DUll to my selfe, and almost dead to these
My many fresh and fragrant Mistresses:
Lost to all Musick now; since every thing
Puts on the semblance here of sorrowing.
Sick is the Land to'th'heart; and doth endure 5
More dangerous faintings by her desp'rate cure.
But if that golden Age wo'd come again,
And *Charles* here Rule, as he before did Raign;

If smooth and unperplext the Seasons were,
As when the *Sweet Maria* lived here: 10
I sho'd delight to have my Curles halfe drown'd
In *Tyrian Dewes*, and Head with Roses crown'd.
And once more yet (ere I am laid out dead)
Knock at a Starre with my exalted Head.[1]

[1] Horace concludes his opening Ode by stating that if Maecenas will rank him among lyric poets, he will touch the stars with his exalted head (*sublimi feriam sidera vertice*).

H–613 *To* Vulcan.

THy sooty *Godhead*, I desire
Still to be ready with thy fire:
That sho'd my Booke despised be,
Acceptance it might find of thee.

H–614 *Like Pattern, like People.*

THis is the height of Justice, that to doe
Thy selfe, which thou put'st other men unto.
As great men lead; the meaner follow on,
Or to the good, or evill action.

H–615 *Purposes.*[1]

NO wrath of Men, or rage of Seas
Can shake a just mans purposes:
No threats of Tyrants, or the Grim
Visage of them can alter him;
But what he doth at first entend, 5
That he holds firmly to the end.

[1] a free rendering of Horace, *Carmina*, III, 3, 1–8.

H–616 *To the Maids to walke abroad.*

COme sit we under yonder Tree,
Where merry as the Maids we'l be.
And as on *Primroses* we sit,
We'l venter (if we can) at wit:

If not, at *Draw-gloves*[1] we will play; 5
So spend some minutes of the day:
Or else spin out the thread of sands,[2]
Playing at *Questions* and *Commands:*
Or tell what strange Tricks Love can do,
By quickly making one of two. 10
Thus we will sit and talke; but tell
No cruell truths of *Philomell,*[3]
Or *Phillis,* whom hard Fate forc't on,
To kill her selfe for *Demophon.*[4]
But Fables we'l relate; how *Jove* 15
Put on all shapes to get a Love:[5]
As now a *Satyr,* then a *Swan;*
A *Bull* but then; and now a man.[6]
Next we will act, how young men wooe;
And sigh, and kiss, as Lovers do: 20
And talke of Brides; and who shall make
That wedding-smock, this Bridal-Cake;
That Dress, this Sprig, that Leaf, this Vine;
That smooth and silken Columbine.
This done, we'l draw lots, who shall buy 25
And guild the Baies and Rosemary:[7]
What Posies for our Wedding Rings;
What Gloves we'l give, and Ribanings:
And smiling at our selves, decree,
Who then the joyning *Priest* shall be. 30
What short sweet Prayers shall be said;
And how the Posset shall be made
With Cream of Lillies (not of Kine)
And *Maiden's-blush,* for spiced wine.
Thus, having talkt, we'l next commend 35
A kiss to each; and *so we'l end.*

[1] a race to take off gloves. [2] (in an hourglass.) [3] Philomela, Athenian princess; after the revenge for her rape by Tereus, she was turned into a nightingale. [4] See H-449, n.1. [5] See H-152, 1–4, 12. [6] Jove's affairs with Antiope, Leda, Europa, Alcmena. [7] H-479, n.2.

H-617 *His own Epitaph.*

AS wearied *Pilgrims,* once possest
Of long'd-for lodging, go to rest:

So I, now having rid my way;
Fix here my Button'd[1] Staffe and stay.
Youth (I confess) hath me mis-led; 5
But Age hath brought me right to Bed.

[1] i.e. with shells from the shrine of St. James the Less at Campostella—the mark of a pilgrim.

H–618

A Nuptiall Verse to Mistresse Elizabeth Lee, *now Lady* Tracie.[1]

SPring with the Larke, most comely Bride, and meet
Your eager Bridegroome with *auspitious* feet.
The Morn's farre spent; and the immortall Sunne
Corrols[2] his cheeke, to see those Rites not done.
Fie, *Lovely maid!* Indeed you are too slow, 5
When to the Temple Love sho'd runne, not go.
Dispatch your dressing then; and quickly wed:
Then feast, and coy't a little; then to bed.
This day is Loves day; and this busie night
Is yours, in which you challeng'd are to fight 10
With such an arm'd, but such an easie Foe,
As will if you yeeld, lye down conquer'd too.
The Field is pitcht; but such must be your warres,
As that your kisses must out-vie the Starres.
Fall down together vanquisht both, and lye 15
Drown'd in the bloud of Rubies there, not die.

[1] daughter of Sir Francis Leigh; married Sir Humphrey Tracy, 3rd Baronet (about 1630?). [2] corals: reddens.

H–619 *The Night-piece, to* Julia.

HEr Eyes the Glow-worme lend thee,
The Shooting Starres attend thee;
And the Elves also,
Whose little eyes glow,
Like the sparks of fire, befriend thee.

2. No *Will-o'th'-Wispe* mis-light thee;
Nor Snake, or Slow-worme[1] bite thee:
But on, on thy way
Not making a stay,
Since Ghost ther's none to affright thee.

3. Let not the darke thee cumber;
What though the Moon do's slumber?
The Starres of the night
Will lend thee their light,
Like Tapers cleare without number.

4. Then *Julia* let me wooe thee,
Thus, thus to come unto me:
And when I shall meet
Thy silv'ry feet,
My soule Ile poure into thee.

[1] small, harmless lizard or blindworm; Herrick probably intends the older meaning, adder.

H–620 *To Sir* Clipseby Crew.

GIve me wine, and give me meate,
To create in me a heate,
That my Pulses high may beate.

2. Cold and hunger never yet
Co'd a noble Verse beget;
But your Boules with Sack repleat.

3. Give me these (my Knight) and try
In a Minutes space how I
Can runne mad, and Prophesie.

4. Then if any Peece proves new,
And rare, Ile say (my dearest *Crew*)
It was full enspir'd by you.

H–621 *Good Luck not lasting.*

IF well the Dice runne, lets applaud the cast:
The happy fortune will not alwayes last.

H–622 *A Kisse.*

WHat is a Kisse? Why this, as some approve;
The sure sweet-Sement, Glue, and Lime[1] of Love.

[1] sticky substance smeared on trees to catch small birds. Cf. Donne, *Sermons*, ed. Potter and Simpson, III, 313: "The Father draws no man, but by the Son; and the Son receives none, but by love, and this cement and glue, of a zealous and a reverentiall love, a holy kisse."

H–623 *Glorie.*

I Make no haste to have my Numbers read.
Seldome comes Glorie till a man be dead.[1]

[1] Cf. Martial, I, 25, 8, *Cineri gloria sera venit,* used by Jonson as the motto of *Underwoods.* An English rendering of it is the motto of the 1659 ed. of Lovelace's *Posthumous Poems:* "Those honours come too late / That on our ashes wait." Cf. H-1022.

H–624 *Poets.*

WAntons we are; and though our words be such,
Our Lives do differ from our Lines by much.[1]

[1] Burton (3,1,1,1, ed. 6, pp. 409–10) mentions a philosopher in life who was a "wanton" in literature, poets who wrote lascivious songs but "were chast, severe, and upright livers," and loosely translates Martial, I, 4, 8, "Howsoever my lines erre, my life is honest." Cf. H-1130.

H–625 *No despight to the dead.*

REproach we may the living; not the dead:
'Tis cowardice to bite the buried.[1]

[1] Ovid, *Amores,* I, 15, 39–40: trans. Jonson, *Poetaster,* I, i, 81–82: "Envy the living, not the dead, doth bite! / For after death all men receive their right."

H–626 *To his Verses.*

WHat will ye (my poor Orphans) do
When I must leave the World (and you)
Who'l give ye then a sheltring shed,
Or credit ye, when I am dead?
Who'l let ye by their fire sit? 5
Although ye have a stock of wit,
Already coin'd to pay for it.
I cannot tell; unlesse there be
Some Race of old humanitie
Left (of the large heart, and long hand) 10
Alive, as Noble *Westmorland;*[1]
Or gallant *Newark;*[2] which brave two
May fost'ring fathers be to you.
If not; expect to be no less
Ill us'd, then Babes left fatherless. 15

[1] See H-112. [2] either Robert Pierrepoint, Viscount Newark (1627), Earl of Kingston (1628), killed in 1643 while fighting for the king; or his son Henry, known as Newark (1628–43); 2nd Earl of Kingston (1643); Marquis of Dorchester (1645).

H–627 *His charge to* Julia *at his death.*

DEarest of thousands, now the time drawes neere,
That with my Lines, my Life must full-stop here.
Cut off thy haires;[1] and let thy Teares be shed
Over my Turfe, when I am buried.
Then for *effusions,*[2] let none wanting be,
Or other Rites that doe belong to me;
As Love shall helpe thee, when thou do'st go hence
Unto thy everlasting residence.

[1] in token of mourning. Cf. Job i.20, Jer. vii.29, Isa. xv.2, and Chapman's trans. of Homer, *Odyssey*, IV, 264–65: "It is the only right that wretched men / Can do dead friends, to cut haire and complaine." [2] Cf. Tibullus, III, 2, where Lygdamus charges Neaera to come to his pyre, with her long hair disordered, to weep and then to sprinkle his bones with old wine and snowy milk, and then to dry them and place them in a marble chamber.

H–628 *Upon Love.*

IN a Dreame, Love bad me go
To the Gallies there to Rowe;
In the Vision I askt, why?
Love as briefly did reply;
'Twas better there to toyle, then prove[1] 5
The turmoiles they endure that love.
I awoke, and then I knew
What Love said was too too true:
Henceforth therefore I will be
As from Love, from trouble free. 10
None pities him that's in the snare,
And warn'd before, wo'd not beware.

[1] undergo, experience.

H–629 *The Coblers Catch.*

COme sit we by the fires side;
And roundly drinke we here;
Till that we see our cheekes Ale-dy'd
And noses tann'd with Beere.

H–630 *Upon* Bran. *Epigram.*

WHat made that mirth last night? the neighbours say,
That *Bran* the Baker did his Breech bewray:[1]
I rather thinke (though they may speake the worst)
'Twas to his Batch,[2] but Leaven laid there first.

[1] betray: to reveal what previously was unnoticed. [2] a quantity of dough set out to rise.

H–631 *Upon* Snare, *an Usurer.*

SNare, ten i'th'hundred[1] calls his wife; and why?
Shee brings in much, by carnall usury.
He by extortion brings in three times more:
Say, who's the worst, th'exactor, or the whore?

[1] 10%.

H–632 *Upon Grudgings.*

GRudgings turnes bread to stones, when to the Poore
He gives an almes, and chides them from his doore.

H–633 Connubii Flores,[1] *or the well-wishes at Weddings.*

CHORUS SACERDOTUM.

1. FRom the Temple to your home
May a thousand blessings come!
And a sweet concurring stream
Of all joyes, to joyn with them.

CHORUS JUVENUM.

2. Happy day
Make no long stay
Here
In thy Sphere;
But give thy place to night,
That she, 10
As Thee,
May be
Partaker of this sight.
And since it was thy care
To see the Younglings wed;
'Tis fit that Night, the Paire,
Sho'd see safe brought to Bed.

CHORUS SENUM.

3. Go to your banquet then, but use delight,
So as to rise still with an appetite.
Love is a thing most nice; and must be fed 20
To such a height; but never surfeited.
What is beyond the mean is ever ill:
'Tis best to feed Love; but not over-fill:
Go then discreetly to the Bed of pleasure;
And this remember, *Vertue keepes the measure.*

CHORUS VIRGINUM.

4. Luckie signes we have discri'd
To encourage on the Bride;
And to these we have espi'd,
Not a kissing *Cupid* flyes
Here about, but has his eyes, 30
To imply your Love is wise.

CHORUS PASTORUM.

5. Here we present a fleece
To make a peece
Of cloth;
Nor Faire, must you be loth
Your Finger to apply
To huswiferie.
Then, then begin
To spin:
And (Sweetling) marke you, what a Web will come 40
Into your Chests, drawn by your painfull[2] Thumb.

CHORUS MATRONARUM.

6. Set you to your Wheele, and wax[3]
Rich, by the Ductile Wool and Flax.
Yarne is an Income; and the Huswives thread
The Larder fils with meat; the Bin with bread.

CHORUS SENUM.

7. Let wealth come in by comely thrift,
And not by any sordid shift:
'Tis haste
Makes waste;
Extreames have still their fault; 50
The softest Fire makes the sweetest Mault.

Who gripes too hard the dry and slip'rie sand,
Holds none at all, or little in his hand.

CHORUS VIRGINUM.

8. Goddesse of Pleasure, Youth and Peace,
Give them the blessing of encrease:
And thou *Lucina,*[4] that do'st heare
The vowes of those, that children beare:
When as her Aprill houre drawes neare,
Be thou then propitious there.

CHORUS JUVENUM.

9. Farre hence be all speech, that may anger move: 60
Sweet words must nourish soft and gentle Love.[5]

CHORUS OMNIUM.

10. Live in the Love of Doves, and having told[6]
The Ravens yeares, go hence more Ripe then old.

[1] wedding flowers. The speakers are choruses of priests, youths, old men, virgins, shepherds, matrons, and all. [2] painstaking. [3] grow. [4] goddess of childbirth. [5] Ovid, *Ars Amoris,* II, 152. [6] counted; lived as long as.

H-634 *To his lovely Mistresses.*

ONe night i'th'yeare, my dearest Beauties, come
And bring those *dew-drink-offerings*[1] to my Tomb.
When thence ye see my reverend Ghost to rise,
And there to lick th'effused sacrifice:
Though palenes be the Livery that I weare, 5
Looke ye not wan, or colourlesse for feare.
Trust me I will not hurt ye; or once shew
The least grim looke, or cast a frown on you:
Nor shall the Tapers when I'm there, burn blew.[2]
This I may do (perhaps) as I glide by, 10
Cast on my Girles a glance, and loving eye:
Or fold mine armes, and sigh, because I've lost
The world so soon, and in it, you the most.
Then these,[3] no feares more on your Fancies fall,
Though then I smile, and speake no words at all. 15

[1] The ancients poured milk and wine as sacrifices for the dead. Herrick asks for dew; cf. the Book of Common Prayer (1559):

"The continuall deawe of thy blessinge." [2] sign of the presence of an evil spirit. [3] other than these.

H–635 *Upon Love.*

A Christall Violl *Cupid* brought,
Which had a juice in it:
Of which who drank, he said no thought
Of Love he sho'd admit.

2. I greedy of the prize, did drinke,
And emptied soon the glasse;
Which burnt me so, that I do thinke
The fire of hell it was.

3. Give me my earthen Cups again,
The Christall I contemne;
Which, though enchas'd with Pearls, contain
A deadly draught in them.

4. And thou O *Cupid!* come not to
My Threshold, since I see,
For all I have, or else can do,
Thou still wilt cozen me.

H–636 *Upon* Gander. *Epigram.*

SInce *Gander* did his prettie Youngling wed;
Gander (they say) doth each night pisse a Bed:
What is the cause? Why *Gander* will reply,
No Goose layes good eggs that is trodden drye.

H–637 *Upon* Lungs. *Epigram.*

LUngs (as some say) ne'r sets him down to eate,
But that his breath do's Fly-blow[1] all the meate.

[1] corrupt. A blowfly spoils food by laying eggs on it.

H–638

The Beggar to Mab, *the* Fairie Queen.

PLease your Grace, from out your Store,[1]
Give an Almes to one that's poore,
That your mickle,[2] may have more.
Black I'm grown for want of meat;
Give me then an Ant to eate; 5
Or the cleft eare of a Mouse
Over-sowr'd in drinke of Souce:[3]
Or *sweet Lady* reach to me
The *Abdomen* of a Bee;
Or commend a *Crickets-hip,* 10
Or his *Huckson,*[4] to my Scrip.[5]
Give for bread, a little bit
Of a Pease, that 'gins to chit,[6]
And my full thanks take for it.
Floure of Fuz-balls,[7] that's too good 15
For a man in needy-hood:
But the Meal of Mill-dust[8] can
Well content a craving man.
Any Orts[9] the Elves refuse
Well will serve the Beggars use. 20
But if this may seem too much
For an Almes; then give me such
Little bits, that nestle there
In the Pris'ners *Panier.*[10]
So a blessing light upon 25
You, and mighty *Oberon:*
That your plenty last till when,
I return your Almes agen.

[1] stock of possessions. [2] much. Prov. xxviii.27, "He that giveth unto the poor, shall not lack." [3] steeped in pickling fluid or brine of the type used for pig's knuckles. [4] hockshin: underside of the thigh. [5] bag for holding provisions. [6] sprout. [7] puffballs—globe-shaped mushrooms. [8] dust from a flourmill. [9] scraps of food. [10] poor prisoner's basket hung out of a jail window for alms.

H-639 *An end decreed.*

LEt's be jocund while we may;
All things have an ending day:
And when once the Work is done;
Fates revolve[1] *no Flax th'ave spun.*

[1] rewind.

H-640 *Upon a child.*

HEre a pretty Baby lies
Sung asleep with Lullabies:
Pray be silent, and not stirre
Th'easie earth that covers her.

H-641 *Painting sometimes permitted.*

IF Nature do deny
Colours, let Art supply.

H-642

Farwell Frost, or welcome the Spring.

FLed are the Frosts, and now the Fields appeare
Re-cloth'd in fresh and verdant Diaper.[1]
Thaw'd are the snowes, and now the lusty Spring
Gives to each Mead a neat enameling.
The Palms put forth their Gemmes,[2] and every Tree 5
Now swaggers in her Leavy gallantry.[3]
The while the *Daulian Minstrell* sweetly sings,
With warbling Notes, her *Tyrrean* sufferings.[4]
What gentle Winds perspire? As if here
Never had been the *Northern Plunderer*[5] 10
To strip the Trees, and Fields, to their distresse,
Leaving them to a pittied nakednesse.
And look how when a frantick Storme doth tear
A stubborn Oake, or Holme[6] (long growing there)
But lul'd to calmnesse, then succeeds a breeze 15
That scarcely stirs the nodding leaves of Trees:

So when this War (which tempest-like doth spoil
Our salt, our Corn, our Honie, Wine, and Oile)
Falls to a temper, and doth mildly cast
His inconsiderate Frenzie off (at last) 20
The gentle Dove may, when these turmoils cease,
Bring in her Bill, once more, *the Branch of Peace.*

[1] patterns and variegations as in patterned linen. [2] buds. [3] magnificence, splendor. [4] while the nightingale (into which Philomela was turned) sings about how she suffered when Tereus, chief of the city of Daulis, raped her and had her tongue torn out. [5] Boreas, the north wind; possibly a reference to the Scots' invasion of England early in the Civil Wars. [6] oak with foliage that resembles holly.

H–643 *The* Hag.

THe Hag[1] is astride,
This night for to ride;
The Devill and shee together:
Through thick, and through thin,
Now out, and then in,
Though ne'r so foule be the weather.

2. A Thorn or a Burr
She takes for a Spurre:
With a lash of a Bramble she rides now,
Through Brakes and through Bryars,
O're Ditches, and Mires,
She followes the Spirit that guides now.

3. No Beast, for his food,
Dares now range the wood;
But husht in his laire he lies lurking:
While mischeifs, by these,
On Land and on Seas,
At noone of Night[2] are a working.

4. The storme will arise,
And trouble the skies;
This night, and more for the wonder,
The ghost from the Tomb
Affrighted shall come,
Cal'd out by the clap of the Thunder.

[1] witch. [2] midnight.

H–644

Upon an old man a Residenciarie.[1]

TRead, Sirs, as lightly as ye can
Upon the grave of this old man.
Twice fortie (bating but one year,
And thrice three weekes) he lived here.
Whom gentle fate translated hence 5
To a more happy Residence.
Yet, Reader, let me tell thee this
(Which from his ghost a promise is)
If here ye will some few teares shed,
He'l never haunt ye now he's dead. 10

[1] residentiary: a parson who resided in a parish; but here the meaning seems to be *old inhabitant*. Claudian's *Epigram* II is about an old man who never went out of his locality.

H–645

Upon Teares.

TEares, though th'are here below the sinners brine,
Above they are the Angels spiced wine.[1]

[1] Cf. Crashaw, "The Weeper" (1646), st. 6: "Angels with their Bottles come; / And draw from these full Eyes of thine, / Their Masters water, their owne Wine."

H–646

Physitians.

PHysitians fight not against men; but these
Combate for men, by conquering the disease.

H–647

The Primitiæ[1] *to Parents.*

OUr *Houshold-gods* our Parents be;
And manners good requires, that we
The first Fruits give to them, who gave
Us hands to get what here we have.

[1] earliest products of the soil; first fruits; the first products of a man's work.

H–648 *Upon* Cob. *Epigram.*

COb clouts[1] his shooes, and as the story tells,
His thumb-nailes-par'd, afford him sperrables.[2]

[1] studs with flat-headed nails. [2] sparables: wedge-shaped, headless nails, used by cobblers.

H–649 *Upon* Lucie. *Epigram.*

SOund Teeth has *Lucie,* pure as Pearl, and small,
With mellow Lips, and luscious there withall.

H–650 *Upon* Skoles. *Epigram.*

SKoles stinks so deadly, that his Breeches loath
His dampish Buttocks furthermore to cloath:
Cloy'd[1] they are up with Arse; but hope, one blast
Will whirle about, and blow them thence at last.

[1] filled, blocked.

H–651 *To* Silvia.

I Am holy, while I stand
Circum-crost[1] by thy pure hand:
But when that is gone; Again,
I, as others, am *Prophane.*

[1] crossed around: her hand around his.

H–652 *To his Closet-Gods.*[1]

WHen I goe Hence ye *Closet-Gods,* I feare
Never againe to have ingression[2] here:
Where I have had, what ever thing co'd be
Pleasant, and precious to my Muse and me.
Besides rare sweets, I had a Book which none 5
Co'd reade the Intext[3] but my selfe alone.

About the Cover of this Book there went
A curious-comely clean *Compartlement:*[4]
And, in the midst, to grace it more, was set
A blushing-pretty-peeping Rubelet: 10
But now 'tis clos'd; and being shut, and seal'd,
Be it, O be it, never more reveal'd!
Keep here still, *Closet-Gods,* 'fore whom I've set
Oblations oft, of sweetest Marmelet.[5]

[1] the tutelary gods or lares of his private room. [2] entrance. Herrick was ejected from Dean Prior in 1647. [3] contents. [4] N.E.D., s.v. "Compartment," suggests that *Compartlement* is a misprint for the variant form *compartiment,* but the 1648 reading seems justified by the consonance of the "l" sounds and the probability that Herrick thought that a root of the word was *partlet,* a collar or band. The meaning is fairly clear: around the cover of the book there was an ornamental square bordering design, elaborately but beautifully contrived, shapely, and free from unevennesses and inequalities. [5] marmalade.

H–653 *A Bacchanalian Verse.*

FIll me a mighty Bowle
Up to the brink:[1]
That I may drink
Unto my *Johnsons* soule.

2. Crowne it agen agen;
And thrice repeat
That happy heat;
To drink to Thee my *Ben.*

3. Well I can quaffe, I see,
To th'number five,
Or nine; but thrive
In frenzie ne'r like thee.

[1] "brim" in the 1648 *Hesperides.*

H–654 *Long lookt for comes at last.*

THough long it be, yeeres may repay the debt;
None loseth that, which he in time may get.

H–655 *To Youth.*

DRink Wine, and live here blithefull, while ye may:
The morrowes life too late is, Live to day.[1]

[1] Martial, V, 58, 7–8; trans. Cowley in "The Danger of Procrastination": "To morrow I will live, the Fool does say; To Day itself's too late, the Wise liv'd Yesterday." Cf. also Martial, I, 15, 12, and H-453.

H–656 *Never too late to dye.*

NO man comes late unto that place from whence
Never man yet had a regredience.[1]

[1] Cf. *Hamlet*, III, i, 79–80, "from whose bourn / No traveller returns."

H–657 *A Hymne to the Muses.*

O! You the Virgins nine!
That doe our soules encline
To noble Discipline!
Nod to this vow of mine:
Come then, and now enspire 5
My violl and my lyre
With your eternall fire:
And make me one entire
Composer in your Quire.
Then I'le your Altars strew 10
With Roses sweet and new;
And ever live a true
Acknowledger of you.

H–658 *On himselfe.*

ILe sing no more, nor will I longer write
Of that sweet Lady, or that gallant Knight:
Ile sing no more of Frosts, Snowes, Dews and Showers;
No more of Groves, Meades, Springs, and wreaths of [Flowers:

Ile write no more, nor will I tell or sing 5
Of *Cupid,* and his wittie coozning:[1]
Ile sing no more of death, or shall the grave
No more my Dirges, and my Trentalls[2] have.

[1] clever deceptions. [2] elegies for the dead, funeral poems, etc.

H–659 *Upon* Jone *and* Jane.

JOne is a wench that's painted;
Jone is a Girle that's tainted;
Yet *Jone* she goes
Like one of those
Whom purity had Sainted. 5

Jane is a Girle that's prittie;
Jane is a wench that's wittie;
Yet, who wo'd think,
Her breath do's stinke,
As so it doth? that's pittie. 10

H–660 *To* Momus.

WHo read'st this Book that I have writ,
And can'st not mend, but carpe at it:
By all the muses! thou shalt be
Anathema to it, and me.

H–661 *Ambition.*

IN wayes to greatnesse, think on this,
That slippery all Ambition is.[1]

[1] So Bacon, "Of Great Place": once high office is attained, "The standing is slippery."

H–662

The Country life, to the honoured Master Endimion Porter, *Groome of the Bed-Chamber*[1] *to His Majesty.*

SWeet Country life, to such unknown,
Whose lives are others, not their own![2]
But serving Courts, and Cities, be
Less happy, less enjoying thee.
Thou never Plow'st the Oceans foame
To seek, and bring rough Pepper home:
Nor to the Eastern Ind dost rove
To bring from thence the scorched Clove.
Nor, with the losse of thy lov'd rest,
Bring'st home the Ingot from the West. 10
No, thy Ambition's Master-piece
Flies no thought higher then a fleece:
Or how to pay thy Hinds, and cleere
All scores;[3] and so to end the yeere:
But walk'st about thine own dear bounds,
Not envying others larger grounds:
For well thou know'st, *'tis not th'extent*
Of Land makes life, but sweet content.
When now the Cock (the Plow-mans Horne)
Calls forth the lilly-wristed Morne; 20
Then to thy corn-fields thou dost goe,
Which though well soyl'd, yet thou dost know,
That the best compost for the Lands
Is the wise Masters Feet, and Hands.
There at the Plough thou find'st thy Teame,
With a Hind whistling there to them:
And cheer'st them up, by singing how
The Kingdoms portion[4] *is the Plow.*
This done, then to th'enameld Meads
Thou go'st; and as thy foot there treads, 30
Thou seest a present God-like Power
Imprinted in each Herbe and Flower:
And smell'st the breath of great-ey'd Kine,
Sweet as the blossomes of the Vine.
Here thou behold'st thy large sleek Neat
Unto the Dew-laps up in meat:

And, as thou look'st, the wanton Steere,
The Heifer, Cow, and Oxe draw neere
To make a pleasing pastime there.
These seen, thou go'st to view thy flocks 40
Of sheep, (safe from the Wolfe and Fox)
And find'st their bellies there as full
Of short sweet grasse, as backs with wool.
And leav'st them (as they feed and fill)
A Shepherd piping on a hill.
For Sports, for Pagentrie, and Playes,
Thou hast thy Eves, and Holydayes:
On which the young men and maids meet,
To exercise their dancing feet:
Tripping the comely country round, 50
With Daffadils and Daisies crown'd.
Thy Wakes, thy Quintels,[5] here thou hast,
Thy May-poles too with Garlands grac't:
Thy Morris-dance; thy Whitsun-ale;
Thy Sheering-feast, which never faile.
Thy Harvest home; thy Wassaile bowle,
That's tost up after Fox i'th'Hole.[6]
Thy Mummeries; thy Twelfe-tide Kings
And Queenes; thy Christmas revellings:
Thy Nut-browne mirth; thy Russet[7] wit; 60
And no man payes too deare for it.
To[8] these, thou hast thy times to goe
And trace the Hare i'th'trecherous Snow:
Thy witty wiles to draw, and get
The Larke into the Trammell net:
Thou hast thy Cockrood,[9] and thy Glade
To take the precious Phesant made:
Thy Lime-twigs,[10] Snares, and Pit-falls then
To catch the pilfring Birds, not Men.
O happy life! if that their good 70
The Husbandmen but understood!
Who all the day themselves doe please,
And Younglings, with such sports as these.
And, lying down, have nought t'affright
Sweet sleep, that makes more short the night.

Cætera desunt——[11]

[1] Endymion Porter (H-117) held this high office in the Royal Household in the 1620's. [2] Cf. Bacon, "Of Great Place": "Men in great place are thrice servants: servants of the sovereign or state;

servants of fame; and servants of business. So as they have no freedom; neither in their persons, nor in their actions, nor in their times." [3] debts. [4] endowment, source of wealth. [5] tilting matches. [6] hopping game. [7] homespun. [8] in addition to. [9] a cockshoot: an open space in a wood across which nets were stretched to catch woodcocks as they shot or darted across it. [10] twigs smeared with sticky substance to capture birds. [11] the rest is lacking; i.e. the poem is incomplete.

H–663 To *Electra.*

I Dare not ask a kisse;
I dare not beg a smile;
Lest having that, or this,
I might grow proud the while.

2. No, no, the utmost share
Of my desire, shall be
Onely to kisse that Aire,
That lately kissed thee.

H–664 *To his worthy friend, Master* Arthur Bartly.[1]

WHen after many Lusters[2] thou shalt be
Wrapt up in Seare-cloth with thine Ancestrie:
When of thy ragg'd *Escutcheons* shall be seene
So little left, as if they ne'r had been:
Thou shalt thy Name have, and thy Fames best trust, 5
Here with the Generation of my Just.[3]

[1] not identified. [2] five-year periods. [3] Ps. xiv.5, "for God is in the generation of the righteous."

H–665 *What kind of Mistresse he would have.*

BE the Mistresse of my choice,
Cleane in manners, cleere in voice:
Be she witty, more then wise;
Pure enough, though not Precise:

Be she shewing in her dresse, 5
Like a civill Wilderness;
That the curious may detect
Order in a sweet neglect:
Be she rowling in her eye,
Tempting all the passers by: 10
And each Ringlet of her haire,
An Enchantment, or a Snare,
For to catch the Lookers on;
But her self held fast by none.
Let her *Lucrece*[1] all day be, 15
Thais[2] in the night, to me.
Be she such, as neither will
Famish me, nor over-fill.

[1] Lucretia revealed to her husband that she had been violated by Sextus and killed herself. See Chaucer, *Legend of Good Women;* Gower, *Confessio Amantis;* Shakespeare, *The Rape of Lucrece.*
[2] Greek courtesan, mistress of Alexander the Great. Cf. Martial, XI, 104, 21–2.

H–666 *Upon Zelot.*

IS *Zelot* pure? he is: ye see he weares
The signe of *Circumcision* in his eares.[1]

[1] His ears had been cropped as a punishment for some crime.

H–667 *The Rosemarie branch.*

GRow for two ends,[1] it matters not at all,
Be't for my *Bridall,* or my *Buriall.*

[1] purposes.

H–668 *Upon Madam* Ursly, *Epigram.*

FOr ropes of pearle, first Madam *Ursly* showes
A chaine of Cornes, pickt from her eares and toes:
Then, next, to match *Tradescant's* curious shels,[1]
Nailes from her fingers mew'd,[2] she shewes: what els?

Why then (forsooth) a Carcanet is shown 5
Of teeth, as deaf[3] as nuts, and all her own.

[1] John Tradescant (d. 1637?) founded a museum; parts of his collections are preserved in Oxford's museums. [2] moulted. [3] hollow.

H–669 *Upon* Crab, *Epigram.*

CRab faces gownes with sundry Furres; 'tis known,
He keeps the Fox-furre for to face his own.

H–670

A Paranæticall, or Advisive Verse, to his friend, Master John Wicks.[1]

IS this a life, to break thy sleep?
To rise as soon as day doth peep?
To tire thy patient Oxe or Asse
By noone, and let thy good dayes passe,
Not knowing This, that *Jove* decrees 5
Some mirth, t'adulce[2] mans miseries?
No; 'tis a life, to have thine oyle,
Without extortion, from thy soyle:
Thy faithfull fields to yeeld thee Graine,
Although with some, yet little paine: 10
To have thy mind, and nuptiall bed,
With feares, and cares uncumbered:[3]
A Pleasing Wife, that by thy side
Lies softly panting like a Bride.
This is to live, and to endeere 15
Those minutes, Time has lent us here.
Then, while Fates suffer, live thou free,
(As is that ayre that circles thee)
And crown thy temples too, and let
Thy servant, not thy own self, sweat, 20
To strut[4] thy barnes with sheafs of Wheat.
Time steals away like to a stream,
And we glide hence away with them.
No sound recalls the houres once fled,
Or Roses, being withered: 25
Nor us (my Friend) when we are lost,
Like to a Deaw, or melted Frost.

Then live we mirthfull, while we should,
And turn the iron Age to Gold.
Let's feast, and frolick, sing, and play, 30
And thus lesse last, then live our Day.
Whose life with care is overcast,
That man's not said to live, but last:
Nor is't a life, seven yeares to tell,
But for to live that half seven well: 35
And that wee'l do; as men, who know,
Some few sands spent, we hence must go,
Both to be blended in the Urn,
From whence there's never a return.

[1] See H-336. [2] sweeten. [3] Cf. Martial, X, 47; trans. Cowley: ". . . Take such a Ground, whose gratitude may be / A fair encouragement for Industry. / . . . Thy active mind in equal temper keep, / In undisturbed peace, yet not in sleep. / . . . Let Rest, which Nature does to darkness wed, / And not Lust, recommend to thee thy Bed." [4] swell.

H-671 *Once seen, and no more.*

THousands each day passe by, which wee,
Once past and gone, no more shall see.

H-672 *Love.*

THis Axiom I have often heard,
Kings ought to be more lov'd, then fear'd.

H-673 *To* Master Denham, *on his Prospective Poem.*[1]

OR lookt I back unto the Times hence flown,
To praise those Muses, and dislike our own?
Or did I walk those *Pean*[2]-Gardens through,
To kick the Flow'rs, and scorn their odours too?[3]
I might (and justly) be reputed (here) 5
One nicely[4] mad, or peevishly severe.
But by *Apollo!* as I worship wit,
(Where I have cause to burn perfumes to it:)

So, I confesse, 'tis somwhat to do well
In our high art, although we can't excell, 10
Like thee; or dare the Buskins to unloose
Of thy brave, bold, and sweet *Maronian* Muse.[5]
But since I'm cal'd (rare *Denham*) to be gone,
Take from thy *Herrick* this conclusion:
'Tis dignity in others, if they be 15
Crown'd Poets; yet live Princes under thee:
The while their wreaths and Purple Robes do shine,
Lesse by their own jemms, then those beams of thine.

[1] *Cooper's Hill* describes the prospect or view near the home of John Denham (1615–69) near Windsor; first published in 1642, it was later revised and enlarged; see the ed. by Theodore Banks (1928). [2] In heraldry, *pean* refers to a black ground powdered with yellow spots: a garden might have such an appearance. A *Paean* is a song to Apollo; if this is intended, Herrick walks through gardens sacred to Apollo, god of poetry; his own *Hesperides* are, in a sense, such a garden of poetry. [3] The question mark may have been substituted for a comma by the printer. The meaning is: *If I looked back . . . or if I walked . . . I might have been reputed,* etc. [4] fastidiously. [5] Virgilian Muse. Cf. Luke iii.16, "one mightier than I cometh, the latchet of whose shoes I am not worthy to unloose."

H–674 *A Hymne, to the* Lares.

IT was, and still my care is,
To worship ye, the *Lares,*
With crowns of greenest Parsley,
And Garlick chives not scarcely:
For favours here to warme me, 5
And not by fire to harme me.
For gladding so my hearth here,
With inoffensive mirth here;
That while the Wassaile Bowle here
With *North-down* Ale doth troule[1] here, 10
No sillable doth fall here,
To marre the mirth at all here.
For which, ô *Chimney-keepers!*
(I dare not call ye Sweepers)
So long as I am able 15
To keep a countrey-table,

Great be my fare, or small cheere,
I'le eat and drink up all here.

[1] troll: circulate from person to person.

H–675

Deniall in women no disheartning to men.

WOmen, although they ne're so goodly make it,[1]
Their fashion is, but to say no, to take it.

[1] although they ever so graciously make a denial.

H–676

Adversity.

LOve is maintain'd by wealth; when all is spent,
Adversity then breeds the discontent.

H–677

To Fortune.

TUmble me down, and I will sit
Upon my ruines (smiling yet:)
Teare me to tatters; yet I'le be
Patient in my necessitie.
Laugh at my scraps of cloaths, and shun 5
Me, as a fear'd infection:
Yet scarre-crow-like I'le walk, as one,
Neglecting thy derision.

H–678

To Anthea.

COme *Anthea,* know thou this,
Love at no time idle is:
Let's be doing, though we play
But at push-pin[1] (half the day:)
Chains of sweet bents[2] let us make, 5
Captive one, or both, to take:

In which bondage we will lie,
Soules transfusing thus, and die.

[1] H-44. [2] grasses.

H–679 *Cruelties.*

NEro commanded; but withdrew his eyes
From the beholding Death, and cruelties.

H–680 *Perseverance.*

HAst thou begun an act? ne're then give o're:
No man despaires to do what's done before.

H–681 *Upon his Verses.*

WHat off-spring other men have got,
The how, where, when, I question not.
These are the Children I have left;
Adopted some; none got by theft.
But all are toucht (like lawfull plate)[1] 5
And no Verse illegitimate.

[1] The fineness of silver and gold utensils was tested by touching, i.e. by rubbing them against a touchstone.

H–682 *Distance betters Dignities.*

KIngs must not oft be seen by publike eyes;
State at a distance adds to dignities.

H–683 *Health.*

HEalth is no other (as the learned hold)
But a just measure both of Heat and Cold.[1]

[1] Herrick simplifies traditional physiology; health was regarded as dependent on a proper balance of hot, cold, moist, and dry. Each

humor (blood, choler, black bile, phlegm) had two of these qualities. A deficiency or excess of any humor caused ill health. For details and references to the "learned," see Lawrence Babb, *The Elizabethan Malady* (1951), pp. 5–12.

H–684 *To Dianeme. A Ceremonie in Glocester.*

I'Le to thee a Simnell[1] bring,
'Gainst thou go'st a *mothering*,
So that, when she blesseth thee,
Half that blessing thou'lt give me.

[1] a bun of fine flour and sometimes currants made for Mid-Lent Sunday when children went "mothering," i.e. visiting parents and exchanging gifts with them. The Epistle read in churches on that Sunday (Gal. iv.21–31) mentions Jerusalem, "the mother of us all."

H–685 *To the King.*[1]

GIve way, give way, now, now my *Charles* shines here,
A Publike Light (in this immensive Sphere.)
Some starres were fixt before; but these are dim,
Compar'd (in this my ample Orbe) to Him.
Draw in your feeble fiers, while that He 5
Appeares but in His Meaner Majestie.
Where, if such glory flashes from His Name,
Which is His Shade, who can abide His Flame!
Princes, and such like Publike Lights as these,
Must not be lookt on, but at distances: 10
For, if we gaze on These brave Lamps too neer,
Our eyes they'l blind, or if not blind, they'l bleer.[2]

[1] Cf. the poem prefaced to *Hesperides* and also H-77, to which this may be a sequel. [2] In Exod. xxxiii.18–20, Moses asks to see God's glory and is told, "Thou canst not see my face: for there shall no man see me and live."

H–686 *The Funerall Rites of the Rose.*

THe Rose was sick, and smiling di'd;
And (being to be sanctifi'd)
About the Bed, there sighing stood
The sweet, and flowrie Sisterhood.
Some hung the head, while some did bring 5
(To wash her) water from the Spring.
Some laid her forth, while other wept,
But all a solemne Fast there kept.
The holy Sisters some among
The sacred *Dirge* and *Trentall* sung. 10
But ah! what sweets smelt every where,
As Heaven had spent all perfumes there.
At last, when prayers for the dead,
And Rites were all accomplished;
They, weeping, spread a Lawnie Loome, 15
And clos'd her up, as in a Tombe.

H–687 *The Rainbow: or curious Covenant.*

MIne eyes, like clouds, were drizling raine,
And as they thus did entertaine
The gentle Beams from *Julia's* sight
To mine eyes level'd opposite:
O Thing admir'd! there did appeare 5
A curious Rainbow smiling there;
Which was the Covenant, that she
No more wo'd drown mine eyes, or me.[1]

[1] Gen. ix.11–13.

H–688 *The last stroke strikes sure.*

THough by well-warding many blowes w'ave past,
That stroke most fear'd is, which is struck the last.

H–689 *Fortune.*

FOrtune's a blind profuser of her own,
Too much she gives to some, enough to none.[1]

[1] Martial, XII, 10, 2; trans. Sir John Harington: "Fortune, they say, doth give too much to many; / But yet she never gave enough to any."

H–690 *Stool-ball.*[1]

1. AT Stool-ball, *Lucia*, let us play,
For Sugar-cakes and Wine;
Or for a Tansie let us pay,
The losse or thine, or mine.

2. If thou, my Deere, a winner be
At trundling of the Ball,[2]
The wager thou shalt have, and me,
And my misfortunes all.

3. But if (my Sweetest) I shall get,
Then I desire but this;
That likewise I may pay the Bet,
And have for all a kisse.

[1] a game like cricket, the *stool* being the wicket, played for a *tansy*, a pudding, omelet, or cake flavored with tansy juice, which is bitter. Cf. the "bitter herbs" of the Passover. [2] at rolling or bowling the ball to the stool.

H–691 *To* Sappho.

LEt us now take time, and play,
Love, and live here while we may;
Drink rich wine; and make good cheere,
While we have our being here:
For, once dead, and laid i'th grave, 5
No return from thence we have.

H–692 *On Poet* Prat, *Epigram.*

PRat He writes Satyres; but herein's the fault,
In no one Satyre there's a mite of salt.[1]

[1] wit, pungency. Col. iv.6, "Let your speech be . . . seasoned with salt."

H–693 *Upon* Tuck, *Epigram.*

AT Post and Paire, or Slam,[1] *Tom Tuck* would play
This Christmas, but his want wherwith, sayes Nay.

[1] card games.

H–694 *Biting of Beggars.*

WHo, railing, drives the Lazar from his door,
Instead of almes, sets dogs upon the poor.

H–695 *The May-pole.*

THe May-pole is up,
Now give me the cup;
I'le drink to the Garlands a-round it:
But first unto those
Whose hands did compose 5
The glory of flowers that crown'd it.

A health to my Girles,
Whose husbands may Earles
Or Lords be, (granting my wishes)
And when that ye wed 10
To the Bridall Bed,
Then multiply all, like to Fishes.

H–696 *Men mind no state*[1] *in sicknesse.*

THat flow of Gallants which approach
To kisse thy hand from out the coach;
That fleet of Lackeyes, which do run
Before thy swift Postilion;[2]
Those strong-hoof'd Mules, which we behold, 5
Rein'd in with Purple, Pearl, and gold,
And shod with silver, prove to be
The drawers of the *axeltree*.[3]
Thy Wife, thy Children, and the state
Of *Persian* Loomes, and *antique* Plate: 10
All these, and more, shall then afford
No joy to thee their sickly Lord.

[1] Men do not care about stateliness and splendor. [2] the rider on the foremost of a set of coach horses. [3] probably a two-wheeled funeral car.

H–697 *Adversity.*

ADversity hurts none, but onely such
Whom whitest Fortune dandled has too much.

H–698 *Want.*

NEed is no vice at all; though here it be,
With men, a loathed inconveniencie.

H–699 *Griefe.*

SOrrowes divided amongst many, lesse
Discruciate[1] a man in deep distresse.

[1] torture.

H–700 *Love palpable.*

I Prest my *Julia's* lips, and in the kisse
Her Soule and Love were palpable in this.

H–701 *No action hard to affection.*

NOthing hard, or harsh can prove
Unto those that truly love.

H–702 *Meane things overcome mighty.*

BY the weak'st means things mighty are o'rethrown,[1]
He's Lord of thy life, who contemnes his own.[2]

[1] I Cor. i.27, "God hath chosen the weak things of the world to confound the things that are mighty." [2] Repeats H-486, 2.

H–703 *Upon* Trigg, *Epigram.*

TRigg having turn'd his sute, he struts in state,
And tells the world, he's now regenerate.

H–704 *Upon* Smeaton.

HOw co'd *Luke Smeaton* weare a shoe, or boot,
Who two and thirty cornes had on a foot.

H–705 *The Bracelet of Pearle: to* Silvia.

I Brake thy Bracelet 'gainst my will;
And, wretched, I did see
Thee discomposed then, and still
Art discontent with me.

One jemme was lost; and I will get
A richer pearle for thee,
Then ever, dearest *Silvia*, yet
Was drunk to *Antonie*.[1]

Or, for revenge, I'le tell thee what
Thou for the breach shalt do; 10
First, crack the strings, and after that,
Cleave thou my heart in two.

[1] by Cleopatra.

H–706 *How Roses came red.*

'TIs said, as *Cupid* danc't among
The *Gods*, he down the Nectar flung;
Which, on the white *Rose* being shed,
Made it for ever after red.

H–707 *Kings.*

MEn are not born Kings, but are men renown'd;
Chose first, confirm'd next, and at last are crown'd.

H–708 *First work, and then wages.*

PRepost'rous is that order, when we run
To ask our wages, e're our work be done.

H–709 *Teares, and Laughter.*

KNew'st thou, one moneth wo'd take thy life away,
Thou'dst weep; but laugh, sho'd it not last a day.

H–710 *Glory.*

GLory no other thing is (*Tullie*[1] sayes)
Then a mans frequent Fame, spoke out with praise.

[1] Cicero, *De Inventione,* II, 15, 166.

H-711 *Possessions.*

THose possessions short-liv'd are,
Into the which we come by warre.

H-712 Laxare fibulam.

TO loose the button, is no lesse,
Then to cast off all bashfulnesse.

H-713 *His returne to London.*

FRom the dull confines of the drooping West,
To see the day spring from the pregnant East,
Ravisht in spirit, I come, nay more, I flie
To thee, blest place of my Nativitie!
Thus, thus with hallowed foot I touch the ground, 5
With thousand blessings by thy Fortune crown'd.
O fruitfull Genius! that bestowest here
An everlasting plenty, yeere by yeere.
O *Place!* O *People!* Manners![1] fram'd to please
All *Nations, Customes, Kindreds, Languages!* 10
I am a free-born *Roman;* suffer then,
That I amongst you live a Citizen.
London my home is: though by hard fate sent
Into a long and irksome banishment;
Yet since cal'd back; henceforward let me be, 15
O native countrey, repossest by thee!
For, rather then I'le to the West return,
I'le beg of thee first here to have mine Urn.
Weak I am grown, and must in short time fall;
Give thou my sacred Reliques Buriall. 20

[1] Cf. H-86, 9.

H-714 *Not every day fit for Verse.*

'TIs not ev'ry day, that I
Fitted am to prophesie:
No, but when the Spirit fils
The fantastick Pannicles:[1]

Full of fier; then I write
As the Godhead doth indite.[2]
Thus inrag'd, my lines are hurl'd,
Like the *Sybells,*[3] through the world.
Look how next the holy fier
Either slakes, or doth retire; 10
So the Fancie cooles, till when
That brave Spirit comes agen.

[1] the cells of the brain which are the seat of imagination and fancy. [2] prescribe, dictate. [3] The Cumaean sibyl (prophetess) wrote her oracles on leaves and left them before her cave, where the wind scattered them.

H–715 *Poverty the greatest pack.*

TO mortall men great loads allotted be,
But of all packs, no pack like poverty.

H–716 *A Beucolick, or discourse of Neatherds.*[1]

1 COme blithefull Neatherds, let us lay
A wager, who the best shall play,
Of thee, or I, the Roundelay,[2]
That fits the businesse of the Day.

Chor. And *Lallage* the Judge shall be,
To give the prize to thee, or me.

2 Content, begin, and I will bet
A Heifer smooth, and black as jet,
In every part alike compleat, 10
And wanton as a Kid as yet.

Chor. And *Lallage* (with cow-like eyes)
Shall be Disposeresse of the prize.

1 Against thy Heifer, I will here
Lay to thy stake a lustie Steere,
With gilded hornes, and burnisht cleere.
Chor. Why then begin, and let us heare
The soft, the sweet, the mellow note
That gently purles from eithers Oat.

2 The stakes are laid: let's now apply
Each one to make his melody: 20
Lal. The equall Umpire shall be I,
Who'l hear, and so judge righteously.

Chor. Much time is spent in prate; begin,
And sooner play, the sooner win.
[*He playes.*

1 That's sweetly touch't, I must confesse:
Thou art a man of worthinesse:
But hark how I can now expresse
My love unto my Neatherdesse.
[*He sings.*

Chor. A suger'd note! and sound as sweet
As Kine, when they at milking meet. 30

1 Now for to win thy Heifer faire,
I'le strike thee such a nimble Ayre,
That thou shalt say (thy selfe) 'tis rare;
And title me without compare.

Chor. Lay by a while your Pipes, and rest,
Since both have here deserved best.

2 To get thy Steerling, once again,
I'le play thee such another strain;
That thou shalt swear, my Pipe do's raigne
Over thine Oat, as Soveraigne. 40
[*He sings.*

Chor. And *Lallage* shall tell by this,
Whose now the prize and wager is.

1 Give me the prize: 2. The day is mine:
1 Not so; my Pipe has silenc't thine:
And hadst thou wager'd twenty Kine,
They were mine own. *Lal.* In love combine.

Chor. And lay we down our Pipes together,
As wearie, not o'recome by either.

[1] a bucolic (pastoral poem) or conversation of cattle herders. [2] a brief simple song, with a refrain; or the music for such a song.

H–717 *True safety.*

'TIs not the Walls, or purple, that defends
A Prince from Foes; but 'tis his Fort of Friends.

H–718 *A Prognostick.*

AS many Lawes and Lawyers do expresse
Nought but a Kingdoms ill-affectednesse:
Ev'n so, those streets and houses do but show
Store of diseases, where Physitians flow.

H–719 *Upon* Julia's *sweat.*

WO'd ye oyle of Blossomes get?
Take it from my *Julia's* sweat:
Oyl of Lillies, and of Spike,[1]
From her moysture take the like:
Let her breath, or let her blow, 5
All rich spices thence will flow.[2]

[1] lavender. [2] Cf. Donne's Elegie VIII.

H–720 *Proof to no purpose.*

YOu see this gentle streame, that glides,
Shov'd on, by quick succeeding Tides:
Trie if this sober streame you can
Follow to th'wilder Ocean:
And see, if there it keeps unspent 5
In that congesting element.
Next, from that world of waters, then
By poares and cavernes back agen
Induc't that[1] inadultrate same
Streame to the Spring from whence it came. 10
This with a wonder when ye do,
As easie, and els easier too:
Then may ye recollect[2] the graines
Of my particular Remaines;
After a thousand Lusters hurld, 15
By ruffling winds, about the world.

[1] i.e. follow that. Water was believed to flow through underground passages and then to rise again to flow from springs. [2] gather again.

H–721 *Fame.*

'TIs still observ'd, that Fame ne're sings
The order,[1] *but the Sum*[2] *of things.*

[1] the progression, i.e. of incidents, actions, etc. [2] the outcome or upshot.

H–722 *By use comes easinesse.*

OFt bend the Bow, and thou with ease shalt do,
What others can't with all their strength put to.

H–723 *To the Genius*[1] *of his house.*

COmmand the Roofe great *Genius*, and from thence
Into this house powre downe thy influence,
That through each room a golden pipe may run
Of living water by thy *Benizon.*[2]
Fulfill the Larders, and with strengthning bread[3] 5
Be evermore these Bynns replenished.
Next, like a Bishop consecrate my ground,
That luckie Fairies here may dance their Round:
And after that, lay downe some silver pence,
The Masters charge and care to recompence. 10
Charme then the chambers; make the beds for ease,
More then for peevish pining sicknesses.
Fix the foundation fast, and let the Roofe
Grow old with time, but yet keep weather-proofe.

[1] tutelary spirits. [2] blessing. Cf. John iv.10, "thou wouldest have asked of him, and he would have given thee living water." [3] Ps. civ.15, "bread which strengtheneth man's heart."

H–724 *His Grange,*[1] *or private wealth.*

THough Clock,
To tell how night drawes hence, I've none,
A Cock,
I have, to sing how day drawes on.

I have
A maid (my *Prew*) by good luck sent,
To save
That little, Fates me gave or lent.
A Hen
I keep, which creeking day by day, 10
Tells when
She goes her long white egg to lay.
A goose
I have, which, with a jealous eare,
Lets loose 15
Her tongue, to tell what danger's neare.
A Lamb
I keep (tame) with my morsells fed,
Whose Dam
An Orphan left him (lately dead.) 20
A Cat
I keep, that playes about my House,
Grown fat,
With eating many a miching[2] Mouse.
To these 25
A **Trasy*[3] I do keep, whereby
I please
The more my rurall privacie:
Which are
But toyes, to give my heart some ease: 30
Where care
None is, slight things do lightly please.

[1] country residence, i.e. the vicarage at Dean Prior. [2] pilfering.
[3]* His Spaniel (Herrick's note).

H–725 *Good precepts, or counsell.*

IN all thy need, be thou possest
Still with a well-prepared brest:
Nor let the shackles make thee sad;
Thou canst but have, what others had.
And this for comfort thou must know, 5
Times that are ill wo'nt still be so.
Clouds will not ever powre down raine;
A sullen day will cleere againe.
First, peales of Thunder we must heare,
Then Lutes and Harpes shall stroke the eare. 10

H–726 *Money makes the mirth.*

WHen all Birds els do of their musick faile,
Money's the still-sweet-singing *Nightingale.*

H–727 *Up tailes all.*[1]

BEgin with a kisse,
Go on too with this:
And thus, thus, thus let us smother
Our lips for a while,
But let's not beguile 5
Our hope of one for the other.

This play, be assur'd,
Long enough has endur'd,
Since more and more is exacted;
For love he doth call 10
For his Uptailes all;
And that's the part to be acted.

[1] refrain of a song beginning "Fly Merry News," in Chappell, *Popular Music of the Olden Time,* I, 196.

H–728 *Upon* Franck.

FRanck wo'd go scoure her teeth; and setting to't,
Twice two fell out, all rotten at the root.

H–729 *Upon* Lucia *dabled in the deaw.*

MY *Lucia* in the deaw did go,
And prettily bedabled so,
Her cloaths held up, she shew'd withall
Her decent[1] legs, cleane, long and small.
I follow'd after to descrie 5
Part of the nak't sincerity;

But still the envious Scene[2] between
Deni'd the Mask[3] I wo'd have seen.

[1] becoming. [2] veil or curtain. [3] play; also a mascle (heraldic term) or voided lozenge.

H–730

Charon *and* Phylomel,[1] *a Dialogue sung.*

Ph. *C*Haron! O gentle *Charon!* let me wooe thee,
By tears and pitie now to come unto mee.
Ch. What voice so sweet and charming do I heare?
Say what thou art.
Ph. I prithee first draw neare.
Ch. A sound I heare, but nothing yet can see,
Speak where thou art.
Ph. O *Charon* pittie me!
I am a bird, and though no name I tell,
My warbling note will say I'm *Phylomel.* 10
Ch. What's that to me, I waft nor fish or fowles,
Nor Beasts (fond[2] thing) but only humane soules.
Ph. Alas for me!
Ch. Shame on thy witching note,
That made me thus hoist saile, and bring my Boat:
But Ile returne; what mischief brought thee hither?
Ph. A deale of Love, and much, much Griefe together.
Ch. What's thy request?
Ph. That since she's now beneath
Who fed my life, I'le follow her in death.[3] 20
Ch. And is that all? I'm gone.
Ph. By love I pray thee,
Ch. Talk not of love, all pray, but few soules pay me.
Ph. Ile give thee vows and tears.
Ch. Can tears pay skores[4]
For mending sails, for patching Boat and Oares?
Ph. I'le beg a penny, or Ile sing so long,
Till thou shalt say, I've paid thee with a song.
Ch. Why then begin, and all the while we make
Our slothfull passage o're the Stygian Lake,
Thou and I'le sing to make these dull Shades merry,
Who els with tears wo'd doubtles drown my ferry.

[1] After the rape of Philomela by her brother-in-law Tereus was avenged, she was turned into a nightingale. Herrick imagines that she asks the boatman of the river Styx to take her to Hades.

[2] foolish. [3] Grosart opines that Philomel is male here, i.e. that Herrick modified the myth; but "who fed my life" probably applies to Xeuxippe, the mother of Philomela and her sister Procne. Since the latter was changed into a swallow, she would, as a bird, have been refused passage. Two of the MSS read *he* instead of *she* and *h* (i.e. *him*) instead of *her*. These may well be the proper readings, the reference being to Philomela's father, Pandion, who is said to have died of grief at the misfortunes of his family (Apollodorus, III, 14, 5 ff.). [4] debts. The text, crowded in the 1648 edition, is here spaced more generously, with two changes: 11 that / that *1648*. 19 Can / can.

H-731 *Upon* Paul. *Epigram.*

PAuls hands do give,[1] what give they bread or meat,
Or money? no, but onely deaw[2] and sweat.
As stones[3] and salt gloves[4] use to give, even so
Pauls hands do give, nought else for ought we know.

[1] one old meaning of *give* is *to become damp, to exude moisture.* [2] moisture exuded by the body. [3] A correspondence between bread and stones, salt and money, seems to be intended. Cf. Matt. vii.9, "what man . . . if his son ask bread, will give him a stone?" [4] Possibly a misprint; Martin suggests *shores.* But *gloves* may symbolize the fastidious and selfish rich who, when asked to give bread and meat, give only stones and salt without meat to put it on.

H-732 *Upon* Sibb. *Epigram.*

SIbb when she saw her face how hard it was,
For anger spat on thee her Looking-glasse:
But weep not *Christall;* for the shame was meant
Not unto thee, but That thou didst present.

H-733

A Ternarie[1] of littles, upon a pipkin[2] of Jellie sent to a Lady.

1. A Little Saint best fits a little Shrine,
A little prop best fits a little Vine,
As my small Cruse best fits my little Wine.

2. A little Seed best fits a little Soyle,
A little Trade best fits a little Toyle:
As my small Jarre best fits my little Oyle.

3. A little Bin best fits a little Bread,
A little Garland fits a little Head:
As my small stuffe best fits my little Shed.

4. A little Hearth best fits a little Fire,
A little Chappell fits a little Quire,
As my small Bell best fits my little Spire.

5. A little streame best fits a little Boat;
A little lead best fits a little Float;
As my small Pipe best fits my little note.

6. A little meat best fits a little bellie,
As sweetly Lady, give me leave to tell ye,
This little Pipkin fits this little Jellie.

[1] set of threes. [2] small earthenware pot.

H–734 *Upon the Roses in* Julias *bosome.*

THrice happie Roses, so much grac't, to have
Within the Bosome of my Love your grave.
Die when ye will, your sepulchre is knowne,
Your Grave her Bosome is, the Lawne the Stone.

H–735 *Maids nay's are nothing.*

MAids nay's are nothing, they are shie
But to desire what they denie.

H–736 *The smell of the Sacrifice.*

THe Gods require the thighes
Of Beeves for sacrifice;
Which rosted, we the steam
Must sacrifice to them:
Who though they do not eat,
Yet love the smell of meat.

H–737 *Lovers how thy come and part.*

A *Gyges* Ring[1] they beare about them still,
To be, and not seen when and where they will.
They tread on clouds, and though they sometimes fall,
They fall like dew, but make no noise at all.
So silently they one to th'other come, 5
As colours steale into the Peare or Plum,
And Aire-like, leave no pression to be seen
Where e're they met, or parting place has been.

[1] Gyges discovered a ring which, when turned, made him visible or invisible (Plato, *Republic,* II).

H–738 *To women, to hide their teeth, if they be rotten or rusty.*

CLose keep your lips, if that you meane
To be accounted inside cleane:
For if you cleave them, we shall see
There in your teeth much Leprosie.

H–739 *In praise of women.*

O *Jupiter,* sho'd I speake ill
Of woman-kind, first die I will;
Since that I know, 'mong all the rest
Of creatures, woman is the best.

H–740 *The Apron of Flowers.*

TO gather Flowers *Sappha* went,
And homeward she did bring
Within her Lawnie Continent,[1]
The treasure of the Spring.

She smiling blusht, and blushing smil'd, 5
And sweetly blushing thus,
She lookt as she'd been got with child
By young *Favonius*.

Her Apron gave (as she did passe)
An Odor more divine, 10
More pleasing too, then ever was
The lap of *Proserpine*.[2]

[1] that which contains, i.e. her apron of fine linen. [2] Cf. *Paradise Lost*, IV.268–71: "Not that faire field / Of *Enna*, where *Proserpin* gathring flours / . . . by gloomie *Dis* [Pluto] / Was gatherd."

H–741 *The Candor*[1] *of* Julias *teeth.*

WHite as *Zenobias*[2] teeth, the which the Girles
Of Rome did weare for their most precious Pearles.

[1] whiteness. [2] Queen Zenobia of Palmyra, a brunette with teeth of pearly whiteness.

H–742 *Upon her weeping.*

SHe wept upon her cheeks, and weeping so,
She seem'd to quench loves fires that there did glow.

H–743 *Another upon her weeping.*

SHe by the River sate, and sitting there,
She wept, and made it deeper by a teare.

H–744 *Delay.*

BReak off Delay, since we but read of one[1]
That ever prosper'd by *Cunctation*.

[1] Fabius Maximus used delaying tactics to hinder Hannibal's advance and thus became known as *Cunctator*, the Delayer. Virgil (*Aeneid*, VI.846) calls him the one man who retrieved the state by delaying.

H–745 *To Sir* John Berkley, *Governour of Exeter.*[1]

STand forth brave man, since Fate has made thee here
The *Hector*[2] over *Aged Exeter;*
Who for a long sad time has weeping stood,
Like a *poore Lady* Lost in Widdowhood:
But feares not now to see her safety sold 5
(As other Townes and Cities were) for gold,
By those ignoble *Births,* which shame the stem
That gave Progermination[3] unto them:
Whose restlesse *Ghosts* shall heare their children sing,
Our Sires betraid their Countrey and their King. 10
True, if this Citie seven times rounded was
With rock, and seven times circumflankt with brasse,
Yet if thou wert not, *Berkley,* loyall proofe,[4]
The Senators down tumbling with the Roofe,
Would into prais'd (but pitied) ruines fall, 15
Leaving no shew, where stood the *Capitoll.*
But thou art just and itchlesse,[5] and dost please
Thy *Genius* with two strength'ning *Buttresses,*
Faith, and *Affection:* which will never slip
To weaken this thy great *Dictator-ship.* 20

[1] John Berkeley, 1607–78, took Exeter in 1643 and governed it till 1646. [2] The fates decreed that Troy should never be destroyed as long as Hector lived. [3] the power to bud and develop branches. [4] of proved and tested loyalty. [5] incorruptible (with no palm itching for bribes).

H–746 *To* Electra. *Love looks for Love.*

LOve love begets, then never be
Unsoft to him who's smooth to thee.
Tygers and Beares (I've heard some say)
For profer'd love will love repay:
None are so harsh, but if they find
Softnesse in others, will be kind;
Affection will affection move,
Then you must like, because I love.

H-747 *Regression spoiles Resolution.*

HAst thou attempted greatnesse? then go on,
Back-turning slackens Resolution.

H-748 *Contention.*

DIscreet and prudent we that Discord call,
That either profits, or not hurts at all.

H-749 *Consultation.*

COnsult[1] ere thou begin'st, that done, go on
With all wise speed for execution.

[1] take counsel.

H-750 *Love dislikes nothing.*[1]

WHatsoever thing I see,
Rich or poore although it be;
'Tis a Mistresse unto mee.

Be my Girle, or faire or browne,
Do's she smile, or do's she frowne: 5
Still I write a Sweet-heart downe.

Be she rough, or smooth of skin;
When I touch, I then begin
For to let Affection in.

Be she bald, or do's she weare 10
Locks incurl'd of other haire;
I shall find enchantment there.

Be she whole, or be she rent,
So my fancie be content,
She's to me most excellent. 15

Be she fat, or be she leane,
Be she sluttish, be she cleane,
I'm a man for ev'ry Sceane.

[1] Cf. H-579.

H–751 *Our own sinnes unseen.*

OTher mens sins wee ever beare in mind;
None sees the fardell[1] *of his faults behind.*

[1] bundle.

H–752 *No Paines, no Gaines.*

IF little labour, little are our gaines:
Mans fortunes are according to his paines.

H–753 *Upon* Slouch.

SLouch he packs up, and goes to sev'rall Faires,
And weekly Markets for to sell his wares:
Meane time that he from place to place do's rome,
His wife her owne ware sells as fast at home.

H–754 *Vertue best united.*[1]

BY so much, vertue is the lesse,
By how much, neere to singlenesse.

[1] i.e. when it consists of a union of particular virtues.

H–755 *The eye.*

A Wanton and lascivious eye
Betrayes the Hearts Adulterie.[1]

[1] II Peter ii.14, "Having eyes full of adultery, and that cannot cease from sin."

H-756

To Prince Charles *upon his coming to Exeter.*[1]

WHat Fate decreed, Time now ha's made us see
A Renovation of the West by Thee.
That Preternaturall Fever, which did threat
Death to our Countrey, now hath lost his heat:
And calmes succeeding, we perceive no more 5
Th'unequall Pulse to beat, as heretofore.
Something there yet remaines for Thee to do;
Then reach those ends that thou wast destin'd to.
Go on with *Sylla's*[2] Fortune; let thy Fate
Make Thee like Him, this, that way fortunate,[3] 10
Apollos[4] Image side with Thee to blesse
Thy Warre (discreetly made) with white successe.
Meane time thy Prophets Watch by Watch shall pray;
While young *Charles* fights, and fighting wins the day.
That done, our smooth-pac't Poems all shall be 15
Sung in the high *Doxologie* of Thee.
Then maids shall strew Thee, and thy Curles from them
Receive (with Songs) a flowrie Diadem.

[1] Aug. 29, 1645. [2] The career of Lucius Cornelius Sulla won him the name of Felix—the Happy; otherwise it offers numerous parallels to the fortunes of Prince Charles. Sulla, in his civil war, defeated an army composed of the dregs of the populace. [3] There is, perhaps, a hint of hope that a brutal retribution like that inflicted by Sulla on the popular party would, in time, fall on the Parliamentarians. [4] Probably a reference to the Emperor Augustus's choice of Apollo as his special patron.

H-757

A Song.

BUrne, or drowne me, choose ye whether,
So I may but die together:
Thus to slay me by degrees,
Is the height of Cruelties.
What needs twenty stabs, when one 5
Strikes me dead as any stone?
O shew mercy then, and be
Kind at once to murder mee.

H–758 *Princes and Favourites.*

PRinces and Fav'rites are most deere, while they
By giving and receiving hold the play:
But the Relation then of both growes poor,
When These can aske, and Kings can give no more.

H–759 *Examples, or like Prince, like People.*

EXamples lead us, and wee likely see,
Such as the Prince is, will his People be.

H–760 *Potentates.*

LOve and the *Graces* evermore do wait
Upon the man that is a Potentate.

H–761 *The Wake.*

COme *Anthea* let us two
Go to Feast, as others do.
Tarts and Custards, Creams and Cakes,
Are the Junketts still at Wakes:[1]
Unto which the Tribes[2] resort, 5
Where the businesse is the sport:
Morris-dancers thou shalt see,
Marian[3] too in Pagentrie:
And a Mimick to devise
Many grinning properties. 10
Players there will be, and those
Base in action[4] as in clothes:
Yet with strutting they will please
The incurious Villages.
Neer the dying of the day, 15
There will be a *Cudgell*-Play,
Where a *Coxcomb* will be broke,
Ere a good *word* can be spoke:

But the anger ends all here,
Drencht in Ale, or drown'd in Beere. 20
Happy Rusticks, best content
With the cheapest Merriment:
And possesse no other feare,
Then to want the Wake next Yeare.

[1] are always the sweetmeats at feasts. [2] families. Cf. Ps. cxxii.4, "Whither the tribes go up." [3] Maid Marian in Mayday pageants; she is Robin Hood's companion in the later versions of his story. [4] dramatic action.

H–762 *The* Peter-*penny.*

FResh strowings allow
To my Sepulcher now,
To make my lodging the sweeter;
A staffe or a wand
Put then in my hand, 5
With a pennie to pay S. *Peter.*[1]

Who has not a Crosse,[2]
Must sit with the losse,
And no whit further must venture;
Since the Porter he 10
Will paid have his fee,
Or els not one there must enter.

Who at a dead lift,[3]
Can't send for a gift
A Pig to the Priest for a Roster,[4] 15
Shall heare his Clarke say,
By yea and by nay,[5]
No pennie, no Pater Noster.

[1] because he holds the keys to heaven. [2] coin. [3] in extreme circumstances. [4] roaster. [5] a substitute for an oath; cf. Matt. v.34–37, "Swear not at all . . . But let your communication be, Yea, yea, Nay, nay."

H-763 *To Doctor* Alablaster.[1]

NOr art thou lesse esteem'd, that I have plac'd
(Amongst mine honour'd) Thee (almost) the last:
In great Processions many lead the way
To him, who is the triumph of the day,
As these have done to Thee, who art the one, 5
One onely glory of a million,
In whom the spirit of the Gods do's dwell,[2]
Firing thy soule, by which thou dost foretell
When this or that vast *Dinastie* must fall
Downe to a *Fillit* more *Imperiall.*[3] 10
When this or that *Horne* shall be broke, and when
Others shall spring up in their place agen:[4]
When times and seasons[5] and all yeares must lie
Drown'd in the Sea of wild Eternitie:[6]
When the *Black Dooms-day Bookes* (as yet unseal'd) 15
Shall by the mighty *Angell* be reveal'd:[7]
And when the Trumpet which thou late hast found[8]
Shall call to Judgment; tell us when the sound
Of this or that great Aprill day[9] shall be,
And next the Gospell wee will credit thee. 20
Meane time like Earth-wormes we will craule below,
And wonder at Those Things that thou dost know.

[1] William Alabaster, 1568–1640, friend of Jonson and Selden and associate of Bishop Williams (Herrick wrote poems to all three), and celebrated for works on mystical theology, *Apparatus in Revelationem Jesu Christi* (Antwerp, 1607); *De Bestia Apocalyptica* (Delft, 1621); *Ecce Sponsus Venit. Tuba Pulchritudinis* (1633); and *Spiraculum Tubarum* (ca. 1633). See his poems in *The Meditative Poem,* ed. Louis Martz, in the Anchor Seventeenth-Century Series. [2] Mindful of Alabaster's apocalyptic writings, Herrick applies to him what Belshazzar said to Daniel (Dan. v.14–16): "I have even heard . . . that the spirit of the gods is in thee . . . that thou canst make interpretations, and dissolve doubts." Alabaster interpreted scriptural prophecies to fit the history of his own times. [3] must fall down in subordination to a more imperial fillet–a heraldic term for what is placed in the chief point of an escutcheon–though Herrick may mean simply a crown. [4] a reference to Alabaster's book on the apocalyptic beast. Cf. Dan. vii.7–8, "a fourth beast . . . had ten horns . . . and behold, there came up among them another little horn, before whom there were three of the first horns pluckt up by the roots"; cf. Dan. viii.8. [5] Acts

i.7, "It is not for you to know the times or the seasons, which the Father hath put in his own power." [6] Cf. Marvell, "To His Coy Mistress," 24: "Desarts of vast Eternity." [7] Rev. x.1–4: an angel had in his hand a little book, open, and John heard a voice tell him "Seal up those things"; in xx.12 he saw the dead "stand before God; and the books were opened." [8] a reference to the last two books mentioned in n.1; both include *tuba*, trumpet, in their titles. [9] Cf. S-4, 34, "till the doom / (The general April of the world) doth Come." *April* derives from *aperio*, open or uncover, and is thus appropriate for Doomsday when the graves open, the bodies are uncovered, and new life opens for the just. I Cor. xv.52, "the trumpet shall sound, and the dead shall be raised incorruptible, and we shall be changed."

H–764 *Upon his Kinswoman Mistresse* Mary Stone.[1]

HEre lies a Virgin, and as sweet
As ere was wrapt in winding sheet.
Her name if next you wo'd have knowne,
The Marble speaks it *Mary Stone:*
Who dying in her blooming yeares, 5
This Stone, for names sake, melts to teares.
If fragrant Virgins you'l but keep
A Fast, while Jets and Marbles weep,
And praying, strew some Roses on her,
You'l do my *Neice*[2] abundant honour. 10

[1] See H-496. [2] Unless one of Herrick's sisters married a Stone, this must be a cousin, a daughter of either Sir Richard Stone, son of Herrick's mother's brother John, or of Richard Stone, son of her brother Richard.

H–765 *Felicitie knowes no Fence.*

OF both our Fortunes good and bad we find
Prosperitie more searching of the mind:
Felicitie flies o're the Wall and Fence,
While misery keeps in with patience.

H–766 *Death ends all woe.*

TIme is the Bound of things, where e're we go,
Fate gives a meeting. Death's the end of woe.

H–767 *A Conjuration, to* Electra.

BY those soft Tods of wooll[1]
With which the aire is full:
By all those Tinctures there,
That paint the *Hemisphere:*
By Dewes and drisling Raine, 5
That swell the Golden Graine:
By all those sweets that be
I'th flowrie Nunnerie:
By silent Nights, and the
Three Formes of *Heccate:*[2] 10
By all Aspects[3] that blesse
The sober *Sorceresse,*
While juice she straines, and pith
To make her Philters with:
By Time, that hastens on 15
Things to perfection:
And by your self, the best
Conjurement of the rest:
O my *Electra!* be
In love with none, but me. 20

[1] masses of clouds; a *tod* is, literally, 28 pounds. [2] The goddess Hecate was often represented in triple form. Among her numerous functions, she protected enchanters and witches and was the queen of ghosts and magic. She was sometimes identified with Diana, "goddess of the triple form," *diva triformis,* as Horace calls her (*Carmina,* III, 22, 4). [3] of the planets.

H–768 *Courage cool'd.*

I Cannot love, as I have lov'd before:
For, I'm grown old; and, with mine age, grown poore:
Love must be fed by wealth: this blood of mine
Must needs wax cold, if wanting bread and wine.

H–769 *The Spell.*

HOly Water come and bring;
Cast in Salt, for seasoning:
Set the Brush for sprinkling:
Sacred Spittle bring ye hither;
Meale and it now mix together; 5
And a little Oyle to either:
Give the Tapers here their light,
Ring the *Saints-Bell*, to affright
Far from hence the evill Sp'rite.

H–770 *His wish to privacie.*

GIve me a Cell
To dwell,
Where no foot hath
A path:
There will I spend, 5
And end
My wearied yeares
In teares.

H–771 *A good Husband.*[1]

A Master of a house (as I have read)
Must be the first man up, and last in bed:
With the Sun rising he must walk his grounds;
See this, View that, and all the other bounds:
Shut every gate; mend every hedge that's torne, 5
Either with old, or plant therein new thorne:
Tread ore his gleab, but with such care, that where
He sets his foot, he leaves rich *compost* there.

[1] husbandman, farmer.

H–772 *A Hymne to* Bacchus.

I Sing thy praise *Iacchus,*
Who with thy *Thyrse* dost thwack us:
And yet thou so dost back us
With boldness that we feare
No *Brutus* entring here; 5
Nor *Cato* the severe.
What though the *Lictors* threat us,
We know they dare not beate us;
So long as thou dost heat us.
When we thy *Orgies* sing, 10
Each Cobler is a King;
Nor dreads he any thing:
And though he doe not rave,
Yet he'l the courage have
To call my *Lord Maior* knave; 15
Besides too, in a brave,
Although he has no riches,
But walks with dangling breeches,
And skirts that want their stiches,
And shewes his naked flitches;[1] 20
Yet he'le be thought or seen,
So good as *George-a-Green;*[2]
And calls his Blouze,[3] his Queene;
And speaks in language keene:
O *Bacchus!* let us be 25
From cares and troubles free;
And thou shalt heare how we
Will chant new *Hymnes* to thee.

[1] sides. [2] The merry pinner (poundkeeper) of Wakefield defeated all contestants in fights with quarterstaffs, defied the tax collector, and defeated Robin Hood and his men. See the play attributed to Robert Greene. [3] wench.

H–773

Upon Pusse *and her Prentice. Epigram.*

PUsse and her Prentice both at Draw-gloves play;
That done, they kisse, and so draw out the day:
At night they draw to Supper; then well fed,
They draw their clothes off both, so draw to bed.

H-774 *Blame the reward of Princes.*

AMong disasters that discention brings,
This not the least is, which belongs to Kings.
If Wars goe well; each for a part layes claime:
If ill, then Kings, not Souldiers beare the blame.

H-775 *Clemency in Kings.*

KIngs must not only cherish up the good,
But must be niggards of the meanest bloud.

H-776 *Anger.*

WRongs if neglected, vanish in short time;
But heard with anger, we confesse the crime.

H-777 *A Psalme or Hymne to the Graces.*

GLory be to the Graces!
That doe in publike places,
Drive thence what ere encumbers,
The listning to my numbers.

Honour be to the Graces! 5
Who doe with sweet embraces,
Shew they are well contented
With what I have invented.

Worship be to the Graces!
Who do from sowre faces, 10
And lungs that wo'd infect me,
For evermore protect me.

H–778 *An Hymne to the Muses.*

HOnour to you who sit!
Neere to the well of wit;
And drink your fill of it.

Glory and worship be!
To you sweet Maids (thrice three) 5
Who still inspire me.

And teach me how to sing
Unto the *Lyrick* string
My measures ravishing.

Then while I sing your praise, 10
My *Priest-hood* crown with bayes
Green, to the end of dayes.

H–779 *Upon* Julia's *Clothes.*

WHen as in silks my *Julia* goes,
Then, then (me thinks) how sweetly flowes
That liquefaction of her clothes.

Next, when I cast mine eyes and see
That brave Vibration each way free; 5
O how that glittering taketh me!

H–780 *Moderation.*

IN things a moderation keepe,
Kings ought to sheare, not skin their sheepe.

H–781 *To Anthea.*

LEts call for *Hymen* if agreed thou art;
Delays in love but crucifie the heart.
Loves thornie Tapers[1] yet neglected lye:
Speak thou the word, they'l kindle by and by.

The nimble howers wooe us on to wed, 5
And *Genius* waits to have us both to bed.
Behold, for us the *Naked Graces* stay
With maunds[2] of roses for to strew the way:
Besides, the most religious Prophet stands
Ready to joyne, as well our hearts as hands. 10
Juno yet smiles; but if she chance to chide,
Ill luck 'twill bode to th'Bridegroome and the Bride.
Tell me *Anthea*, dost thou fondly dread
The loss of that we call a Maydenhead?
Come, Ile instruct thee. Know, the vestall fier 15
Is not by mariage quencht, but flames the higher.

[1] torches carried at weddings. [2] baskets.

H-782 *Upon* Prew *his Maid.*

IN this little Urne is laid
Prewdence Baldwin (once my maid)
From whose happy spark here let
Spring the purple Violet.

H-783 *The Invitation.*

TO sup with thee thou didst me home invite;
And mad'st a promise that mine appetite
Sho'd meet and tire, on such lautitious[1] meat,
The like not *Heliogabalus*[2] did eat:
And richer Wine wo'dst give to me (thy guest) 5
Then Roman *Sylla*[3] powr'd out at his feast.
I came; (tis true) and lookt for Fowle of price,
The bastard *Phenix;* bird of *Paradice;*[4]
And for no less then Aromatick Wine
Of *Maydens-blush,* commixt with *Jessimine.*[5] 10
Cleane was the herth, the mantle[6] larded jet;
Which wanting *Lar,*[7] and smoke, hung weeping wet;
At last, i'th'noone of winter, did appeare
A ragd-soust[8]-neats-foot with sick[9] vineger:
And in a burnisht Flagonet stood by 15
Beere small as Comfort, dead as Charity.
At which amaz'd, and pondring on the food,
How cold it was, and how it child my blood;

I curst the master; and I damn'd the souce;
And swore I'de got the ague of the house. 20
Well, when to eat thou dost me next desire,
I'le bring a Fever; since thou keep'st no fire.

[1] sumptuous. [2] Roman Emperor. His voluptuous indulgences are described by Lampridian, Herodian, and Dio Cassius. [3] See H-756. Sulla was notorious for gross sensuality. [4] The brightly colored, plumed bird of paradise was called the bastard or spurious phoenix. [5] of the pink rose mixed with jasmine. [6] mantlepiece. Herrick probably means that the hearth was bare (without fire, fowl roasting, kettles, etc.), but Martin thinks *larded* may mean "greased and polished"; Grosart explains *larded jet* as "greasily flaked or streaked, not merely with smoke, but with soot." [7] Sacrifices to the tutelary spirit of a household were ordinarily burned in the fire on the hearth; but in this case fire and lar were lacking. [8] pickled. [9] corrupted.

H-784 Ceremonies for Christmasse.

COme, bring with a noise,
My merrie merrie boyes,
The Christmas Log to the firing;
While my good Dame, she
Bids ye all be free; 5
And drink to your hearts desiring.

With the last yeeres brand
Light the new block, And
For good successe in his spending,[1]
On your Psaltries[2] play, 10
That sweet luck may
Come while the Log is a teending.[3]

Drink now the strong Beere,
Cut the white loafe here,
The while the meat is a shredding; 15
For the rare Mince-Pie
And the Plums stand by
To fill the Paste that's a kneading.

[1] in its consumption by the fire. [2] harp-like ten-stringed instruments. [3] kindling.

H–785 *Christmasse-Eve, another Ceremonie.*

COme guard this night the Christmas-Pie,
That the Thiefe, though ne'r so slie,
With his Flesh-hooks, don't come nie
To catch it

From him, who all alone sits there, 5
Having his eyes still in his eare,
And a deale of nightly feare
To watch it.

H–786 *Another to the Maids.*

WAsh your hands, or else the fire
Will not teend[1] to your desire;
Unwasht hands, ye Maidens, know,
Dead[2] the Fire, though ye blow.

[1] kindle. [2] deaden.

H–787 *Another.*

WAssaile[1] the Trees, that they may beare
You many a Plum, and many a Peare:
For more or lesse fruits they will bring,
As you doe give them Wassailing.

[1] drink healths to (usually in spiced ale).

H–788 *Power and Peace.*

'TIs never, or but seldome knowne,
Power and Peace to keep one Throne.

H-789 *To his deare Valentine, Mistresse* Margaret Falconbrige.[1]

NOw is your turne (my Dearest) to be set
A Jem in this eternall Coronet:
'Twas rich before; but since your Name is downe,
It sparkles now like *Ariadne's* Crowne.[2]
Blaze by this Sphere for ever:[3] Or this doe, 5
Let Me and It shine evermore by you.

[1] daughter of Thomas F. See H-483. [2] Cretan princess. She married Bacchus, who gave her a golden crown which was later placed among the stars. [3] blaze by means of the inclusion of your name in this coronet of poems.

H-790 *To* Oenone.

SWeet *Oenone*, doe but say
Love thou dost, though Love sayes Nay.
Speak me faire; for Lovers be
Gently kill'd by Flatterie.

H-791 *Verses.*

WHo will not honour Noble Numbers, when
Verses out-live the bravest deeds of men?

H-792 *Happinesse.*

THat Happines do's still the longest thrive,
Where Joyes and Griefs have Turns Alternative.

H-793 *Things of choice, long a comming.*

WE pray 'gainst Warre, yet we enjoy no Peace;
Desire deferr'd is, that it may encrease.

H–794 *Poetry perpetuates the Poet.*

HEre I my selfe might likewise die,
And utterly forgotten lye,
But that eternall Poetrie
Repullulation[1] gives me here
Unto the thirtieth thousand yeere,[2] 5
When all now dead shall re-appeare.

[1] regeneration. [2] See H-515, n.6.

H–795 *Upon* Bice.

BIce laughs, when no man speaks; and doth protest
It is his own breech there that breaks the jest.

H–796 *Upon* Trencherman.

TOm shifts the Trenchers;[1] yet he never can
Endure that luke-warme name of Serving-man:
Serve or not serve, let *Tom* doe what he can,
He is a serving, who's a Trencher-man.

[1] platters on which food is served.

H–797 *Kisses.*

GIve me the food that satisfies a Guest:
Kisses are but dry banquets to a Feast.

H–798 *Orpheus.*

ORpheus he went (as Poets tell)
To fetch *Euridice* from Hell;
And had her; but it was upon
This short but strict condition:
Backward he should not looke while he 5
Led her through Hells obscuritie:

But ah! it hapned as he made
His passage through that dreadfull shade:
Revolve he did his loving eye;
(For gentle feare, or jelousie) 10
And looking back, that look did sever
Him and *Euridice* for ever.

H–799

Upon Comely *a good speaker but an ill singer,* Epigram.

COmely Acts well; and when he speaks his part,
He doth it with the sweetest tones of Art:
But when he sings a *Psalme*, ther's none can be
More curst for singing out of tune then he.

H–800

Any way for wealth.

E'Ene all Religious courses to be rich
Hath been reherst, by *Joell Michelditch:*
But now perceiving that it still do's please
The sterner Fates, to cross his purposes;
He tacks about, and now he doth profess 5
Rich he will be by all unrighteousness:
Thus if our ship fails of her Anchor hold,
We'l love the Divell, so he lands the gold.

H–801

Upon an old Woman.

OLd widdow *Prouse* to do her neighbours evill
Wo'd give (some say) her soule unto the Devill.
Well, when sh'as kild, that Pig, Goose, Cock or Hen,
What wo'd she give to get that soule agen?

H–802

Upon Pearch. *Epigram.*

THou writes in Prose, how sweet all Virgins be;
But ther's not one, doth praise the smell of thee.

H–803 *To* Sapho.

SApho, I will chuse to go
Where the Northern winds do blow
Endlesse Ice, and endlesse Snow:
Rather then I once wo'd see,
But a Winters face in thee, 5
To benumme my hopes and me.

H–804 *To his faithfull friend, Master* John Crofts,[1] *Cup-bearer to the King.*

FOr all thy many courtesies to me,
Nothing I have (my *Crofts*) to send to Thee
For the requitall; save this only one
Halfe of my just remuneration.
For since I've travail'd all this Realm throughout 5
To seeke, and find some few *Immortals* out
To *circumspangle* this my spacious Sphere,
(As Lamps for everlasting shining here:)
And having fixt Thee in mine *Orbe* a Starre
(Amongst the rest) both bright and singular; 10
The present Age will tell the world thou art
If not to th'whole, yet satisfy'd in part.
As for the rest, being too great a summe
Here to be paid; Ile pay't i'th'world to come.

[1] 1598–1664; son of Sir John Crofts of Saxham (See Carew's "To Saxham"); accompanied Lord Herbert of Cherbury to Paris, 1619; author of three "Hymnes" set by Henry Lawes. Davenant also addressed a poem to him.

H–805 *The Bride-Cake.*

THis day my *Julia* thou must make
For Mistresse Bride, the wedding Cake:
Knead but the Dow and it will be
To paste of Almonds turn'd by thee:
Or kisse it thou, but once, or twice, 5
And for the Bride-Cake ther'l be Spice.

H–806

To be merry.

LEts now take our time;
While w'are in our Prime;
And old, old Age is a farre off:
For the evill evill dayes[1]
Will come on apace; 5
Before we can be aware of.

[1] Eccles. xii.1, "Remember now thy Creator in the days of thy youth, while the evil days come not, nor the years draw nigh, when thou shalt say, I have no pleasure in them."

H–807

Buriall.

MAn may want Land to live in; but for all,
Nature finds out some place for buriall.

H–808

Lenitie.

'TIs the Chyrurgions praise, and height of Art,
Not to cut off, but cure the vicious part.

H–809

Penitence.

WHo after his transgression doth repent,
Is halfe, or altogether innocent.

H–810

Griefe.

COnsider sorrowes, how they are aright:
Griefe, if't be great, 'tis short; if long, 'tis light.

H–811

The Maiden-blush.

SO look the mornings when the Sun
Paints them with fresh Vermilion:
So Cherries blush, and Kathern[1] Peares,
And Apricocks, in youthfull yeares:

So Corrolls looke more lovely Red, 5
And Rubies lately polished:
So purest Diaper[2] doth shine,
Stain'd by the Beames of Clarret wine:
As *Julia* looks when she doth dress
Her either cheeke with bashfullness. 10

[1] a variety named after St. Catharine. [2] a textile, usually linen, so woven that reflections reveal patterns in it.

H-812 *The Meane.*

IMparitie doth ever discord bring:
The Mean the Musique makes in every thing.

H-813 *Haste hurtfull.*

HAste is unhappy: What we Rashly do
Is both unluckie; I, and foolish too.
Where War with rashnesse is attempted, there
The Soldiers leave the Field with equall feare.

H-814 *Purgatory.*

REaders wee ent[r]eat ye pray
For the soule of *Lucia;*
That in little time she be
From her *Purgatory* free:
In th'*intrim* she desires 5
That your teares may coole her fires.

H-815 *The Cloud.*

SEest thou that Cloud that rides in State
Part *Ruby-like,* part *Candidate?*[1]
It is no other then the Bed
Where *Venus* sleeps (halfe smothered.)

[1] literally, *robed in white.*

H–816 *Upon* Loach.

SEeal'd up with Night-gum, *Loach* each morning lyes,
Till his Wife licking, so unglews his eyes.
No question then, but such a lick is sweet,
When a warm tongue do's with such Ambers[1] meet.

[1] liquidambars: yellowish, sticky gums.

H–817 *The Amber Bead.*

I Saw a Flie within a Beade
Of Amber cleanly buried:
The Urne was little, but the room
More rich then *Cleopatra's* Tombe.

H–818

To my dearest Sister Mistresse Mercie Herrick.[1]

WHen ere I go, or what so ere befalls
Me in mine Age, or forraign Funerals,
This Blessing I will leave thee, ere I go,
Prosper thy Basket, and therein thy Dow.[2]
Feed on the paste of Filberts, or else knead 5
And Bake the floure of Amber for thy bread.
Balm may thy Trees drop, and thy Springs runne oyle
And everlasting Harvest crown thy Soile!
These I but wish for; but thy selfe shall see,
The Blessing fall in mellow times on Thee. 10

[1] Since she married John Wingfield in 1611, this poem was probably written before that date. See H-590. [2] Deut. xxviii.5, "Blessed shall be thy basket and thy store [*margin: Or* dough, *or* kneading trough]."

H–819 *The Transfiguration.*

IMmortall clothing I put on,[1]
So soone as *Julia* I am gon
To mine eternall Mansion.[2]

Thou, thou art here, to humane sight
Cloth'd all with incorrupted light;[3]
But yet how more admir'dly bright

Wilt thou appear, when thou art set
In thy refulgent Thronelet,
That shin'st thus in thy counterfeit?

[1] II Esdras ii.45, "these be they that have put off the mortal clothing, and put on the immortal." [2] John xiv.2, "In my Father's house are many mansions." [3] Wisd. of Sol. xviii.4, "the uncorrupt light"; Ps. cxxxii.9, "clothed with righteousness"; Isa. lxi.10, "he hath clothed me with the garments of salvation, he hath covered me with the robe of righteousness."

H–820 *Suffer that thou canst not shift.*

DO's Fortune rend thee? Beare with thy hard Fate:
Vertuous instructions ne'r are delicate.[1]
Say, do's she frown? still countermand her threats:
Vertue best loves those children that she beates.[2]

[1] Seneca, *De Providentia,* IV, 12, trans. Lodge: "Virtuous instructions are never delicate." [2] Rev. iii.19, "As many as I love, I rebuke and chasten." Prov. iii.12, "whom the Lord loveth, he correcteth, even as a father the son."

H–821 *To the Passenger.*

IF I lye unburied Sir,
These my Reliques, (pray) interre:
'Tis religious[1] part to see
Stones, or turfes to cover me.
One word more I had to say;
But it skills[2] not; go your way;

He that wants a buriall roome
For a Stone, ha's Heaven his Tombe.[3]

[1] "religions"—if the "n" was accidentally turned by the printer of the 1648 ed. [2] matters. [3] Lucan, *Pharsalia,* VII, 819, trans. May: "they obtaine / Heavens coverture, that have no urnes at all."

H–822

Upon Nodes.

WHere ever *Nodes* do's in the Summer come,
He prayes his Harvest may be well brought home.
What store of Corn has carefull *Nodes,* thinke you,
Whose Field his foot is, and whose Barn his shooe?

H–823

TO THE KING,
Upon his taking of *Leicester.*[1]

THis Day is Yours *Great CHARLES!* and in this War
Your Fate, and Ours, alike Victorious are.
In her white Stole; now Victory do's rest
Enspher'd with Palm on Your Triumphant Crest.
Fortune is now Your Captive; other Kings
Hold but her hands; You hold both hands and wings.

[1] May 31, 1645.

H–824

To Julia, *in her Dawn, or Day-breake.*

BY the next kindling of the day
My *Julia* thou shalt see,
Ere *Ave-Mary* thou canst say
Ile come and visit thee.

Yet ere thou counsel'st with thy Glasse, 5
Appeare thou to mine eyes
As smooth, and nak't, as she that was
The prime of *Paradice.*

If blush thou must, then blush thou through
A Lawn, that thou mayst looke 10
As purest Pearles, or Pebles do
When peeping through a Brooke.

As Lillies shrin'd in Christall, so
Do thou to me appeare;
Or Damask Roses, when they grow 15
To sweet acquaintance there.[1]

[1] Cf. Martial, VIII, 68, 5–8; Matthew Prior, "Non Pareil," 9–12: "Lillies and roses there combine, / More beauteous than in flow'ry field; / Transparent is Her skin, so fine, / To this each crystal stream must yield."

H–825 *Counsell.*

'TWas *Cesars* saying:[1] *Kings no lesse Conquerors are*
By their wise Counsell, then they be by Warre.

[1] *De Bell. Civ.* I, 72.

H–826 *Bad Princes pill[1] their People.*

LIke those infernall Deities which eate
The best of all the sacrificed meate;
And leave their servants, but the smoak and sweat:
So many *Kings,* and *Primates*[2] too there are,
Who claim the Fat, and Fleshie for their share,
And leave their Subjects but the starved ware.

[1] despoil. [2] chiefs, leaders, especially bishops, for the next line probably refers to I Sam. ii.13–16 which tells how, if need be by force, the priest took the fat and fleshy parts of the sacrifices.

H–827 *Most Words, lesse Workes.*

IN desp'rate cases, all, or most are known
Commanders, *few for execution.*[1]

[1] few for carrying out the orders.

H–828 *To* Dianeme.

I Co'd but see thee yesterday
Stung by a fretfull Bee;
And I the Javelin suckt away,
And heal'd the wound in thee.

A thousand thorns, and Bryars and Stings, 5
I have in my poore Brest;
Yet ne'r can see that salve which brings
My Passions any rest.

As Love shall helpe me, I admire[1]
How thou canst sit and smile, 10
To see me bleed, and not desire
To stench the blood the while.

If thou compos'd of gentle mould
Art so unkind to me;
What dismall Stories will be told 15
Of those that cruell be?

[1] wonder.

H–829 *Upon* Tap.

TAp (better known then trusted) as we heare
Sold his old Mothers Spectacles for Beere:
And not unlikely; rather too then fail,
He'l sell her Eyes, and Nose, for Beere and Ale.

H–830 *His Losse.*

ALl has been plundered from me, but my wit;
Fortune her selfe can lay no claim to it.

H–831 *Draw, and Drinke.*

MIlk stil your Fountains, and your Springs, for why?
The more th'are drawn, the lesse they wil grow dry.

H–832 *Upon* Punchin. *Epigram.*

GIve me a reason why men call
Punchin a dry *plant-animall*.
Because as Plants by water grow,
Punchin by Beere and Ale, spreads so.

H–833 *To* Oenone.

THou sayest Loves Dart
Hath prickt thy heart;
And thou do'st languish too:
If one poore prick,
Can make thee sick, 5
Say, what wo'd many do?

H–834 *Upon* Blinks. *Epigram.*

TOm Blinks his Nose is full of wheales, and these
Tom calls not pimples, but *Pimpleides:*[1]
Sometimes (in mirth) he sayes each whelk's a sparke
(When drunke with Beere) to light him home, i'th'dark.

[1] something belonging to Pimpla, a hill and fountain sacred to the Muses; by analogy with Pleiades, a constellation.

H–835 *Upon* Adam Peapes. *Epigram.*

PEapes he do's strut, and pick his Teeth, as if
His jawes had tir'd on some large Chine[1] of Beefe.
But nothing so; The Dinner *Adam* had,
Was cheese full ripe with Teares, with Bread as sad.[2]

[1] back cut. [2] not risen properly or imperfectly baked.

H–836 *To* Electra.

SHall I go to Love and tell,
Thou art all turn'd isicle?
Shall I say her Altars be
Disadorn'd, and scorn'd by thee?
O beware! in time submit; 5
Love has yet no wrathfull fit:
If her patience turns to ire,
Love is then consuming fire.

H–837 *To Mistresse* Amie Potter.[1]

AI me! I love, give him your hand to kisse
Who both your wooer, and your Poet is.
Nature has pre-compos'd us both to Love;
Your part's to grant; my Scean must be to move.
Deare, can you like, and liking love your Poet? 5
If you say (I)[2] Blush-guiltinesse will shew it.
Mine eyes must wooe you; (though I sigh the while)
True Love is tonguelesse as a Crocodile.[3]
And you may find in Love these differing Parts;
Wooers have Tongues of Ice, but burning hearts. 10

[1] daughter of Herrick's predecessor at Dean Prior, Barnaby Potter, who became Bishop of Carlisle. [2] (aye). [3] So Pliny taught (*Hist. Nat.* VIII, 37).

H–838 *Upon a Maide.*

HEre she lyes (in Bed of Spice)
Faire as *Eve* in Paradice:
For her beauty it was such
Poets co'd not praise too much.
Virgins Come, and in a Ring 5
Her supreamest *Requiem* sing;
Then depart, but see ye tread
Lightly, lightly ore the dead.

H–839 *Upon* Love.

LOve is a Circle, and an Endlesse Sphere;
From good to good, revolving here, and there.[1]

[1] See H-29.

H–840 *Beauty.*

BEauti's no other but a lovely Grace
Of lively colours, flowing from the face.[1]

[1] Cf. John Bodenham, *Politeuphia:* "Of Beauty": "Beauty is a seemly composition of all the members, wherein all the parts with a certain grace agree together."

H–841 *Upon Love.*

SOme salve to every sore, we may apply;
Only for my wound there's no remedy.[1]
Yet if my *Julia* kisse me, there will be
A soveraign balme found out to cure me.

[1] Ovid, *Metamorphoses,* I, 523, trans. Sandys: "Ay me, that herbs can Love no cure afford." Cf. H-157. Burton, 3,2,5,1 (ed. 6, p. 541): "Some are of opinion that this love cannot be cured."

H–842

Upon Hanch *a Schoolmaster. Epigram.*

HAnch, since he (lately) did interre his wife,
He weepes and sighs (as weary of his life.)
Say, is't for reall griefe he mourns? not so;
Teares have their springs from joy, as well as woe.

H-843 *Upon* Peason. *Epigram.*

LOng Locks of late our Zelot *Peason* weares,
Not for to hide his high and mighty eares;
No, but because he wo'd not have it seen,
That Stubble stands, where once large eares have been.[1]

[1] i.e. his ears had been cut off as a punishment for his fanaticism.

H-844 *To his Booke.*

MAke haste away, and let one be
A friendly Patron unto thee:
Lest rapt from hence, I see thee lye
Torn for the use of Pasterie:
Or see thy injur'd Leaves serve well, 5
To make loose Gownes[1] for Mackarell:
Or see the Grocers in a trice,
Make hoods of thee to serve out Spice.

[1] wrappers. Catullus, XCV, 8; Martial, IV, 86, 8; and numerous other classical works refer to wrapping fish in poetry; Milton echoes them in his First Defence when he refers to "harangues predestined to wrap up mackerels."

H-845 *Readinesse.*

THe readinesse of doing, doth expresse
No other, but the doers willingnesse.

H-846 *Writing.*

WHen words we want, Love teacheth to endite;
And what we blush to speake, she bids us write.[1]

[1] The line translates Ovid, *Heroides,* IV, 10, as does H-74, 2.

H–847 *Society.*

TWo things do make society to stand;
The first *Commerce* is, and the next *Command.*

H–848 *Upon a Maid.*

GOne she is a long, long way,
But she has decreed a day
Back to come, (and make no stay.)
So we keepe till her returne
Here, her ashes, or her Urne. 5

H–849 *Satisfaction for sufferings.*

FOr all our workes, a recompence is sure:
'Tis sweet to thinke on what was hard t'endure.[1]

[1] Seneca, *Hercules Furens*, 656–7.

H–850 *The delaying Bride.*

WHy so slowly do you move
To the centre of your love?
On your niceness though we wait,
Yet the houres say 'tis late:
Coynesse takes us to a measure; 5
But o'racted deads the pleasure.[1]
Go to Bed, and care not when
Cheerfull day shall spring agen.
One *Brave Captain*[2] did command
(By his word) the Sun to stand: 10
One short charme if you but say
Will enforce the Moon to stay,
Till you warn her hence (away)
T'ave your blushes seen by day.

[1] Probably based on Martial, IV, 38. [2] Joshua.

H–851

To Master Henry Lawes, *the excellent Composer of his Lyricks.*[1]

TOuch but thy Lire (my *Harrie*) and I heare
From thee some raptures of the rare *Gotire.*[2]
Then if thy voice commingle with the String
I heare in thee rare *Laniere*[3] to sing;
Or curious *Wilson:*[4] Tell me, canst thou be 5
Less then *Apollo,* that usurp'st such Three?
Three, unto whom the whole world give applause;
Yet their Three praises, praise but One; that's *Lawes.*

[1] See Willa McLung Evans, *Henry Lawes* (New York, 1941). [2] H-111, n.3. [3] H-213, n.2. [4] H-111, n.3.

H–852

Age unfit for Love.[1]

MAidens tell me I am old;
Let me in my Glasse behold
Whether smooth or not I be,
Or if haire remaines to me.
Well, or be't or be't not so, 5
This for certainty I know;
Ill it fits old men to play,
When that Death bids come away.

[1] Based on *Anacreontea,* VII, with a changed ending. Cf. Stanley's version, "The old Lover XI" (*Poems,* 1651): "By the women I am told / 'Lasse Anacreon thou grow'st old, / Take thy glasse and look else, there / Thou wilt see thy temples bare; / Whether I be bald or no / That I know not, this I know, / Pleasures, as lesse time to try / Old men have, they more should ply."

H–853

The Bed-man, or Grave-maker.

THou hast made many Houses for the Dead;
When my Lot calls me to be buried,
For Love or Pittie, prethee let there be
I'th'Church-yard, made, one Tenement for me.

H–854 *To Anthea.*

ANthea I am going hence
With some small stock of innocence:
But yet those blessed gates I see
Withstanding entrance unto me.
To pray for me doe thou begin, 5
The Porter then will let me in.

H–855 *Need.*

WHo begs to die for feare of humane need,
Wisheth his body, not his soule, good speed.

H–856 *To* Julia.

I Am zeallesse, prethee pray
For my well-fare (*Julia*)
For I thinke the gods require
Male perfumes,[1] but Female fire.

[1] Virgil, Eclogue VIII, 65, asks to have "male frankincense" (*mascula thura*) burned. Cf. N-83, 76.

H–857 *On* Julias *lips.*

SWeet are my *Julia's* lips and cleane,
As if or'e washt in Hippocrene.[1]

[1] fountain sacred to the Muses on Mt. Helicon.

H–858 *Twilight.*

TWilight, no other thing is, Poets[1] say,
Then the last part of night, and first of day.

[1] e.g. Ovid, *Heroides,* XIV, 21–2.

H–859 *To his Friend, Master* J. Jincks.

LOve, love me now, because I place
Thee here among my righteous race:
The bastard Slips[1] may droop and die
Wanting both Root, and Earth; but thy
Immortall selfe, shall boldly trust 5
To live for ever, with my Just.

[1] Wisd. of Sol. iv.3, "the multiplying brood of the ungodly shall not thrive, nor take deep rooting from bastard slips, nor lay any fast foundation."

H–860 *On himselfe.*

IF that my Fate has now fulfill'd my yeere,
And so soone stopt my longer living here;
What was't (ye Gods!) a dying man to save,
But while he met[1] with his Paternall grave;
Though while we living 'bout the world do roame, 5
We love to rest in peacefull Urnes at home,
Where we may snug, and close together lye
By the dead bones of our deare Ancestrie.

[1] What was it but to save a dying man until he met.

H–861 *Kings and Tyrants.*

TWixt Kings and Tyrants there's this difference known;
Kings seek their Subjects good: Tyrants their owne.[1]

[1] Aristotle's distinction (*Politics,* III, 7), frequently cited by other writers; e.g. Milton, *Commonplace Book* (Yale ed. of his *Complete Prose,* I, 443): " 'The tyrant seeks what benefits himself, the king what benefits his subjects'."

H–862 *Crosses.*

OUr Crosses are no other then the rods,
And our Diseases, Vultures of the Gods:
Each griefe we feele, that likewise is a Kite
Sent forth by them, our flesh to eate, or bite.

H–863 *Upon Love.*[1]

LOve brought me to a silent Grove,
And shew'd me there a Tree,
Where some had hang'd themselves for love,
And gave a Twist to me.

The Halter was of silk, and gold, 5
That he reacht forth unto me:
No otherwise, then if he would
By dainty things undo me.

He bade me then that Neck-lace use;
And told me too, he maketh 10
A glorious end by such a Noose,
His Death for Love that taketh.

'Twas but a dream; but had I been
There really alone;
My desp'rate feares, in love, had seen 15
Mine Execution.

[1] Written in the manner of George Herbert.

H–864 *No difference i'th'dark.*

NIght makes no difference 'twixt the Priest and Clark;
Jone as my Lady is as good i'th'dark.[1]

[1] Cf. H-586, 5–6.

H–865 *The Body.*

THe Body is the Soules poore house, or home,
Whose Ribs the Laths are, and whose Flesh the Loame.

H–866 *To* Sapho.

THou saist thou lov'st me *Sapho;* I say no;
But would to Love I could beleeve 'twas so!
Pardon my feares (sweet *Sapho,*) I desire
That thou be righteous found; and I the Lyer.

H–867 *Out of Time, out of Tune.*

WE blame, nay we despise her paines
That wets her Garden when it raines:
But when the drought has dri'd the knot;[1]
Then let her use the watring pot.
We pray for showers (at our need) 5
To drench, but not to drown our seed.

[1] flowerbed.

H–868 *To his Booke.*

TAke mine advise, and go not neere
Those faces (sower as Vineger.)
For these, and Nobler numbers can
Ne'r please the *supercillious* man.

H–869 *To his Honour'd friend,* *Sir* Thomas Heale.[1]

STand by the *Magick* of my powerfull Rhymes
'Gainst all the indignation of the Times.
Age shall not wrong thee; or one jot abate
Of thy both Great, and everlasting fate.
While others perish, here's thy life decreed 5
Because begot of my *Immortall* seed.

[1] or Hele; baronet, 1627; active in Devonshire affairs. Line 2 may refer to his being disabled in Jan. 1644, from his seat in Parliament as member for Plymouth or, more probably, to the criticism in his county made when he sided with the king.

H–870

The Sacrifice, by way of Discourse betwixt himselfe and Julia.

Herr. COme and let's in solemn wise
Both addresse to sacrifice:
Old Religion first commands
That we wash our hearts, and hands.
Is the beast exempt from staine, 5
Altar cleane, no fire prophane?
Are the Garlands, Is the Nard[1]
Jul. Ready here? All well prepar'd,
With the Wine that must be shed
(Twixt the hornes) upon the head 10
Of the holy Beast we bring
For our Trespasse-offering.
Herr. All is well; now next to these
Put we on pure Surplices;
And with Chaplets crown'd, we'l rost 15
With perfumes the Holocaust:[2]
And (while we the gods invoke)
Reade acceptance by the smoake.

[1] an aromatic balsam or an aromatic plant used to make ointment.
[2] the complete sacrificial offering.

H–871

To Apollo.

THou mighty Lord and master of the Lyre,
Unshorn[1] *Apollo*, come, and re-inspire
My fingers so, the Lyrick-strings to move,
That I may play, and sing a Hymne to Love.

[1] H-178, n.1.

H–872

On Love.[1]

LOve is a kind of warre; Hence those who feare,
No cowards must his royall Ensignes beare.

[1] Based on Ovid, *Ars Amoris*, II, 233–4.

H–873 *Another.*

WHere love begins, there dead thy first desire:
A sparke neglected makes a mighty fire.

H–874 *An Hymne to* Cupid.

THou, thou that bear'st the sway
With whom the Sea-Nimphs play;
And *Venus*, every way:
When I embrace thy knee;
And make short pray'rs to thee: 5
In love, then prosper me.
This day I goe to wooe;
Instruct me how to doe
This worke thou put'st me too.
From shame my face keepe free, 10
From scorne I begge of thee,
Love to deliver me:
So shall I sing thy praise;
And to thee Altars raise,
Unto the end of daies. 15

H–875 *To* Electra.

LEt not thy Tomb-stone er'e be laid by me:
Nor let my Herse, be wept upon by thee:
But let that instant when thou dy'st be known,
The minute of mine *expiration.*
One knell be rung for both; and let one grave 5
To hold us two, an endlesse honour have.

H–876 *How his soule came ensnared.*

MY soule would one day goe and seeke
For Roses, and in *Julia's* cheeke,
A richess of those sweets she found,
(As in an other *Rosamond.*)

But gathering Roses as she was; 5
(Not knowing what would come to passe)
It chanst a ringlet of her haire,
Caught my poore soule, as in a snare:[1]
Which ever since has been in thrall,
Yet freedome, shee enjoyes withall. 10

[1] Cf. Marvell, "The Fair Singer," 8–9: "My dis-intangled Soul it self might save, / Breaking the curled trammels of her hair."

H–877 *Factions.*

THe factions of the great ones call,
To side with them, the Commons[1] all.

[1] the common people.

H–878 *Kisses Loathsome.*

I Abhor the slimie kisse,
(Which to me most loathsome is.)
Those lips please me which are plac't
Close, but not too strictly lac't:
Yeilding I wo'd have them; yet 5
Not a wimbling[1] Tongue admit:
What sho'd poking-sticks[2] make there,
When the ruffe is set elsewhere?

[1] hole-boring, penetrating. [2] rods of wood or bone used to straighten the flutings of a ruff.

H–879 *Upon Reape.*

REapes eyes so rawe are, that (it seemes) the flyes
Mistake the flesh, and flye-blow[1] both his eyes;
So that an Angler, for a daies expence,[2]
May baite his hooke, with maggots taken thence.

[1] putrefy, by laying their eggs to hatch there. [2] use.

H–880 *Upon Teage.*

TEage has told lyes so long, that when *Teage* tells
Truth, yet *Teages* truths are untruths, (nothing else.)

H–881 *Upon* Julia's *haire, bundled up in a golden net.*

TEll me, what needs[1] those rich deceits,
These golden Toyles, and Trammel-nets,[2]
To take thine haires when they are knowne
Already tame, and all thine owne?
'Tis I am wild, and more then haires 5
Deserve these Mashes[3] and those snares.
Set free thy Tresses, let them flow
As aires doe breathe, or winds doe blow:
And let such curious Net-works be
Lesse set for them, then spred for me. 10

[1] what need is there for. [2] fishnets. [3] meshes.

H–882 *Upon* Truggin.[1]

TRuggin a Footman was; but now, growne lame,
Truggin now lives but to belye his name.

[1] pronounced *trudgin'*.

H–883 *The showre of Blossomes.*

LOve in a showre of Blossomes came
Down, and halfe drown'd me with the same:
The Blooms that fell were white and red;
But with such sweets commingled,
As whether (this) I cannot tell 5
My sight was pleas'd more, or my smell:

But true it was, as I rowl'd there,
Without a thought of hurt, or feare;
Love turn'd himselfe into a Bee,
And with his Javelin wounded me: 10
From which mishap this use I make,
Where most sweets are, there lyes a Snake.
Kisses and Favours are sweet things;
But Those have thorns, and These have stings.

I–884 *Upon* Spenke.

SPenke has a strong breath, yet short Prayers saith:
Not out of want of breath, but want of faith.

I–885 *A defence for Women.*

NAught[1] are all Women: I say no,
Since for one Bad, one Good I know:
For *Clytemnestra*[2] most unkind,
Loving *Alcestis*[3] there we find:
For one *Medea*[4] that was bad, 5
A good *Penelope*[5] was had:
For wanton *Lais*,[6] then we have
Chaste *Lucrece*,[7] or a wife as grave:
And thus through Woman-kind we see
A Good and Bad. *Sirs credit me.*[8] 10

[1] worthless, bad. [2] Agamemnon's unfaithful wife murdered him. [3] She accepted death as a substitute for her husband. [4] She deceived her father, murdered her brother, induced two girls to boil their father, contrived the death of her husband's second wife, killed her own children, tried to poison Theseus, and killed her brother Perses. [5] Ulysses' faithful wife. [6] a rapacious Corinthian courtesan. [7] Blackmailed into adultery, she told all to her husband and father, made them swear to avenge the crime, and stabbed herself. [8] Cf. Plutarch, "The vertuous Deeds of Women," in his *Morals*, trans. Holland (1657), p. 397 ff.

H–886 *Upon* Lulls.

LUlls swears he is all heart; but you'l suppose
By his *Probossis* that he is all nose.[1]

[1] Martial, XII, 88.

H–887 *Slavery.*

'TIs liberty to serve one Lord; but he
Who many serves, serves base servility.[1]

[1] Matt. vi.24, "No man can serve two masters."

H–888 *Charmes.*

BRing the holy crust of Bread,
Lay it underneath the head;
'Tis a certain Charm to keep
Hags away, while Children sleep.

H–889 *Another.*

LEt the superstitious wife
Neer the childs heart lay a knife:
Point be up, and Haft be downe;
(While she gossips in the towne)
This 'mongst other mystick charms 5
Keeps the sleeping child from harms.

H–890 *Another to bring in the Witch.*

TO house[1] the Hag, you must doe this;
Commix with Meale a little Pisse
Of him bewitcht:[2] then forthwith make
A little Wafer or a Cake;
And this rawly bak't will bring 5
The old Hag in. No surer thing.

[1] to attract into your house (in order to identify and then bring to punishment). [2] of the person bewitched by her.

H-891 *Another Charme for Stables.*

HAng up Hooks, and Sheers to scare
Hence the Hag, that rides the Mare,
Till they be all over wet,
With the mire, and the sweat:
This observ'd, the Manes shall be 5
Of your horses, all knot-free.

H-892

Ceremonies for Candlemasse[1] *Eve.*

DOwn with the Rosemary and Bayes,
Down with the Misleto;
In stead of Holly, now up-raise
The greener Box (for show.)

The Holly hitherto did sway; 5
Let Box now domineere;
Untill the dancing Easter-day,[2]
Or Easters Eve appeare.

Then youthfull Box which now hath grace,
Your houses to renew; 10
Grown old, surrender must his place,
Unto the crisped Yew.

When Yew is out, then Birch comes in,
And many Flowers beside;
Both of a fresh, and fragrant kinne 15
To honour Whitsontide.

Green Rushes then, and sweetest Bents,
With cooler Oken boughs;
Come in for comely ornaments,
To re-adorn the house. 20
Thus times do shift; each thing his turne do's hold;
New things succeed, as former things grow old.

[1] festival (Feb. 2) of the Presentation of Christ to the Temple by the Virgin Mary. [2] a reference to the popular superstition that the sun dances on Easter day. Sir Thomas Browne attacks the error, though he would like to believe in such a "sympathetical exultation" (*Pseudodoxia Epidemica*, V, xxii, 16; ed. Keynes. III, 148).

H–893

The Ceremonies for Candlemasse day.

KIndle the Christmas Brand,[1] and then
Till Sunne-set, let it burne;
Which quencht, then lay it up agen,
Till Christmas next returne.

Part must be kept wherewith to teend
The Christmas Log next yeare;
And where 'tis safely kept, the Fiend,
Can do no mischiefe (there.)

[1] log.

H–894

Upon Candlemasse day.

ENd now the White-loafe,[1] and the Pye,
And let all sports with[2] Christmas dye.

[1] made of fine white flour. [2] associated with.

H–895

Surfeits.

BAd are all surfeits: but Physitians call
That surfeit tooke by bread, the worst of all.

H–896

Upon Nis.

NIs, he makes Verses; but the Lines he writes,
Serve but for matter to make Paper-kites.

H–897

To Biancha, *to blesse him.*

WO'd I wooe, and wo'd I winne,
Wo'd I well my worke begin?
Wo'd I evermore be crown'd
With the end that I propound?

Wo'd I frustrate, or prevent
All Aspects malevolent?
Thwart all Wizzards, and with these
Dead all black contingencies:
Place my words, and all works else
In most happy Parallels? 10
All will prosper, if so be
I be kist, or blest by thee.

H–898 Julia's *Churching, or Purification.*[1]

PUt on thy *Holy Fillitings,*[2] and so
To th'Temple with the sober *Midwife* go.
Attended thus (in a most solemn wise)
By those who serve the Child-bed misteries.
Burn first thine incense; next, when as thou see'st 5
The candid[3] Stole thrown ore the *Pious Priest;*
With reverend Curtsies come, and to him bring
Thy free (and not decurted)[4] offering.
All Rites well ended, with faire Auspice come
(As to the breaking of a Bride-Cake) home: 10
Where ceremonious *Hymen* shall for thee
Provide a second *Epithalamie.*
She who keeps chastly to her husbands side
Is not for one, but every night his Bride:
And stealing still with love, and feare to Bed, 15
Brings him not one, but many a Maiden-head.

[1] after childbirth, when thanks are given for safe delivery. [2] head-bands. [3] white. [4] generous, not curtailed.

H–899 *To his Book.*

BEfore the Press scarce one co'd see
A little-peeping-part of thee:
But since th'art Printed, thou dost call
To shew thy nakedness to all.
My care for thee is now the less; 5
(Having resign'd thy shamefac'tness:)

Go with thy Faults and Fates; yet stay
And take this sentence, then away;
Whom one belov'd will not suffice,
She'l runne to all adulteries. 10

H–900 *Teares.*

TEares most prevaile; with teares too thou mayst move
Rocks to relent, and coyest maids to love.

H–901 *To his friend to avoid contention of words.*

WOrds beget Anger; Anger brings forth blowes:
Blowes make of dearest friends immortall Foes.
For which prevention (Sociate) let there be
Betwixt us two no more *Logomachie*.[1]
Farre better 'twere for either to be mute, 5
Then for to murder friendship, by dispute.

[1] argument.

H–902 *Truth.*

TRuth is best found out by the time, and eyes;
Falsehood winnes credit by uncertainties.

H–903 *Upon* Prickles. *Epigram.*

PRickles is waspish, and puts forth his sting,
For Bread, Drinke, Butter, Cheese; for every thing
That *Prickles* buyes, puts *Prickles* out of frame;
How well his nature's fitted to his name!

H–904 *The Eyes before the Eares.*

WE credit most our sight; one eye doth please
Our trust farre more then ten eare-witnesses.

H–905 *Want.*

WAnt is a softer Wax, that takes thereon,
This, that, and every base impression.

H–906 *To a Friend.*

LOoke in my Book, and herein see,
Life endlesse sign'd[1] to thee and me.
We o're the tombes, and Fates shall flye;
While other generations dye.

[1] assigned. Cf. the motto on the title page of *Hesperides.*

H–907 *Upon Master* William Lawes, *the rare Musitian.*[1]

SHo'd I not put on Blacks,[2] when each one here
Comes with his Cypresse, and devotes a teare?
Sho'd I not grieve (my *Lawes*) when every Lute,
Violl, and Voice, is (by thy losse) struck mute?
Thy loss brave man! whose Numbers have been hurl'd, 5
And no less prais'd, then spread throughout the world.
Some have Thee call'd *Amphion;* some of us,
Nam'd thee *Terpander,* or sweet *Orpheus:*[3]
Some this, some that, but all in this agree,
Musique had both her birth, and death with Thee. 10

[1] Henry Lawes' brother, killed 1645 while in the Royalist army. He set H-208 to music. [2] mourning clothes. [3] Amphion's harping lured stones to form the Theban wall; Terpander founded the Sparta school of music; Orpheus charmed beasts with his lyre.

H–908 *A song upon* Silvia.

FRom me my *Silvia* ranne away,
And running therewithall;
A *Primrose* Banke did cross her way,
And gave my Love a fall.

But trust me now I dare not say,
What I by chance did see;
But such the Drap'ry did betray
That fully ravisht me.

H–909 *The Hony-combe.*

IF thou hast found an honie-combe,
Eate thou not all, but taste on some:
For if thou eat'st it to excess;
That sweetness turnes to Loathsomness.[1]
Taste it to Temper;[2] then 'twill be
Marrow, and Manna unto thee.

[1] Prov. xxv.27, "It is not good to eat much honey"; xxvii.7, "The full soul loatheth an honey-comb." [2] moderation.

H–910 *Upon* Ben. Johnson.

HEre lyes *Johnson* with the rest
Of the Poets; but the Best.
Reader, wo'dst thou more have known?
Aske his Story, not this Stone.
That will speake what this can't tell
Of his glory. *So farewell.*

H–911 *An Ode for him.*

AH *Ben!*
Say how, or when
Shall we thy Guests
Meet at those *Lyrick* Feasts,
Made at the *Sun*, 5
The *Dog*, the triple *Tunne*?[1]
Where we such clusters had,
As made us nobly wild, not mad;
And yet each Verse of thine
Out-did the meate, out-did the frolick wine. 10

My *Ben*
Or come agen:
Or send to us,
Thy wits great over-plus;
But teach us yet 15
Wisely to husband it;
Lest we that Tallent spend:
And having once brought to an end
That precious stock; the store
Of such a wit the world sho'd have no more. 20

[1] taverns.

H–912 *Upon a Virgin.*

SPend Harmless shade thy nightly Houres,
Selecting here, both Herbs, and Flowers;
Of which make Garlands here, and there,
To dress thy silent sepulchre.
Nor do thou feare the want of these,
In everlasting Properties.
Since we fresh strewings will bring hither,
Farre faster then the first can wither.

H–913 *Blame.*

IN Battailes what disasters fall,
The King he beares the blame of all.

H–914 *A request to the Graces.*

POnder my words, if so that any be
Known guilty here of incivility:
Let what is graceless, discompos'd, and rude,
With sweetness, smoothness, softness, be endu'd.
Teach it to blush, to curtsie, lisp, and shew 5
Demure, but yet, full of temptation too.
Numbers[1] *ne'r tickle, or but lightly please,*
Unlesse they have some wanton carriages.[2]
This if ye do, each Piece will here be good,
And gracefull made, by your neate Sisterhood. 10

[1] verses. [2] meanings. Cf. Martial, I, 35, 11.

H–915 *Upon himselfe.*

I Lately fri'd, but now behold
I freeze as fast, and shake for cold.
And in good faith I'd thought it strange
T'ave found in me this sudden change;
But that I understood by dreames,
These only were but Loves extreames;
Who fires with hope the Lovers heart,
And starves with cold the self-same part.

H–916 *Multitude.*

WE Trust not to the multitude in Warre,
But to the stout; and those that skilfull are.

H–917 *Feare.*

MAn must do well out of a good intent;
Not for the servile feare of punishment.

H–918 *To Master* Kellam.

WHat can my *Kellam* drink his Sack
In Goblets to the brim,
And see his *Robin Herrick* lack,
Yet send no Boules to him?

For love or pitie to his Muse,
(That she may flow in Verse)
Contemne to recommend a Cruse,
But send to her a Tearce.[1]

[1] give disapproval to consigning a small bottle, but send to her a tierce (42 gallons).

H–919

Happinesse to hospitalitie, or a hearty wish to good house-keeping.

FIrst, may the hand of bounty bring
Into the daily offering
Of full provision; such a store,
Till that the Cooke cries, Bring no more.
Upon your hogsheads never fall 5
A drought of wine, ale, beere (at all)
But, like full clouds, may they from thence
Diffuse their mighty influence.
Next, let the Lord, and Ladie here
Enjoy a Christning yeare by yeare; 10
And this *good blessing* back them still,
T'ave Boyes, and Gyrles too, as they will.
Then from the porch may many a Bride
Unto the Holy Temple ride:
And thence return, (short prayers seyd) 15
A wife most richly married.
Last, may the Bride and Bridegroome be
Untoucht by cold *sterility;*
But in their springing blood so play,
As that in *Lusters* few they may, 20
By laughing too, and lying downe,
People a *City* or a *Towne.*

H–920

Cunctation[1] *in Correction.*

THe *Lictors* bundl'd up their rods: beside,
Knit them with knots (with much adoe unty'd)
That if (unknitting) men wo'd yet repent,
They might escape the lash of punishment.[2]

[1] delay. [2] Cf. Plutarch, "Roman Questions," LXXXII, in *The Morals*, trans. Holland (1657, p. 718): "*What is the reason that before . . . the head Magistrate there be carried bundles of rods, together with hatchets. . .* ? Is it . . . because that to undo and unbind the said bundles yeeldeth some time and space for choler to coole . . . which is the cause otherwhiles that they change their minds, and do not proceed to punishment?"

H–921 *Present Government grievous.*

MEn are suspicious; prone to discontent:
Subjects still[1] *loath the present Government.*[2]

[1] always. [2] Cf. Hooker, *Laws of Ecclesiastical Polity,* opening of Book I: "He that goeth about to persuade a multitude that they are not so well governed as they ought to be, shall never want attentive and favorable hearers."

H–922 *Rest Refreshes.*

LAy by the good a while; a resting field
Will, after ease, a richer harvest yeild:
Trees this year beare; next, they their wealth with-hold:
Continuall reaping makes a land wax old.[1]

[1] Ovid, *Ars Amoris,* III, 82.

H–923 *Revenge.*

MAns disposition is for to requite
An injurie, before a benefite:
Thanksgiving is a burden, and a paine;
Revenge is pleasing to us, as our gaine.

H–924 *The first marrs or makes.*

IN all our high designments, 'twill appeare,
The first event breeds confidence or feare.

H–925 *Beginning, difficult.*

HArd are the two first staires unto a Crowne;
Which got, the third, bids him a King come downe.

H-926 *Faith four-square.*

FAith is a thing that's four-square; let it fall
This way or that, it not declines at all.

H-927 *The present time best pleaseth.*

PRaise they that will Times past, I joy to see
My selfe now live: *this age best pleaseth mee.*

H-928 *Cloathes, are conspirators.*

THough from without no foes at all we feare;
We shall be wounded by the cloathes we weare.

H-929 *Cruelty.*

TIs but a dog-like madnesse in bad Kings,
For to delight in wounds and murderings.
As some plants prosper best by cuts and blowes;[1]
So Kings by killing doe encrease their foes.

[1] Cf. Falstaff in *Henry IV*, Pt. I, II, iv: "the camomile, the more it is trodden on, the faster it grows."

H-930 *Faire after foule.*

TEares quickly drie: griefes will in time decay:
A cleare will come after a cloudy day.

H-931 *Hunger.*

ASke me what hunger is, and Ile reply,
'Tis but a fierce desire of hot and drie.[1]

[1] the qualities of the element of fire and the humor of choler—opposite those of phlegm, which is cold and moist. Cf. H-683.

H–932 *Bad wages for good service.*

IN this misfortune Kings doe most excell,
To heare the worst from men, when they doe well.

H–933 *The End.*

COnquer we shall, but we must first contend;
'Tis not the Fight that crowns us, but the end.

H–934 *The Bondman.*

BInd me but to thee with thine haire,
And quickly I shall be
Made by that fetter or that snare
A bondman unto thee.

Or if thou tak'st that bond away,
Then bore me through the eare;
And by the Law I ought to stay
For ever with thee here.[1]

[1] Cf. Exod. xxi.5–6, "if the servant shall plainly say, I love my master, my wife, and my children, I will not go out free: Then . . . his master shall bore his ear through with an awl; and he shall serve him for ever."

H–935 *Choose for the best.*

GIve house-roome to the best; *'Tis never known*
Vertue and pleasure, both to dwell in one.

H–936 *To* Silvia.

PArdon my trespasse (*Silvia*) I confesse,
My kisse out-went the bounds of shamfastnesse:
None is discreet at all times; no, *not Jove*
Himselfe, at one time, can be wise, and Love.[1]

[1] Burton, "Democritus to the Reader" (ed. 6, p. 72): "That Lovers are mad, I think no man will deny. *Amare simul et sapere, ipsi Jovi non datur, Jupiter* himself cannot intend both at once."

H–937 *Faire shewes deceive.*

SMooth was the Sea, and seem'd to call
To[1] prettie girles to play withall:
Who padling there, the Sea soone frown'd,
And on a sudden both were drown'd.
What credit can we give to seas,
Who, kissing, kill such Saints as these?

[1] i.e. two.

H–938 *His wish.*

FAt be my Hinde;[1] unlearned be my wife;
Peacefull my night; my day devoid of strife:[2]
To these a comely off-spring I desire,
Singing about my everlasting fire.

[1] rustic servant. [2] Martial, II, 90, 9–10; trans. Courthope: "My slave content, not very learn'd my wife, / Dreamless my sleep, and without suits my life." (W. J. Courthope, *Selections from Martial*, 1914). The 1648 reading "Peacefull by night" is clearly not intended.

H–939
Upon Julia's *washing her self in the river.*

HOw fierce was I, when I did see
My *Julia* wash her self in thee!
So *Lillies* thorough Christall look:
So purest pebbles in the brook:
As in the River *Julia* did, 5
Halfe with a Lawne of water hid,
Into thy streames my self I threw,
And strugling there, I kist thee too;
And more had done (it is confest)
Had not thy waves forbad the rest. 10

H–940 *A Meane in our Meanes.*

THough Frankinsense the *Deities* require,
We must not give all to the hallowed fire.
Such be our gifts, and such be our expence,
As for our selves to leave some frankinsence.

H–941 *Upon* Clunn.

A Rowle of Parchment *Clunn* about him beares,
Charg'd with the Armes of all his Ancestors:
And seems halfe ravisht, when he looks upon
That *Bar,* this *Bend;* that *Fess,* this *Cheveron;*
This *Manch,* that *Moone;* this *Martlet,* and that *Mound;*
This counterchange[1] of *Perle* and *Diamond.*
What joy can *Clun* have in that Coat, or this,
When as his owne still out at elboes is?

[1] interchange or reversal: the terms are heraldic; e.g. *diamond* is the black color in nobles' coats of arms.

H–942 *Upon* Cupid.[1]

LOve, like a Beggar, came to me
With Hose and Doublet torne:
His Shirt bedangling from his knee,
With Hat and Shooes out-worne.

He askt an almes; I gave him bread, 5
And meat too, for his need:
Of which, when he had fully fed,
He wisht me all *Good speed.*

Away he went, but as he turn'd
(In faith I know not how) 10
He toucht me so, as that I burn'd,
And am tormented now.

Love's silent flames, and fires obscure
Then crept into my heart;
And though I saw no Bow, I'm sure, 15
His finger was the dart.

[1] Cf. *Anacreontea,* XXXIII.

H–943 *Upon* Blisse.

BLisse (last night drunk) did kisse his mothers knee:
Where he will kisse (next drunk) conjecture ye.

H–944 *Upon* Burr.

BUrr is a smell-feast,[1] and a man alone,
That (where meat is) will be a hanger on.

[1] one who smells out feasts and goes to them uninvited: he is a man in one respect only—that he will be a hanger-on where food is.

H–945 *Upon* Megg.

MEgg yesterday was troubled with a Pose,[1]
Which, this night hardned, sodders up her nose.

[1] mucus discharge.

H–946 *An Hymne to Love.*

I Will confesse
With Cheerfulnesse,
Love is a thing so likes me,
That let her lay[1]
On me all day,
Ile kiss the hand that strikes me.

2. I will not, I,
Now blubb'ring, cry,
It (Ah!) too late repents me,
That I did fall
To love at all,
Since love so much contents me.

3. No, no, Ile be
In fetters free;
While others they sit wringing
Their hands for paine;
Ile entertaine
The wounds of love with singing.

4. With Flowers and Wine,
And Cakes Divine,
To strike me I will tempt thee:
Which done; no more
Ile come before
Thee and thine Altars emptie.

[1] lay blows.

H–947

To his honoured and most Ingenious friend Master Charles Cotton.[1]

FOr brave comportment, wit without offence,
Words fully flowing, yet of influence:
Thou art that man of men, the man alone,
Worthy the Publique Admiration:
Who with thine owne eyes read'st what we doe write, 5
And giv'st our Numbers *Euphonie*, and weight.
Tel'st when a Verse springs high, how understood
To be, or not borne of the Royall-blood.
What State[2] above, what *Symmetrie* below,
Lines have, or sho'd have, thou the best canst show. 10
For which (my *Charles*) it is my pride to be,
Not so much knowne, as to be lov'd of thee.
Long may I live so, and my wreath of *Bayes*,
Be lesse anothers *Laurell*, then thy praise.

[1] possibly the poet (1630–87) who, with Herrick, contributed to *Lachrymae Musarum* (1649), but probably his father, whom Clarendon (*Life*, ed. 1827, I, 36) described as "the greatest ornament of the town," with "such a pleasantness and gaiety of humour, such a sweetness and gentleness of nature and such a civility and delightfulness of conversation, that no man . . . appeared a more accomplished person." [2] stateliness, elevation, dignity.

H–948 *Women uselesse.*

WHat need we marry Women, when
Without their use we may have men?
And such as will in short time be,
For murder fit, or mutinie;
As *Cadmus* once a new way found, 5
By throwing teeth into the ground:
(From which poore seed, and rudely sown)
Sprung up a War-like Nation.
So let us Yron, Silver, Gold,
Brasse, Leade or Tinne, throw into th'mould;[1] 10
And we shall see in little space
Rise up of men, a fighting race.
If this can be, say then, what need
Have we of Women or their seed?

[1] possibly a reference to the sacrifice of plate to raise funds for the Royalist forces.

H–949 *Love is a sirrup.*

LOve is a sirrup; and who er'e we see
Sick and surcharg'd with this sacietie:[1]
Shall by this pleasing trespasse quickly prove,
Ther's loathsomnesse e'en in the sweets of love.

[1] satiety (probably a printer's misreading).

H–950 *Leven.*[1]

LOve is a Leven, and a loving kisse
The Leven of a loving sweet-heart is.

[1] leaven: that which causes swelling. Levin: lightning, or any bright light or flame.

H–951 *Repletion.*

PHysitians say Repletion springs
More from the sweet then sower things.

H–952 *On Himselfe.*

WEepe for the dead, for they have lost this light:[1]
And weepe for me, lost in an endlesse night.
Or mourne, or make a Marble Verse for me,
Who writ for many. *Benedicite.*

[1] Ecclus. xxii.11, "Weep for the dead, for he hath lost the light."

H–953 *No man without Money.*

NO man such rare parts hath, that he can swim,
If favour or occasion helpe not him.

H–954 *On Himselfe.*

LOst to the world; lost to my selfe; alone
Here now I rest under this Marble stone:
In depth of silence, heard, and seene of none.

H–955 *To Master* Leonard Willan[1] *his peculiar friend.*

I Will be short, and having quickly hurl'd
This line about, live Thou throughout the world;
Who art a man for all Sceanes; unto whom
(What's hard to others) nothing's troublesome.
Can'st write the *Comick, Tragick* straine, and fall 5
From these to penne the pleasing Pastorall:
Who fli'st at all heights: Prose and Verse run'st through;
Find'st here a fault, and mend'st the trespasse too:

For which I might extoll thee, but speake lesse,
Because thy selfe art comming to the Presse: 10
And then sho'd I in praising thee be slow,
Posterity will pay thee what I owe.

[1] author of a pastoral, *Astraea*, 1651; a tragedy, *Orgula*, 1658; and a verse translation of Aesop, 1651.

H-956 *To his worthy friend Master* John Hall,[1] *Student of Grayes-Inne.*

TEll me young man, or did the Muses bring
Thee lesse to taste, then to drink up their spring;
That none hereafter sho'd be thought, or be
A Poet, or a Poet-like but Thee.
What was thy Birth, thy starre that makes thee knowne, 5
At twice ten yeares, a prime and publike one?[2]
Tell us thy Nation, kindred, or the whence
Thou had'st, and hast thy *mighty influence*,
That makes thee lov'd, and of the men desir'd,
And no lesse prais'd, then of the maides admir'd.[3] 10
Put on thy Laurell then; and in that trimme
Be thou *Apollo*, or the type of him:
Or let the *Unshorne God* lend thee his Lyre,
And next to him, be Master of the Quire.

[1] 1627–56; *Poems*, 1647; his essays, *Horae Vacivae* "amazed not only the University"—he entered St. John's, Cambridge, in 1646—"but the more serious part of men in the three Nations" (John Davies). See P. S. Havens' article in *Huntington Lib. Bull.*, Nov. 1934; R. F. Jones, *Ancients and Moderns* (1936), pp. 100–3; introd. to A. K. Croston's ed. of Hall's *Advancement of Learning* (1646). [2] This statement and the description of Hall as of Gray's Inn, which he entered in May, 1647, suggest that the poem was composed in the latter half of 1647. [3] In the summer of 1647, Hall married a gentlewoman much sought by other suitors.

H–957 *To* Julia.

OFfer thy gift; but first the Law commands
Thee *Julia*, first, to *sanctifie* thy hands:
Doe that my *Julia* which the rites require,
Then boldly give thine incense to the fire.

H–958 *To the most comely and proper Mistresse* Elizabeth Finch.[1]

HAnsome you are, and Proper you will be
Despight of all your infortunitie:
Live long and lovely, but yet grow no lesse
In that your owne prefixed comelinesse:
Spend on that stock:[2] and when your life must fall,
Leave others Beauty, to set up withall.

[1] not identified. Cf. H-1006. [2] i.e. make use throughout your life of that stock or supply of comeliness which you have already achieved.

H–959 *Upon* Ralph.

RAlph pares his nayles, his warts, his cornes, and *Raph*
In sev'rall tills, and boxes keepes 'em safe;
Instead of Harts-horne (if he speakes the troth)
To make a lustie-gellie[1] for his broth.

[1] jelly: gelatin. Sliced stag horn was boiled to produce ammonia; so *lusty* refers to the potency of Ralph's mixture.

H–960 *To his Booke.*

IF hap it must, that I must see thee lye
Absyrtus-like[1] all torne confusedly:
With solemne tears, and with much grief of heart,
Ile recollect[2] thee (weeping) part by part;
And having washt thee, close thee in a chest
With spice; that done, Ile leave thee to thy rest.

[1] Medea tore her brother Absyrtus into pieces and scattered them to delay her father's pursuit of her and Jason. [2] re-collect.

H-961

TO THE KING,

Upon his welcome to Hampton-Court.

Set and Sung.[1]

WElcome, *Great Cesar*, welcome now you are,
As dearest Peace, after destructive Warre:
Welcome as slumbers; or as beds of ease
After our long, and peevish sicknesses.
O *Pompe of Glory!* Welcome now, and come 5
To re-possess once more your long'd-for home.
A thousand Altars smoake; a thousand thighes
Of Beeves here ready stand for Sacrifice.
Enter and prosper, while our eyes doe waite
For an *Ascendent* throughly *Auspicate:* 10
Under which signe we may the former stone
Lay of our safeties new foundation:
That done; *O Cesar*, live, and be to us,
Our *Fate*, our *Fortune*, and our *Genius;*[2]
To whose free knees we may our temples tye 15
As to a still protecting Deitie.
That sho'd you stirre, we and our Altars too
May (*Great Augustus*) *goe along with You.*
Chor. Long live the King; and to accomplish this,
We'l from our owne, adde far more years to his. 20

[1] On Aug. 24, 1647, Charles I, in custody of the army, was moved to Hampton Court. He still hoped to play factions against each other and to gain a settlement to his liking. No confirming evidence that the poem was set to music or sung has been discovered. [2] In *Notes and Observations* (Oxford, 1646), John Gregory remarks (pp. 29–33) that the ancients did nothing "inauspicatò" when they founded or took possession of a city: they propitiated the genius of the place with sacrifices and took cognizance of the city's ascendant

—the sign of the zodiac which was rising when the first stone was laid. By such means they insured that the "Fortune and Genius of the City" were favorable.

H–962

Ultimus Heroum:[1]

OR,

To the most learned, and to the right Honourable,
Henry, *Marquesse of* Dorchester.[2]

ANd as time past when *Cato* the Severe
Entred the circumspacious Theater;
In reverence of his person, every one
Stood as he had been turn'd from flesh to stone:
E'ne so my numbers will astonisht be 5
If but lookt on; struck dead, if scan'd by Thee.

[1] The Greatest of the Illustrious. [2] Henry Pierrepoint, second Earl of Kingston, 1643, was created Marquis of Dorchester in 1645. John Collop dedicated *Poesis Rediviva* (1656) to him, praising him as "The most Honourable, who in the worst of times dare to be good." See H-626, n.2.

H–963

To his Muse, another to the same.

TEll that Brave Man, fain thou wo'dst have access
To kiss his hands, but that for fearfullness;
Or else because th'art like a modest Bride,
Ready to blush to death, sho'd he but chide.

H–964

Upon Vineger.

VIneger is no other I define,
Then the dead Corps, or carkase of the Wine.

H-965 *Upon* Mudge.

MUdge every morning to the Postern[1] comes,
(His teeth all out) to rince and wash his gummes.

[1] back door.

H-966

To his learned friend Master John Harmar,[1] *Phisitian to the Colledge of* Westminster.

WHen first I find those Numbers thou do'st write;
To be most soft, terce, sweet, and perpolite:[2]
Next, when I see Thee towring in the skie,
In an expansion[3] no less large, then high;
Then, in that compass,[4] sayling here and there, 5
And with Circumgyration[5] every where;
Following with love[6] and active heate thy game,
And then at last to truss[7] the Epigram;
I must confess, distinction none I see
Between *Domitians Martiall*[8] then, and Thee. 10
But this I know, should *Jupiter* agen
Descend from heaven, to re-converse with men;
The Romane Language full, and superfine,
If *Iove* wo'd speake, he wo'd accept of thine.

[1] John Harmar, 1594–1670; teacher at various schools, including Westminster; Professor of Greek at Oxford during the Commonwealth. His numerous works (See Wood, *Athenae*, ed. Bliss, III, 919–20) include an apology for Bishop Williams, to whom H-146 was written. John Philipott (*Poems*, 1646; ed. L. C. Martin, p. 34), praises him in Latin verse for knowledge of medicine and credits him with *De Lue Venereâ*, though no copy is known. Harmar almost certainly wrote the Latin verses below Herrick's portrait in the frontispiece to *Hesperides*. [2] highly polished. [3] when I see thee soaring in the sky (like a hawk), in an expanse. [4] range. [5] wheeling round. [6] intentness (hawking term). [7] Trussing, in falconry, is a hawk's raising its prey aloft and then descending with it to the ground. [8] Martial addressed adulatory epigrams to the Emperor Domitian.

H-967 *Upon his Spaniell* Tracie.

NOw thou art dead, no eye shall ever see,
For shape and service, *Spaniell* like to thee.
This shall my love doe, give thy sad death one
Teare, that deserves of me a million.

H-968 *The deluge.*

DRowning, drowning, I espie
Coming from my *Julia's* eye:
'Tis some solace in our smart,
To have friends to beare a part:
I have none; but must be sure 5
Th'inundation to endure.
Shall not times hereafter tell
This for no meane *miracle;*
When the waters by their fall
Threatn'd ruine unto all? 10
Yet the deluge here was known,
Of a world to drowne but One.

H-969 *Upon* Lupes.

LUpes for the outside of his suite has paide;
But for his heart,[1] he cannot have it made:
The reason is, his credit cannot get
The inward carbage[2] for his cloathes as yet.

[1] even to save his heart; "for the life of him"; despite his utmost efforts. [2] Herrick seems to intend *garbage*—that which is functionally related to garb; i.e. lining, trimming, padding. Cf. H-195, 6, "In-laid Garbage." *Cabbage,* perhaps a corrupt form of *carbage,* was a term used for shreds and pieces of cloth. Cf. H-970.

H-970 *Raggs.*

WHat are our patches, tatters, raggs, and rents,
But the base dregs and lees of vestiments?

H–971 *Strength to support Soveraignty.*

LEt Kings and Rulers, learne this line from me;
Where power is weake, unsafe is Majestie.

H–972 *Upon Tubbs.*

FOr thirty yeares, *Tubbs* has been proud and poor,
'Tis now his habit, which he can't give ore.

H–973 *Crutches.*

THou seest me *Lucia* this year droope,
Three *Zodiaks* fill'd more I shall stoope;
Let Crutches then provided be
To shore up my debilitie.
Then while thou laugh'st; Ile, sighing, crie, 5
A *Ruine underpropt* am I:
Do'n[1] will I then my *Beadsmans*[2] gown,
And when so feeble I am grown,
As my weake shoulders cannot beare
The burden of a *Grashopper:*[3] 10
Yet with the bench of aged sires,
When I and they keep tearmly[4] fires;
With my weake voice Ile sing, or say
Some Odes I made of *Lucia:*
Then will I heave my wither'd hand 15
To *Jove* the Mighty for to stand
Thy faithfull friend, and to poure downe
Upon thee many a *Benizon.*

[1] do on: don. [2] one who prays for a benefactor; inmate of an almshouse. [3] Eccles. xii.5, "And the grasshopper shall be a burden, and desire shall fail: because man goeth to his long home, and the mourners go about the streets." [4] termly; periodically; occurring at each term of a college or similar body. But the word here may refer to the need for fires' warmth felt by men at the term or final limit of their lives.

H-974

To Julia.

HOly waters hither bring
For the sacred sprinkling:
Baptize me and thee, and so
Let us to the Altar go.
And (ere we our rites commence)
Wash our hands in innocence.
Then I'le be the *Rex Sacrorum*,[1]
Thou the Queen of *Peace and Quorum.*[2]

[1] sacrificing priest. [2] A Justice of the Peace and Quorum is one without whom a committee of justices cannot act.

H-975

Upon Case.

CAse is a Lawyer, that near[1] pleads alone,
But when he hears the like confusion,
As when the disagreeing Commons throw
About their House, their clamorous I, or No:
Then *Case*, as loud as any *Serjant* there,
Cries out (my Lord, my Lord) the Case is clear:
But when all's husht, *Case* then a fish more mute,
Bestirs his Hand, but starves in hand the Suite.

[1] never. The poem echoes Martial, I, 97.

H-976

To Perenna.

I A *Dirge* will pen for thee;
Thou a *Trentall* make for me:
That the Monks and Fryers together,
Here may sing the rest of either:
Next, I'm sure, the Nuns will have
Candlemas[1] to grace the Grave.

[1] a celebration or display involving many candles.

H-977 *To his Sister in Law, Mistresse* Susanna Herrick.[1]

THe Person crowns the Place; your lot doth fall
Last,[2] yet to be with These a Principall.
How ere it fortuned; know for Truth, I meant
You a fore-leader in this Testament.

[1] wife of Nicholas Herrick. [2] i.e. last of the poems addressed to members of his family in a special manuscript volume of such poems. See H-522.

H-978 *Upon the Lady* Crew.[1]

THis Stone can tell the storie of my life,
What was my Birth, to whom I was a Wife:
In teeming years, how soon my Sun was set,
Where now I rest, these may be known by *Jet*.
For other things, my many Children be
The best and truest *Chronicles* of me.

[1] See H-283, n.1.

H-979 *On* Tomasin Parsons.[1]

GRow up in Beauty, as thou do'st begin,
And be of all admired, *Tomasin*.

[1] Second daughter of John Parsons, organist of Westminster Abbey. Archbishop Laud's secretary, William Dell, based the following undated statement on allegations made by his servant: "Thomsen Parsons hath a Bastard lately shee was brought to bedd at Greenwich. // Mr Herricque a Minister possest of a very good Living in Devonshire hath not resided thereon haveing noe Lycence for his non-residence & not being Chapline to any Noble man or man qualifyed by Law as I heare, his Lodging is on the little Amrie at Nicholas Weilkes his house where the said Thomsen Parsons lives." (PRO: C.S.P.Dom. [1640?], CCCCLXXIV, no. 77). It is noteworthy that the two statements are separate; that Herrick is accused of absenteeism, not paternity; that Herrick would hardly have published a poem to the mother of an illegitimate child; and that there is no evidence that Herrick's superiors hesitated to allow him to stay at Dean Prior. Cf. H-136.

H–980 *Ceremony upon Candlemas Eve.*

DOwn with the Rosemary, and so
Down with the Baies, & misletoe:
Down with the Holly, Ivie, all,
Wherewith ye drest the Christmas Hall:
That so the superstitious find
No one least Branch there left behind:
For look how many leaves there be
Neglected there (maids trust to me)
So many *Goblins* you shall see.

H–981 *Suspicion makes secure.*

HE that will live of all cares dispossest,
Must shun the bad, I, and suspect the best.

H–982 *Upon* Spokes.

SPokes when he sees a rosted Pig, he swears
Nothing he loves on't but the chaps and ears:
But carve to him the fat flanks; and he shall
Rid these, and those, and part by part eat all.

H–983
To his kinsman Master Thomas Herrick,[1]
who desired to be in his Book.

WElcome to this my Colledge, and though late
Tha'st got a place here (standing candidate)[2]
It matters not, since thou art chosen one
Here of my great and good foundation.

[1] probably the eldest son of Herrick's brother Nicholas. [2] i.e. aspiring to a place of honor.

H–984 *A Bucolick betwixt Two:*
Lacon *and* Thyrsis.

Lacon. FOr a kiss or two, confesse,
What doth cause this pensiveness?
Thou most lovely Neat-heardesse:[1]
Why so lonely on the hill?
Why thy pipe by thee so still, 5
That ere while was heard so shrill?

Tell me, do thy kine now fail
To fulfill the milkin-paile?
Say, what is't that thou do'st aile?

Thyr. None of these; but out, alas! 10
A mischance is come to pass,
And I'le tell thee what it was:
See mine eyes are weeping ripe,
Lacon. Tell, and I'le lay down my Pipe.

Thyr. I have lost my lovely steere, 15
That to me was far more deer
Then these kine, which I milke here.
Broad of fore-head, large of eye,
Party colour'd like a Pie;
Smooth in each limb as a die; 20
Clear of hoof, and clear of horn;
Sharply pointed as a thorn:
With a neck by yoke unworn.
From the which hung down by strings,
Balls of Cowslips, Daisie rings, 25
Enterplac't with ribbanings.
Faultless every way for shape;
Not a straw co'd him escape;
Ever gamesome as an ape:
But yet harmless as a sheep. 30
(Pardon, *Lacon* if I weep)
Tears will spring, where woes are deep.
Now (ai me) (ai me.) Last night
Came a mad dog, and did bite,
I, and kil'd my dear delight. 35

Lacon. Alack for grief!
Thyr. But I'le be brief,

Hence I must, for time doth call
Me, and my sad Play-mates all,
To his Ev'ning Funerall. 40
Live long, *Lacon*, so *adew*.
Lacon. Mournfull maid farewell to you;
Earth afford ye flowers to strew.

[1] female herder of cattle.

H–985 *Upon* Sapho.

LOok upon *Sapho's* lip, and you will swear,
There is a love-like-leven rising there.

H–986 *Upon* Faunus.

WE read how *Faunus*, he the shepheards *God*,
His wife to death whipt with a *Mirtle Rod*.[1]
The Rod (perhaps) was better'd by the name;
But had it been of Birch, the death's the same.

[1] "Flavius a soothsayer had a wife, who used secretly to drink wine, and when she . . . was taken in the manner by her husband, she was well beaten by him with myrtle rods" (Plutarch, "Roman Questions," *Morals*, trans. Holland, 1657, pp. 700–1).

H–987 *The Quintell.*[1]

UP with the Quintill, that the Rout,
May fart for joy, as well as shout:
Either's welcome, Stinke or Civit,[2]
If we take it, as they give it.

[1] quintain: tilting post. [2] civet: a musky substance from glands in the anal pouch of the civet, used for perfumes.

H–988 *A Bachanalian Verse.*

DRinke up
Your Cup,
But not spill Wine;
For if you
Do,
'Tis an ill signe;

2. That we
Foresee,
You are cloy'd here,
If so, no
Hoe,[1]
But avoid here.

[1] whoa: stop!

H–989 *Care a good keeper.*

CAre keepes the Conquest; 'tis no lesse renowne,
To keepe a Citie, then to winne a Towne.

H–990 *Rules for our reach.*

MEn must have Bounds how farre to walke; for we
Are made farre worse, by lawless liberty.

H–991 *To* Biancha.

AH *Biancha!* now I see,
It is Noone and past with me:
In a while it will strike one;
Then *Biancha,* I am gone.

Some *effusions* let me have,
Offer'd on my holy Grave;
Then, *Biancha,* let me rest
With my face towards the East.[1]

[1] in order to salute the Sun of Righteousness at the Resurrection.

H–992

To the handsome Mistresse Grace Potter.[1]

AS is your name, so is your comely face,
Toucht every where with such diffused grace,
As that in all that *admirable round,*
There is not one least *solecisme*[2] found;
And as that part, so every portion else,
Keepes line for line with *Beauties Parallels.*

[1] Daughter of Herrick's predecessor at Dean Prior and sister of Amy Potter; H-837. [2] The word ordinarily refers to an impropriety in speech or, by extension, an incongruity; but the conceit here is geometrical: Herrick may derive the word from Greek *solos,* a spherical mass of iron, and *schizo,* split; i.e. not the smallest cleft is found in the roundness of her face.

H–993

Anacreontike.

I Must
Not trust
Here to any;
Bereav'd,
Deceiv'd 5
By so many:
As one
Undone
By my losses;
Comply 10
Will I
With my crosses.
Yet still
I will

Not be grieving; 15
Since thence
And hence
Comes relieving.
But this
Sweet is 20
In our mourning;
Times bad
And sad
Are a turning:
And he 25
Whom we
See dejected;
Next day
Wee may
See erected. 30

H–994 *More modest, more manly.*

'TIs still observ'd, those men most valiant are,
That are most modest ere they come to warre.

H–995 *Not to covet much where little is the charge.*

WHy sho'd we covet much, when as we know,
W'ave more to beare our charge,[1] then way to go?

[1] expenses.

H–996 *Anacrontick Verse.*[1]

BRisk methinks I am, and fine,
When I drinke my capring wine:
Then to love I do encline;
When I drinke my wanton wine:
And I wish all maidens mine, 5
When I drinke my sprightly wine:

Well I sup, and well I dine,
When I drinke my frolick wine:
But I languish, lowre, and Pine,
When I want my fragrant wine. 10

[1] Cf. Stanley, "Anacreon XXXIX," *Poems,* 1651, lines 7 ff.: "Full of Wine my head I crown / Roving loosely up and down; / Full of Wine I praise the life / Calmly ignorant of strife; / Full of Wine I court some Fair, / And *Cythera's* worth declare; / Full of Wine my close thoughts I / To my Jovial Friends unty: / Wine makes Age with new years sprout: / Wine deni'd, my life goes out."

H–997 *Upon Pennie.*

BRown bread *Tom Pennie* eates, and must of right,
Because his stock will not hold out for white.

H–998 *Patience in Princes.*

KIngs must not use the Axe for each offence:
Princes cure some faults by their patience.

H–999 *Feare gets force.*

DEspaire takes heart, when ther's no hope to speed:
The Coward then takes Armes, and do's the deed.

H–1000 *Parcell-gil't[1]-Poetry.*

LEt's strive to be the best; the Gods, we know it,
Pillars and men, hate an indifferent Poet.[2]

[1] partly gilded: a term applied to bowls, cups, etc. gilded on the inside, in contrast to massy gold plate. [2] Horace, *Ars Poetica,* 372–3, states that neither men, nor gods, nor columns tolerate a mediocre poet. Books were often exposed for sale around pillars.

H–1001

Upon Love, by way of question and answer.

I Bring ye love, *Quest.* What will love do?
Ans. Like, and dislike ye:
I bring ye love: *Quest.* What will love do?
Ans. Stroake ye to strike ye.
I bring ye love: *Quest.* What will Love do? 5
Ans. Love will be-foole ye:
I bring ye love: *Quest.* What will love do?
Ans. Heate ye to coole ye:
I bring ye love: *Quest.* What will love do?
Ans. Love gifts will send ye: 10
I bring ye love: *Quest.* What will love do?
Ans. Stock ye to spend ye:
I bring ye love: *Quest.* What will love do?
Ans. Love will fulfill ye:
I bring ye love: *Quest.* What will love do? 15
Ans. Kisse ye, to kill ye.

H–1002

To the Lord Hopton, *on his fight in* Cornwall.[1]

GO on brave *Hopton,* to effectuate that
Which wee, and times to come, shall wonder at.
Lift up thy Sword; next, suffer it to fall,
And by that *One blow* set an end to all.

[1] Ralph Hopton, 1598–1652; winner of Royalist victories in Cornwall; created Baron Hopton, Sept. 4, 1643. Apparently Herrick wrote the poem before the victories and added the title later.

H–1003 *His Grange.*[1]

HOw well contented in this private *Grange*
Spend I my life (that's subject unto change:)
Under whose Roofe with *Mosse-worke* wrought, there I
Kisse my *Brown wife*, and *black Posterity*.

[1] a riddle poem: what is it that nests in a storage place for seeds, nuts, or the like, under a roof of twisted mosses, and has a brown mate and black children?

H–1004 *Leprosie in houses.*

WHen to a House I come, and see
The *Genius* wastefull, more then free:
The servants *thumblesse*,[1] yet to eat,
With lawlesse tooth the floure of wheate:[2]
The Sonnes to suck the milke of Kine, 5
More then the teats of Discipline:
The Daughters wild and loose in dresse;
Their cheekes unstain'd with shamefac'tnesse:
The Husband drunke, the Wife to be
A Baud to[3] incivility: 10
I must confesse, I there descrie,
A House spred through with *Leprosie*.

[1] clumsy or helpless, according to Martin, who follows *O.E.D.*, which cites only this passage for this sense. But, in keeping with *lawlesse* in the next line, Herrick probably means that the servants are not *under the thumb* or direction of a proper domestic authority. [2] yet I see that they are allowed to eat, without anyone's disciplining their appetites, the best kind of flour. Cf. Ecclus. xvii.16, "he nourisheth with discipline." [3] a promoter of.

H–1005 *Good manners at meat.*

THis rule of manners I will teach my guests,
To come with their own bellies unto feasts:
Not to eat equall portions; but to rise
Farc't[1] with the food, that may themselves suffice.

[1] stuffed.

H–1006 Anthea's *Retractation.*

ANthea laught, and fearing lest excesse
Might stretch the cords of civill comelinesse:
She with a dainty blush rebuk't her face;
And cal'd each line back to his *rule* and *space.*

H–1007 *Comforts in Crosses.*

BE not dismaide, though crosses cast thee downe;
Thy fall is but the rising to a Crowne.

H–1008 *Seeke and finde.*

ATtempt the end, and never stand to doubt;
Nothing's so hard, but search will find it out.

H–1009 *Rest.*

ON with thy worke, though thou beest hardly prest;
Labour is held up, by the hope of rest.

H–1010 *Leprosie in Cloathes.*

WHen flowing garments I behold
Enspir'd[1] with *Purple, Pearle,* and *Gold;*
I think no other but I see
In them a glorious leprosie
That do's infect, and make the rent 5
More mortall in the vestiment.
As flowrie vestures doe descrie[2]
The wearers rich immodestie;
So plaine and simple cloathes doe show
Where vertue walkes, not those that flow. 10

[1] literally, *blown into, inflated;* but with a hint of Latin *en* and *spira:* wrapped within; i.e. linings or inlays of purple, pearl, and

gold are visible through slashes or slits in the garments, especially when their wearer's motions cause them to inflate; the "rent" in line 5 is such a slit. [2] reveal.

H–1011 *Upon* Buggins.

BUggins is Drunke all night, all day he sleepes;
This is the Levell-coyle[1] that *Buggins* keeps.

[1] A player in the game of level-coil or hitch-buttock "keeps level-coil" or remains passive after he has been ejected from his seat and supplanted in it by another, whose turn to be ejected would then follow. Buggins observes such passivity by being drunk all night and asleep all day.

H–1012

Great Maladies, long Medicines.

TO an old soare a long cure must goe on;
Great faults require great satisfaction.

H–1013 *His Answer to a friend.*

YOu aske me what I doe, and how I live?
And (Noble friend) this answer I must give:
Drooping, I draw on to the vaults of death,
Or'e which you'l walk, when I am laid beneath.

H–1014 *The Begger.*

SHall I a daily Begger be,
For loves sake asking almes of thee?
Still shall I crave, and never get
A hope of my desired bit?
Ah cruell maides! Ile goe my way, 5
Whereas (perchance) my fortunes may
Finde out a Threshold or a doore,
That may far sooner speed the poore:
Where thrice we knock, and none will heare,
Cold comfort still I'm sure lives there. 10

H–1015 *Bastards.*

OUr Bastard-children are but like to Plate,
Made by the Coyners illegitimate.

H–1016 *His change.*

MY many cares and much distress,
Has made me like a wilderness:
Or (discompos'd) I'm like a rude,
And all confused multitude:
Out of my comely manners worne; 5
And as in meanes, in minde all torne.

H–1017 *The Vision.*

ME thought I saw (as I did dreame in bed)
A crawling Vine about *Anacreon's* head:
Flusht was his face; his haires with oyle did shine;
And as he spake, his mouth ranne ore with wine.
Tipled he was; and tipling lispt withall; 5
And lisping reeld, and reeling like to fall.
A young *Enchantresse* close by him did stand
Tapping his plump thighes with a *mirtle* wand:
She smil'd; he kist; and kissing, cull'd[1] her too;
And being cup-shot, more he co'd not doe. 10
For which (me thought) in prittie anger she
Snatcht off his Crown, and gave the wreath to me:
Since when (me thinks) my braines about doe swim,
And I am wilde and wanton like to him.

[1] colled: hugged, "necked."

H–1018 *A vow to* Venus.

HAppily I had a sight
Of my dearest deare last night;
Make her this day smile on me,
And Ile Roses give to thee.

H–1019 *On his Booke.*

THe bound (almost) now of my book I see,
But yet no end of those therein or me:
Here we begin new life; while thousands quite
Are lost, and theirs, in everlasting night.

H–1020 *A sonnet of* Perilla.

THen did I live when I did see
Perilla smile on none but me.
But (ah!) by starres malignant crost,
The life I got I quickly lost:
But yet a way there doth remaine, 5
For me embalm'd to live againe;
And that's to love me; in which state
Ile live as one *Regenerate.*

H–1021 *Bad may be better.*

MAn may at first transgress, but next do well:
Vice doth in some but lodge a while, not dwell.

H–1022 *Posting to Printing.*

LEt others to the Printing Presse run fast,
Since after death comes glory, *Ile not haste.*

H–1023 *Rapine brings Ruine.*

WHat's got by Justice is establisht sure;
No Kingdomes got by Rapine long endure.

H–1024 *Comfort to a youth that had lost his Love.*

WHat needs complaints,
When she a place
Has with the race
Of Saints?
In endlesse mirth, 5
She thinks not on
What's said or done
In earth:
She sees no teares,
Or any tone 10
Of thy deep grone
She heares:
Nor do's she minde,
Or think on't now,
That ever thou 15
Wast kind.
But chang'd above,
She likes not there,
As she did here,
Thy Love. 20
Forbeare therefore,
And Lull asleepe
Thy woes and weep
No more.

H–1025 *Upon* Boreman. *Epigram.*[1]

BOreman takes tole, cheats, flatters, lyes, yet *Boreman*,
For all the Divell helps, will be a poore man.

[1] Martial, XI, 66; in the Amsterdam, 1704 ed. of Martial, Thomas Farnaby notes the popular saying, "He hath too many occupations to thrive."

H–1026

Saint Distaffs day,[1] *or the morrow after Twelfth day.*

PArtly worke and partly play
Ye must on S. *Distaffs* day:
From the Plough soone free your teame;
Then come home and fother[2] them.
If the Maides a spinning goe, 5
Burne the flax, and fire the tow:[3]
Scorch their plackets,[4] but beware
That ye singe no maiden-haire.
Bring in pailes of water then,
Let the Maides bewash the men. 10
Give S. *Distaffe* all the right,
Then bid Christmas sport *good-night.*
And next morrow, every one
To his owne vocation.

[1] Jan. 7, the day after the Feast of the Epiphany and the 13th day after Christmas, when women resumed their spinning after the holidays. A distaff is a cleft rod on which wool or flax is wound. [2] fodder: feed. [3] the hard, coarse part of flax or hemp. [4] aprons or petticoats.

H–1027

Sufferance.

IN the hope of ease to come,
Let's endure one[1] Martyrdome.

[1] Martin suggests that *one* is a misprint for *our;* but the point seems to be that it is better to endure one martyrdom in this life than eternal suffering. Cf. Donne, Holy Sonnet X, 13: "One short sleepe past, wee wake eternally."

H–1028

His tears to Thamasis.[1]

I Send, I send here my supremest kiss
To thee my *silver-footed Thamasis.*
No more shall I reiterate[2] thy Strand,[3]
Whereon so many Stately Structures stand:

Nor in the summers sweeter evenings go, 5
To bath in thee (as thousand others doe.)
No more shall I a long thy christall glide,
In Barge (with boughes and rushes beautifi'd)
With soft-smooth Virgins (for our chast disport)
To *Richmond, Kingstone,* and to *Hampton-Court:*[4] 10
Never againe shall I with Finnie-Ore[5]
Put from, or draw unto the faithfull shore:
And Landing here, or safely Landing there,
Make way to my *Beloved Westminster:*[6]
Or to the *Golden-cheap-side,*[7] where the earth 15
Of *Julia Herrick* gave to me my Birth.
May all clean *Nimphs* and curious water Dames,
With Swan-like-state, flote up and down thy streams:
No drought upon thy wanton waters fall
To make them Leane, and languishing at all. 20
No ruffling winds come hither to disease[8]
Thy pure, and *Silver-wristed Naides.*
Keep up your state ye streams; and as ye spring,
Never make sick your Banks by surfeiting.
Grow young with Tydes, and though I see ye never, 25
Receive this vow, *so fare-ye-well for ever.*

[1] the Thames. [2] walk and re-walk along. [3] the shore of the river between the cities of London and Westminster, especially the street called The Strand, which lies nearby. [4] palaces and parks up the Thames from Westminster. [5] fin-like oar. [6] Herrick probably lived in or near Westminster before and after his going to Devonshire; but there is no evidence that he attended Westminster School. See notes to H-966, H-979. [7] Cheapside was the goldsmith's quarter. [8] dis-ease: disturb, with a play on disease: infect.

H–1029 *Pardons.*

THose ends in War the best contentment bring,
Whose Peace is made up with a Pardoning.

H–1030 *Peace not Permanent.*

GReat Cities seldome rest: If there be none
T'invade from far: They'l finde worse foes at home.

H–1031 *Truth and Errour.*

TWixt Truth and Errour, there's this difference known,
Errour is fruitfull, Truth is onely one.

H–1032 *Things mortall still mutable.*

THings are uncertain, and the more we get,
The more on ycie pavements we are set.

H–1033 *Studies to be supported.*

STudies themselves will languish and decay,
When either price, or praise is ta'ne away.

H–1034 *Wit punisht, prospers most.*

DRead not the shackles: on with thine intent;
Good wits get more fame by their punishment.

H–1035
Twelfe night, or King *and* Queene.[1]

NOw, now the mirth comes
With the cake full of plums,
Where Beane's the *King* of the sport here;
Beside we must know,
The Pea also 5
Must revell, as *Queene*, in the Court here.

Begin then to chuse,
(This night as ye use)
Who shall for the present delight here,
Be a *King* by the lot, 10
And who shall not
Be Twelfe-day *Queene* for the night here.

Which knowne, let us make
Joy-sops with the cake;[2]
And let not a man then be seen here, 15
Who unurg'd will not drinke
To the base from the brink
A health to the King and the Queene here.

Next crowne the bowle full
With gentle lambs-wooll;[3] 20
Adde sugar, nutmeg and ginger,
With store of ale too;
And thus ye must doe
To make the wassaile a swinger.[4]

Give then to the King 25
And Queene wassailing;[5]
And though with ale ye be whet here;
Yet part ye from hence,
As free from offence,
As when ye innocent met here. 30

[1] In the revels on Jan. 6, the eve of the Feast of the Epiphany, a plum cake containing a bean was served to the men and one containing a pea to the women. The recipients became King and Queen of the celebrations. [2] bits of cake, instead of the usual toast, in the liquor drunk to wish each other joy. [3] apple pulp. [4] a whopper. [5] i.e., drink to their health.

H–1036 *His desire.*

GIve me a man that is not dull,
When all the world with rifts is full:
But unamaz'd dares clearely sing,
When as the roof's a tottering:
And, though it falls, continues still 5
Tickling the *Citterne*[1] with his quill.

[1] cithern: a musical instrument strung with wires, played with a plectrum.

H–1037 *Caution in Councell.*

KNow when to speake; for many times it brings
Danger to give the best advice to Kings.

H–1038 *Moderation.*

LEt moderation on thy passions waite
Who loves too much, too much the lov'd will hate.

H–1039 *Advice the best actor.*

STill take advice; though counsels when they flye
At randome, sometimes hit most happily.

H–1040 *Conformity is comely.*

COnformity gives comelinesse to things.
And equall shares exclude all murmerings.

H–1041 *Lawes.*

WHo violates the Customes, hurts the Health,
Not of one man, but all the Common-wealth.

H–1042 *The meane.*

TIs much among the filthy to be clean;
Our heat of youth can hardly keep the mean.

H–1043 *Like loves his like.*

LIke will to like,[1] each Creature loves his kinde;
Chaste words proceed still from a bashfull minde.

[1] Cf. *Proverbes or Adagies, gathered out of the Chiliades of Erasmus, by Richard Taverner* (1569), 8r–8v: "*Aequalis aequadem delectat.* Like deliteth the like. . . . *Simile gaudet simili.* The like deliteth in the like: or as the English man saith. Like will to like."

H–1044 *His hope or sheat-Anchor.*

AMong these Tempests great and manifold
My Ship has here one only Anchor-hold;
That is my hope; which if that slip, I'm one
Wildred in this vast watry *Region.*

H–1045 *Comfort in Calamity.*

TIs no discomfort in the world to fall,
When the great Crack[1] not Crushes one, but all.

[1] the crack or thunderpeal of doom.

H–1046 *Twilight.*

THe Twi-light is no other thing (we say)
Then Night now gone, and yet not sprung the Day.[1]

[1] Cf. H-858.

H–1047 *False Mourning.*

HE who wears Blacks, and mournes not for the Dead,
Do's but deride the Party buried.

H–1048 *The will makes the work, or consent makes the Cure.*

NO grief is grown so desperate, but the ill
Is halfe way cured, if the party will.

H–1049 *Diet.*

IF wholsome Diet can re-cure a man,
What need of Physick, or Physitian?

H–1050 *Smart.*

STripes justly given yerk us[1] (with their fall)
But causelesse whipping smarts the most of all.

[1] cause us to wince.

H–1051 *The Tinkers Song.*

ALong, come along,
Let's meet in a throng
Here of Tinkers;
And quaffe up a Bowle
As big as a Cowle[1] 5
To Beer Drinkers.
The pole of the Hop
Place in the Ale-shop
to Bethwack us;
If ever we think 10
So much as to drink
Unto *Bacchus*.
Who frolick will be,
For little cost he
Must not vary, 15
From Beer-broth at all,
So much as to call
For Canary.[2]

[1] a tub, especially one used in brewing. [2] wine.

H–1052 *His Comfort.*

THe only comfort of my life
Is, that I never yet had wife;
Nor will hereafter; since I know
Who Weds, ore-buyes[1] his weal with woe.

[1] overbuys: purchases at too high a price.

H–1053 *Sincerity.*[1]

WAsh clean the Vessell, lest ye soure
What ever Liquor in ye powre.

[1] purity.

H–1054 *To Anthea.*

SIck is *Anthea,* sickly is the spring,
The Primrose sick, and sickly every thing:
The while my deer *Anthea* do's but droop,
The *Tulips, Lillies, Daffadills* do *stoop;*
But when again sh'as got her healthfull houre, 5
Each bending then, will rise a proper flower.

H–1055 *Nor buying or selling.*

NOw, if you love me, tell me,
For as I will not sell ye,
So not one cross[1] to buy thee
Ile give, if thou deny me.

[1] coin.

H–1056 *To his peculiar friend Master* John Wicks.[1]

SInce shed or Cottage I have none,
I sing the more, that thou hast one;
To whose glad threshold, and free door
I may a Poet come, though poor;
And eat with thee a savory bit, 5
Paying but common thanks for it.
Yet sho'd I chance, (my *Wicks*) to see
An over-leven-looke[2] in thee,
To soure the Bread, and turn the Beer
To an exalted[3] vineger; 10
Or sho'dst thou prize me as a Dish
Of thrice-boyl'd-worts,[4] or third dayes fish;
I'de rather hungry go and come,
Then to thy house be Burdensome;
Yet, in my depth of grief, I'de be 15
One that sho'd drop his *Beads* for[5] thee.

[1] H-336, n.2. [2] over-leavened: sour. The 1648 ed. has "looks". [3] changed in nature from what it was. [4] worts: vegetables and plants, especially of the cabbage family. [5] say prayers for.

H–1057 *The more mighty, the more mercifull.*

WHo may do most, do's least: The bravest will
Shew mercy there, where they have power to kill.

H–1058 *After Autumne, Winter.*

DIe ere long I'm sure, I shall;
After leaves, the tree must fall.

H–1059 *A good death.*

FOr truth I may this sentence tell,
No man dies ill, that liveth well.

H–1060 *Recompence.*

WHo plants an Olive, but to eate the Oile?
Reward, we know, is the chiefe end of toile.

H–1061 *On Fortune.*

THis is my comfort, when she's most unkind,
She can but spoile me of my Meanes, not Mind.

H–1062

To Sir George Parrie,[1] *Doctor of the Civill Law.*

I Have my Laurel Chaplet on my head,
If 'mongst these many Numbers to be read,
But one by you be hug'd and cherished.

Peruse my Measures thoroughly, and where
Your judgement finds a guilty Poem, there 5
Be you a Judge; but not a Judge severe.

The meane passe by, or over, none contemne;
The good applaud: the peccant lesse condemne,
Since *Absolution* you can give to them.

Stand forth Brave Man, here to the publique sight; 10
And in my Booke now claim a two-fold right:
The first as *Doctor*, and the last as *Knight.*

[1] A George Parry, son of Henry, Bishop of Worcester, became Recorder of Exeter and is probably to be identified with the Dr. George Parry, Chancellor to the Bishop of Exeter, who was knighted in 1644 at Oxford.

H–1063 *Charmes.*

THis Ile tell ye by the way,
Maidens when ye Leavens lay,[1]
Crosse your Dow, and your dispatch,
Will be better for your Batch.[2]

[1] when you lay leavened dough aside to rise. [2] Put cross marks on the dough and your disposing of it in this manner will be the better for this batch of bread.

H–1064 *Another.*

IN the morning when ye rise
Wash your hands, and cleanse your eyes.
Next be sure ye have a care,
To disperse the water farre.
For as farre as that doth light, 5
So farre keepes the evill Spright.

H–1065 *Another.*

IF ye feare to be affrighted
When ye are (by chance) benighted:
In your Pocket for a trust,
Carrie nothing but a Crust:
For that holy piece of Bread, 5
Charmes the danger, and the dread.

H–1066 *Upon* Gorgonius.

UNto *Pastillus* ranke *Gorgonius* came,
To have a tooth twitcht out of's native frame.
Drawn was his tooth; but stanke so, that some say,
The Barber[1] stopt his Nose, and ranne away.

[1] In the seventeenth century, barbers were also dentists and surgeons.

H–1067 *Gentlenesse.*

THat Prince must govern with a gentle hand,
Who will have love comply with his command.

H–1068

A Dialogue betwixt himselfe and Mistresse Elizabeth Wheeler, *under the name of* Amarillis.[1]

MY dearest Love, since thou wilt go,
And leave me here behind thee;
For love or pitie let me know
The place where I may find thee.

Amaril. In country Meadowes pearl'd with Dew, 5
And set about with Lillies;
There filling Maunds[2] with Cowslips, you
May find your *Amarillis.*

Her. What have the Meades to do with thee,
Or with thy youthfull houres? 10
Live thou at Court, where thou mayst be
The *Queen* of men, not flowers.

Let Country wenches make 'em fine
With Poesies, since 'tis fitter
For thee with richest Jemmes to shine, 15
And like the Starres to glitter.

Amaril. You set too high a rate upon
A Shepheardess so homely;
Her. Believe it (dearest) ther's not one
I'th'Court that's halfe so comly. 20

I prithee stay. (*Am.*) I must away,
Lets kiss first, then we'l sever.
Ambo.[3] And though we bid adieu to day,
Wee shall not part for ever.

[1] H-130. [2] wicker baskets. [3] both.

H–1069

To Julia.

HElp me, *Julia,* for to pray,
Mattens sing, or Mattens say:
This I know, the Fiend will fly
Far away, if thou beest by.
Bring the Holy-water hither; 5
Let us wash, and pray together:
When our Beads are thus united,
Then the Foe will fly affrighted.

H–1070

To Roses in Julia's *Bosome.*

ROses, you can never die,
Since the place wherein ye lye,
Heat and moisture mixt are so,
As to make ye ever grow.

H–1071

To the Honoured, Master Endimion Porter.[1]

WHen to thy Porch I come, and (ravisht) see
The State[2] of Poets there attending Thee:
Those *Bardes,* and I, all in a *Chorus* sing,
We are Thy *Prophets*[3] *Porter; Thou our King.*

[1] H-117. [2] court or council; a college or group with common functions. Cf. H-1080, 4. [3] Latin *vates:* inspired bards. Cf. II Chron. xxxiv.22, "Huldah the prophetess . . . . dwelt in Jerusalem in the college."

H–1072

Speake in season.

WHen times are troubled, then forbeare; but speak,
When a cleare day, out of a Cloud do's break.

H–1073 *Obedience.*

THe Power of Princes rests in the Consent
Of onely those, who are obedient:[1]
Which if away, proud Scepters then will lye
Low, and of Thrones the Ancient *Majesty.*

[1] Cf. Sir William Cornwallis, *Discourses upon Seneca the Tragedian* (1601), sig. C4, "The state of a prince is upheld by his subjects opinion, his Maiestie begetteth reverence, so long as his power fitteth it selfe to justice. . . : nothing assisteth another, that is not againe by that assisted."

H–1074 *Another on the same.*

NO man so well a Kingdome Rules, as He,
Who hath himselfe obaid the Soveraignty.[1]

[1] Cf. *Proverbes . . . gathered out of . . . Erasmus, by Richard Taverner* (1569), 3r: "*Nemo bene imperat, nisi qui perverit imperio.* No man can be a good ruler, onlesse he hath been first ruled."

H–1075 *Of Love.*

1. INstruct me now, what love will do;
2. 'Twill make a tongless man to wooe.
1. Inform me next, what love will do;
2. 'Twill strangely make a one of too.
1. Teach me besides, what love wil do;
2. 'Twill quickly mar, and make ye too.
1. Tell me, now last, what love will do;
2. 'Twill hurt and heal a heart pierc'd through.

H–1076 *Upon Trap.*

TRap, of a Player turn'd a Priest now is;
Behold a suddaine *Metamorphosis.*
If Tythe-pigs faile,[1] then will he shift the scean,
And, from a Priest, turne Player once again.

[1] if pigs owed to pay tithes are lacking.

H–1077 *Upon Grubs.*

GRubs loves his Wife and Children, while that they
Can live by love, or else grow fat by Play:
But when they call or cry on *Grubs* for meat;
Instead of Bread, *Grubs* gives them stones to eat.
He raves, he rends, and while he thus doth tear,[1] 5
His Wife and Children fast to death for fear.

[1] Cf. Hamlet at the beginning of Act III, sc. ii: "it offends me to the soul to hear a . . . fellow tear a passion to tatters."

H–1078 *Upon Dol.*

NO question but *Dols* cheecks wo'd soon rost dry,
Were they not basted by her either eye.

H–1079 *Upon Hog.*

HOg has a place i'th'Kitchen, and his share
The flimsie Livers, and blew Gizzards are.

H–1080

The School or[1] *Perl*[2] *of* Putney,
the Mistress of all singular manners,
Mistresse Portman.

WHether I was my selfe, or else did see
Out of my self[3] that *Glorious Hierarchie!*
Or whether those (in orders rare) or these
Made up One State[4] of *Sixtie Venuses;*
Or whether *Fairies, Syrens, Nymphes* they were, 5
Or *Muses,* on their mountaine sitting there;
Or some enchanted Place, I do not know
(Or *Sharon,*[5] where eternall Roses grow.)
This I am sure; I Ravisht stood, as one
Confus'd in utter Admiration. 10

Me thought I saw them stir, and gently move,
And look as all were capable of Love:
And in their motion smelt much like to flowers
Enspir'd by th'Sun-beams after dews and showers.
There did I see the *Reverend Rectresse* stand, 15
Who with her eyes-gleam, or a glance of hand,
Those spirits rais'd; and with like precepts then
(As with a *Magick*) laid them all agen:
(*A happy Realme! When no compulsive Law,
Or fear of it, but Love keeps all in awe.*) 20
Live you *great Mistresse* of your Arts, and be
A nursing Mother so to Majesty;
As those your Ladies may in time be seene,
For Grace and Carriage, every one a Queene.
One Birth their Parents gave them; but their new, 25
And better Being, they receive from You.
*Mans former Birth is grace-lesse; but the state
Of life comes in, when he's Regenerate.*

[1] misprint for *of*? [2] The Latin for *pearl* is *margarita;* so this teacher of manners and deportment was probably named Margaret Portman; but she has not been identified. Grosart found entries in Putney Parish Register for a Mary Portman who died in 1671. Evelyn, on April 17, 1649, went "To Putney by Water in barge with divers Ladys, to see the *Schooles* or *Colledges* of the Young Gentlewomen." [3] i.e. in an ecstasy or vision. Cf. II Cor. xii.3–4, "I knew such a man (whether in the body, or out of the body, I cannot tell: God knoweth) How that he was caught up into paradise." [4] court, society. [5] Song of Sol. ii.1.

H–1081 *To* Perenna.

THou say'st I'm dull; if edge-lesse so I be,
Ile whet my lips, and sharpen Love on thee.

H–1082 *On himselfe.*

LEt me not live, if I not love,
Since I as yet did never prove,
Where Pleasures met; at last, doe find,
All Pleasures meet in Woman-kind.

H–1083

On Love.

THat love 'twixt men do's ever longest last
Where War and Peace the Dice by turns doe cast.

H–1084

Another on Love.

LOve's of it self, too sweet; the best of all
Is, when loves hony has a dash of gall.

H–1085

Upon Gut.

SCience[1] puffs up, sayes *Gut,* when either Pease
Make him thus swell, or windy Cabbages.

[1] knowledge. Cf. I Cor. viii.1, "Knowledge puffeth up."

H–1086

Upon Chub.

WHen *Chub* brings in his harvest, still he cries,
Aha my boyes! heres wheat for Christmas Pies!
Soone after, he for beere so scores[1] his wheat,
That at the tide,[2] he has not bread to eate.

[1] to get beer he runs up such a debt to be paid by his wheat or the proceeds from selling it. [2] i.e. Christmas tide.

H–1087

Pleasures Pernicious.

WHere Pleasures rule a Kingdome, never there
Is sober virtue, seen to move her sphere.

H–1088

On himself.

A Wearied Pilgrim, I have wandred here
Twice five and twenty (bate[1] me but one yeer)
Long I have lasted in this world; (tis true)
But yet those yeers that I have liv'd, but few.

Who by his gray Haires, doth his lusters tell, 5
Lives not those yeers, but he that lives them well.
One man has reatch't his sixty yeers, but he
Of all those three-score, has not liv'd halfe three:
He lives, who lives to virtue: men who cast
Their ends for Pleasure, do not live, but last. 10

[1] deduct. If these figures are to be taken literally, the poem was written in 1640.

H–1089

To Master Laurence Swetnaham.[1]

REad thou my Lines, my *Swetnaham,* if there be
A fault, tis hid, if it be voic't by thee.
Thy mouth will make the sourest numbers please;
How will it drop pure hony, speaking these?

[1] A Lawrence Swettenham was buried at St. Margaret's, Westminster, in 1648, and a Larence Sweatnam in the East Cloister of Westminster Abbey in 1673.

H–1090

His Covenant or Protestation to Julia.

WHy do'st thou wound, and break my heart?
As if we sho'd for ever part?
Hast thou not heard an Oath from me,
After a day, or two, or three,
I wo'd come back and live with thee? 5
Take, if thou do'st distrust that Vowe;
This second Protestation now.
Upon thy cheeke that spangel'd Teare,
Which sits as Dew of Roses there:
That Teare shall scarce be dri'd before 10
Ile kisse the Threshold of thy dore.
Then weepe not sweet; but thus much know,
I'm halfe return'd before I go.

H–1091 *On himselfe.*

I Will no longer kiss,
I can no longer stay;
The way of all Flesh is,
That I must go this day:
Since longer I can't live, 5
My frolick Youths adieu;
My Lamp to you Ile give,
And all my troubles too.

H–1092

To the most accomplisht Gentleman
Master Michael Oulsworth.[1]

NOr thinke that Thou in this my Booke art worst,
Because not plac't here with the midst, or first.
Since Fame that sides with these, or goes before
Those, that must live with Thee for evermore.
That Fame, and Fames rear'd Pillar, thou shalt see 5
In the next sheet[2] *Brave Man* to follow Thee.
Fix on That Columne then, and never fall;
Held up by Fames *eternall Pedestall.*

[1] Michael Oldisworth, 1591–1660?; secretary to William, 3rd Earl of Pembroke and then to Philip, Earl of Pembroke and Montgomery (H-359); M.P., 1624; 1640, elected for Plympton, Devon, but sat in the Long Parliament for Salisbury, which also chose him. Though Oldisworth's death date is sometimes given as 1654, he appears to have been among the Rumpers who returned to the House in 1659–60. He was satirized by Royalist pamphleteers and wrote a pamphlet on the diversity of names in Great Britain. [2] This line is the last one on p. 380 (Sig. Cc3[v]) of the 1648 *Hesperides;* "The Pillar of Fame" (H-1129) occurs on p. 398 (Cc7[v]).

H–1093 *To his Girles who would have him sportfull.*

ALas I can't, for tell me how
Can I be gamesome (aged now)

Besides ye see me daily grow
Here Winter-like, to Frost and Snow.
And I ere long, my Girles shall see, 5
Ye quake for cold to looke on me.

H–1094 *Truth and falsehood.*

TRuth by her own simplicity is known,
Falsehood by Varnish and Vermillion.[1]

[1] Cf. *Proverbes . . . of Erasmus, by Richard Taverner* (1569), 14v–15r: "*Veritas simplex oratio.* Trouthes tale is simple, he that meaneth good faith, goeth not about to glose his communication with painted wordes. Plaine and homely men call a figge, a figge, and a spade a spade. Rhetorike and coloringe of spech, proveth manye times a mans matter to be naught."

H–1095 *His last request to* Julia.

I Have been wanton, and too bold I feare,
To chafe o're much the Virgins cheek or eare:
Beg for my Pardon *Julia; He doth winne*
Grace with the Gods, who's sorry for his sinne.
That done, my *Julia,* dearest *Julia,* come, 5
And go with me to chuse my Buriall roome:
My Fates are ended; when thy *Herrick* dyes,
Claspe thou his Book, then close thou up his Eyes.

H–1096 *On himselfe.*

ONe Eare tingles; some there be,
That are snarling now at me:
Be they those that *Homer* bit,
I will give them thanks for it.

H–1097 *Upon Kings.*

KIngs must be dauntlesse: Subjects will contemne
Those, who want Hearts, and weare a Diadem.

H–1098 *To his Girles.*

WAnton Wenches doe not bring
For my haires black colouring:
For my Locks (Girles) let 'em be
Gray or white, all's one to me.

H–1099 *Upon* Spur.

SPur jingles now, and sweares by no meane oathes,
He's double honour'd since h'as got gay cloathes:
Most like his Suite, and all commend the Trim;
And thus they praise the Sumpter;[1] but not him:
As to the Goddesse, people did conferre 5
Worship, and not to'th'Asse that carried her.[2]

[1] beasts of burden, or the packs they bore, or their drivers; but here Herrick seems to refer to the man's clothing and, probably, the harness and its trimming (including jingling bells); or he may mean *sumptuosity*. [2] a reference to the fable of the ass who bore an Egyptian goddess and thought that the people knelt to him.

H–1100 *To his Brother* Nicolas Herrick.[1]

WHat others have with cheapnesse seene, and ease,
In Varnisht maps; by'th'helpe of Compasses:
Or reade in Volumes, and those Bookes (with all
Their large Narrations, *Incanonicall*)[2]
Thou hast beheld those seas, and Countries farre; 5
And tel'st to us, what once they were, and are.
So that with bold truth, thou canst now relate
This Kingdomes fortune, and that Empires fate:
Canst talke to us of *Sharon;*[3] where a spring
Of Roses have an endlesse flourishing. 10
Of *Sion, Sinai, Nebo*, and with them,
Make knowne to us the now *Jerusalem*.
The Mount of *Olives; Calverie*, and where
Is (and hast seene) *thy Saviours Sepulcher*.

So that the man that will but lay his eares, 15
As *Inapostate*, to[4] the thing he heares,
Shall by his hearing quickly come to see
The truth of Travails lesse in bookes then Thee.

[1] the 3rd son in Herrick's parents' family, born two years before Robert. He became a merchant, trading to the Levant, and married Susanna Salter, who bore him three sons and three daughters. [2] their exaggerated travel stories, which are untrustworthy because of their "tall tales." [3] Sharon is a Palestinian plain; Zion, a height in Jerusalem; Sinai, the mountain on which Moses received the Ten Commandments; Nebo or Pisgah, a mountain or ridge to the east of the Dead Sea's north end. [4] as reliant upon the truth of.

H-1101 *The Voice and Violl.*

RAre[1] is the voice it selfe; but when we sing
To'th Lute or Violl, then 'tis ravishing.

[1] excellent.

H-1102 *Warre.*

IF Kings and kingdomes, once distracted be,
The sword of war must trie the Soveraignty.

H-1103 *A King and no King.*

THat Prince, who may doe nothing but what's just,
Rules but by leave, and takes his Crowne on trust.

H-1104 *Plots not still prosperous.*

ALl are not ill Plots, that doe sometimes faile;
Nor those false vows, which oft times don't prevaile.

H-1105 *Flatterie.*

WHat is't that wasts a Prince? example showes,
'Tis flatterie spends a King, more then his foes.

H–1106 *Upon* Rumpe.

RUmpe is a Turne-broach,[1] yet he seldome can
Steale a swolne sop out of the Dripping pan.

[1] a turnspit; one who rotates a spit over a fire to roast meat.

H–1107 *Upon* Shopter.

OLd Widow *Shopter,* when so ere she cryes,
Lets drip a certain Gravie from her eyes.

H–1108 *Upon* Deb.

IF felt and heard, (unseen) thou dost me please;
If seen, thou lik'st me, *Deb,* in none of these.

H–1109 *Excesse.*

EXcesse is sluttish: keepe the meane; for why?
Vertue's clean Conclave[1] is sobriety.

[1] literally, *something which has a key;* hence, *inner chamber, home, dwelling place.*

H–1110 *Upon* Croot.

ONe silver spoon shines in the house of *Croot;*
Who cannot buie,[1] or steale a second to't.

[1] buy.

H–1111 *The soul is the salt.*

THe body's salt, the soule is; which when gon,
The flesh soone sucks in putrifaction.

H–1112

Upon Flood, *or a thankfull man.*

FLood, if he has for him and his a bit,
He sayes his fore and after Grace for it:
If meate he wants, then Grace he sayes to see
His hungry belly borne by Legs *Jaile-free.*
Thus have, or have not, all alike is good, 5
To this our poore, yet ever patient *Flood.*

H–1113

Upon Pimpe.

WHen *Pimpes* feet sweat (as they doe often use)[1]
There springs a sope-like-lather in his shoos.

[1] i.e. use to do: are wont to do.

H–1114

Upon Luske.

IN Den'-shire Kerzie[1] *Lusk* (when he was dead)
Wo'd shrouded be, and therewith buried.
When his Assignes askt him the reason why?
He said, because he got his wealth thereby.

[1] kersey: a coarse woolen cloth made chiefly in Devonshire and Kent in the 17th century.

H–1115

Foolishnesse.

IN's *Tusc'lanes, Tullie* doth confesse,[1]
No plague ther's like to foolishnesse.

[1] In his *Tusculan Disputations,* III, iv, 9, Cicero admits that.

H–1116 *Upon* Rush.

RUsh saves his shooes, in wet and snowie wether;
And feares in summer to weare out the lether:
This is strong thrift that warie *Rush* doth use
Summer and Winter still to save his shooes.

H–1117 *Abstinence.*

AGainst diseases here the strongest fence
Is the defensive vertue, Abstinence.

H–1118 *No danger to men desperate.*

WHen feare admits no hope of safety, then
Necessity makes dastards valiant men.

H–1119 *Sauce for sorrowes.*

ALthough our suffering meet with no reliefe,
An equall mind is the best sauce for griefe.

H–1120 *To* Cupid.

I Have a leaden, thou a shaft of gold;
Thou kil'st with heate, and I strike dead with cold.
Let's trie of us who shall the first expire;
Or thou by frost, or I by quenchlesse fire:
Extreames are fatall, where they once doe strike, 5
And bring to'th'heart destruction both alike.

H–1121 *Distrust.*

WHat ever men for Loyalty pretend,
'Tis Wisdomes part to doubt a faithfull friend.

H–1122 *The Hagg.*

THe staffe is now greas'd,
And very well pleas'd,
She cockes out her Arse at the parting,
To an old Ram Goat,
That rattles i'th'throat, 5
Halfe choakt with the stink of her farting.

In a dirtie Haire-lace
She leads on a brace
Of black-bore-cats[1] to attend her;
Who scratch at the Moone,
And threaten at noone 10
Of night from Heaven for to rend her.

A hunting she goes;
A crackt horne she blowes;
At which the hounds fall a bounding;
While th'Moone in her sphere 15
Peepes trembling for feare,
And night's afraid of the sounding.

[1] black male cats.

H–1123 *The mount of the Muses.*

AFter thy labour take thine ease,
Here with the sweet *Pierides.*[1]
But if so be that men will not
Give thee the Laurell Crowne for lot;[2]
Be yet assur'd, thou shalt have one 5
Not subject to corruption.[3]

[1] the Muses. [2] for thy portion. [3] I Cor. ix.25, "And every man that striveth for the mastery is temperate in all things. Now, they do it to obtain a corruptible crown, but we an incorruptible."

H–1124 *On Himselfe.*

IL'e write no more of Love; but now repent
Of all those times that I in it have spent.
Ile write no more of life; but wish twas ended,
And that my dust was to the earth commended.

H–1125 *To his Booke.*

GOe thou forth my booke, though late;
Yet be timely fortunate.
It may chance good-luck may send
Thee a kinsman, or a friend,
That may harbour thee, when I, 5
With my fates neglected lye.
If thou know'st not where to dwell,
See, the fier's by: *Farewell.*

H–1126 *The end of his worke.*

PArt of the worke remaines; one part is past:
And here my ship rides having Anchor cast.

H–1127 *To Crowne it.*

MY wearied Barke, O Let it now be Crown'd!
The Haven reacht to which I first was bound.

H–1128 *On Himselfe.*

THe worke is done: young men, and maidens set
Upon my curles the *Mirtle Coronet,*
Washt with sweet ointments; Thus at last I come
To suffer in the Muses *Martyrdome:*
But with this comfort, if my blood be shed, 5
The Muses will weare blackes, when I am dead.

H–1129 ## *The pillar of Fame.*[1]

FAmes pillar here, at last, we set,
Out-during[2] *Marble, Brasse,* or *Jet,*
Charm'd and enchanted so,
As to withstand the blow
Of overthrow:
Nor shall the seas,
Or OUTRAGES
Of storms orebear
What we up-rear,
Tho Kingdoms fal,
This pillar never shall
Decline or waste at all;
But stand for ever by his owne
Firme and well fixt foundation.

[1] On the popularity of shaped verse of this kind see Puttenham, *Arte of English Poesie,* 1578. [2] outlasting.

H–1130

To his Book's end this last line he'd have plac't,
Jocond his Muse was; but his Life was chast.

FINIS.

Noble Numbers

HIS
NOBLE NUMBERS:

OR,

HIS PIOUS PIECES,

Wherein (amongſt other things)

he ſings the Birth of his CHRIST:
and ſighes for his *Saviours* ſuffe-
ring on the *Croſſe*.

HESIOD.

Ἴδμεν ψεύδεα πολλὰ λέγειν ἐτύμοισιν ὁμοῖα.
Ἴδμεν δ', εὖτ' ἐθέλωμεν, ἀληθέα μυθήσασθαι.

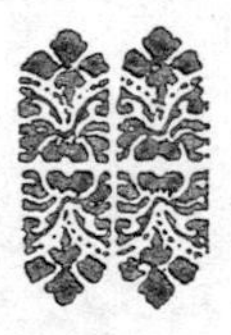

LONDON.
Printed for *John Williams*, and *Francis Eglesfield*.
1647.

A Note on the Title Page

The Greek is quoted from Hesiod's *Theogony*, 27–28: "We know how to say many things that bear the guise of truth, and we also know when we intend to state the truth."

The date, 1647, suggests that Herrick may have originally intended to have *Noble Numbers* precede *Hesperides*, which is dated 1648. If so, he seems to have changed his mind before typesetting began, for the signatures of *Noble Numbers* run Aa–Ee, not A–E. The probability is that he prepared both collections in 1647 and dated both manuscript title pages accordingly, but that the setting up of the type for the main title page was left to the last, by which time 1648 had arrived or was near.

HIS
Noble Numbers:
OR,
His pious Pieces.

N–1 *His Confession.*

LOok how our foule Dayes do exceed our faire;
And as our bad, more then our good Works are:
Ev'n so those Lines, pen'd by my wanton Wit,
Treble the number of these good I've writ.[1]
Things precious are least num'rous: Men are prone
To do ten Bad, for one Good Action.

[1] *Hesperides* contains more than four times as many poems as *Noble Numbers* and more than five times as many lines; but many of the poems in *Hesperides* could be classified as "pious Pieces."

N–2 *His Prayer for Absolution.*

FOr Those my unbaptized Rhimes,
Writ in my wild unhallowed Times;
For every sentence, clause and word,
That's not inlaid with Thee, (my Lord)
Forgive me God, and blot each Line 5
Out of my Book, that is not Thine.
But if, 'mongst all, thou find'st here one
Worthy thy Benediction;
That One of all the rest, shall be
The Glory of my Work, and Me. 10

N–3 *To finde God.*[1]

WEigh me the Fire; or, canst thou find
A way to measure out the Wind;
Distinguish all those Floods that are
Mixt in that watrie Theater;[2]
And tast thou them as saltlesse there, 5
As in their Channell first they were.[3]
Tell[4] me the People that do keep
Within the Kingdomes of the Deep;
Or fetch me back that Cloud againe,
Beshiver'd into seeds of Raine; 10
Tell me the motes, dust,[5] sands,[6] and speares
Of Corn, when Summer shakes his eares;
Shew me that world of Starres, and whence
They noiselesse spill their Influence:
This if thou canst; then shew me Him 15
That rides the glorious *Cherubim.*[7]

[1] The "impossibility theme" (Cf. Donne's "Goe, and catche a falling starre" and Marvell's "Had we but World enough, and time") was much used by 17th-century poets; here Herrick varies the theme to build up to a miraculous climax: *IF* you can perform all these "impossibilities," then show me the supreme sight, the vision of God. [2] the oceans. [3] Cf. II Esdras iv.5–7, "weigh me the weight of the fire, or measure me the blast of the wind . . . how many springs are in the beginning of the deep, or how many springs are above the firmament." Cf. H-720. [4] count. Cf. Gen. xv.5, "tell the stars, if thou be able to number them"; Ps. cxlvii.4, "He telleth the number of the stars." [5] Gen. xiii.16, "if a man can number the dust of the earth." [6] Ecclus. i.2–3, "Who can number the sand of the sea, and the drops of rain, and the days of eternity? Who can find out the height of heaven, and the breadth of the earth, and the deep, and wisdom." [7] Ps. xviii.10, "he rode upon a cherub"; cf. Ezek. i.

N–4 *What God is.*

GOD is above the sphere of our esteem,
And is the best known, not defining Him.

N–5 *Upon God.*

GOD is not onely said to be
An *Ens*, but *Supraentitie*.

N–6 *Mercy and Love.*

GOD hath two wings, which He doth ever move,
The one is Mercy, and the next is Love:
Under the first the Sinners ever trust;
And with the last he still directs the Just.

N–7 *Gods Anger without Affection.*

GOD when He's angry here with any one,
His wrath is free from perturbation;
And when we think His looks are sowre and grim,
The alteration is in us, not Him.

N–8 *God not to be comprehended.*

'TIs hard to finde God, but to comprehend
Him, as He is, is labour without end.

N–9 *Gods part.*

PRayers and Praises are those spotlesse two
Lambs, by the Law, which God requires as due.[1]

[1] The Mosaic law required the daily sacrifice of two lambs: Exod. xxix.38–42; Numb. xxviii.3–10; Lev. xiv.10.

N–10 *Affliction.*

GOD n'ere afflicts us more then our desert,
Though He may seem to over-act His part:
Somtimes He strikes us more then flesh can beare;
But yet still lesse then Grace can suffer here.

N–11 *Three fatall Sisters.*

THree fatall Sisters wait upon each sin;
First, Fear and Shame without, then Guilt within.

N–12 *Silence.*

SUffer thy legs, but not thy tongue to walk:[1]
God, the most Wise, is sparing of His talk.

[1] Ps. lxxiii.9: the foolish "set their mouth against the heavens, and their tongue walketh through the earth"; Prov. xvii.27–28, "He that hath knowledge spareth his words . . . and he that shutteth his lips, is esteemed a man of understanding."

N–13 *Mirth.*

TRue mirth resides not in the smiling skin:
The sweetest solace is to act no sin.

N–14 *Loading and unloading.*

GOD loads, and unloads, (thus His work begins)
To load with blessings, and unload from sins.

N–15 *Gods Mercy.*

GOD's boundlesse mercy is (to sinfull man)
Like to the ever-wealthy Ocean:
Which though it sends forth thousand streams, 'tis ne're
Known, or els seen to be the emptier:
And though it takes all in, 'tis yet no more 5
Full, and fild-full, then when full-fild before.

N–16 *Prayers must have Poise.*

GOD He rejects all Prayers that are sleight,
And want their Poise: words ought to have their weight.

N–17 *To God: an Anthem, sung in the Chappell at White-Hall,[1] before the King.*

Verse.[2] MY God, I'm wounded by my sin,
And sore without, and sick within:
Ver. Chor. I come to Thee, in hope to find
Salve for my body, and my mind.
Verse. In *Gilead* though no Balme be found,
To ease this smart, or cure this wound;[3]
Ver. Chor. Yet, Lord, I know there is with Thee
All saving health,[4] and help for me.
Verse. Then reach Thou forth that hand of Thine,
That powres in oyle, as well as wine.
Ver. Chor. And let it work, for I'le endure
The utmost smart, so Thou wilt cure.

[1] W. C. Hazlitt conjectured that Herrick may have had some subordinate post in the Chapel Royal. Cf. N-96, N-97, N-98, N-102. [2] The versicle is said or sung by the officiating priest, with responses by the choir. [3] Jer. viii.22, "Is there no balm in Gilead? is there no physician there?" [4] Ps. lxvii.2, "thy saving health among all nations."

N–18 *Upon God.*

GOD is all fore-part; for, we never see
Any part backward in the Deitie.[1]

[1] Cf. Exod. xxxiii.23, "thou shalt see my back parts."

N–19 *Calling, and correcting.*

GOD is not onely mercifull, to call
Men to repent, but when He strikes withall.

N–20 *No escaping the scourging.*

GOD scourgeth some severely, some He spares;[1]
But all in smart have lesse, or greater shares.

[1] Tobit xiii.2, "he doth scourge, and hath mercy"; Heb. xii.6, "whom the Lord loveth he chasteneth, and scourgeth every son whom he receiveth"; Rev. iii.19, "As many as I love, I rebuke and chasten."

N–21 *The Rod.*

GOD's Rod doth watch while men do sleep; and then
The Rod doth sleep, while vigilant are men.

N–22 *God has a twofold part.*

GOD when for sin He makes His Children smart,
His own He acts not, but anothers part:
But when by stripes He saves them,[1] then 'tis known,
He comes to play the part that is His own.

[1] Isa. liii.5, "and with his stripes we are healed"; I Pet. ii.24, "by whose stripes ye were healed."

N–23 *God is One.*

GOD, as He is most Holy knowne;
So He is said to be most One.

N–24 *Persecutions profitable.*

AFflictions they most profitable are
To the beholder, and the sufferer:
Bettering them both, but by a double straine,
The first by patience, and the last by paine.

N–25 *To God.*

DO with me, God! as Thou didst deal with *John*,
(Who writ that heavenly *Revelation*)
Let me (like him) first cracks of thunder heare;[1]
Then let the Harps inchantments strike mine eare;[2]
Here give me thornes;[3] there, in thy Kingdome, set 5
Upon my head the golden coronet;
There give me day; but here my dreadfull night:
My sackcloth here; but there my *Stole* of white.

[1] Rev. vi.1, "the Lamb opened one of the seals, and I heard, as it were the noise of thunder. . . ." [2] Rev. xiv.2, "I heard a voice from heaven . . . as the voice of a great thunder; and I heard the voice of harpers harping with their harps." [3] II Cor. xii.7, "And lest I should be exalted above measure . . . there was given to me a thorn in the flesh."

N–26 *Whips.*

GOD has his whips here to a twofold end,
The bad to punish, and the good t'amend.

N–27 *Gods Providence.*

IF all transgressions here should have their pay,
What need there then be of a reckning day:
If God should punish no sin, here, of men,
His Providence who would not question then?

N–28 *Temptation.*

THose Saints, which God loves best,
The Devill tempts not least.

N–29 *His Ejaculation to God.*

MY God! looke on me with thine eye
Of pittie, not of scrutinie;
For if thou dost, thou then shalt see
Nothing but loathsome sores in mee.
O then! for mercies sake, behold 5
These my irruptions manifold;
And heale me with thy looke, or touch:
But if thou wilt not deigne so much,
Because I'me odious in thy sight,
Speak but the word, and cure me quite.[1] 10

[1] Matt. viii.8, "speak the word only, and my servant shall be healed."

N–30 *Gods gifts not soone granted.*

GOD heares us when we pray, but yet defers
His gifts, to exercise[1] Petitioners:
And though a while He makes Requesters stay,
With Princely hand He'l recompence delay.

[1] I Tim. iv.7, "exercise thyself rather unto godliness."

N–31 *Persecutions purifie.*

GOD strikes His Church, but 'tis to this intent,
To make, not marre her, by this punishment:
So where He gives the bitter Pills, be sure,
'Tis not to poyson, but to make thee pure.

N–32 *Pardon.*

GOD pardons those, who do through frailty sin;
But never those that persevere therein.

N–33

An Ode of the Birth of our Saviour.

1. IN Numbers, and but these few,
I sing Thy Birth, Oh JESU!
Thou prettie Babie, borne here,
With sup'rabundant scorn here:
Who for Thy Princely Port here,
Hadst for Thy place
Of Birth, a base
Out-stable for thy Court here.

2. Instead of neat Inclosures
Of inter-woven Osiers;[1]
Instead of fragrant Posies
Of Daffadills, and Roses;
Thy cradle, Kingly Stranger,
As Gospell tells,
Was nothing els,
But, here, a homely manger.

3. But we with Silks, (not Cruells)[2]
With sundry precious Jewells,
And Lilly-work will dresse Thee;
And as we dispossesse thee
Of clouts,[3] wee'l make a chamber,
Sweet Babe, for Thee,
Of Ivorie,
And plaister'd round with Amber.

4. The Jewes they did disdaine Thee,
But we will entertaine Thee
With Glories to await here
Upon Thy Princely State here,
And more for love, then pittie.
From yeere to yeere
Wee'l make Thee, here,
A Free-born of our Citie.

[1] i.e. cradles. [2] worsteds used for embroidery. [3] swaddling clothes.

N–34 *Lip labour.*

IN the old Scripture I have often read,
The calfe without meale n'ere was offered;[1]
To figure to us, nothing more then this,
Without the heart, lip-labour[2] nothing is.

[1] Num. xv.9, "Then shall he bring with a bullock a meat-offering . . . of flour mingled with . . . oil." (*Meat* here refers to cakes of fine flour; Lev. ii.1). A calf is ordered sacrificed with such a "meat" offering in Lev. ix.2–4, but one may not "often read" of such conjunctions in the Bible. [2] Prov. xiv.23, "In all labour there is profit: but the talk of the lips tendeth only to penury"; Ps. xvii.1–3, "give ear unto my prayer that goeth not out of feigned lips. . . . Thou hast proved mine heart." Cf. Hos. xiv.2, "so will we render the calves of our lips."

N–35 *The Heart.*

IN Prayer the Lips ne're act the winning part,
Without the sweet concurrence of the Heart.

N–36 *Eare-rings.*

WHy wore th'Egyptians Jewells in the Eare?
But for to teach us, all the grace is there,
When we obey, by acting what we heare.

N–37 *Sin seen.*

WHen once the sin has fully acted been,
Then is the horror of the trespasse seen.

N–38 *Upon Time.*[1]

TIme was upon
The wing, to flie away;
And I cal'd on
Him but a while to stay;
But he'd be gone, 5
For ought that I could say.

He held out then,
A Writing, as he went;
And askt me, when
False man would be content 10
To pay agen,[2]
What God and Nature lent.

An houre-glasse,
In which were sands but few,
As he did passe, 15
He shew'd, and told me too,
Mine end near was,
And so away he flew.

[1] The similarity of this poem to those by George Herbert is apparent. [2] repay.

N-39 *His Petition.*

IF warre, or want shall make me grow so poore
As for to beg my bread from doore to doore;
Lord! let me never act that beggars part,
Who hath thee in his mouth, not in his heart.[1]
He who asks almes in that so sacred Name, 5
Without due reverence, playes the cheaters game.

[1] Ecclus. xxi.26, "The heart of fools is in their mouth, but the mouth of the wise is in their heart."

N-40 *To God.*

THou hast promis'd, Lord, to be
With me in my miserie;
Suffer me to be so bold,
As to speak, Lord, say and hold.[1]

[1] i.e. hold firm to what you have promised.

N–41 *His Letanie, to the Holy Spirit.*

1. IN the houre of my distresse,
When temptations me oppresse,
And when I my sins confesse,
Sweet Spirit comfort me!

2. When I lie within my bed,
Sick in heart, and sick in head,
And with doubts discomforted,
Sweet Spirit comfort me!

3. When the house doth sigh and weep,
And the world is drown'd in sleep,
Yet mine eyes the watch do keep;
Sweet Spirit comfort me!

4. When the artlesse Doctor sees
No one hope, but of his Fees,
And his skill runs on the lees;[1]
Sweet Spirit comfort me!

5. When his Potion and his Pill,
His,[2] or none, or little skill,
Meet for nothing, but to kill;
Sweet Spirit comfort me!

6. When the passing-bell doth tole,
And the Furies in a shole
Come to fright a parting soule;
Sweet Spirit comfort me!

7. When the tapers now burne blew,[3]
And the comforters are few,
And that number more then true;
Sweet Spirit comfort me!

8. When the Priest his last hath praid,
And I nod to what is said,
'Cause my speech is now decaid;
Sweet Spirit comfort me!

9. When (God knowes) I'm tost about,
Either with despaire, or doubt;
Yet before the glasse be out,
Sweet Spirit comfort me!

10. When the Tempter me pursu'th
With the sins of all my youth,
And halfe damns me with untruth;
Sweet Spirit comfort me!

11. When the flames and hellish cries
Fright mine eares, and fright mine eyes,
And all terrors me surprize;
Sweet Spirit comfort me!

12. When the Judgment is reveal'd,
And that open'd which was seal'd,[4]
When to Thee I have appeal'd;
Sweet Spirit comfort me!

[1] a drinking term: is drained to the last drop; i.e., is almost exhausted. Accordingly he is "artlesse" (stanza 4) in being without ability to cure or relieve the patient. [2] amended to "has" by some editors. [3] a sign of the presence of devils or evil spirits. [4] Rev. vi and viii.1.

N–42 *Thanksgiving.*

THanksgiving for a former, doth invite
God to bestow a second benefit.

N–43 *Cock-crow.*

BEll-man of Night, if I about shall go
For to denie my Master, do thou crow.
Thou stop'st S. *Peter* in the midst of sin;[1]
Stay me, by crowing, ere I do begin;
Better it is, premonish'd, for to shun 5
A sin, then fall to weeping when 'tis done.

[1] Matt. xxvi.74–75.

N–44

All things run well for the Righteous.

ADverse and prosperous Fortunes both work on
Here, for the righteous mans salvation:
Be he oppos'd, or be he not withstood,
All serve to th'Augmentation of his good.[1]

[1] Rom. viii.28, "all things work together for good, to them that love God."

N–45

Paine ends in Pleasure.

AFflictions bring us joy in times to come,
When sins, by stripes, to us grow wearisome.[1]

[1] John xvi.20, "ye shall be sorrowful, but your sorrow shall be turned into joy"; cf. Heb. xiii.11.

N–46

To God.

I'Le come, I'le creep, (though Thou dost threat)
Humbly unto Thy Mercy-seat:
When I am there, this then I'le do,
Give Thee a Dart, and Dagger too;
Next, when I have my faults confest, 5
Naked I'le shew a sighing brest;
Which if that can't Thy pittie wooe,
Then let Thy Justice do the rest,
And strike it through.

N–47

A Thanksgiving to God, for his House.

LOrd, Thou hast given me a cell
Wherein to dwell;
And little house, whose humble Roof
Is weather-proof;

Under the sparres of which I lie 5
Both soft, and drie;
Where Thou my chamber for to ward
Hast set a Guard
Of harmlesse thoughts, to watch and keep
Me, while I sleep. 10
Low is my porch, as is my Fate,
Both void of state;
And yet the threshold of my doore
Is worn by'th poore,
Who thither come, and freely get 15
Good words, or meat:
Like as my Parlour, so my Hall
And Kitchin's small:
A little Butterie, and therein
A little Byn, 20
Which keeps my little loafe of Bread
Unchipt, unflead:[1]
Some brittle sticks of Thorne or Briar
Make me a fire,
Close by whose living coale I sit, 25
And glow like it.
Lord, I confesse too, when I dine,
The Pulse is Thine,
And all those other Bits, that bee
There plac'd by Thee; 30
The Worts, the Purslain, and the Messe
Of Water-cresse,
Which of Thy kindnesse Thou hast sent;
And my content
Makes those, and my beloved Beet, 35
To be more sweet.
'Tis thou that crown'st my glittering Hearth
With guiltlesse mirth;
And giv'st me Wassaile Bowles to drink,
Spic'd to the brink. 40
Lord, 'tis thy plenty-dropping hand,
That soiles my land;
And giv'st me, for my Bushell sowne,
Twice ten for one:
Thou mak'st my teeming Hen to lay 45
Her egg each day:
Besides my healthfull Ewes to beare
Me twins each yeare:

The while the conduits of my Kine
Run Creame, (for Wine.) 50
All these, and better Thou dost send
Me, to this end,
That I should render, for my part,
A thankfull heart;
Which, fir'd with incense, I resigne, 55
As wholly Thine;
But the acceptance, that must be,
My Christ, by Thee.

[1] unflayed, i.e. intact, unaffected by mice or mould.

N–48 *To God.*

MAke, make me Thine, my gracious God,
Or with thy staffe, or with thy rod;[1]
And be the blow too what it will,
Lord, I will kisse it, though it kill:
Beat me, bruise me, rack me, rend me,[2] 5
Yet, in torments, I'le commend Thee:
Examine me with fire, and prove me
To the full, yet I will love Thee:
Nor shalt thou give so deep a wound,
But I as patient will be found. 10

[1] Here and in N-241 Herrick thinks that the rod of Ps. xxiii.4 ("thy rod and thy staff they comfort me") is a twig or switch used to deliver light blows. [2] Ps. vii.9, "the righteous God trieth the heart and reins"; Ps. xxvi.1–2, "Judge me, O Lord . . . Examine me . . . and prove me; try my reins and my heart."

N–49 *Another, to God.*

LOrd, do not beat me,
Since I do sob and crie,
And swowne away to die,
Ere Thou dost threat me.

Lord, do not scourge me, 5
If I by lies and oaths
Have soil'd my selfe, or cloaths,
But rather purge me.

N–50 *None truly happy here.*

HAppy's that man, to whom God gives
A stock of Goods, whereby he lives
Neer to the wishes of his heart:
No man is blest through ev'ry part.

N–51 *To his ever-loving God.*

CAn I not come to Thee, my God, for[1] these
So very-many-meeting hindrances,
That slack my pace; but yet not make me stay?
Who slowly goes, rids[2] (in the end) his way.
Cleere Thou my paths, or shorten Thou my miles, 5
Remove the barrs, or lift me o're the stiles:
Since rough the way is, help me when I call,
And take me up; or els prevent the fall.
I kenn my home; and it affords some ease,
To see far off the smoaking Villages. 10
Fain would I rest; yet covet not to die,
For feare of future-biting penurie:
No, no, (my God) Thou know'st my wishes be
To leave this life, not loving it, but Thee.

[1] because of. [2] makes progress along.

N–52 *Another.*

THou bidst me come; I cannot come; for why,
Thou dwel'st aloft, and I want wings to flie.
To mount my Soule, she must have pineons given;
For, 'tis no easie way from Earth to Heaven.

N–53 *To Death.*

THou bidst me come away,
And I'le no longer stay,
Then for to shed some teares
For faults of former yeares;

And to repent some crimes,
Done in the present times:
And next, to take a bit
Of Bread, and Wine with it:
To d'on my robes of love,[1]
Fit for the place above; 10
To gird my loynes about
With charity throughout;
And so to travaile hence
With feet of innocence:
These done, I'le onely crie 15
God mercy; and so die.

[1] Isa. lxi.10, "he hath clothed me with the garments of salvation, he hath covered me with the robe of righteousness."

N–54 *Neutrality loathsome.*

GOD will have all, or none; serve Him, or fall
Down before *Baal, Bel,* or *Belial:*[1]
Either be hot, or cold: God doth despise,
Abhorre, and spew out all Neutralities.[2]

[1] I Kings xviii.21, "if the Lord be God, follow him: but if Baal, then follow him." [2] Rev. iii.15–16, "I know thy works, that thou art neither cold nor hot: I would thou wert cold or hot. So then, because thou art lukewarm, . . . I will spue thee out of my mouth."

N–55 *Welcome what comes.*

WHatever comes, let's be content withall:
Among Gods Blessings, there is no one small.

N–56 *To his angrie God.*

THrough all the night
Thou dost me fright,
And hold'st mine eyes from sleeping;[1]
And day, by day,
My Cup can say, 5
My wine is mixt with weeping.[2]

Thou dost my bread
With ashes knead,
Each evening and each morrow:
Mine eye and eare 10
Do see, and heare
The coming in of sorrow.

Thy scourge of steele,
(Ay me!) I feele,
Upon me beating ever: 15
While my sick heart
With dismall smart
Is disacquainted never.

Long, long, I'm sure,
This can't endure; 20
But in short time 'twill please Thee,
My gentle God,
To burn the rod,
Or strike so as to ease me.

[1] Ps. lxxvii.4, "Thou holdest mine eyes waking." [2] Ps. cii.9, "I have eaten ashes like bread, and mingled my drink with weeping."

N–57 *Patience, or Comforts in Crosses.*[1]

ABundant plagues I late have had,
Yet none of these have made me sad:
For why, my Saviour, with the sense
Of suffring gives me patience.

[1] adversities.

N–58 *Eternitie.*

1 O Yeares! and Age! Farewell:
Behold I go,
Where I do know
Infinitie to dwell.

2 And these mine eyes shall see
All times, how they
Are lost i'th'Sea
Of vast Eternitie.

3 Where never Moone shall sway
The Starres; but she,
And Night, shall be
Drown'd in one endlesse Day.

N–59 *To his Saviour, a Child; a Present, by a child.*

GO prettie child, and beare this Flower
Unto thy little Saviour;
And tell Him, by that Bud now blown,
He is the *Rose of Sharon*[1] known:
When thou hast said so, stick it there 5
Upon his Bibb, or Stomacher:
And tell Him, (for good handsell[2] too)
That thou hast brought a Whistle new,
Made of a clean strait oaten reed,
To charme his cries, (at time of need:) 10
Tell Him, for Corall, thou hast none;
But if thou hadst, He sho'd have one;
But poore thou art, and knowne to be
Even as monilesse, as He.
Lastly, if thou canst win a kisse 15
From those mellifluous lips of his;[3]
Then never take a second on,
To spoile the first impression.

[1] Song of Sol. ii, chapter heading: "1 *The mutual love of Christ and his church*"; 1, "I am the rose of Sharon." [2] gift, initial payment, pledge. [3] Song of Sol. iv.3, "Thy lips are like a thread of scarlet, and thy speech is comely."

N–60 *The New-yeeres Gift.*

LEt others look for Pearle and Gold,
Tissues, or Tabbies[1] manifold:
One onely lock of that sweet Hay
Whereon the blessed Babie lay,
Or one poore Swadling-clout, shall be 5
The richest New-yeeres Gift to me.

[1] silk taffetas.

N–61 *To God.*

IF any thing delight me for to print
My Book, 'tis this; that *Thou, my God, art in't.*

N–62 *God, and the King.*

HOw am I bound to Two! God, who doth give
The mind; the King, the meanes whereby I live.

N–63 *Gods mirth, Mans mourning.*

WHere God is merry, there write down thy fears:
What He with laughter speaks, heare thou with tears.[1]

[1] Ps. ii.4–5, "He that sitteth in the heavens shall laugh: the Lord shall have them in derision. Then shall he speak unto them in his wrath"; Prov. i.26, "I also will laugh at your calamity; I will mock when your fear cometh."

N–64 *Honours are hindrances.*

GIve me Honours: what are these,
But the pleasing hindrances?
Stiles, and stops, and stayes, that come
In the way 'twixt me, and home:
Cleer the walk, and then shall I 5
To my heaven lesse run, then flie.

N–65 *The Parasceve, or Preparation.*[1]

TO a Love-Feast[2] we both invited are:
The figur'd Damask, or pure Diaper,[3]
Over the golden Altar now is spread,
With Bread, and Wine, and Vessells furnished;
The *sacred Towell*, and the *holy Eure*[4] 5
Are ready by, to make the Guests all pure:

Let's go (my *Alma*)[5] yet e're we receive,
Fit, fit it is, we have our *Parasceve.*
Who to that *sweet Bread*[6] unprepar'd doth come
Better he starv'd, then but to tast one crumme. 10

[1] Mark xv.42, "when the even was come (because it was the preparation, that is, the day before the sabbath)." [2] a meal in token of brotherly love eaten by the early Christians in connection with the Eucharist; Herrick uses it poetically for the sacrament of the Lord's Supper. [3] linen. [4] ewer, flagon. [5] Soul. [6] the consecrated bread.

N–66 *To God.*

GOD gives not onely corne, for need,
But likewise sup'rabundant seed;
Bread for our service, bread for shew;
Meat for our meales, and fragments too:
He gives not poorly, taking some 5
Between the finger, and the thumb;
But, for our glut, and for our store,
Fine flowre prest down, and running o're.

N–67 *A will to be working.*

ALthough we cannot turne the fervent fit
Of sin, we must strive 'gainst the streame of it:
And howsoe're we have the conquest mist;
'Tis for our glory, that we did resist.

N–68 *Christs part.*

CHRIST, He requires still, wheresoere He comes,
To feed, or lodge, to have the best of Roomes:
Give Him the choice; grant Him the nobler part
Of all the House: the best of all's the Heart.

N–69 *Riches and Poverty.*

GOD co'd have made all rich, or all men poore;
But why He did not, let me tell wherefore:
Had all been rich, where then had Patience been?
Had all been poore, who had His Bounty seen?

N–70 *Sobriety in Search.*

TO seek of[1] God more then we well can find,
Argues a strong distemper of the mind.

[1] To try to find knowledge and insight into the nature of. Cf. Adam's last speech in *Paradise Lost* XII, 557–60: "Greatly instructed I shall hence depart, / Greatly in peace of thought, and have my fill / Of knowledge, what this vessel can contain; / Beyond which was my folly to aspire."

N–71 *Almes.*

GIve, if thou canst, an Almes; if not, afford,
Instead of that, a sweet and gentle word:
God crowns our goodnesse, where so ere He sees,
On our part, wanting all abilities.

N–72 *To his Conscience.*

CAn I not sin, but thou wilt be
My private *Protonotarie*?[1]
Can I not wooe thee to passe by
A short and sweet iniquity?
I'le cast a mist and cloud, upon 5
My delicate transgression,
So utter dark, as that no eye
Shall see the hug'd[2] impietie:
Gifts blind the wise,[3] and bribes do please,
And winde[4] all other witnesses: 10
And wilt not thou, with gold, be ti'd
To lay thy pen and ink aside?

That in the mirk[5] and tonguelesse night,
Wanton I may, and thou not write?
It will not be: And, therefore, now, 15
For times to come, I'le make this Vow,
From aberrations to live free;
So I'le not feare the Judge, or thee.

[1] chief recording clerk in a court. [2] hugged, cherished. Cf. Job xxiv.15, where the sinner "waiteth for the twilight, saying, No eye shall see me." [3] Deut. xvi.19, "a gift doth blind the eyes of the wise." [4] pervert. [5] murky.

N–73 *To his Saviour.*

LORD, I confesse, that Thou alone art able
To purifie this my *Augean* stable:[1]
Be the Seas water, and the Land all Sope,
Yet if Thy Bloud not wash me, there's no hope.

[1] The stables of Augeas, King of Elis, contained a thirty-year accumulation of filth from 3000 oxen. Hercules (sometimes regarded as a type of Christ) was set the task of cleansing the stable.

N–74 *To God.*

GOD is all-sufferance[1] here; here He doth show
No Arrow nockt,[2] onely a stringlesse Bow:[3]
His Arrowes flie; and all his stones are hurl'd
Against the wicked, in another world.

[1] Ps. lxxxvi.15, "But thou, O Lord, art a God full of compassion, and gracious: long-suffering, and plenteous in mercy and truth." [2] notched to fit a bowstring. To make his point that God punishes the wicked with the arrows and stones of His wrath in the afterlife, Herrick concentrates on the numerous scriptural passages which call God all-suffering and ignores those in which He readies his arrows (Ps. xxi.12) or will let them fly in this world (e.g. Numb. xxiv.8, Ps. xxxviii.2). [3] the rainbow signifying God's covenant with Noah and his descendants, Gen. ix.11–17.

N–75 *His Dreame.*

I Dreamt, last night, Thou didst transfuse
Oyle from Thy Jarre, into my creuze;
And powring still, Thy wealthy store,
The vessell full, did then run ore:
Me thought, I did Thy bounty chide, 5
To see the waste; but 'twas repli'd
By Thee, Deare God, God gives man seed
Oft-times for wast, as for his need.
Then I co'd say, that house is bare,
That has not bread, and some to spare. 10

N–76 *Gods Bounty.*

GOds Bounty, that ebbs lesse and lesse,
As men do wane in thankfulnesse.

N–77 *To his sweet Saviour.*[1]

NIght hath no wings, to him that cannot sleep;
And Time seems then, not for to flie, but creep;
Slowly her chariot drives, as if that she
Had broke her wheele, or crackt her axeltree.
Just so it is with me, who list'ning, pray 5
The winds, to blow the tedious night away;
That I might see the cheerfull peeping day.
Sick is my heart; O Saviour! do Thou please
To make my bed soft in my sicknesses:
Lighten my candle, so that I beneath 10
Sleep not for ever in the vaults of death:[2]
Let me Thy voice betimes i'th morning heare;[3]
Call, and I'le come; say Thou, the when, and where:
Draw me, but first, and after Thee I'le run,
And make no one stop, till my race be done. 15

[1] Martin suggests that Herrick had in mind Quarles, *Emblems* (1635), I, xiv, on Ps. xiii.3, "lighten mine eyes"; III, i, on Isa. xxvi.9, "My soul hath desired thee in the night"; and (for lines 14–15), IV, viii, on Song of Sol. i.3–4, "Draw me; we will follow

[*margin:* or run] after thee by the favour of thy good Oyntments." [2] Ps. xviii.28, "For thou wilt light my candle: the Lord my God will enlighten my darkness." [3] Ps. cxliii.8, "Cause me to hear thy loving-kindness in the morning."

N–78 *His Creed.*

I Do believe, that die I must,
And be return'd from out my dust:
I do believe, that when I rise,
Christ I shall see, with these same eyes:[1]
I do believe, that I must come, 5
With others, to the dreadfull Doome:
I do believe, the bad must goe
From thence, to everlasting woe:
I do believe, the good, and I,
Shall live with Him eternally: 10
I do believe, I shall inherit
Heaven, by Christs mercies, not my merit:
I do believe, the One in Three,
And Three in perfect Unitie:
Lastly, that JESUS is a Deed 15
Of Gift from God: *And heres my Creed.*

[1] Job xix.26, "yet in my flesh shall I see God."

N–79 *Temptations.*

TEmptations hurt not, though they have accesse:
Satan o'recomes none, but by willingnesse.

N–80 *The Lamp.*

WHen a mans Faith is frozen up, as dead;
Then is the Lamp and oyle extinguished.

N–81 *Sorrowes.*

SOrrowes our portion are: Ere hence we goe,
Crosses we must have; or, hereafter woe.

N–82 *Penitencie.*

A Mans transgression God do's then remit,
When man he makes a Penitent for it.

N–83

The Dirge of Jephthahs *Daughter:*[1] *sung by the Virgins.*

1 O Thou, the wonder of all dayes!
O Paragon, and Pearle of praise!
O Virgin-martyr, ever blest
Above the rest
Of all the Maiden-Traine! We come,
And bring fresh strewings to thy Tombe.

2 Thus, thus, and thus we compasse round
Thy harmlesse and unhaunted Ground;
And as we sing thy Dirge, we will
The Daffadill,
And other flowers, lay upon
(The Altar of our love) thy Stone.

3 Thou wonder of all Maids, li'st here,
Of Daughters all, the Deerest Deere;
The eye[2] of Virgins; nay, the Queen
Of this smooth Green,
And all sweet Meades; from whence we get
The Primrose, and the Violet.

4 Too soon, too deere did *Jephthah* buy,
By thy sad losse, our liberty:
His was the Bond and Cov'nant, yet
Thou paid'st the debt,
Lamented Maid! he won the day,
But for the conquest thou didst pay.

5 Thy Father brought with him along
The Olive branch, and Victors Song:
He slew the Ammonites, we know,
But to thy woe;
And in the purchase of our Peace,
The Cure was worse then the Disease.

6 For which obedient zeale of thine,
We offer here, before thy Shrine,
Our sighs for Storax, teares for Wine;
And to make fine,
And fresh thy Herse-cloth,[3] we will, here,
Foure times bestrew thee ev'ry yeere.

7 Receive, for this thy praise, our teares:
Receive this offering of our Haires:[4]
Receive these Christall Vialls fil'd
With teares, distil'd
From teeming eyes; to these we bring,
Each Maid, her silver Filleting,

8 To guild thy Tombe; besides, these Caules,[5]
These Laces, Ribbands, and these Faules,[6]
These Veiles, wherewith we use to hide
The Bashfull Bride,
When we conduct her to her Groome:
All, all we lay upon thy Tombe.

9 No more, no more, since thou art dead,
Shall we ere bring coy Brides to bed;
No more, at yeerly Festivalls
We Cowslip balls,
Or chaines of Columbines shall make,
For this, or that occasions sake.

10 No, no; our Maiden-pleasures be
Wrapt in the winding-sheet, with thee:
'Tis we are dead, though not i'th grave:
Or, if we have
One seed of life left, 'tis to keep
A Lent for thee, to fast and weep.

11 Sleep in thy peace, thy bed of Spice;
And make this place all Paradise:
May Sweets grow here! and smoke from hence,
Fat Frankincense:
Let Balme, and Cassia send their scent
From out thy Maiden-Monument.

12 May no Wolfe howle, or Screech-Owle stir
A wing about thy Sepulcher!
No boysterous winds, or stormes, come hither,
To starve, or wither
Thy soft sweet Earth! but (like a spring)
Love keep it ever flourishing.

13 May all shie Maids, at wonted hours,
Come forth, to strew thy Tombe with flow'rs:
May Virgins, when they come to mourn,
Male-Incense[7] burn
Upon thine Altar! then return,
And leave thee sleeping in thy Urn.

[1] Jephthah's daughter allowed herself to be sacrificed in fulfillment of her father's vow to offer up whatever came to meet him from his house if he defeated the Ammonites; "the daughters of Israel went yearly to lament with [*margin:* or talk with] the daughter of Jephthah the Gileadite four days in a year." Before the sacrifice "she went with her companions, and bewailed her virginity upon the mountains." (Judges xi.30–40). [2] most cherished. [3] i.e. the turf or tomb covering her. Cf. stanza 8. [4] in token of grief. Cf. Jer. vii.29, "Cut off thine hair, O Jerusalem, and cast it away, and take up a lamentation on the high places." [5] netted caps or hairnets. [6] falls: veils which fall down over the face or collars which fall flat round the neck. [7] See H-856, n.1.

N–84 *To God, on his sicknesse.*

WHat though my Harp, and Violl[1] be
Both hung upon the Willow-tree?[2]
What though my bed be now my grave,
And for my house I darknesse have?[3]
What though my healthfull dayes are fled, 5
And I lie numbred with the dead?
Yet I have hope, by Thy great power,
To spring; though now a wither'd flower.

[1] Isa. v.11–12, "Woe unto them that rise up early in the morning, that they may follow strong drink, that continue until night, till wine inflame them. And the harp and the viol . . . are in their feasts: but they regard not the work of the Lord." [2] Ps. cxxxvii.2, "We hanged our harps upon the willows." [3] Job xvii.13, "the grave is mine house: I have made my bed in the darkness."

N–85 *Sins loath'd, and yet lov'd.*

SHame checks our first attempts; but then 'tis prov'd,
Sins first dislik'd, are after that belov'd.

N–86 *Sin.*

SIn leads the way, but as it goes, it feels
The following plague still treading on his heels.

N–87 *Upon God.*

GOD when He takes my goods and chattels hence,
Gives me a portion, giving patience:
What is in God is God; if so it be,
He patience gives; He gives himselfe to me.

N–88 *Faith.*

WHat here we hope for, we shall once[1] inherit:
By Faith we all walk here, not by the Spirit.[2]

[1] at some future time, once and for all. [2] Gal. v.5, "For we through the Spirit, wait for the hope of righteousness by faith." Gal. v.16, "Walk in the Spirit, and ye shall not fulfil the lust of the flesh."

N–89 *Humility.*

HUmble we must be, if to Heaven we go:
High is the roof there; but the gate is low:
When e're thou speak'st, look with a lowly eye:
Grace is increased by humility.[1]

[1] Prov. iii.34, "he giveth grace unto the lowly."

N–90 *Teares.*

OUr present Teares here (not our present laughter)
Are but the handsells of[1] our joyes hereafter.

[1] token payments for; pledges of sincerity requisite to.

N–91 *Sin and Strife.*

AFter true sorrow for our sinnes, our strife
Must last with Satan, to the end of life.

N–92 *An Ode, or Psalme, to God.*

DEer God,
If thy smart Rod
Here did not make me sorrie,
I sho'd not be
With Thine, or Thee, 5
In Thy eternall Glorie.

But since
Thou didst convince[1]
My sinnes, by gently striking;
Add still to those 10
First stripes, new blowes,
According to Thy liking.

Feare me,[2]
Or scourging teare me;
That thus from vices driven, 15
I may from Hell
Flie up, to dwell
With Thee, and Thine in Heaven.

[1] overcome. [2] make me afraid.

N–93 *Graces for Children.*

WHat God gives, and what we take,
'Tis a gift for Christ His sake:
Be the meale of Beanes and Pease,
God be thank'd for those, and these:
Have we flesh, or have we fish, 5
All are Fragments from His dish.
He His Church save, and the King,
And our Peace here, like a Spring,
Make it ever flourishing.

N–94 *God to be first serv'd.*

HOnour thy Parents; but good manners call
Thee to adore thy God, the first of all.

N–95 *Another Grace for a Child.*

HEre a little child I stand,
Heaving up my either hand;
Cold as Paddocks[1] though they be,
Here I lift them up to Thee,
For a Benizon[2] to fall 5
On our meat, and on us all. *Amen.*

[1] frogs or toads. [2] blessing.

N–96

A Christmas Caroll, *sung to the King in the Presence at* White-Hall.

Chor. WHat sweeter musick can we bring,
Then a Caroll, for to sing
The Birth of this our heavenly King?
Awake the Voice! Awake the String!
Heart, Eare, and Eye, and every thing 5

Awake! the while the active Finger
Runs division[1] with the Singer.

From the Flourish[2] they came to the Song.[3]

1 Dark and dull night, flie hence away,
And give the honour to this Day,
That sees *December* turn'd to *May*. 10

2 If we may ask the reason, say;
The why, and wherefore all things here
Seem like the Spring-time of the yeere?

3 Why do's the chilling Winters morne
Smile, like a field beset with corne? 15
Or smell, like to a Meade new-shorne,
Thus, on the sudden? 4. Come and see
The cause, why things thus fragrant be:
'Tis He is borne, whose quickning Birth
Gives life and luster, publike mirth, 20
To Heaven, and the under-Earth.

Chor. We see Him come, and know him ours,
Who, with His Sun-shine, and His showers,
Turnes all the patient ground to flowers.

1 The Darling of the world is come, 25
And fit it is, we finde a roome
To welcome Him. 2. The nobler part
Of all the house here, is the heart,

Chor. Which we will give Him; and bequeath
This Hollie, and this Ivie Wreath, 30
To do Him honour; who's our King,
And Lord of all this Revelling.

The Musicall Part[4] was composed by
Master Henry Lawes.[5]

[1] divides a succession of long notes into many small ones. [2] fanfare of horns, trumpets, or the like. [3] the numbers indicate different voices. [4] not extant. [5] See H-851.

N–97

The New-yeeres Gift, or Circumcisions[1] *Song, sung to the King in the Presence at White-Hall.*

1 PRepare for Songs; He's come, He's come;
And be it sin here to be dumb,
And not with Lutes to fill the roome.

2 Cast Holy Water all about,
And have a care no fire gos out, 5
But 'cense the porch, and place throughout.

3 The Altars all on fier be;
The Storax fries; and ye may see,
How heart and hand do all agree,
To make things sweet. *Chor.* Yet all less sweet then He. 10

4 Bring Him along, most pious Priest,
And tell us then, when as thou seest
His gently-gliding, Dove-like eyes,
And hear'st His whimp'ring, and His cries;
How canst thou this Babe circumcise? 15

5 Ye must not be more pitifull then wise;
For, now unlesse ye see Him bleed,
Which makes the Bapti'me; 'tis decreed,
The Birth is fruitlesse: *Chor.* Then the *work God speed.*

1 Touch gently, gently touch; and here 20
Spring Tulips up through all the yeere;
And from His sacred Bloud, here shed,
May Roses grow, to crown His own deare Head.

Chor. Back, back again; each thing is done
With zeale alike, as 'twas begun; 25
Now singing, homeward let us carrie
The Babe unto His Mother *Marie;*
And when we have the Child commended
To her warm bosome, then our Rites are ended.

Composed by Master *Henry Lawes.*

[1] the festival of the Circumcision of Christ, Jan. 1.

N–98

Another New-yeeres Gift, or Song for the Circumcision.

1 HEnce, hence prophane, and none appeare
With any thing unhallowed, here:
No jot of Leven[1] must be found
Conceal'd in this most holy Ground:

2 What is corrupt, or sowr'd with sin, 5
Leave that without, then enter in;
Chor. But let no Christmas mirth begin
Before ye purge, and circumcise
Your hearts, and hands, lips, eares, and eyes.

3 Then, like a perfum'd Altar, see 10
That all things sweet, and clean may be:
For, here's a Babe, that (like a *Bride*)
Will *blush to death,* if ought be spi'd
Ill-scenting, or unpurifi'd.

Chor. The room is cens'd: help, help t'invoke 15
Heaven to come down, the while we choke
The Temple, with a cloud of smoke.

4 Come then, and gently touch the Birth
Of Him, who's Lord of Heav'n and Earth;

5 And softly handle Him: y'ad need, 20
Because the *prettie Babe* do's bleed.
Poore-pittied Child! who from Thy Stall
Bring'st, in Thy Blood, a Balm, that shall
Be the best New-yeares Gift to all.

1 Let's blesse the Babe: And, as we sing 25
His praise; so let us blesse the King:

Chor. Long may He live, till He hath told
His New-yeeres trebled to His old:[2]
And, when that's done, to re-aspire
A new-borne *Phœnix* from His own chast fire.[3] 30

[1] Exod. xxxiv.25, "Thou shalt not offer the blood of my sacrifice with leaven." Cf. I Cor. v.6–8. [2] Long may King Charles I live, until he has counted or lived a number of New Years which is three

times the number that he has already lived. [3] i.e. after his death may he live again in his son, the product of his own chaste love for his Queen.

N–99 *Gods Pardon.*

WHen I shall sin, pardon my trespasse here;
For, once in hell, none knowes Remission there.

N–100 *Sin.*

SIn once[1] reacht up to Gods eternall Sphere,
And was committed, not remitted there.

[1] when Satan rebelled.

N–101 *Evill.*

EVill no Nature hath; the losse of good
Is that which gives to sin a livelihood.

N–102

The Star-Song:[1] A Caroll to the King; sung at White-Hall.

The Flourish of Musick: then followed the Song

1 TEll us, thou cleere and heavenly Tongue,
Where is the Babe but lately sprung?
Lies He the Lillie-banks among?[2]

2 Or say, if this new Birth of ours
Sleeps, laid within some Ark of Flowers, 5
Spangled with deaw-light; thou canst cleere
All doubts, and manifest the where.

3 Declare to us, bright Star, if we shall seek
Him in the Mornings blushing cheek,
Or search the beds of Spices through, 10
To find him out?

Star. No, this ye need not do;
But only come, and see Him rest
A Princely Babe in's Mothers Brest.

Chor. He's seen, He's seen, why then a Round, 15
Let's kisse the sweet and holy ground;
And all rejoyce, that we have found
A King, before conception crown'd.

4 Come then, come then, and let us bring
Unto our prettie *Twelfth-Tide King*, 20
Each one his severall offering;

Chor. And when night comes, wee'l give Him wassailing:
And that His treble Honours[3] may be seen,
Wee'l chuse Him King, and make His Mother Queen.

[1] sung for the Epiphany, the festival commemorating the manifestation of Christ to the Gentiles, represented by the three Magi. It was celebrated on the twelfth day after Christmas, Jan. 6. On a secular level the poem may also be a compliment to King Charles and his Queen on the birth of Prince Charles, which was accompanied by a noonday star. See notes on the prefatory poem to *Hesperides*. [2] Song of Sol. ii.16, "he feedeth among the lillies." [3] the gifts of gold, frankincense, and myrrh, brought by the Magi.

N–103 *To God.*

WIth golden Censers, and with Incense, here,
Before Thy Virgin-Altar I appeare,
To pay Thee that I owe, since what I see
In, or without; all, all belongs to Thee:
Where shall I now begin to make, for one 5
Least loane of Thine, half Restitution?
Alas! I cannot pay a jot; therefore
I'le kisse the Tally,[1] and confesse the score.[2]
Ten thousand Talents lent me, Thou dost write:
'Tis true, my God; *but I can't pay one mite.* 10

[1] stick, on one side of which notches were cut to show the amount of a debt. [2] and acknowledge the amount owed.

N–104 *To his deere God.*

I'Le hope no more,
For things that will not come;
And, if they do, they prove but cumbersome;
Wealth brings much woe:
And, since it fortunes so; 5
'Tis better to be poore,
Then so t'abound,
As to be drown'd,
Or overwhelm'd with store.

Pale care, avant, 10
I'le learn to be content
With that small stock, Thy Bounty gave or lent.
What may conduce
To my most healthfull use,
Almighty God me grant; 15
But that, or this,
That hurtfull is,
Denie Thy suppliant.

N–105 *To God, his good will.*

GOld I have none, but I present my need,
O Thou, that crown'st the will, where wants the deed.
Where Rams are wanting, or large Bullocks thighs,
There a poor Lamb's a plenteous sacrifice.
Take then his Vowes, who, if he had it, would 5
Devote to Thee, both incense, myrrhe, and gold,
Upon an Altar rear'd by Him, and crown'd
Both with the *Rubie, Pearle,* and *Diamond.*

N–106 *On Heaven.*

PErmit mine eyes to see
Part, or the whole of Thee,
O happy place!
Where all have Grace,
And Garlands shar'd, 5
For their reward;

Where each chast Soule
In long white stole,
And Palmes in hand,
Do ravisht stand; 10
So in a ring,
The praises sing
Of Three in One,
That fill the Throne;
While Harps, and Violls then 15
To Voices, say, *Amen.*

N–107

The Summe, and the Satisfaction.

LAst night I drew up mine Account,
And found my Debits to amount
To such a height, as for to tell
How I sho'd pay, 's impossible:
Well, this I'le do; my mighty score 5
Thy mercy-seat I'le lay before;
But therewithall I'le bring the Band,[1]
Which, in full force, did daring[2] stand,
Till my Redeemer (on the Tree)
Made void for millions, as for me. 10
Then, if Thou bidst me pay, or go
Unto the prison, I'le say, no;
Christ having paid, I nothing owe:
For, this is sure, the Debt is dead
By Law, the Bond once *cancelled.* 15

[1] bond; covenant for a debt. [2] terrifying.

N–108

Good men afflicted most.

GOD makes not good men wantons,[1] but doth bring
Them to the field,[2] and, there, to skirmishing;
With trialls those, with terrors these He proves,
And hazards those most, whom the most He loves:
For *Sceva,*[3] darts; for *Cocles,*[4] dangers; thus 5
He finds a fire for mighty *Mutius;*[5]
Death for stout *Cato;*[6] and besides all these,
A poyson too He has for *Socrates;*

Torments for high *Attilius;*[7] and, with want,
Brings in *Fabricius*[8] for a Combatant: 10
But, bastard-slips,[9] and such as He dislikes,
He never brings them once to th'push of Pikes.

[1] spoiled, undisciplined persons. Seneca, *De Providentia,* I, 6; trans. Thomas Lodge (1614): "He maketh not a good man a wanton." [2] battlefield; ibid. III, 4: "fortune . . . seeketh for the strongest to match her . . . attempteth the most confident and couragious sort of men . . . tryeth her fire upon *Mutius,* povertie in *Fabricius,* banishment in *Rutilus,* torments in *Regulus,* poyson in *Socrates,* death in *Cato.*" [3] Scaeva, a centurion in Caesar's army, caught 120 darts on his shield at the siege of Dyrrachium. [4] Horatius Cocles defended the bridgehead leading to Rome against the Etruscans while the bridge was being destroyed. See Macaulay's *Lays of Ancient Rome.* [5] Mutius, called *Scaevola,* "left-handed," because, as a prisoner, he held his right hand in a fire, thus showing indifference to death. [6] Cato of Utica philosophically committed suicide when his military situation was hopeless. See Addison's *Cato* (1713) and the first canto of Dante's *Purgatorio.* [7] Atilius Regulus, a prisoner of the Carthaginians, was sent by them to Rome to propose peace, under oath to return if he failed to obtain it. He advised the Romans to continue the war and then returned to torture and death in Carthage. [8] Fabricius Luscinus, though a man "with want," that is, a lack of possessions, resisted the efforts of King Pyrrhus to corrupt him with wealth. [9] See H-859, n.1.

N–109 *Good Christians.*

PLay their offensive and defensive parts,
Till they be hid o're with a wood of darts.[1]

[1] See N-108, n.3.

N–110 *The Will the cause of Woe.*

WHen man is punisht, he is plagued still,
Not for the fault of Nature, but of will.

N–111 *To Heaven.*

OPen thy gates
To him, who weeping waits,
And might come in,
But that held back by sin.
Let mercy be 5
So kind, to set me free,
And I will strait
Come in, or force the gate.

N–112 *The Recompence.*

ALL I have lost, that co'd be rapt from me;
And fare it well: yet *Herrick*, if so be
Thy Deerest Saviour renders thee but one
Smile, that one smile's full restitution.

N–113 *To God.*

PArdon me God, (once more I Thee intreat)
That I have plac'd Thee in so meane a seat,
Where round about Thou seest but all things vaine,
Uncircumcis'd, unseason'd, and prophane.
But as Heavens publike and immortall Eye 5
Looks on the filth, but is not soil'd thereby;
So Thou, my God, may'st on this impure look,
But take no tincture from my sinfull Book:
Let but one beame of Glory on it shine,
And that will make me, and my Work divine. 10

N–114 *To God.*

LOrd, I am like to *Misletoe*,
Which has no root, and cannot grow,
Or prosper, but by that same tree
It clings about; so I by Thee.

What need I then to feare at all, 5
So long as I about Thee craule?
But if that Tree sho'd fall, and die,
Tumble shall heav'n, and down will I.

N–115 *His wish to God.*

I Would to God, that mine old age might have
Before my last, but here a living grave,
Some one poore Almes-house; there to lie, or stir,
Ghost-like, as in my meaner sepulcher;
A little piggin,[1] and a pipkin[2] by, 5
To hold things fitting my necessity;
Which, rightly us'd, both in their time and place,
Might me excite to fore, and after-grace.
Thy Crosse, my *Christ*, fixt 'fore mine eyes sho'd be,
Not to adore that, but to worship Thee. 10
So, here the remnant of my dayes I'd spend,
Reading Thy Bible, and my Book; *so end.*

[1] a small pail, usually of wood. [2] a small earthenware pot.

N–116 *Satan.*

WHen we 'gainst Satan stoutly fight, the more
He teares and tugs us, then he did before;
Neglecting once to cast a frown on those
Whom ease makes his, without the help of blowes.

N–117 *Hell.*

HEll is no other, but a soundlesse[1] pit,
Where no one beame of comfort peeps in it.

[1] fathomless.

N–118

The way.

WHen I a ship see on the Seas,
Cuft with those watrie savages,[1]
And therewithall, behold, it hath
In all that way no beaten path;
Then, with a wonder, I confesse, 5
Thou art our way i'th wildernesse:[2]
And while we blunder in the dark,
Thou art our candle there, or spark.

[1] buffeted by those watery rugged wildernesses. [2] Isa. xliii.19, "I will even make a way in the wilderness."

N–119

Great grief, great glory.

THe lesse our sorrowes here and suffrings cease,
The more our Crownes of Glory there increase.

N–120

Hell.

HEll is the place where whipping-cheer[1] abounds,
But no one Jailor[2] there to wash the wounds.

[1] flogging (a jocular usage). [2] i.e. no one is Jailor. When St. Paul and St. Silas were whipped in Philippi, their jailer was converted and washed their wounds (Acts xvi.23–33).

N–121

The Bell-man.

ALong the dark, and silent night,
With my Lantern, and my Light,
And the tinkling of my Bell,
Thus I walk, and this I tell:
Death and dreadfulnesse call on, 5
To the gen'rall Session;
To whose dismall Barre, we there
All accompts must come to cleere:

Scores of sins w'ave made here many,
Wip't out few, (God knowes) if any. 10
Rise ye Debters then, and fall
To make paiment, while I call.
Ponder this, when I am gone;
By the clock 'tis almost *One*.

N–122 *The goodnesse of his God.*

WHen Winds and Seas do rage,
And threaten to undo me,
Thou dost their wrath asswage,
If I but call unto Thee.

A mighty storm last night 5
Did seek my soule to swallow,
But by the peep of light
A gentle calme did follow.

What need I then despaire,
Though ills stand round about me; 10
Since mischiefs neither dare
To bark, or bite, without Thee?[1]

[1] without permission from Thee.

N–123 *The Widdowes teares: or, Dirge of* Dorcas.[1]

1. COme pitie us, all ye, who see
Our Harps hung on the Willow-tree:
Come pitie us, ye Passers by,
Who see, or heare poor Widdowes crie:
Come pitie us; and bring your eares, 5
And eyes, to pitie Widdowes teares.
Chor. And when you are come hither;
Then we will keep
A Fast, and weep
Our eyes out all together. 10

2. For *Tabitha*, who dead lies here,
Clean washt, and laid out for the Beere;
O modest Matrons, weep and waile!
For now the Corne and Wine must faile:

The Basket and the Bynn of Bread, 15
Wherewith so many soules were fed
Chor. Stand empty here for ever:
And ah! the Poore,
At thy worne Doore,
Shall be releeved never. 20

3. Woe worth[2] the Time, woe worth the day,
That reav'd[3] us of thee *Tabitha!*
For we have lost, with thee, the Meale,
The Bits, the Morsells, and the deale[4]
Of gentle Paste, and yeelding Dow, 25
That Thou on Widdowes didst bestow.
Chor. All's gone, and Death hath taken
Away from us
Our Maundie;[5] thus,
Thy Widdowes stand forsaken. 30

4. Ah *Dorcas, Dorcas!* now adieu
We bid the Creuse[6] and Pannier too:
I and the flesh, for and[7] the fish,
Dol'd to us in That Lordly dish.
We take our leaves now of the Loome, 35
From whence the house-wives cloth did come:
Chor. The web affords now nothing;
Thou being dead,
The woosted thred
Is cut, that made us clothing. 40

5. Farewell the Flax and Reaming[8] wooll,
With which thy house was plentifull.
Farewell the Coats, the Garments, and
The Sheets, the Rugs, made by thy hand.
Farewell thy Fier and thy Light, 45
That ne're went out by Day or Night:
Chor. No, or thy zeale so speedy,
That found a way
By peep of day,
To feed and cloth the Needy. 50

6. But, ah, alas! the Almond Bough,
And Olive Branch is wither'd now.
The Wine Presse now is ta'ne from us,
The Saffron and the Calamus.[9]
The Spice and Spiknard hence is gone, 55
The Storax and the Cynamon,

Chor. The Caroll of our gladnesse
Ha's taken wing,
And our late spring
Of mirth is turn'd to sadnesse. 60

7. How wise wast thou in all thy waies!
How worthy of respect and praise!
How Matron-like didst thou go drest!
How soberly above the rest
Of those that prank it with their Plumes; 65
And jet it with their choice purfumes.
Chor. Thy vestures were not flowing:
Nor did the street
Accuse thy feet
Of mincing in their going. 70

8. And though thou here li'st dead, we see
A deale of beauty yet in thee.
How sweetly shewes thy smiling face,
Thy lips with all diffused grace![10]
Thy hands (though cold) yet spotlesse, white, 75
And comely as the Chrysolite.[11]
Chor. Thy belly like a hill is,
Or as a neat
Cleane heap of wheat,
All set about with Lillies.[12] 80

Sleep with thy beauties here, while we
Will shew these garments made by thee;
These were the Coats, in these are read
The monuments of *Dorcas* dead.
These were thy Acts, and thou shalt have 85
These hung, as honours o're thy Grave,
Chor. And after us (distressed)
Sho'd fame be dumb;
Thy very Tomb
Would cry out, *Thou art blessed.* 90

[1] a dirge for Dorcas, also known as Tabitha. She was a woman "full of good works, and alms-deeds which she did." But she died and St. Peter was brought to the room where her corpse lay; "and all the widows stood by him weeping, and showing the coats and garments which Dorcas made while she was with them" (Acts ix.32–39). [2] a curse upon. [3] bereaved. [4] portions. [5] alms. [6] cruse, containing wine or oil for them. [7] and also. [8] foamy. [9] an aromatic plant (Exod. xxx.23, "sweet calamus"). [10] Ps. xlv.2,

"grace is poured into thy lips." [11] a precious stone of a transparent gold color mixed with green; peridot. [12] Song of Sol. vii.2, "thy belly is like an heap of wheat, set about with lilies."

N–124 *To God, in time of plundering.*

RApine has yet tooke nought from me;
But if it please my God, I be
Brought at the last to th'utmost bit,
God make me thankfull still for it.
I have been gratefull for my store: 5
Let me say grace when there's no more.

N–125 *To his Saviour. The New yeers gift.*

THat little prettie bleeding part
Of Foreskin send to me:
And Ile returne a bleeding Heart,
For New-yeers gift to thee.

Rich is the Jemme that thou did'st send, 5
Mine's faulty too, and small:
But yet this Gift Thou wilt commend,
Because I send Thee *all*.

N–126 *Doomes-Day.*

LEt not that Day Gods Friends and Servants scare:
The Bench is then their place;[1] and not the Barre.

[1] I Cor. vi.2, "the saints shall judge the world."

N–127 *The Poores Portion.*

THe sup'rabundance of my store,
That is the portion of the poore:
Wheat, Barley, Rie, or Oats; what is't
But he takes tole of? all the Griest.

Two raiments have I: *Christ* then makes
This Law;[1] that He and I part stakes.[2]
Or have I two loaves; then I use
The poore to cut, and I to chuse.[3]

Luke iii,11. [2] divide equally. [3] then my custom is to have the
oor divide them, after which I choose the half which I want.

N–128

The white Island: or place of the Blest.

IN this world (the *Isle of Dreames*)
While we sit by sorrowes streames,
Teares and terrors are our theames
Reciting:

But when once from hence we flie, 5
More and more approaching nigh
Unto young Eternitie
Uniting:

In that *whiter Island*, where
Things are evermore sincere; 10
Candor here, and lustre there
Delighting:

There no monstrous fancies shall
Out of hell an horrour call,
To create (or cause at all) 15
Affrighting.

There in calm and cooling sleep
We our eyes shall never steep;
But eternall watch shall keep,
Attending 20

Pleasures, such as shall pursue
Me immortaliz'd, and you;
And fresh joyes, as never too
Have ending.

N–129

To Christ.

I Crawle, I creep; my *Christ,* I come
To Thee, for curing *Balsamum:*
Thou hast, nay more, Thou art the Tree,
Affording salve of Soveraigntie.[1]
My mouth I'le lay unto Thy wound 5
Bleeding, that no Blood touch the ground:
For, rather then one drop shall fall
To wast, my JESU, I'le take all.

[1] supreme efficacy.

N–130

To God.

GOD! to my little meale and oyle,
Add but a bit of flesh, to boyle:
And Thou my Pipkinnet[1] shalt see,
Give a *wave-offring*[2] unto Thee.

[1] potlet. [2] In Exod. xxix.24 the Israelites are told to wave (*margin:* shake to and fro) certain offerings. Herrick refers to the movements of his mixture as it boils.

N–131

Free Welcome.

GOD He refuseth no man; but makes way
For All that now come, or hereafter may.

N–132

Gods Grace.

GODS Grace deserves here to be daily fed,
That, thus increast, it might be perfected.

N–133

Coming to Christ.

TO him, who longs unto his CHRIST to go,
Celerity even it self is slow.

N–134 *Correction.*

GOD had but one Son free from sin; but none
Of all His sonnes free from correction.

N–135 *Gods Bounty.*

GOD, as He's potent, so He's likewise known,
To give us more then Hope can fix upon.

N–136 *Knowledge.*

SCience in God, is known to be
A Substance, not a Qualitie.[1]

[1] i.e. God's knowledge is essential, not adventitious.

N–137 *Salutation.*

CHRIST, I have read, did to His Chaplains say,
Sending them forth, *Salute no man by'th way:*[1]
Not, that He taught His Ministers to be
Unsmooth, or sowre, to all civilitie;
But to instruct them, to avoid all snares
Of tardidation[2] in the Lords Affaires.
Manners are good: but till his errand ends,
Salute we must, nor Strangers, Kin, or Friends.

[1] Luke x.4. [2] delay.

N–138 *Lasciviousnesse.*

LAsciviousnesse is known to be
The sister to saturitie.[1]

[1] fullness, excess, or glut.

N–139 *Teares.*

GOD from our eyes all teares hereafter wipes,
And gives His Children kisses then, not stripes.

N–140 *Gods Blessing.*

IN vain our labours are, whatsoe're they be,
Unlesse God gives the *Benedicite.*

N–141 *God, and Lord.*

GOD, is His Name of Nature; but that word
Implies His Power, *when He's cal'd the LORD.*[1]

[1] i.e. as men are called men because it is their nature to be men, and angels are called angels because their nature is angelic, so God, in accordance with His nature, is called God; but when He is called the Lord, *that* word implies His power.

N–142 *The Judgment-Day*

GOD hides from man the reck'ning Day, that He
May feare it ever for uncertaintie:
That being ignorant of that one, he may
Expect the coming of it ev'ry day.

N–143 *Angells.*

ANgells are called Gods;[1] yet of them, none
Are Gods, but by *participation:*
As Just Men are intitled Gods, yet none
Are Gods, of them, but by Adoption.

[1] Ps. lxxxii.6—and frequently in *Paradise Lost.*

N–144

Long life.

THe longer thred of life we spin,
The more occasion still to sin.

N–145

Teares.

THe teares of Saints more sweet by farre,
Then all the songs of sinners are.

N–146

Manna.

THat Manna, which God on His people cast,
Fitted it self to ev'ry Feeders tast.[1]

[1] Wisd. of Sol. xvi.20: God sent his people "from heaven bread prepared without their labour, able to content every man's delight, and agreeing to every taste."

N–147

Reverence.

TRue rev'rence is (as *Cassiodore*[1] doth prove)
The feare of God, commixt with cleanly love.

[1] Cassiodorus, 6th-century statesman, historian, and divine: commentary on Ps. xxxiv.

N–148

Mercy.

MErcy, the wise Athenians held to be
Not an Affection,[1] but a *Deitie.*[2]

[1] i.e. not something merely in the mind. [2] According to Pausanias, *Attica,* I, 17, 1, there was an altar to the goddess Mercy in Athens.

N–149

Wages.

AFter this life, the wages shall
Not shar'd alike be unto all.

N–150

Temptation.

GOD tempteth no one (as S. *Aug'stine* saith)[1]
For any ill; but, for the proof of Faith:
Unto temptation God exposeth some;
But none, of purpose, to be overcome.

[1] Such statements occur frequently in St. Augustine's writings; e.g. Serm. II, on God's temptation of Abraham, and Epist. CCV, *Ad Consentium.*

N–151

Gods hands.

GOds Hands are round, and smooth, that gifts may fall
Freely from them, and hold none back at all.

N–152

Labour.

LAbour we must, and labour hard
I'th *Forum* here, or *Vineyard.*

N–153

Mora Sponsi, *the stay of the Bridegroome.*

THe time the Bridegroom stayes from hence,
Is but the time of penitence.

N–154 *Roaring.*[1]

ROaring is nothing but a weeping part,
Forc'd from the mighty dolour of the heart.

[1] an act of weeping. Cf. Ps. xxxviii.8–9, "I have roared by reason of the disquietness of my heart . . . and my groaning is not hid from thee."

N–155 *The Eucharist.*

HE that is hurt seeks help: sin is the wound;
The salve for this i'th Eucharist is found.

N–156 *Sin severely punisht.*

GOD in His own Day will be then severe,
To punish great sins, who small faults whipt here.

N–157 Montes Scripturarum, *the Mounts of the Scriptures.*

THe Mountains of the Scriptures are (some say)
Moses, and *Jesus,* called *Joshua:*
The *Prophets* Mountains of the Old are meant;
Th' *Apostles* Mounts of the *New Testament.*

N–158 *Prayer.*

A Prayer, that is said alone,
Starves, having no companion.
Great things ask for, when thou dost pray,
And those great are, which ne're decay.
Pray not for silver, rust eats this; 5
Ask not for gold, which metall is:
Nor yet for houses, which are here
But earth: *such vowes nere reach Gods eare.*

N–159 *Christs sadnesse.*

CHrist was not sad, i'th garden, for His own
Passion, but for His sheeps dispersion.

N–160 *God heares us.*

GOD, who's in Heav'n, will hear from thence;
If not to'th sound, yet, to the sense.

N–161 *God.*

GOD (as the learned *Damascen*[1] doth write)
A *Sea of Substance* is, *Indefinite.*

[1] St. John of Damascus, *De Fide Orthodoxa,* I, 9.

N–162 *Clouds.*

HE that ascended in a cloud, shall come
In clouds, descending to the publike *Doome.*

N–163 *Comforts in contentions.*

THe same, who crownes the Conquerour, will be
A Coadjutor in the Agonie.

N–164 *Heaven.*

HEav'n is most faire; but fairer He
That made that fairest Canopie.

N–165 *God.*

IN God there's nothing, but 'tis known to be
Ev'n God Himself, in perfect *Entitie.*

N–166 *His Power.*

GOD can do all things, save but what are known
For to imply a contradiction.

N–167 *Christs words on the Crosse,* My God, My God.[1]

CHrist, when He hung the dreadfull Crosse upon,
Had (as it were) a *Dereliction;*[2]
In this regard, in those great terrors He
Had no one *Beame* from Gods sweet Majestie.

[1] Matt. xxvii.46, "My God, my God, Why hast thou forsaken me?"
[2] a condition of being forsaken. The word derives from Ps. xxii.1, *Quare me dereliquisti?* "Why hast thou forsaken me?" Herrick probably takes it from John Gregory, *Notes and Observations upon some Passages of Scripture* (1646), p. 5, "*Our Saviour . . . in that great case of dereliction.*"

N–168 *JEHOVAH.*

JEHOVAH, as *Boëtius*[1] saith,
No number of the *Plurall* hath.

[1] Boethius, *De Trinitate,* 3.

N–169 *Confusion of face.*[1]

GOd then confounds mans face, when He not hears
The Vowes of those, who are Petitioners.

[1] Ezra ix.7, "for our iniquities have we . . . been delivered . . . to the sword . . . and to confusion of face." Cf. Dan. ix.7–8.

N–170 *Another.*

THe shame of mans face is no more
Then prayers repel'd, (sayes *Cassiodore.*)[1]

[1] Cassiodorus on Ps. xxxiii. Cf. Ps. xliv.15, "My confusion is continually before me, and the shame of my face hath covered me."

N–171 *Beggars.*

JAcob Gods Beggar was;[1] and so we wait
(Though ne're so rich) all beggars at His Gate.

[1] when he wrestled with the angel and asked to be released (Gen. xxxii.26). Hos. xii.4 recalls that Jacob "made supplication unto him."

N–172 *Good, and bad.*

THe Bad among the Good are here mixt ever:
The Good without the Bad are here plac'd never.

N–173 *Sin.*

SIn no Existence; Nature none it hath,
Or Good at all, (as learn'd *Aquinas* saith.)[1]

[1] Aquinas, *Contra Gentes,* II, 41, 6.

N–174 *Martha, Martha.*

THe repetition of the name[1] made known
No other, then *Christs* full Affection.

[1] Luke x.41, "Jesus answered . . . Martha, Martha, thou art careful, and troubled about many things."

N–175 *Youth, and Age.*

GOD on our Youth bestowes but little ease;
But on our Age most sweet *Indulgences.*

N–176 *Gods Power.*

GOD is so potent, as His Power can
Draw out of *bad* a soveraigne *good* to man.

N–177 *Paradise.*

PAradise is (as from the Learn'd I gather)
A quire of blest Soules circling in the Father.[1]

[1] Herrick modifies a statement attributed to Psellus by J. Gregory (See N-167, n.2), p. 75: *"The Chaldean Paradise is a Quire of divine powers incircling the Father."*

N–178 *Observation.*

THe Jewes, when they built Houses (I have read)[1]
One part thereof left still unfinished:
To make them, thereby, mindfull of their own
Cities most sad and dire destruction.

[1] in Gregory, *Notes,* "To the Reader," which refers to Leo of Modena, *Degli Riti Hebraici,* Pt. I.

N–179 *The Asse.*

GOD did forbid the Israelites, to bring
An Asse unto Him, for an *offering:*
Onely, by this dull creature, to expresse
His detestation to all slothfulnesse.

N–180 *Observation.*

THe Virgin-Mother stood[1] at distance (there)
From her Sonnes Crosse, not shedding once a teare:
Because the Law forbad to sit and crie
For those, who did as malefactors die.
So she, to keep her mighty woes in awe, 5
Tortur'd her love, not to transgresse the Law.
Observe we may, how *Mary Joses*[2] then,
And th'other *Mary* (*Mary Magdalen*)
Sate by the Grave; and sadly sitting there,
Shed for their Master many a bitter teare: 10
But 'twas not till their *dearest Lord* was dead;
And then to weep they both were licensed.

[1] Gregory, *Notes,* pp. 24–27, explains that when a criminal was killed, mourners were not allowed by Jewish and Roman law to adopt the sitting posture which was customary for mourning.
[2] Mary, the mother of James and Joses. Matt. xxvii.56–61.

N–181 *Tapers.*

THose Tapers, which we set upon the grave,
In fun'rall pomp, but this importance have;
That soules departed are not put out quite;
But, as they walk't here in their *vestures* white,
So live in Heaven, in everlasting light.[1] 5

[1] Gregory, *Notes,* p. 111: "funerall Tapers . . . shew, that the departed soules are not quite put out, but having walked here as the children of the *Light,* are now gone to walke before God in the *Light* of the *Living.*"

N–182 *Christs Birth.*

ONe Birth our Saviour had; the like none yet
Was, or will be a *second* like to it.

N–183 *The Virgin* Mary.

TO work a *wonder*, God would have her shown,
At once, a Bud, and yet a *Rose full-blowne*.

N–184 *Another*.

AS Sun-beames pierce the glasse, and streaming in,
No crack or Schisme leave i'th subtill skin:
So the Divine Hand work't, and brake no thred,
But, in a *Mother*, kept a *maiden-head*.

N–185 *God*.

GOD, in the *holy Tongue*, they call
The Place that filleth *All in all*.[1]

[1] Gregory, *Notes*, p. 135: "All things are full of God. He is therefore called . . . *Hammakom, the Place*. Or that Fulnesse which filleth *All* in *All*."

N–186 *Another of God*.

GOD's said to leave this place, and for to come
Nearer to that place, then to other some:
Of locall motion, in no least respect,
But only by impression of effect.[1]

[1] Gregory, *Notes*, pp. 137–138: "God is said to be nearer to this man then to that, more in one place then in another. Thus he is said to depart from some and come to others, to leave this place and to abide in that, not by Essential application of himselfe (much lesse by locall motion) but by Impression of Effect."

N–187

Another.

GOD is *Jehovah* cal'd; which name of His
Implies or *Essence*, or the *He* that Is.[1]

[1] Gregory, *Notes*, p. 138: "As he is to all and in all places, he is called . . . *Jehovah, He* that is, or Essence."

N–188

Gods presence.

GOD's evident, and may be said to be
Present with just men, to the veritie:
But with the wicked if He doth comply,
'Tis (as S. *Bernard* saith) but seemingly.[1]

[1] Gregory, *Notes*, p. 138: According to St. Bernard, God is present with just men "*in veritate,* In deed, but with the wicked dissemblingly . . . *in dissimulatione.*"

N–189

Gods Dwelling.

GOD's said to dwell there, wheresoever He
Puts down some prints of His high Majestie:
As when to man He comes, and there doth place
His *holy Spirit*, or doth plant His *Grace*.[1]

[1] Gregory, *Notes*, p. 138: God "*is said to dwell there* (saith *Maimon*) *where he putteth the markes or evidences of His Majesty and presence.* And he doth this by his *Grace* and *Holy Spirit.*"

N–190

The Virgin Mary.

THe *Virgin Marie* was (as I have read)
The *House of God*, by *Christ* inhabited;
Into the which He enter'd: but, the Doore
Once shut, was never to be open'd more.[1]

[1] Gregory, *Notes*, p. 86: Jacob's observation "this is none other but the house of God, and this is the gate of heaven" (Gen. xxviii.17), "*is to be meant of the Virgin Mary, who became as it*

were another Heaven, truly to be call'd the House of God, as wherein the Son of God . . . inhabited . . . and it shall not be set open the second time, according to . . . Ezekiel" (xliv.2).

N–191 *To God.*

GOD's undivided, *One* in *Persons Three;*
And *Three* in *Inconfused Unity:*
Originall of Essence there is none
'Twixt God the *Father, Holy Ghost,* and *Sonne:*
And though the *Father* be the first of *Three,* 5
'Tis but by *Order,* not by *Entitie.*

N–192 *Upon Woman and* Mary.[1]

SO long (it seem'd) as *Maries* Faith was small,
Christ did her *Woman,* not her *Mary* call:
But no more *Woman,* being strong in Faith;
But *Mary* cal'd then (as S. *Ambrose* saith.)[2]

[1] St. Mary Magdalen. Luke vii.44; John xx.15–16. [2] St. Ambrose, *Expos. in Lucam,* X, 161 ff.

N–193 *North and South.*[1]

THe *Jewes* their beds, and offices of ease,
Plac't *North* and *South,* for these cleane purposes;
That mans uncomely froth might not molest
Gods wayes and walks, which lie still East and West.

[1] based on a passage in Gregory's *Notes,* chap. XIX, pp. 92–93, which concludes, "*That the uncomely Necessities of Nature . . . might not fall into the Walke and Wayes of God, whose Schecina or dwelling presence lyeth West and East.*"

N–194 *Sabbaths.*

S*Abbaths* are threefold, (as S. *Austine*[1] sayes:)
The first of Time, or Sabbath here of Dayes;
The second is a Conscience trespasse-free;
The last the *Sabbath of Eternitie.*

[1] St. Augustine, *Serm.* CCCLXIII, and *Serm.* CCLXX, 5.

N–195 *The Fast, or Lent.*

NOah the first was (as Tradition sayes)[1]
That did ordaine the Fast of forty Dayes.

[1] according to Gregory, *Notes,* p. 28.

N–196 *Sin.*

THere is no evill that we do commit,
But hath th'extraction of some good from it:
As when we sin; God, the great *Chymist,* thence
Drawes out th'*Elixar* of true penitence.

N–197 *God.*

GOD is more here, then in another place,
Not by His *Essence,* but commerce of *Grace.*

N–198 *This, and the next World.*

GOD hath this world for many made; 'tis true:
But He hath made the world to come for few.

N–199 *Ease.*

GOD gives to none so absolute an Ease,
As not to know, or feel some *Grievances.*

N–200 *Beginnings and Endings.*

PAul, he began ill, but he ended well;
Judas began well, but he foulely fell:
In godlinesse, not the beginnings, so
Much as the ends are to be lookt unto.

N–201 *Temporall goods.*

THese temp'rall goods God (the most Wise) commends
To th'good and bad, in common, for two ends:
First, that these goods none here may o're esteem,
Because the wicked do partake of them:
Next, that these ills none cowardly may shun; 5
Being, oft here, the just mans portion.

N–202 *Hell fire.*

THe fire of Hell this strange condition hath,
To burn, not shine (as learned *Basil* saith.)[1]

[1] In his homily on Ps. xxviii St. Basil observes that fire has the double power of burning and shining.

N–203 Abels *Bloud.*[1]

SPeak, did the Bloud of *Abel* cry
To God for vengeance? yes say I;
Ev'n as the sprinkled bloud cal'd on
God, for an expiation.

[1] Heb. xii.24, "to the blood of sprinkling, that speaketh better things than that of Abel." Herrick versifies a passage in Gregory's *Notes*, p. 118. Cf. John Diodati, *Pious Annotations upon the Holy Bible* (3rd ed. London, 1681) on Heb. xii.24: "*That speaketh*–which as one should say, presents it selfe before God, not to desire vengeance of the murtherous Jews, as *Abels* bloud did against *Cain, Gen.* 4.10. but to obtain favour and pardon for them."

N–204 *Another.*[1]

THe bloud of *Abel* was a thing
Of such a rev'rend reckoning,
As that the old World thought it fit,
Especially to sweare by it.

[1] a versifying of a passage in Gregory, p. 118.

N–205

A Position in the Hebrew Divinity.

ONe man repentant is of more esteem
With God, then one, that never sin'd 'gainst Him.[1]

[1] In comment upon Luke xv.10 ("There is joy in the presence of the angels of God, over one sinner that repenteth"), Gregory, p. 134, writes, "The words have a reflexe upon that old position in Hebrew Divinity . . . *That a Repenting man is of greater esteeme in the sight of God, then one that never fell away.*"

N–206

Penitence.

THe Doctors, in the Talmud, say,
That in this world, one onely day
In true repentance spent, will be
More worth, then Heav'ns Eternitie.[1]

[1] Gregory, p. 135: "The Doctours in the *Talmud* say . . . *one day spent here in true Repentance, is more worth then Eternity it selfe, or all the dayes of Heaven in the other world.*"

N–207

Gods presence.[1]

GOD's present ev'ry where; but most of all
Present by Union *Hypostaticall:*
God, He is there, where's nothing else (Schooles say)
And nothing else is there, *where He's away.*

[1] based on Gregory, pp. 135–36.

N–208

The Resurrection possible, and probable.[1]

FOr each one Body, that i'th earth is sowne,
There's an up-rising but of one for one:
But for each Graine, that in the ground is thrown,
Threescore or fourescore spring up thence for one:

So that the wonder is not halfe so great, 5
Of ours, as is the rising of the wheat.

[1] a versifying of a passage in Gregory, pp. 128–29, in comment upon I Cor. xv.36.

N–209 *Christs suffering.*

JUstly our *dearest Saviour* may abhorre us,
Who hath more suffer'd by us farre, then for us.

N–210 *Sinners.*

SInners confounded are a twofold way,
Either as when (the learned Schoolemen say)
Mens sins destroyed are, when they repent;
Or when, for sins, men suffer punishment.

N–211 *Temptations.*

NO man is tempted so, but may o'recome,
If that he has a will to Masterdome.

N–212 *Pittie, and punishment.*

GOD doth embrace the good with love; and gaines
The good by mercy, as the bad by paines.

N–213 *Gods price, and mans price.*

GOd bought man here with his hearts blood expence;
And man sold God here for base *thirty pence.*

N–214 *Christs Action.*

CHRIST never did so great a work, but there
His humane Nature did, in part, appeare:
Or, ne're so meane a peece, but men might see
Therein some beames of His Divinitie:
So that, in all He did, there did combine 5
His Humane Nature, and His Part Divine.

N–215 *Predestination.*

PRedestination is the Cause alone
Of many standing, but of fall to none.[1]

[1] The doctrine of predestination propounded here and in the following poems is obviously not Calvinistic. Cf. Edward Reynolds, *A Treatise of the Passions and Faculties of the Soul of Man* (1640), 4th ed., 1658, p. 1095: "It is true indeed, *Gods Prescience* implies a necessity of our working after that manner, as he foreknows: but this is *Necessitas* only *Infallibilitatis,* in regard of his undeceivable knowledge, which ever foresees things as they will certainly come to passe by the free and natural workings of the Agents, whence they proceed. It is not *Necessitas Coactionis,* or *Determinationis,* whereby the Will of man is without any other disposition or propension in it self, enforced or unspontaneously determined to the producing of such effects. The Actions of Gods Will or Knowledge within himself, do sweetly consist with the native liberty of mans will; He can effect all his purposes by the genuine and proper agency of Second Causes, and is never necessitated to violate or alter the manner of our working for the effecting of his own. . . . nothing is done which God in all respects doth will shall not be done with the secret Will of his good pleasure . . . yet he doth not so work his Will out of mens, as thereby to constrain and take away theirs. . . . This were an Argument of weaknesse, as if he were not able to bring his own Ends about but by chaining and fettering his oppugners from exercising the freedome which he first gave them. . . . as sundry times Gods *Revealed Will* is broken . . . so alwayes his *Secret Will* is performed, even by the free and self moving Operations of those who set themselves stubbornly to oppose it."

N–216 *Another.*

ARt thou not destin'd? then, with hast, go on
To make thy faire *Predestination:*
If thou canst change thy life, God then will please
To change, or call back, His past *Sentences.*

N–217 *Sin.*

SIn never slew a soule, unlesse there went
Along with it some tempting blandishment.

N–218 *Another.*

SIn is an act so free, that if we shall
Say, 'tis not free, 'tis then no sin at all.

N–219 *Another.*

SIn is the cause of death; and sin's alone
The cause of Gods *Predestination:*
And from Gods *Prescience* of mans sin doth flow
Our *Destination* to eternall woe.

N–220 *Prescience.*

GOds *Prescience makes none sinfull;* but th'offence
Of man's the chief cause of Gods *Prescience.*

N–221 *Christ.*

TO all our wounds, here, whatsoe're they be,
Christ is the one sufficient *Remedie.*

N–222 *Christs Incarnation.*

CHRIST took our Nature on Him, not that He
'Bove all things lov'd it, for the puritie:
No, but He drest Him with our humane Trim,
Because our flesh stood most in need of Him.

N–223 *Heaven.*

HEaven is not given for our good works here:
Yet it is given to the *Labourer.*

N–224 *Gods keyes.*

GOD has *foure keyes,* which He reserves alone;
The first of *Raine,*[1] the key of *Hell* next known:[2]
With the third key He opes and shuts the wombe;[3]
And with the *fourth key* He unlocks the tombe.

[1] Deut. xi.17, "he shut up the heaven that there be no rain." Rev. xi.3–6, "I will give power unto my two witnesses . . . to shut heaven, that it rain not in the days of their prophecy." I Kings viii.35, "When the heaven is shut up, and there is no rain." II Chron. vii.13, "If I shut up the heaven that there be no rain." [2] Rev. i.18, "I am alive for evermore, Amen; and have the keys of hell and of death." Diodati (See N-203, n.1) interprets these keys as "the absolute power over these things, to condemn unto them, and to free from them at my pleasure." [3] Gen. xxx.22; I Sam. i.6; Job iii.10; Isa. lxvi.9.

N–225 *Sin.*

THere's no constraint to do amisse,
Whereas but one enforcement is.

N–226 *Almes.*

GIve unto all, lest he, whom thou deni'st,
May chance to be no other man, but *Christ.*

N–227

Hell fire.

ONe onely fire has Hell; but yet it shall,
Not after one sort, there excruciate all:
But look, how each transgressor onward went
Boldly in sin, shall feel more punishment.

N–228

To keep a true Lent.

1 IS this a Fast, to keep
The Larder leane?
And cleane
From fat of Veales, and Sheep?

2 Is it to quit the dish
Of Flesh, yet still
To fill
The platter high with Fish?

3 Is it to fast an houre,
Or rag'd[1] to go,
Or show
A down-cast look, and sowre?[2]

4 No: 'tis a Fast, to dole
Thy sheaf of wheat,
And meat,
Unto the hungry Soule.[3]

5 It is to fast from strife,
From old debate,
And hate;[4]
To circumcise thy life.[5]

6 To shew a heart grief-rent;[6]
To sterve thy sin,
Not Bin;
And that's to keep thy Lent.

[1] ragged. [2] Cf. Isa. lviii.5, "Is it such a fast that I have chosen? a day for a man to afflict his soul? is it to bow down his head as a bulrush . . . , wilt thou call this a fast and an acceptable day unto the Lord?" [3] Ibid. 7, "Is it not to deal thy bread to the hungry . . . ?" [4] Ibid. 4, "Behold, ye fast for strife and debate,

and to smite with the fist of wickedness: ye shall not fast as ye do this day, to make your voices to be heard on high." [5] Rom. ii.29, "he is a Jew which is one inwardly; and circumcision is that of the heart, in the spirit, and not in the letter." [6] Joel ii.13, "rend your heart, and not your garments."

N–229 *No time in Eternitie.*

BY houres we all live here, in Heaven is known
No spring of Time, or Times succession.

N–230 *His Meditation upon Death.*

BE those few hours, which I have yet to spend,
Blest with the Meditation of my end:
Though they be few in number, I'm content;
If otherwise, I stand indifferent:
Nor makes it matter, *Nestors* yeers[1] to tell, 5
If man lives long, and if he live not well.
A multitude of dayes still heaped on,
Seldome brings order, but confusion.
Might I make choice, long life sho'd be with-stood;
Nor wo'd I care how short it were, if good: 10
Which to effect, let ev'ry passing Bell
Possesse my thoughts,[2] next comes my dolefull knell:
And when the night perswades me to my bed,
I'le thinke I'm going to be buried:
So shall the Blankets which come over me, 15
Present those Turfs, which once must cover me:
And with as firme behaviour I will meet
The sheet I sleep in, as my Winding-sheet.
When sleep shall bath his body in mine eyes,
I will believe, that then my body dies: 20
And if I chance to wake, and rise thereon,
I'le have in mind my Resurrection,
Which must produce me[3] to that *Gen'rall Doome,*
To which the Pesant, so the Prince must come,
To heare the Judge give sentence on the Throne, 25
Without the least hope of affection.[4]
Teares, at that day, shall make but weake defence;
When Hell and Horrour fright the Conscience.

Let me, though late, yet at the last, begin
To shun the least Temptation to a sin; 30
Though to be tempted be no sin, untill
Man to th'alluring object gives his will.
Such let my life assure me, when my breath
Goes theeving from me, I am safe in death;
Which is the height of comfort, when I fall, 35
I rise triumphant in my Funerall.

[1] King Nestor of Pylos, called by Homer the *Gerenian*, an epithet thought by some to derive from the Greek word for old age. In the *Iliad* he had survived two generations of men; therefore his years must have numbered at least 70. [2] let every bell tolled for someone's dying occupy my thoughts with the idea that. [3] lead me forth. [4] partiality.

N–231 *Cloaths for Continuance.*

THose Garments lasting evermore,[1]
Are works of mercy to the poore,
Which neither Tettar, Time, or Moth
Shall fray that silke, or fret this cloth.[2]

[1] Isa. lxi.10, "he hath clothed me with the garments of salvation, he hath covered me with the robe of righteousness." Isa. xxiii.18, "durable clothing." [2] Matt. vi.19, "Lay not up for yourselves treasures upon earth, where moth and rust doth corrupt." Luke xii.33, "provide yourselves bags which wax not old, a treasure in the heavens that faileth not, where no . . . moth corrupteth."

N–232 *To God.*

COme to me God; but do not come
To me, as to the gen'rall Doome,
In power; or come Thou in that state,
When Thou Thy Lawes didst promulgate,
When as the Mountaine quak'd for dread,[1] 5
And sullen clouds bound up his head.[2]
No, lay thy stately terrours by,
To talke with me familiarly;
For if Thy thunder-claps I heare,
I shall lesse swoone, then die for feare. 10

Speake thou of love and I'le reply
By way of *Epithalamie*,
Or sing of *mercy*, and I'le suit
To it my Violl and my Lute:
Thus let Thy lips but love distill, 15
Then come my God, and hap what will.

[1] before God called Moses to ascend Mt. Sinai to receive the Ten Commandments, Exod. xix.18. [2] Exod. xix.16, "there were thunders and lightnings, and a thick cloud upon the mount."

N–233 *The Soule.*

WHen once the Soule has lost her way,
O then, how restlesse do's she stray![1]
And having not her God for light,
How do's she erre in endlesse night!

[1] Cf. Marvell, "On a Drop of Dew," which he compares to the soul: "long divided from the Sphear / Restless it roules and unsecure, / Trembling lest it grow impure."

N–234 *The Judgement day.*

IN doing justice, God shall then be known,
Who shewing mercy here, few priz'd, or none.

N–235 *Sufferings.*

WE merit all we suffer, and by far
More stripes, then God layes on the sufferer.

N–236 *Paine and pleasure.*

GOd suffers not His Saints, and Servants deere,
To have continuall paine, or pleasure here:
But look how night succeeds the day, so He
Gives them by turnes their grief and jollitie.

N–237 *Gods presence.*

GOD is *all-present* to what e're we do,
And as *all-present*, so *all-filling* too.

N–238 *Another.*

THat there's a God, we all do know,
But what God is, we cannot show.

N–239 *The poore mans part.*

TEll me rich man, for what intent
Thou load'st with gold thy vestiment?
When as the poore crie out, to us
Belongs all gold superfluous.[1]

[1] Prov. iii.27, "Withhold not good from them [*Margin:* Heb. *the owners thereof*] to whom it is due." Gregory, p. 59, cites part of this passage in Latin, adding that giving to the poor is but giving them their own.

N–240 *The right hand.*

GOD has a Right Hand, but is quite bereft
Of that, which we do nominate the Left.[1]

[1] The left hand symbolized the unpropitious, evil, dishonest, sinister, and unfortunate, and as such would be unappropriate, metaphorically, for God. There seems to be no reference in the Bible to God's left hand, though "the hands of the mighty God of Jacob" are mentioned in Gen. xlix.24.

N–241 *The Staffe and Rod.*

TWo instruments belong unto our God;
The one a *Staffe* is, and the next a *Rod:*
That if the twig sho'd chance too much to smart,
The staffe might come to play the friendly part.[1]

[1] See N-48, n.1; cf. N-261.

N–242 *God sparing in scourging.*

GOD still rewards us more then our desert:
But when He strikes, He quarter-acts His part.[1]

[1] i.e. he lessens the force of the blows by three-fourths.

N–243 *Confession.*

COnfession twofold is (as *Austine* sayes,)
The first of *sin* is, and the next of *praise:*[1]
If ill it goes with thee, thy faults confesse:
If well, then chant Gods praise with cheerfulnesse.

[1] St. Augustine, *Enarr. in Ps. xxix,* II, 19.

N–244 *Gods descent.*

GOD is then said for to descend, when He
Doth, here on earth, some thing of novitie;[1]
As when, in humane nature He works more
Then ever, yet, the like was done before.[2]

[1] novelty; i.e. something miraculous, contrary to the usual course of nature. [2] i.e. He effects something unprecedented, of a kind that was never done before.

N–245

No coming to God without Christ.

GOod and great God! How sho'd I feare
To come to Thee, if *Christ* not there!
Co'd I but think, He would not be
Present, to plead my cause for me;
To Hell I'd rather run, then I 5
Wo'd see Thy Face, and He not by.

N–246

Another, to God.

THough Thou beest all that *Active Love*,
Which heats those ravisht Soules above;
And though all joyes spring from the glance
Of Thy most winning countenance;
Yet sowre and grim Thou'dst seem to me; 5
If through my *Christ* I saw not Thee.

N–247

The Resurrection.

THat *Christ* did die, the *Pagan* saith;
But that He rose, that's *Christians* Faith.

N–248

Coheires.

WE are Coheires with *Christ;* nor shall His own
Heire-ship be lesse, by our adoption:
The number here of Heires, shall from the state
Of His great *Birth-right* nothing derogate.

N–249

The number of two.

GOD hates the *Duall Number;* being known
The lucklesse number of division:
And when He blest each sev'rall Day, whereon
He did His *curious operation;*[1]

'Tis never read there (as the Fathers say,) 5
God blest His work done on the *second day:*
Wherefore two prayers ought not to be said,
Or by our selves, or from the Pulpit read.

[1] His excellent, exact, well-thought-out, and ingenious work of creation. Herrick refers to the ancient (Rabbinical?) notion that "God saw that it was good" was not added after the second day of creation (Gen. i.6–7) because it was the first disuniting of what He had created.

N–250 *Hardning of hearts.*

GOD's said our hearts to harden[1] then,
When as His grace not supples men.

[1] John xii.40, "He hath blinded their eyes, and hardened their heart." Cf. Exod. vii.13.

N–251 *The Rose.*

BEfore Mans fall, the Rose was born
(S. *Ambrose* sayes)[1] without the Thorn:
But, for Mans fault, then was the Thorn,
Without the fragrant Rose-bud, born;
But ne're the Rose without the Thorn. 5

[1] St. Ambrose, *Hexaemeron,* III, 11.

N–252

Gods time must end our trouble.

GOD doth not promise here to man, that He
Will free him quickly from his miserie;
But in His own time, and when He thinks fit,
Then He will give a happy end to it.

N–253 *Baptisme.*

THe strength of *Baptisme,* that's within;
It saves the soule, by drowning sin.

N–254 *Gold and Frankincense.*

GOld serves for Tribute to the King;
The *Frankincense* for Gods Offring.

N–255 *To God.*

GOD, who me gives a will for to repent,
Will add a power, to keep me innocent;
That I shall ne're that trespasse recommit,
When I have done true Penance here for it.

N–256 *The chewing the Cud.*

WHen well we speak, and nothing do that's good,
We not divide the *Hoof*, but chew the *Cud:*
But when good words, by good works, have their proof,
We then both chew the *Cud,* and cleave the *Hoof.*[1]

[1] Lev. xi.3–7 permits the eating of cloven-footed, cud-chewing animals but denounces as unclean animals which have undivided hooves or do not chew cud. So, speaking good without performance is unclean, but their combination is pleasing to God.

N–257 *Christs twofold coming.*

THy former coming was to cure
My soules most desp'rate *Calenture;*[1]
Thy second *Advent,* that must be
To heale my Earths infirmitie.

[1] inflammation, fever.

N–258 *To God, his gift.*

AS my little Pot doth boyle,
We will keep this *Levell-Coyle;*[1]
That a *Wave,* and I will bring
To my God, a *Heave-offering.*

[1] a game whose name derives from French *lever le cul,* "to lift up or remove the buttock," i.e. to rise from one's place and give it to another. As his pot boils, Herrick will observe such a practice. The boiling will wave the meat to and fro, in a manner like the waving of an offering by a priest (See N-130, n.2), and Herrick will give to God (i.e. to charity) the meat he lifted off the fire, although as a priest he is himself entitled to such a "heave-offering" (Numb. xv.20; xviii.11).

N–259 *Gods Anger.*

GOD can't be wrathfull; but we may conclude,
Wrathfull He may be, by similitude:
God's wrathfull said to be, when He doth do
That without *wrath,* which wrath doth *force us* to.

N–260 *Gods Commands.*

IN Gods Commands, ne're ask the reason why;
Let thy *obedience* be the best Reply.

N–261 *To God.*

IF I have plaid the *Truant,* or have here
Fail'd in my part; O! Thou that art my *deare,*
My *mild,* my *loving Tutor, Lord and God!*
Correct my errors gently with Thy Rod.
I know, that faults will many here be found, 5
But where sin swells, there let Thy grace abound.

N–262

To God.

THe work is done; now let my *Lawrell* be
Given by none, but by Thy selfe, to me:
That done, with Honour Thou dost me create
Thy *Poet,* and Thy *Prophet Lawreat.*

N–263

Good Friday: Rex Tragicus, *or Christ going to His Crosse.*

PUt off Thy Robe of *Purple,*[1] then go on
To the sad place of execution:
Thine houre is come;[2] and the Tormentor stands
Ready, to pierce Thy tender Feet, and Hands.
Long before this, the base, the dull, the rude, 5
Th'inconstant, and unpurged Multitude
Yawne for Thy coming; some e're this time crie,
How He deferres, how loath He is to die!
Amongst this scumme, the Souldier, with his speare,
And that sowre Fellow, with his *vineger,* 10
His *spunge,* and *stick,*[3] do ask why Thou dost stay?
So do the *Skurfe* and *Bran*[4] too: Go Thy way,
Thy way, Thou guiltlesse man, and satisfie
By Thine approach, each their beholding eye.
Not as a thief, shalt Thou ascend the mount, 15
But like a Person of some high account:
The *Crosse* shall be Thy *Stage;* and Thou shalt there
The spacious field have for Thy *Theater.*
Thou art that *Roscius,*[5] and that markt-out man,
That must this day act the Tragedian, 20
To wonder and affrightment: Thou art He,
Whom all the flux of Nations[6] comes to see;
Not those poor Theeves that act their parts with Thee:
Those act without regard, when once a *King,*
And *God,* as Thou art, comes to suffering. 25
No, No, this *Scene* from Thee takes life and sense,
And soule and spirit[,] plot, and excellence.
Why then begin, great King! ascend Thy Throne,
And thence proceed, to act Thy Passion

To such an height, to such a period rais'd, 30
As Hell, and Earth, and Heav'n may stand amaz'd.
God, and good Angells guide Thee; and so blesse
Thee in Thy severall parts of bitternesse;
That those, who see Thee nail'd unto the Tree,
May (though they scorn Thee) praise and pitie Thee. 35
And we (Thy Lovers) while we see Thee keep
The Lawes of Action,[7] will both sigh, and weep;
And bring our Spices, to embalm Thee dead;
That done, wee'l see Thee sweetly buried.

[1] Mark xv.17–20, "they clothed him with purple. . . . And when they had mocked him they took off the purple from him." [2] John xiii.1. [3] Matt. xxvii.48. [4] the scum of the population and the coarse ones. [5] tragic actor. [6] Lam. i.12, "Is it nothing to you, all ye that pass by?" Rev. vii.9, "a great multitude, which no man could number, of all nations, and kindreds, and people." [7] theatrical term: the rules for acting a role on the stage–in this instance, that of the Tragic King.

N–264

His words to Christ, going to the Crosse.

WHen Thou wast taken, Lord, I oft have read,
All Thy Disciples Thee forsook, and fled.
Let their example not a pattern be
For me to flie, but now to follow Thee.

N–265

Another, to his Saviour.

IF Thou beest taken, *God* forbid,
I flie fromThee, as others did:
But if Thou wilt so honour me,
As to accept my companie,
I'le follow Thee, hap, hap what shall, 5
Both to the *Judge*, and *Judgment-Hall:*
And, if I see Thee posted there,
To be all-flayd with whipping-cheere,
I'le take my share; or els, my God,
Thy stripes I'le kisse, or burn the *Rod.* 10

N–266

His Saviours words, going to the Crosse.

HAve, have ye no regard, all ye
Who passe this way,[1] to pitie me,
Who am a man of miserie![2]

A man both bruis'd, and broke, and one
Who suffers not here for mine own, 5
But for my friends *transgression!*[3]

Ah! *Sions Daughters,* do not feare[4]
The *Crosse,* the *Cords,* the *Nailes,* the *Speare,*
The *Myrrhe,* the *Gall,* the *Vineger:*

For *Christ,* your loving Saviour, hath 10
Drunk up the wine of Gods fierce wrath;[5]
Onely, there's left a little froth,

Lesse for to tast, then for to shew,
What bitter cups had been your due,
Had He not drank them up for *you.* 15

[1] See N-263, n.6. [2] Isa. liii.3, "a man of sorrows, and acquainted with grief." [3] ibid. 4–5, "we did esteem him stricken, smitten of God, and afflicted. But he was wounded for our transgressions, he was bruised for our iniquities." [4] Luke xxiii.28, "Daughters of Jerusalem, weep not for me." [5] Cf. Isa. li.17, "which hast drunk . . . the cup of his fury."

N–267

His Anthem, to Christ on the Crosse.

WHen I behold Thee, almost slain,
With one, and all parts, full of pain:
When I Thy gentle Heart do see
Pierc't through, and dropping bloud, for me,
I'le call, and cry out, Thanks to Thee.

Vers. But yet it wounds my soule, to think,
That for my sin, Thou, Thou must drink,
Even Thou alone, the *bitter cup*
Of *furie,* and of *vengeance* up.

Chor. Lord, I'le not see Thee to drink all
The *Vineger,* the *Myrrhe,* the *Gall:*

Ver. Chor. But I will sip a little wine;
Which done, Lord say, *The rest is mine.*

N–268

This Crosse-Tree here
Doth Jesus *beare,*
Who sweet'ned first,
The Death accurs't.
Here all things ready are, make hast, make hast away; 5
For, long this work wil be, & very short this Day.
Why then, go on to act: Here's wonders to be done,
Before the last least sand of Thy ninth houre be run;
Or e're dark Clouds do dull, or dead the Mid-dayes Sun.
Act when Thou wilt, 10
Bloud will be spilt;
Pure Balm, that shall
Bring Health to All.
Why then, Begin
To powre first in 15
Some Drops of Wine,
In stead of Brine,
To search the Wound,
So long unsound:
And, when that's done, 20
Let Oyle, next, run,
To cure the Sore
Sinne made before.
And O! Deare Christ,
E'en as Thou di'st, 25
Look down, and see
Us weepe for Thee.
And tho (Love knows)
Thy dreadfull Woes
Wee cannot ease; 30
Yet doe Thou please,
Who Mercie art,
T'accept each Heart,
That gladly would
Helpe, if it could. 35
Meane while, let mee,
Beneath this Tree,
This Honour have,
To make my grave.

N–269

To his Saviours Sepulcher: his Devotion.

HAile holy, and all-honour'd Tomb,
By no ill haunted; here I come,
With shoes put off, to tread thy Roome.
I'le not prophane, by soile of sin,
Thy Doore, as I do enter in: 5
For I have washt both hand and heart,
This, that, and ev'ry other part;
So that I dare, with farre lesse feare,
Then full affection, enter here.
Thus, thus I come to kisse Thy Stone 10
With a warm lip, and solemne one:
And as I kisse, I'le here and there
Dresse Thee with flowrie Diaper.
How sweet this place is! as from hence
Flow'd all *Panchaia's* Frankincense; 15
Or rich *Arabia* did commix,
Here, all her rare *Aromaticks*.
Let me live ever here, and stir
No one step from this *Sepulcher*.
Ravisht I am! and down I lie, 20
Confus'd, in this brave Extasie.
Here let me rest; and let me have
This for my *Heaven*, that was Thy *Grave:*
And, coveting no higher sphere,
I'le my Eternitie spend here. 25

N–270

His Offering, with the rest, at the Sepulcher.

TO joyn with them, who here confer
Gifts to my Saviours Sepulcher;
Devotion bids me hither bring
Somwhat for my Thank-Offering.
Loe! Thus I give a Virgin-Flower, 5
To dresse my Maiden-Saviour.

N–271 *His coming to the Sepulcher.*

HEnce they have born my Lord: Behold! the Stone
Is rowl'd away; and my sweet Saviour's gone!
Tell me, white Angell; what is now become
Of Him, we lately seal'd up in this Tombe?
Is He, from hence, gone to the shades beneath, 5
To vanquish Hell, as here He conquer'd Death?
If so; I'le thither follow, without feare;
And live in Hell, if that my *Christ* stayes there.

N–272

OF all the good things whatsoe're we do,
God is the ΑΡΧΗ, and the ΤΕΛΟΣ[1] too.

[1] the Beginning and the End. Rev. i.8, "I am Alpha and Omega, the beginning and the ending, saith the Lord."

A Supplement

A Supplement of Poems Not Included in the 1648 Edition

The following 12 poems and others inserted above near works to which they are related were not included in *Hesperides* and *Noble Numbers* but were attributed to Herrick in seventeenth-century sources. He was certainly the author of S-1 and S-2 and probably of the others; but the evidence is inconclusive. Martin prints 25 other poems in his edition because internal evidence or proximity to works known to be Herrick's or attribution to "R.H." suggests his authorship. But without stronger evidence, such attributions are little more than guesses. Manuscript collections of seventeenth-century writings contain hundreds of anonymous poems which could, with more or less plausibility, be attributed to Herrick.

The procedures followed in editing the supplementary poems have been deliberately varied, partly because it is interesting for a reader to see what the sources are like, chiefly because the nature of the sources varied and required different degrees of editing if a minimum intelligibility was to be achieved. Titles of MSS poems have been italicized.

–1

Upon Master FLETCHERS *Incomparable Playes.*[1]

Apollo sings, his harpe resounds; give roome,
For now behold the golden Pompe is come,
Thy Pompe of Playes which thousands come to see,
With admiration both of them and thee,
O Volume worthy leafe, by leafe and cover 5
To be with juice of Cedar washt all over;[2]
Here's words with lines, and lines with Scenes consent,
To raise an Act to full astonishment;
Here melting numbers, words of power to move
Young men to swoone, and Maides to dye for love. 10
Love lyes a bleeding here, *Evadne* there
Swells with brave rage, yet comely every where,
Here's a *mad lover,* there that high designe
Of *King and no King*[3] (and the rare Plott thine)
So that when 'ere wee circumvolve our Eyes, 15
Such rich, such fresh, such sweet varietyes,
Ravish our spirits, that entranc't wee see
None writes lov's passion in the world, like Thee.

[1] Printed in *Comedies and Tragedies by Francis Beaumont and John Fletcher* (1645), folio e; by "Rob. Herrick." [2] as a preservative. [3] references to *Philaster, or Love lies a-bleeding; The Mad Lover;* and A *King and no King.*

S–2

The New Charon,
Upon the death of *Henry* Lord *Hastings.*[1]

The Musical part being set by Master Henry Lawes.

The Speakers,
Charon and Eucosmeia.

Euc. *Charon,* O *Charon,* draw thy Boat to th' shore,
And to thy many, take in one soul more.
Cha. Who calls? who calls?
Euc. One overwhelm'd with ruth;
Have pity either on my Tears or Youth, 5
And take me in, who am in deep Distress;
But first cast off thy wonted Churlishness.
Cha. I will be gentle as that Air which yeelds
A breath of Balm along th'*Elizean* fields.
Speak, what art thou? 10
Euc. One, once that had a lover,
Then which, thy self ne'er wafted sweeter over.
He was—
Cha. Say what.
Eu. Ay me, my woes are deep. 15
Euc. He was an *Hastings;* and that one Name has
In it all Good, that is, and ever was.
He was my *Life,* my *Love,* my *Joy;* but di'd
Some hours before I shou'd have been his Bride.
Chorus. *Thus, thus the Gods celestial still decree,* 20
For Humane Joy, Contingent Misery.
Euc. The *hallowed Tapers* all prepared were,
And *Hymen* call'd to bless the Rites.
Cha. Stop there.
Euc. Great are my woes. 25
Cha. And great must that Grief be,
That makes grim *Charon* thus to pity thee.
But now come in.
Euc. More let me yet relate.
Cha. I cannot stay; more souls for waftage wait, 30
And I must hence.

Eu. Yet let me thus much know,
Departing hence, where Good and Bad souls go.
Cha. Those souls which ne'er were drencht in pleasures stream,
The Fields of *Pluto* are reserv'd for them; 35
Where, drest with garlands, there they walk the ground,
Whose blessed Youth with endless flow'rs is crown'd.
But such as have been drown'd in this wilde Sea,
For those is kept the Gulf of *Hecate;*
Where, with their own contagion they are fed; 40
And there do punish, and are punished.
This known, the rest of thy sad story tell,
When on the Flood that nine times circles Hell
Chorus. *We sail along, to visit mortals never;*
But there to live, where Love shall last for ever. 45

[1] From *Lachrymae Musarum; The Tears of the Muses: exprest in Elegies written by divers persons of Nobility and Worth upon the death of the most hopefull Henry Lord Hastings. . . . Collected and set forth by R*[ichard] *B*[rome] (1649), pp. 38–39. Attributed, at the end, to "Rob. Herrick." Son of the 6th Earl of Huntington, Hastings died at the age of 19 on June 24, 1649, just before his marriage was to have taken place to Elizabeth, daughter of the physician Sir Theodore Turquet de Mayerne. The name Eucosmeia, given to her in this poem, derives from the Greek *eukosmos,* well-ordered, decorous, graceful, well-adorned. Cf. H-730.

S–3 *My Daughter's Dowry.*[1]

Ere I go hence and be no more[2]
Seen to the world, I'll quit[3] the score
I owe unto a female child;[4]
And that is this—a verse instyled
My[5] *Daughter's Dowry;* having which, 5
I'll leave her[6] then completely rich.

Instead of gold, pearls, rubies, bonds,
Long forfeited[7] pawned[8] diamonds,
Or antique pledges, house, or land,
I give thee this, that shall withstand 10
The blow of Ruin and of Chance.[9]
These[10] hurt not thine inheritance,

For 'tis fee simple;[11] and no rent
Thou Fortune[12] ow'st for tenement.[13]
However after times will 'praise[14] 15
This portion, my Prophetic Bays[15]
Cannot deliver up to th' trust;[16]
Yet I sleep pleased[17] in my dust.
As for thy birth and better seeds[18]—
Those which must grow to Virtuous Deeds— 20
Thou didst derive from this[19] old stem[20]
Love, Peace,[21] and Mercy: cherish them.
Which, like a Vestal[22] Virgin, ply
With holy fire lest it[23] die.
Grow up by mild means[24] to know 25
At what time to say aye and[25] no.
Let manners teach thee where to be
More comely flowing, where less free.
These bring thy husband like to those
Old coins and medals we expose 30
To the sight[26] but never part with. Next,
As in a more conspicuous text
(The[27] forehead), let therein be sign'd
The maiden candor of thy mind;
And under it,[28] two chaste-born spies 35
To bar out bold adulteries
(For through those optics pass[29] the darts
Of lust which set[30] on fire our hearts.)
On either side of these, quick ears
There must be plac'd to season[31] fears, 40
Which sweeten love, yet ne'er come nigh
The brands[32] of wilder jealousy.
Then let each cheek of thine intice
His soul, as to a bed of spice
Where he may roll and loose his sense 45
As in a cloud[33] of frankincense.
A lip enkindled[34] with that coal
With which love warms and chafes[35] the soul
Bring to him next; and in it show[36]
Love's cherries from such fires grow 50
And have their harvest—which must stand
The gathering of the lip, not hand.
Then unto these, be it thy care
To clothe thy words in gentle air
That, smooth as oil, sweet, soft, and clean 55
As is the childish bloom of bean,

They may fall down and stroke, as the
Beams of the sun the peaceful sea.
 White[37] hands as smooth as mercies bring
Him for his better cherishing, 60
That, when thou dost his neck ensnare
Or with thy wrist or fettering[38] hair,
He may, a prisoner, there discry
Bondage more loved than liberty.
 A nature so well form'd, so wrought 65
To calm and temper,[39] let be brought
With thee, that should he but incline
To roughness, clasp him like a vine.
Or like as wool meets steel, give way
Unto the passion, not it[40] stay: 70
(Wrath, if resisted, over-boils;
If not, it dies, or else recoils).
 And lastly, see thou bring to him
Somewhat peculiar in[41] each limb.
 And I do charge[42] thee to be known 75
By n' other face than[43] by thine own.
Let it, in love's name, be kept sleek,
Yet to be found when he shall seek
It, and not, instead of saint,
Give up his worship to the paint. 80
For,[44] trust me girl, she[45] overdoes
Who by a double proxy woos.[46]
 But, lest I should forget his bed,
Be sure thou bring'st[47] a maidenhead
That is a margarite;[48] which, lost, 85
Thou bring'st into[49] his bed a frost
Or a cold poison, which his blood
Benumbs like that[50] forgetful flood.[51]
 Now, for some jewels to supply
The want of ear-ring[52] bravery: 90
For public[53] eyes, take only these,
Ne'er travelled for[54] beyond the seas
(They're nobly home-bred, yet have price[55]
Beyond the far fetcht[56] merchandize):
Obedience, wise distrust, peace. Shy 95
Distance and sweet urbanity,
Safe modesty, love, patience,[57] fear
Of offending, temperance, dear
Constancy, bashfulness, and all
The virtues less or cardinal 100

Take, with my blessing; and go forth
Injewelled with thy native worth.
And now, if there a man be found
That looks for such prepared ground,
Let him but with indifferent skill 105
So good a soil bestock and till,
He may ere long, with such[58] a wife,
Nourish in's breast a Tree of Life.

[1] Text based on H (Harvard MS Eng 626F, f.31v); variants from A (Bodleian MS Ashmole 38, p. 94); spelling modernized; punctuation almost entirely supplied by the editor, who is also responsible for the space after line 6 and the paragraphing. Readers should remember that punctuation is conjectural and that other combinations of lines and phrases are sometimes possible. Martin, p. 407, prints the text of MS A but adds a comma at the end of line 15 and expands abbreviations. There is no reason to believe that the spelling and sparse punctuation of the MSS in any way reflect Herrick's intentions. [2] Ps. xxxix.13, "before I go hence, and be no more." [3] pay off (A: *give*). Cf. N-103, 7–8. [4] Cf. H-443, 92. [5] So in both MSS; but in A the heading replaces *My* with *Mr Hericke his.* [6] (A: *thee*). [7] (A: *forfaite*). Cf. H-338, 4: "To keep my Bond still free from forfeiture." [8] (A: *pawnèd*). [9] Cf. H-323, 9–12. [10] i.e. ruin and chance. [11] absolute possession. [12] (H: *for time*). [13] tenure. Cf. H-552, 8–10. [14] appraise, ed. conj. (AH: *praise*). A pun on the two senses of praise and 'praise is probably intended. [15] (H: *layes*). Cf. H-197, 92. [16] (A: *to'th rust*). The meaning in H seems to be that the poetic dowry is not of a nature which can be formally transferred by legal means in trust for her. Cf. H-202, 7 and H-664, 5. [17] (A: *I keepe peacefull*). [18] Cf. H-186, 20: "sacred seeds of thee." [19] (A: *that*). [20] Cf. H-451, 3. [21] (A: *Love and*). The line is parenthesized in the MSS. [22] Cf. H-781, 15–16: "the vestall fier / Is not by marriage quencht, but flames the higher." [23] (A: *least that itt*). [24] (A: *upp with Mylder Lawes*). [25] (A: *or*). [26] (A: *To'th shew*). [27] (A: *thy*). [28] (H: *those*). [29] (A: *fly*). [30] (A: *setts*). [31] (*placed, for season'd*). [32] (A: *Plague*). [33] (A: *bedd*). [34] (A: *Inkyndled* H: *unkindled*). [35] (A: *Chafes and warmes*). [36] show that. [37] conjectural reading credited to P. Simpson by Martin. (*W^th^* is the abbreviation used in A; it is normally used for *with.* H: *With*). [38] (A: *flattering*). [39] (A: *Too Calme A tempest*). [40] (A: *to*). [41] (A: *to*). [42] (A: *I charge*). [43] (A: *but*). [44] (H: *And*). [45] (H: *hee*). [46] (AH: *woes*); who woos (with a pun on *brings woes*) by proxy using her double (her painted face) for that purpose. [47] (A: *bringe*). [48] pearl. [49] (A: *unto*). [50] (A: *the*). [51] Lethe. Cf. H-201, 50. [52] (A: *Eare rings*). (H: *earing*). Pun on erring? [53] (A: *pup-*

like). [54] (A: *travylde for*). (H: *travaile far*). Puns on *travailled* and *far*? [55] (H: *prize*). [56] (A: *fare-fetch*). [57] (A: *Lov'd Patience*). (H: *Love Patience*). [58] (A: *have*).

S–4

Master Herrick's Farewell unto Poetry.[1]

I have beheld[2] two lovers in a night
Hatched[3] o'er with moonshine, from their stolen delight[4]
(When this to that and that to this had given
A kiss to such a jewel of the heaven,[5]
Or while that each[6] from other's breath did drink[7] 5
Health[8] to the rose, the violet, or pink)
Call'd on the sudden by the jealous mother,
Some stricter mistress,[9] or suspicious other,[10]
(Urging divorcement worse than death to these[11]
By the soon[12], jingling of some sleepy[13] keys) 10
Part with a hasty kiss; and in that[14] show
How stay they would, but forc'd they are, to go.
Even such are we,[15] and, in our parting, do
No otherwise than as those former two
Natures like ours. We, who have spent our time 15
Both from the morning to the evening chime,
(Nay, till the bellman of the night had tolled[16]
Past noon of night) yet wear the hours, not cold
Nor dull'd with iron sleep, but have outworn[17]
The first[18] and fairest flourish of the morn 20
With flame and rapture, drinking to the odd
Number of nine,[19] which makes us full with god.[20]
And in that mystic frenzy, we have hurled,
As with a tempest, nature through the world,
And in a whirlwind twirl'd her home, aghast 25
At that which in her ecstasy had passed.
Thus, crowned with rosebuds, sack, thou mad'st me fly
Like firedrakes,[21] yet did'st me no harm thereby.
O thou almighty nature[22] who dost[23] give
True heat wherewith humanity doth live 30
Beyond its stinted circle; giving food,
White[24] fame, and resurrection to the good;
Soaring them up 'bove ruin, till the doom
(The general April[25] of the world) doth come,

That makes all equal; many thousands should, 35
Were't not for thee, have crumbled into mould
And, with their cerecloths rotted, not to show[26]
Whether the world such spirits had or no;
Whereas by thee, those and a million since,
Nor fate nor envy can their fames convince.[27] 40
Homer, Musaeus, Ovid, Maro,[28] more
Of those god-full prophets long before
Hold their eternal fires; and ours of late
(Thy mercy helping) shall resist strong fate
Nor stoop to th' center, but survive[29] as long 45
As fame or rumor hath a[30] trump or tongue.
But unto me be only hoarse,[31] since now
(Heaven and my soul bear record of my vow),
I my desires screw from thee and direct
Them and my thoughts to that sublime[32] respect 50
And conscience unto priesthood.[33] 'Tis not need,
The scarecrow unto mankind, that doth breed
Wiser conclusions in me, since I know
I've more to bear my charge than way to go;[34]
Or, had I not, I'd stop the spreading itch 55
Of craving more, so in conceit be rich.[35]
But 'tis the god of nature who intends
And shapes my functions for more glorious ends.

Guest[36] so depart. Yet stay a while to see
The lines of sorrow that lie drawn in[37] me, 60
In speech, in picture, no otherwise than when,
Judgment and death denounc'd[38] 'gainst guilty men,
Each takes a weeping farewell, racked in mind
With joys before and pleasure left behind,
Shaking the head whilst each to each doth mourn, 65
With thought[39] they go whence they must ne'er return.
So, with like looks as once the ministrel[40]
Cast, leading his Eurydice through hell,
I strike thy loves and greedily pursue
Thee with mine eyes, or in or out of view. 70
So looked the Grecian orator[41] when sent
From's native country into banishment,
Throwing his eyeballs backward to survey
The smoke of his beloved Attica.
So Tully[42] look'd when, from the breasts of Rome 75
The sad soul went, not with his love, but doom,

Shooting his eye-darts 'gainst it to surprise
It or to draw the city to his eyes.
Such is my parting with thee. And to prove
There was not onely varnish in my love 80
But substance too, receive this pearly tear,
Frozen with grief, and place it in thine ear.
Then part in name of peace, and softly on,
With numerous[43] feet, to hoofy[44] Helicon.
And when thou art upon that forked hill 85
Among the thrice three sacred virgins,[45] fill
A full-brimmed bowl of fury and of rage,
And quaff it to the prophets of our age.
When drunk with rapture, curse the blind and lame
Base ballad-mongers who usurp thy name 90
And foul thy altar: charm some into frogs,
Some to be rats, and others to be hogs—
Into the loathsom'st shapes thou canst devise
To make fools hate them only by disguise.
Thus, with a kiss of warmth and love, I part, 95
Not so but that some relic in my heart
Shall stand for ever, though I do address
Chiefly my self to what I do[46] profess:[47]
Know yet, rare soul, when my diviner muse[48]
Shall want a handmaid, as she oft will use, 100
Be ready then[49] in me, to wait upon her
Though as a servant, yet a maid of honor.
The crown of duty is our duty. Well
Doing's the fruit of doing well. Farewell.

[1] Text based on A (Bodleian MS Ashmole 38, p. 106; variants from B (B.M. Add MS 22603 f.30v); C (Huntington MS HM 198, p. 14); and R (Bodleian MS Rawl poet 160 f.46v); spelling modernized; punctuation largely supplied by the editor, who is also responsible for the paragraphing. Some variants which do not affect sense (e.g. headings such as *Herickes Farewell to Poetrie*) are not recorded. Martin, pp. 410 and 493 prints the text of A with the variants which occur in B, C, and R. [2] (R: *Even as yow see*). [3] a night crisscrossed or streaked with moonlight and shadow-lines: *hatch* is a jewelers' term used for lines in engraving or for inlays. Cf. H-223, 92. [4] The basic construction is: I have beheld lovers who, called from their delight by someone else, part with a hasty kiss. [5] When each lover had given the other a kiss in tribute to such a heaven which, by night, seemed bejewelled or inlaid by the moonlight. [6] (B: *while the Earth*). [7] each lover drank in from the other's breath. [8] (A: *Healthes*). [9] tutoress.

[10] other person. [11] i.e. prompting a separation which these lovers regarded as worse than death. [12] i.e. the guardian's warning jingle seemed too soon to the lovers. [13] i.e. the guardian responsible for the girl is sleepy and wishes her to return to the house so that the doors may be locked. (B: *the sleepinge keyes*). [14] by that kiss. [15] Poetry and Herrick. [16] or *told.* [17] i.e. we nevertheless continue to wear out or pass away the hours and are neither cold nor dulled by iron sleep; on the contrary, we have outworn, etc. Grosart interprets as follows: *yet were the hours not old, nor dulled,* etc., but *wear* seems meant to parallel *outworn.* The MSS all read *old,* but we have conjecturally substituted *cold* since it contrasts with *flame* in line 21 and with other heat references. [18] (ABR: *fresh*). [19] (A: *wyne*). In *Carmina,* III, XIX, 9–12, Horace calls for the drinking of a health to the new moon and midnight and urges that the draught be mixed with three or nine measures of wine. Cf. H-653, 11. [20] Bacchus—an echo of Horace, *Carmina,* II, XIX, 6. [21] will-o'-the-wisps, ignis fatuus. [22] Poetry. [23] (A: *did'st*). [24] W. C. Hazlitt's conjectural reading; the MSS read "(While Fame)". [25] See H-763, n.9. [26] i.e. would not be able to show. [27] Because of Poetry, the fame of those many thousands (line 35) and the fame of a million others since them cannot be overwhelmed by fate or envy. [28] Virgil. [29] (Nor . . . survive / C: *not stooping downe, but she survives*). [30] (A: *or*). [31] i.e. Poetry (Herrick's Muse) will now speak to him only hoarsely. [32] (A: *sublim'd*). [33] This statement suggests that this poem was written when Herrick was looking forward to his ordination (1623). [34] i.e. I have more money to pay my expenses than I have road to travel. [35] and thus I would be rich in mind and imagination, though not in fact. [36] i.e. Poetry, who has been his guest for many years. Herrick may also mean *ghost* in the sense of an inspiration, spirit or breath; cf. line 5. The MSS read *Guesse* or *Ghesse;* Hazlitt conjectured that *kiss* was intended, but, as Martin notes, citing *O.E.D.,* there is no need to conjecture. [37] (BCR: *and*). [38] having been denounced. The meaning seems to be as follows: Stay to see me appear not otherwise than men do when, having been sentenced to death, each of them takes a weeping farewell. Line 61 is parenthesized in the MSS. [39] with thought that. [40] Orpheus. [41] Demosthenes. [42] Cicero. [43] rhythmical. [44] a reference to Pegasus. [45] the nine Muses. [46] (AR: *must*). [47] the priesthood. [48] Urania, the Muse of sacred poetry. [49] (A: *thou*).

S–5

Upon a Carved Cherrystone Sent to Wear in the Tip of the Lady Jemmonia Walgrave's Ear, a Death's Head on the One Side and Her Face on the Other.[1]

Lady, I entreat you, wear
This little pendant in your ear.
'Tis no jewell of great prize
Or in regard of merchandize;
But deep mystery, not the stone, 5
Gives it estimation.
Read it[2] then, and, in a view,
See th'epitomè of you;
For what life and death confines
Looks through the passage of these lines; 10
Whose carved measures do descry
A scripture how you live and die.
Kiss it then, before your lip
Commends it to your ear's soft tip.
And, the while you do survey 15
This Janus, looking double way,[3]
With a tear, you must compare
To what you must be, what you are.
Know, time past, this cherrystone
Had a sweet complexion, 20
Skin and color, flesh and blood,
Dainty taste for ladies' food.
All's now fled save this, a lone
Poor relic of the beauty – bone!
And that so little, we despair[4] 25
It ever, dangling, smil'd i'th'air.
So must that fair face of yours
(As this looking-glass assures)
Fade and scarce leave to be shown
There ever livéd such a one. 30
And, when another age shall bring
Your lean scalp to censuring,[5]
Though the Sexton truly swear
Here Jemmonia's titles were–
In this ragg'd escutcheon– 35
Most[6] may smile; believe will none;

Or their height of faith may grow
But to this: to think 'twas so.
 This lesson you must pierce to th' truth
And know (fair mistress), of your youth,[7] 40
Death with it still walks along
From mattins to the evensong,
From the pickax, to the spade,
To the tomb where't must be laid.
 Whether in the morn, or noon, 45
Of your beauty, Death comes soon.
And though his visage hung i'th'ear
Doth not to the sight appear,
At each warning, he's as much
Known to th' hearing as the touch. 50

Place, then, this mirror to the view
Of those virgins, whose brisk hue
Of lines and colors makes them scorn
This livery, which the Greek[8] hath worn.
Let them read this book and learn 55
Their airy colors to discern.[9]
 'Twixt this and them, this Gorgon,[10] shown,
 Turns the beholders into stone.

[1] Text, eclectic; spelling and punctuation modernized. Title, a composite of headings in various MSS. Based on B.M. MSS Rawl poet 160 f.28; Add 30982 f.66; Sloane 1446 f.62v; Harvard MS 626F f.35v; Rosenbach MSS 239/27, pp. 310–11. [2] penetrate into the mystery, and read this poem which interprets it. [3] The carved cherrystone is like the god Janus in that it has faces looking in opposite directions. [4] doubt that. [5] i.e. when, after years in the earth, the remains of her body are dug up to make room for another. Cf. Yorick's fate in *Hamlet*. [6] most people. [7] concerning your youth, that. [8] Perseus killed the Gorgon Medusa, who had the power of turning to stone any object upon which she fixed her eyes. He gave the head to Minerva, who placed it in the center of her aegis or shield. [9] i.e. to see that their beauty ends in death. [10] this death's head (skull and crossbones). [Martin records on p. 495 of his edition the variants in all the MSS except the one in the Rosenbach Foundation Library. They are as follows. Heading: One a cherry stone haveinge a deaths head one the outside, and a gentle woman on the other. 2 of great prize / for the price. 7 a / the. 10 Look / Looke. 12 you / wee. 14 Commends / Commend. 19 time past / in times past. 24 the beauty–bone! / a beautious stone;. 26 i'th'air / in t'hayre. 32 scalp to / scull (?) to the. 33–38 OMITTED. 39 pierce to th' / know the. 40 (fair mistress) / vice-m^{r}. 41 with it still /

still with itt. 42 OMITTED. 45 or / or in the. 46 comes / doe come. 47 his visage hung / this visage hang'd. 49 warning, he's / moveinge theres. 50 to / in. 50 as the / 'ith. 51 then / you. 51 to / in. 53 lines / Limbes. 54 Greek hath / Greekes have]

S–6 *The Description*[1]

Of a Woman,

Whose head, befringéd with bescatter'd tresses,
Seems like Apollo's when the morn he blesses,[2]
Or like unto Aurora, when she sets
Her long dishevell'd rose-crowned trammel-nets.[3]
Her forehead smooth, full, polish'd, bright and high, 5
Bares[4] in itself a graceful majesty;
Under the which, two crawling eyebrows twine,
Like to the tendrills of a flatt'ring vine;
Under whose shades, two starry, sparkling eyes
Are beautifi'd with fair, fring'd canopies. 10
Her comely nose, with uniformal grace,
Like purest white, stands in the middle place,
Parting the pair, as we may well suppose,
Each cheek resembling still a damask rose;
Which, like a garden, manifestly show 15
How roses, lillies, and carnations grow;
Which, sweetly mixéd both with white and red,
Like rose leaves, white and red seem mingléd.
Their Nature, for a sweet allurement, sets
Two smelling, swelling,[5] bashfull cherrilets; 20
The which, with ruby redness being tipp'd,
Do speak a virgin, merry cherry-lipp'd;
Over the which, a meet,[6] sweet skin is drawn,
Which makes them show like roses under lawn.
These be the ruby portals and divine 25
Which ope themselves to show an holy shrine
Whose breath is rich perfume that, to the sense,
Smells like the burnt Sabæan frankincense;
In which, the tongue, though but a member small,
Stands guarded with a rosy, hilly wall; 30
And her white teeth, which in the gums are set,
Like pearl and gold make one rich carcenet.[7]
Next doth her chin with dimpled beauty strive
For his[8] plump, white, and smooth prerogative;

At whose fair top, to please the sight, there grows 35
The blessed[9] image of a blushing rose,
Moved by the chin, whose motion causeth this:
That both her lips do part, do meet, do kiss.
Her ears, which like two labyrinths are placed
On either side, with rich, rare jewels grac'd, 40
Moving a question—whether that, by them,
The gem is grac'd, or they grac'd by the gem.
But the foundation of this architect
Is the swan-staining,[10] fair, rare, stately neck;
Which, with ambitious humbleness, stands under, 45
Bearing aloft this rich, round world of wonder;
In which the veins implanted seem to lie,
Like loving vines, hid under ivory,
So full of claret that whoso pricks a vine
May see it sprout forth streams of muscadine. 50
Her breast (a place for Beauty's throne most fit),
Bears up two globes, where Love and Pleasure sit;
Which, headed with two rich, round rubies, show
Like wanton rosebuds growing out of snow;
And, in the milky valley that's between, 55
Sits Cupid, kissing of his mother queen,
Fing'ring the paps that feel like sleaved[11] silk,
And, press'd a little, they will weep new milk.
Then comes the belly, seated next below,
Like a fair mountain of Riphean[12] snow; 60
Where Nature, in the whiteness without spot,
Hath, in the middle, tied a Gordian knot;[13]
Or else, that she on that white, waxen hill,
Hath sealed the promise[14] of her utmost skill.[15]
But now my Muse hath spied a dark descent 65
From this so peerless, precious prominent—
A milky high way that direction yields
Unto the port mouth of th'Elysian fields—
A place desir'd of all, but got by these,
Whom Love admits to this Hesperides. 70
Here's golden fruit, that far exceeds all price,
Growing in this love-guarded paradise.
Above the entrance, there is written this:
This is the portal to the bower of bliss;
Through midst thereof, a crystal stream there flows, 75
Passing the sweet sweet of a musky rose.
Now, Love invites me to survey her thighs,
Swelling, in likeness to two crystal skies,

With plump, soft flesh of metal pure and fine,
Resembling shields both smooth[16] and crystaline. 80
Hence rise those two ambitious hills that look
Into the middlemost, sight-pleasing crook;
Which, for the better beautifying, shrouds
Its humble self 'twixt two aspiring clouds;
Which, to the knees, by Nature fast'n'd on, 85
Derive their ever well-grac'd motion.
Her legs, with two clear calves, like silver tried,
Kindly[17] swell up with little, pretty pride,
Leaving a distance for the beauteous small[18]
To beautify the leg and foot withal. 90
Then, lowly, but most lovely, stand the feet,
Round, short, and clear, like pounded spices sweet;
And, whatsoever thing they tread upon,
They make it scent like bruised cinnamon.
The lovely shoulders now allure the eye 95
To see two tablets of pure ivory;
From which, two arms, like branches, seem to spread,
With tender rind, and silver coloréd,
With little hands, and fingers long and small
To grace a lute, a viol virginal. 100
In length, each finger doth his next excel,
Each richly headed with a pearly shell,
Richer than that fair, precious, virtuous[19] horn
That arms the forehead of the unicorn.
Thus every part in contrariety 105
Meets in the whole and makes a harmony,
As diverse strings do singly disagree
But, form'd by number, make sweet melody.
Unto the idol of the life[20] divine
I consecrate this loving work of mine, 110
Bowing my lips unto that stately root
Whence beauty springs; and thus I kiss thy foot.

[1] Text, modernized in spelling and punctuation, based on a comparison of Bodleian MSS Ashmole 38, p. 88; Harl 6057 f.42; Rawlinson poet 160 f.105 (printed in Martin's ed.); Huntington MS 198, p. 8; and *Recreation for Ingenious Head-peeces* (1645), under "Fancies and Fantasticks," preceded by an engraving. In the first of these the poem is attributed to Herrick; in the second to R.W. (Rowland Watkins?). Though the ideas and vocabulary are partially Herrickian, the style is often unlike his. If he wrote the poem, he was, perhaps, experimenting to see how many phrases

and clauses he could hang, one on another. In genre, the poem is a verse character: the device of having the first line carry on syntactically from a title phrase is frequent in prose characters. Some of the more significant variants are placed in parentheses in the notes below. [2] (*dresses*). [3] hair nets. [4] (*bares*). [5] (*Two seeming smiling*). [6] (*neat*). [7] band or chain of jewels. (*cabinet*). [8] its. [9] (*fairest*). [10] The meaning probably is that her swanlike neck sustains the architecture of walls, labyrinths, etc., already mentioned by the poet. In this sense the neck is a foundation sustaining the "world of wonder" (line 46) above it. However, "staining" may refer to the claret-red veins hidden under the swanlike whiteness of the neck. [11] composed of slender, flossy filaments. The Rawlinson MS reads "sleeded," which is attractive both for its sound and the suggestion of sledding on snowy whiteness. [12] According to Ptolemy, the Riphaei were mountains in north Europe; in *Georgics,* IV, 518, Virgil refers to the Riphean plains that never lose their frost. [13] The knot tying together parts of the chariot of the Phrygian king, Gordius, was so artfully made that its ends could not be perceived. [14] (*primrose*). [15] i.e. hath put a seal of approval on her accomplishment of everything that the exercise of her artistry gave promise of achieving. But if *primrose* is the poet's intention, he means that on the white hill of the belly, Nature has placed a seal, the navel, which is primrose-shaped and is made with Nature's greatest skill. [16] (*pure*). [17] appropriate to their nature and species. [18] the small of the leg. [19] potent. [20] (*work*).

S–7 *Upon parting:*[1]

Goe hence away, and in thy parting know
Tis not my voice, but heavens, that bidds thee goe;
Spring hence thy faith, nor thinke it ill desert
I finde in thee, that makes me thus to part,
But voice of fame, and voice of heaven have thunderd 5
We both were lost, if both of us not sunderd;
Fould now thine armes, and in thy last looke reare
One Sighe of love, and coole it with a teare;
Since part we must Let's kisse, that done retire
With as cold frost, as erst we mett with fire; 10
With such white vowes as fate can nere dissever
But truth knitt fast; and so farewell for ever.

[1] Text from B.M. MS Harl 6917 f.82v. Initial letters editorially capitalized in lines 2, 6, 7, 8, 9, 10, 12. Ascribed to "Ro Herrick" in MS Folger 1669.2, f.270v.

S–8 *To a Mayd.*[1]

1.

Fayre Mayd, you did but cast your eyes erewhile,
Your ripening eyes,
Upon a Banke of Camomile,
And straight a blushing Birth
Of Strawberryes
Began to smile
And all to gild the earth.

2.

Would you have Cherry harvest here
Still last? then doe no more
But kisse yon Sicamore,
That Mirtle, or that Bay;
And Cherryes will appeare
Not onely ripe for that one day
But dangling all the yeare.

[1] From B.M. Add MS 33998 f.82v; commas added at the ends of lines 1, 2, 10; initial capital letters supplied for lines 2, 5, 6, 7, 9, 10, 11, 13, 14. The poem was printed in *The Academy of Complements* (1650), p. 231 with the following variants: 8 cherry / every. 10 yon / your. 12 Cherryes / Berries. 13 that one / this whole

S–9 *To a disdaynefull fayre.*[1]

1.

Thou maist be proud, and be thou so for me;
Yet know, there is a death for me and thee:
Whenas, poore souls, our softer frailties must
Be lost in blended dust,
That Charnell house that keepes us both shall signe
No neat distinction twixt thy bones and mine.

2.

And when to Hell[2] our two lean soules [are come],[3]
Where that just judge shall give to each his doome,
Think'st thou thy pride, forme, colour, there can fee
Him not to censure thee?
Know, wretched soule, a judge thou there shalt finde
Who not respects the body, but the minde.

3.

And for my plea, in acorne cups Ile show
Those two last teares which from mine eyes did flow.
And all my sighs through silke-worme bags shall sound
Thou gav'st me deadly wound.
Can Justice then, when these have sworne thy guilt,
Ah! not revenge the blood that thou hast spilt?

[1] From Bodleian MS Don c 57, f.41, attributed to "Herick"; title from *E* (B.M. MS Egerton 2013 f.10, with music by John Hilton; lines 1–6 only); the first stanza also occurs in *A* (B.M. Add MS 33998 f.82v). In Thomas Pestell, *The Poems*, ed. Hannah Buchan (Oxford, 1940), p. 59, "The Patchd Song. 1636" is a restoration of this poem, probably based on imperfect memory. [2] the place of the dead. [3] missing words conjectured by ed. Variants: 2 is / rests *A*. 2 me and thee *A* / thee and me *Don, E*. 3 softer / weaker *A*. 3 that / which *E*. 6 neat / neare *E*.

S–10 *Epitaph on a man who had a Scold to his Wife.*[1]

1.

Nay, read, and spare not, Passenger;[2]
My sence is now past feeling,
Who to my Grave a wound did beare
Within, past Physicks healing.

2.

But doe not, if thou be to wed,
To read my story, tarry;
Least thou envy me this cold Bed,
Rather then live to marry.

3.

For a long strife with a leud Wife
(Worst of all Ills beside)
Made me grow weary of my life;
So I fell sicke and dyde.

[1] From B.M. Add MS 33998 f.33v. Commas changed to semicolons at the ends of lines 1 and 11; comma inserted after "story" in line 6. Initial letters capitalized in lines 2–4, 6–8, 10–12. R. G. Howarth in *Notes and Queries* (June, 1958), p. 249 points out that this poem "was claimed by Thomas Jordan in his *Claraphil and Clarinda: In a Forest of Fancies*, ?1650, as 'An Epitaph on Himself' and again in his *A Nursery of Novelties in Variety of Poetry*, ?1665,

as 'An Epitaph supposed to be written by a Gentleman on himself, who dyed of a Disease, called by the name of a Bad Wife'; but since Jordan appropriated the work of others, only the complete title of this piece renders it more likely to be his than Herrick's."

S–11 *Orpheus and Pluto.*[1]

Orph: Howl not you Ghosts and Furies while I sing
Accents of grief to your Infernal King.

Pluto! O Pluto! pity my sad tears!
Plu: What heavenly rapture, this, doth pierce our ears?
Hark! hark! What art thou that call'st to Hell? 5
Orph: Orpheus, the poor Thracian min[i]strel[2]
Plu: What cam'st thou here for?
Orph: Justice.
Plu: What's thy plea?
Orph: To crave again my dear Euridice.
Plu: Com'st thou for her whom Fate's too hasty sheers
Cut off but in the blossom of her years? 10
Orph: For her I come.
Plu: Fond man, she's ours by fate.
Orph: Yet Love's entreaty never comes too late.
Plu: What should Infernall Jove[3] do? – Deign to warn
The Fatal Sisters to retwist the yarn?[4]
Orph: But oh! it is in Pluto's power to do it 15
If he but nod and put the Parcae to it.
Let Love move Pluto – let my grief tormenting –
And jointly both move Pluto to repenting.
Plu: Can we in justice do it?
Orph: Jove may.
Plu: And who 20
Dares speak 'gainst that which Jove is pleased to do?
Orph: Call back her fate and give a new beginning
To the cut web, and bless the thread in spinning.
Plu: Why, then, triumph! Go take her hence; and tell[5]
Thy music fetch'd Euridice from Hell.

Such are thy measures, Music, such thy charms 25
That it the Furies of their brands disarms.
Such were thy active numbers, Music, then
When thou build'st Thebes and cast it down again.

[1] Text based on Bodleian Library MS Don c 57, f.53v; title, nearly all the punctuation, modernized spelling, and attributions of the

speeches provided by the editor; Martin in his ed. supplies the same title but assigns the speeches to Orpheus and Pluto quite differently. The MS attributes the musical setting and poem to Robert Ramsay and "Mr. Heyrick." Cf. H-730 and S-2. For the background, see H-798. [2] "Minstrell" in the MS; but the word occurs frequently with three syllables in Herrick's period. [3] Cf. H-336, 28. [4] Cf. H-639, 4: *"Fates revolve no Flax th'ave spun."* [5] relate that.

S–12 *Parkinson's Shade to the House of Mr. Pallavicine Taking his Death Ill.*[1]

Will you still lament, and raise
A shade from rest?
Do you love, and will molest
A harmless Ghost with ayes?[2]
Babram, by my love, forbear 5
To shed a tear
Or spend a groan, unless for tombs
You'll have me come to haunt your rooms.
Ah! should I prove
A Goblin to the place I love? 10
No, no; rather let me keep
My peaceful urn
Than to the common light return
And want my silken sleep.[3]
I am old and love to be 15
'Mongst ancestry,[4]
Where in charnels we compare
Our grandsires' bones to those which are
In these days, when
The age breeds boys, not men. 20
But howsoever these defaults
Have fate alike in vaults,
This[5] from the dead: prepare to come;
For me and you benignant earth has room.
Meanwhile, God's benison and good men's vows 25
Prevent[6] your acts. Peace guard this house.
Exit Parkinson.

[1] Text: Huntington Library MS HM 198, p. 30; spelling modernized; punctuation supplied. The Palavicino estate at Babraham

(or Babram, line 5) was inherited by Tobias (or Toby or Tobit), 3rd son of Sir Horatio Palavicino, after the death of his brother Henry, the 2nd son (knighted 1611), in 1615. Both married daughters of Sir Oliver Cromwell. [2] i.e. sounds of grief. [3] Cf. H-106, 38: "silken slumbers." [4] Cf. H-860. [5] This message I bring you. [6] guide and favor.

INDEX OF TITLES AND FIRST LINES

Titles of poems appear in small capitals; first lines in italics. First lines of two-line poems have been omitted.

THE ANCHOR SEVENTEENTH-CENTURY SERIES

The Anchor Anthology of Short Fiction of the Seventeenth Century

SELECTED AND EDITED BY CHARLES C. MISH AC–1

The Complete English Poetry of John Milton

ARRANGED IN CHRONOLOGICAL ORDER WITH AN INTRODUCTION, NOTES, AND VARIANTS BY JOHN T. SHAWCROSS AC–2

The Complete Poetry of Robert Herrick

EDITED WITH AN INTRODUCTION AND NOTES BY J. MAX PATRICK AC–3

The Complete Poetry of Ben Jonson

EDITED WITH AN INTRODUCTION, NOTES, AND VARIANTS BY WILLIAM B. HUNTER, JR. AC–4

The Anchor Anthology of Jacobean Drama, VOLUME I

EDITED WITH AN INTRODUCTION, NOTES, AND VARIANTS BY RICHARD C. HARRIER AC–5a

OTHER ANCHOR BOOKS OF INTEREST

BIOGRAPHY, AUTOBIOGRAPHY AND LETTERS

ANDRADE, E. N. da C. Sir Isaac Newton, A151
BEETHOVEN, LUDWIG VAN Beethoven: Letters, Journals and Conversations, Trans. & Ed. Hamburger, A206
BENDIX, REINHARD Max Weber: An Intellectual Portrait, A281
COLETTE My Mother's House and The Vagabond, A62
CONNOLLY, CYRIL Enemies of Promise and Other Essays, A194
CONRAD, JOSEPH The Mirror of the Sea and A Personal Record, A207
DICKINSON, EMILY Selected Poems and Letters of Emily Dickinson, Ed. Linscott, A192
DUPEE, F. W. Henry James: His Life and Writings, A68
ESSLIN, MARTIN Brecht: The Man and His Work, A245
GEIRINGER, KARL Brahms: His Life and Work, A245
GONCOURT, EDMOND & JULES DE The Goncourt Journals (1851–1870), A158
GRAVES, ROBERT Good-Bye to All That, A123
HIMMELFARB, GERTRUDE Darwin and the Darwinian Revolution, A325
JAMES, HENRY The Selected Letters of Henry James, Ed. Edel, A204
KEATS, JOHN The Selected Letters of John Keats, Ed. Trilling, A70
KROPOTKIN, PETER Memoirs of a Revolutionist, Ed. Rogers, A287
LAWRENCE, D. H. Selected Letters of D. H. Lawrence, Ed. Trilling, A236
LEWIS, D. B. WYNDHAM François Villon, A147
LOWRIE, WALTER A Short Life of Kierkegaard, A273
NEALE, J. E. Queen Elizabeth I, A105
NICOLSON, HAROLD Tennyson, A284
PHILLIPS, DR. HARLAN B., ed. Felix Frankfurter Reminisces, A310
RAHV, PHILIP, ed. Discovery of Europe, A208
RILKE, RAINER MARIA Selected Letters of Rainer Maria Rilke, Ed. Moore, A223
SHATTUCK, ROGER The Banquet Years, A238
STEEGMULLER, FRANCIS The Grand Mademoiselle, A205
TAYLOR, A. E. Socrates, A9
TRELAWNY, E. J. The Last Days of Shelley and Byron, A225
WILSON, EDMUND A Piece of My Mind, A143
YEATS, WILLIAM BUTLER The Autobiography of William Butler Yeats, A142

ESSAYS, BELLES LETTRES & LITERARY CRITICISM

AUERBACH, ERICH Mimesis, A107
BARZUN, JACQUES Classic, Romantic and Modern, A255
BATE, WALTER JACKSON Prefaces to Criticism, A165
BAUDELAIRE, CHARLES The Mirror of Art, A84
BEERBOHM, MAX A Selection from *Around Theatres*, A226
BERGSON, HENRI Laughter (with Meredith's *Essay on Comedy*) in Comedy, A87
BLACKMUR, R. P. Form and Value in Modern Poetry, A96
BRANDEIS, IRMA The Ladder of Vision, A320
BROOKS, VAN WYCK America's Coming-of-Age, A129
CARY, JOYCE Art and Reality, A260
CASTIGLIONE, BALDESAR The Book of the Courtier, A186
CHASE, RICHARD The American Novel and Its Tradition, A116
CONNOLLY, CYRIL Enemies of Promise and Other Essays, A194
DUMAS, ALEXANDRE Adventures in Spain, A211
DUPEE, F. W. Henry James: His Life and Writings, A68
EDEL, LEON Literary Biography, A188
FERGUSSON, FRANCIS The Human Image in Dramatic Literature, A124
——— The Idea of a Theater, A4

OTHER ANCHOR BOOKS OF INTEREST